Managing Humanitari

Praise for the book...

'A "must-read" for students of the humanitarian relief system and a "must-have on the shelf" for planners and managers of emergency programmes. It combines comprehensive coverage of issues with incisive comments and well-balanced judgments &and, it is clearly-written.'

David Hulme, Professor in Development Studies, Institute for Development Policy and Management, Manchester University, UK.

'This book is a must-read for all serious practitioners who work at the sharp end in the delivery of humanitarian and developmental outcomes to disaster affected populations. Eric covers the spectrum from the theoretical underpinnings to the practicalities of managing an NGO in the field. It is a "how to" book that will greatly assist in the professionalization of our programmes and will remain very close at hand during the conduct of our future operations.'

Marc Preston, CEO, Australian Aid International.

'Eric James has created a handbook that makes you wonder how humanitarian agencies ever got along without it! As an academic, I admire its clarity and comprehensiveness; as a practitioner and consultant, I will add this to my toolkit as an indispensable resource.'

Dirk Salomons, Director, Humanitarian Affairs Program, School of International and Public Service Columbia University.

'An essential addition to the aid worker's tool kit. This comprehensive guide should be a part of every humanitarian NGO's orientation for new staff. A handy reference for all of the major tasks required for the successful establishment of an emergency mission which will likely help NGO staff to avoid the pitfalls and unintended consequences of decisions that are often, necessarily, taken on the fly.'

Peter Medway, Director of Operations, International Medical Corps UK.

'In combining a Textbook and Field Manual Dr James has demystified relief work for today's generation of relief workers. This unique and perfect balance of analyses and practical guides and check-lists makes any field worker or manager's job immeasurably more productive and rewarding. For years to come, every course on humanitarian relief will use this book and every relief worker will carry one in his to-go kit. CEOs and HR departments would be wise to order in bulk for all staff and new recruits. If every staff of every NGO had a copy of this book the humanitarian field would very simply advance by light years.'

Farshad Rastegar, President and CEO, Relief International, Los Angeles.

'This is a useful reference tool for anyone starting out in their career in humanitarian work.'

Graham MacKay, Deputy Humanitarian Director, Oxfam

Managing Humanitarian Relief
An operational guide for NGOs

Eric James

PRACTICAL ACTION
Publishing

Intermediate Technology Publications Ltd
trading as Practical Action Publishing
Schumacher Centre for Technology and Development
Bourton on Dunsmore, Rugby,
Warwickshire CV23 9QZ, UK
www.practicalactionpublishing.org

First published 2008

ISBN 978 1 85339 669 4

Since 1974, Practical Action Publishing has published and disseminated
books and information in support of international development work
throughout the world. Practical Action Publishing (formerly ITDG
Publishing) is a trading name of Intermediate Technology Publications Ltd
(Company Reg. No. 1159018), the wholly owned publishing company of
Intermediate Technology Development Group Ltd (working name Practical
Action). Practical Action Publishing trades only in support of its parent
charity objectives and any profits are covenanted back to Practical Action
(Charity Reg. No. 247257, Group VAT Registration No. 880 9924 76).

Cover concept by Heather Williams and Clinton Cahill
Cover design by Mercer Design
Illustrations by Clinton Cahill
Typeset by SJI Services
Printed by Replika Press

Contents

Tables

Figures

Boxes

Photos

Acronyms

ACBAR:	Agency Coordinating Body for Afghan Relief
ALNAP:	Active Learning Network for Accountability and Performance in Humanitarian Action
ALP:	Accelerated Learning Programme
AI:	Appreciative Inquiry
AIDCO:	(EU) Aid Cooperation Office
AOB:	Any Other Business
ARI:	Acute Respiratory Infection
AUSAID:	Australian Aid
BCG:	Bacillus Calmette-Guérin
BINGO:	Big International NGO
BMI:	Body Mass Index
BOQ:	Bill Of Quantity
BPRM:	Bureau of Population, Refugees and Migration
CAFF:	Children Associated with Fighting Forces
CBO:	Community-Based Organization
CD:	Country Director
CDC:	Community Disaster Committee
CEDAW:	Convention on the Elimination of all forms of Discrimination Against Women
CFW:	Cash for Work
CPA:	Child Protection Agency
CSB:	Corn-Soya Based
CTC:	Community Outreach Centre
CV:	Curriculum Vitae
CWC:	Child Welfare Committee
CHA:	(Sri Lanka) Coordination of Humanitarian Affairs
CIDA:	Canadian International Development Agency
CIMIC:	Civil–Military Coordination Centre
CMCC:	Civil–Military Coordination Centre
CMOC:	Civil–Military Operations Centre
CMR:	Crude Mortality Rate
CPM:	Critical Path Method and the

CRC: Convention on the Rights of the Child
CSP: Country Strategy Papers
DART: (US) Disaster Assistance Response Team
DDR: Disarm, Demobilize and Reintegrate
DEC: (UK) Disaster Emergencies Committee
DFID: (UK) Department for International Development
DOTS: Directly Observed Therapy/Short (course for treating TB)
DSM: Dry Soya Milk
ECCD: Early Childhood Care and Development
ECHO: European Committee Humanitarian Office
EPI: Expanded Programme of Immunization
EVI: Extremely Vulnerable Individuals
FAO: (UN) Food and Agriculture Organization
FFP: Food for Peace
FFW: Food For Work
FGD: Focus Group Discussion
FGM: Female Genital Mutilation
FIFO: First In, First Out (warehouse management)
FPA: Framework Partnership Agreement
FTR: Family Tracing and Reunification
GAAP: Generally Accepted Accounting Practices
GBV: Gender-Based Violence
GHP: Global Humanitarian Platform
GIS: Geographic Information System
GPS: Global Positioning System
HAC: Humanitarian Aid Committee
HAP: Humanitarian Accountability Project
HDI: Human Development Index
HF: High [radio] Frequency
HFA: Height-For-Age
HIC: Humanitarian Information Centre
HOC: Humanitarian Operations Centre
HQ: Headquarters
HR: Human Resources
HRM: Human Resources Management
IASC: Inter-Agency Standing Committee
ICRC: International Committee of the Red Cross
ICS: Incident Command System
ICT: Information and Communication Technology

ICVA:	International Council of Voluntary Agencies
IDP:	Internally Displaced Person
IFRC:	International Federation of the Red Cross
IGO:	Inter-governmental Organization
IHL:	International Humanitarian Law
IMS:	Incident Management System
INGO:	International Non-Governmental Organization
INMARSAT:	International Maritime Satellite Organization
IO:	International Organization
IOM:	International Office of Migration
KAP:	Knowledge, Attitudes and Practice surveys
kbps:	Kilo-bytes per second
kVA:	kilowatt
LNGO:	Local (National) Non-governmental Organization
MCH:	Maternal and Child Health
MCI:	Mass Casualty Incident
MDD:	Micro-Nutrients Deficiency
M&E:	Monitoring and Evaluation
MISP:	Minimum Initial Service Package (reproductive health)
MOSS:	Minimum Operating Security Standards
MOU:	Memorandum of Understanding
MSR:	Main Supply Routes
MUAC:	Mid-Upper Arm Circumference measurement
NFI:	Non-Food Item
NGO:	Non-Governmental Organization
OD:	Organizational Development
OFDA:	(USAID) Office of US Foreign Disaster Assistance
OJT:	On-the-Job Training
ORT/S:	Oral Rehydration Therapy/Solution (or Salts)
OTI:	(US) Office of Transition initiatives
PAHO:	Pan-American Health Organization
PEM:	Protein-Energy Malnutrition
PEP:	Post-Exposure Prophylaxis
PERT:	Programme Evaluation and Review Technique
PHC:	Primary Health Care
PM:	Project/Programme Manager
PLA:	Participatory Learning and Action
PLWH/A:	People Living With HIV/AIDS
PSA:	Public Service Announcement

PTT:	Push-To-Talk button
PTSD:	Post-Traumatic Stress Disorder
PVO:	Private Voluntary Organization
PRA:	Participatory Rural Assessment (or Appraisal)
RRA:	Rapid Rural Assessment (or Appraisal)
SAR:	Search And Rescue
SFP:	Supplementary Feeding Programme
SLA:	Sustainable Livelihood Approach
SMART:	Specific, Measurable, Achievable, Realistic and Time-bound
SOP:	Standard Operating Procedure
SOW:	Scope of Work
STI:	Sexually Transmitted Infection
SUMA:	SUpply and MAnagement system
SWOT:	Strengths, Weaknesses, Opportunities and Threats analysis
TBA:	Traditional Birth Attendant
TFC:	Therapeutic Feeding Centre
TFP:	Therapeutic Feeding Programme
TOR:	Terms of Reference
TOT:	Training of Trainers
UAM:	Unaccompanied Minors
UNDP:	UN Development Programme
UNDPKO:	UN Department of Peacekeeping Operations
UNDSS:	UN Department of Safety and Security
UNFPA:	UN Family Planning Agency
UNHAS:	UN Humanitarian Air Service
UNHCR:	UN High Commissioner for Refugees
UNICEF:	UN International Children's Emergency Fund
UNOCHA:	UN Office for the Coordination of Humanitarian Affairs
UPS:	Uninterrupted Power Supply
USAID:	US Agency for International Development
UXO:	Unexploded Ordnance
VHF:	Very High [radio] Frequency
VIP:	Ventilated Pit Latrine
VLOM:	Village-Level Operation and Maintenance
VNR:	Video News Release
VOICE:	Voluntary Organizations in Cooperation in Emergencies
VoIP:	Voice over Internet Protocol
WAFF:	Women Associated with Fighting Forces
WFA:	Weight-For-Age

WFP: UN World Food Programme
WFH: Weight-For-Height
WHO: UN World Health Organization
ZOPP: Zielorientierte Projekplanung

Foreword: A brief overview of humanitarianism today

When some people are in dire straits, other people want to help. Be it a hurricane or a war, a drought or a tsunami, crisis situations call for a humanitarian response. It sounds simple. Someone is in need; someone else responds, saving a life and allowing that person to get back on his or her feet. Would that it were this simple!

Relief work helps. It saves lives and, if done correctly, can save livelihoods, relieve human suffering and help people begin to build new lives. But the modern world of humanitarian response is beset by problems and pitfalls. These stem in part from the recent dramatic growth of this sector and the proliferation of its agencies and funds. Everyone has got into this act – from the private sector to multilateral agencies, from governments to international NGOs, not to mention the plethora of licit and illicit groups on the ground in the emergency area. Relief workers often find themselves in a world of uncoordinated, highly competitive agencies working with cross-cutting purposes.

Within this reality there is a multiplicity of ways of doing business. Some agencies get it right. Their staff focus on saving human lives and livelihoods within a specific economic and social system: they listen to local people; they build from the reality on the ground; they preserve and enhance local capacities; they tailor their response to the local situation, not employing a one-strategy-fits-all mentality to each disaster. They use local knowledge, experts and organizations in combination with outside intervention to create an effective response.

Good practitioners understand that politics pervades everything. All aid flows out of and into politically charged environments. All aid is politically charged, no matter how much agencies shout that they are apolitical. It is particularly true, since many humanitarian agencies are funded in large part by governments or international agencies. Practitioners are split over how to respond within this political environment. A few strive to maintain neutrality in extremely difficult situations; most use neutrality as a cover; still others toss out the concept and work in solidarity with one or more of the political actors on the scene. The recent focus on the war on terror by some of the largest donors adds a particular political dimension, bringing into close scrutiny all aspects of work, including the identities and intentions of your work colleagues.

Humanitarian responses are complex and as intricate as the complex emergencies they are trying to help. One key issue for all is ethics: the personal ethics of each aid worker, the institutional ethics of agencies working in extreme situations and the industry ethics of the whole humanitarian sector. It seems that for some the humanitarian imperative means intervention at any cost; it is the intervention that is morally right. For others, the humanitarian impulse must be tempered by attention to the most effective form of intervention. This may not be providing a direct response; it may be advocating or lobbying. Principles, standards, codes of conduct and ethical best practices have helped bring these issues to the fore. They deserve even more attention.

Response to emergencies and humanitarian aid cannot by separated from the historical, economic, ethical, social and political forces that shape society. Countries, communities and individuals come into each crisis with a history and will come out of it with a reality transformed by the response to the crisis. Emergency responses affect the economic and socio-political systems in which people live. It is therefore essential for practitioners to be focused on the long term, even when concrete actions are short-term. While aid givers must focus on the logistics and the how-to of effective aid, they must also be aware of how their actions affect the broader economic, social, psychological and political forces of the country and the community.

This then begs the question of what is the overall purpose of humanitarian intervention. In part, it is to save lives and reduce human suffering over time. In part, it is to ensure that the intervention helps build systems that will allow people to do more than just survive – or at least not destroy local systems that will allow for rebuilding to occur. Ultimately all people want to live in a society in which they are able to flourish and to have secure and meaningful lives: a major goal of human development.

At the end of the day the practitioner is there to act, to put together a programme of action to help people in extreme crisis. This requires knowledge of operational systems: from logistics to personnel management, from evaluation to complex budgetary statements. This book is an important hands-on manual for both the experienced field hand and the person going out into the field for the first time. It tells us what we can do – the nitty-gritty detail of how to act in an emergency. It will answer your questions as they come up. It will help you make fewer mistakes. It is recommended as a reference book to keep with you as you go into the field.

Eric James gives the relief worker practical tools for effective work. In these pages, James explains how to do many tasks, such as developing a full monitoring system, creating a step-by-step recruitment procedure for staff, producing an office equipment procurement checklist, and even labelling keys and changing locks on doors of newly rented apartments. These are the nuts and bolts a practitioner needs when faced with the complexity and multiplicity of tasks at hand in an emergency. Like in any craft, these tools by themselves do not make a good final product. This will depend on the holder of the tools, the sensitivity of the intervener and the human and political skill of the practitioner. But this manual will be a welcomed companion to the crafter of solutions in the field.

John Hammock
Associate Professor of Public Policy
Gerald J. and Dorothy R. Friedman School of Nutrition Science and Policy and the Fletcher School, Tufts University
Founder and Former Director, Alan Shawn Feinstein International Famine Center

Acknowledgements

In preparing this book, I have benefited from the reviews by and support of my friends, colleagues and specialists. For this, I am thankful for the encouragement and technical comments provided by Wayne Bleier, Martha Bregan, Bruce Britton, Edward and Michael Bizub, Koenraad Van Brabant, Andrea Becklund, John Cindric, Gwen Desplats, Marc James, Cristana Falcone, Giorgio Francia, Toby Fenwick, Nick Gnanathurai, Lotta Hagman, Joan Kellenburg, Erin Kenny, Chris Nixon, Christie Scott, Marcus Skinner, Gregg Swanson, Patrick Wandabusi and Mike Wessells. At IDPM, I would like to thank Jenny Peterson, Joanne Tippett, Siobhan McGrath and George Holmes. Special thanks go to Clint Cahill for his hard work and skill. I'd also like to thank the anonymous reviewers, but of course, all errors and omissions are mine. Finally, I would like to thank my mother for her love and constant support. This book is dedicated to her.

About the author

Since 1995, Eric James has managed humanitarian emergency programmes for a number of NGOs in Central and South Asia, the Balkans and sub-Saharan Africa. He was educated in international relations, public health and humanitarianism in the US and the UK.

Introduction

The purpose of this book

This book is meant to provide practical information for relief workers. It is an attempt to provide an accessible book that bridges the gap between theory and practice, between what is written by academia, practitioners and the technical manuals. It is based on well-known, proven, reliable and appropriate methods as well as my own field experience and that of my reviewers.

There now exists an informative body of work written about the development industry. Unfortunately, most of it is not immediately useful to those working in the field and the breadth of subjects relief workers face seems to require a small library and a high-speed internet connection. Much of the other stuff can be misleading or written by or for (or both) people who don't work in the field. NGOs need to mature and professionalize further – their role now is too important not to take seriously.

Successful NGOs are normally identified by the focus on their core missions; usually by making a significant positive impact on the beneficiaries of their projects. Some organizations, however, get away without having effective systems, policies and procedures, but they are almost certainly not working as well as they good be. There is probably inefficiency and needless strain on staff. This book can serve as a remedy.

Who this book is for

This book provides a practical guide for the relief workers who oversee a range of activities and are called upon to do a myriad of tasks while managing emergency programmes. It will benefit most delegates, supervisors, project managers, programme or field coordinators, country directors, representatives or whatever position title NGO staff may have in the field. For those new to the field, the information here should provide a useful primer while those familiar with these sectors may use them as an *aide mémoire* or for training material. This book will also help staff working in headquarters, academia and on development programmes. Moreover, this book is written for the non-specialist and is not written as a technical manual but is rather general guidance for managers and others involved in providing humanitarian relief.

Anyone who has worked in an emergency situation knows that they are messy affairs with significant differences from normal work environments. For a variety of reasons, people working as logisticians are called upon to write proposals, doctors may need to buy generators, nutritionists perform human resource management and accountants are asked to understand the basics of therapeutic feeding. It is worth adding that, as with the majority of writing on international development, the focus here is primarily on International (Northern) NGOs. Most information here, however, applies and should be helpful for Local (or 'national' or Southern) NGOs.

How this book is structured

Managing Humanitarian Relief brings together critical information 'under one roof'. It is organized into 21 chapters. The first chapters focus on general understanding of the relief industry, how people are affected by emergencies and what is often the response. Then a general cycle is followed from assessing an emergency to opening a programme to its closing. Along the way, a number of subjects that relief workers should be familiar with such as project management, proposal writing and capacity building are covered as well as other important aspects of any relief programme including logistics, security and coordination. The annex contains essential references as well as a selected bibliography and glossary.

As much as possible, this book is organized to be 'user friendly' in terms of its readability. Where appropriate, boxed text, checklists and 'step-by-step' explanations are provided as well as an extensive glossary and annexes of reference information to help readers who have little time while working in emergencies.

A typical day for a relief worker may involve half or more of these subjects and not in a neat order. They do not have the luxury of saying 'I'd rather not know the basics of this project sector, or how radios work, or how to lessen stress among my staff'. The reason for the breadth of this book is that managers in the field are faced with at least all of the subjects presented here during an emergency.

Important assumptions

Everything that follows in this book was written with several important assumptions. First, this book is about how to manage relief-oriented NGOs effectively. It is not a 'cook book' or 'repair manual' for solving disasters and complex emergencies. And it is not a substitute for other resources, in-depth study, training, or informed action. As this book can be used as reference or to gain basic familiarity with a topic, it is hoped that this book will help relief workers become better informed and well-rounded professionals.

Second, this is an operational book (as opposed to academic, descriptive or critical work) so it is assumed that only certain parts or chapters will be 'usable' to any given reader. An attempt was made to cover a range of topics that relief workers will find useful, but not every topic could be covered in comprehensively. Readers are encouraged to seek more information, do more research, and ask more questions in the field.

Third, every effort was made to source material properly and this is noted throughout the book. In the annex, the best sources are cited and they serve as references for that particular section. Some of the material is 'common knowledge' and information picked up over the years passed on randomly through conversations and in work environments. In such cases, the originator of the material is not known. For example, the UN's guidance on HIV+ mothers breastfeeding children has flip-flopped for and against over the years. This seems to be a common research problem but this presented a challenge in preparing a book of this scope.

Fourth, it is important to be aware that improving procedures and the mechanics of an organization will not improve the assistance delivered. The reality in the field, however, is that far too many NGOs have the right mission and aims, but simply do a poor job because they are disorganized, operate without systems or lack the tools that would enable them to make better decisions. With solid systems and by following good practice, goals can be communicated, linkages developed and a fuller realization of objectives achieved.

Finally, it is assumed that the local context in which the reader finds themselves will be taken into account and adjusted accordingly. Some could argue that providing a little knowledge could cause harm, but too often in emergencies people make decisions with no knowledge let alone accurate information, experience or wisdom. Given the state of the field, this book assumes some information will push people in the right direction and at least prevent a failure or two. For the most part, the answers to the problems we seek to resolve are out there. People affected by emergencies usually handle problems themselves and the external aid that comes is just that - a bit of help. Relief workers must strive to do all they can in keeping with humanitarian basic principles including the principle of doing nothing if it were to cause harm.

Disclaimer: The information presented here is for purposes of information only. It is based on the idea that when no information is available (a common occurrence in emergency situations), some information is better than none. The author takes no responsibility if the information presented in this book is used unwisely or in isolation from other information. If you find better methods or approaches, run with it and share what you know with others.

CHAPTER 1
Understanding emergencies and disaster-affected populations

The purpose of this chapter is to provide an understanding of emergencies, problems that arise out of responses, a brief history of the development industry and the response to problems and issues for the future. This chapter discusses:
- What is an emergency
- The role of NGOs in emergency situations
- Humanitarian principles
- Problems and dilemmas of the international emergency response system
- Standardized initiatives and approaches

The start of the 21st century is following the pattern set in the previous century when more than 150 million people died as a result of war. Conflicts in Africa, parts of Asia and other areas seem no closer to resolution than they were 10–15 years ago. Natural disasters, from tsunamis to tropical storms, continue to take their toll. Indicators anticipate increased devastation wrought by environmental degradation.

While not all doom and gloom, the development industry that supports the international response to emergencies will likely grow for years to come. Yet the development industry is ill-equipped and, sometimes literally, outgunned. From many corners, there has been a call for improvements in the industry, for 'smart aid' that can deal with these problems. After so many failures, more thoughtful and holistic approaches, incorporating solutions at different levels, have come forward during the last decade. Relief workers need to be aware of these issues and how they can make on-the-ground decisions for better results.

Deciding what the problems are in the first place can be much more difficult than prescribing the solutions. In the field, many staff have neither a clear diagnosis of their problems nor a set of solutions. This chapter provides different ways to think about the problems encountered while running an emergency programme as well as many possible solutions.

While it is possible to effectively implement good programmes without a well-stocked office or without knowing much about capacity building, success is doubtful without knowing the principles and approaches of current good practice. For this reason, the focus of this chapter may be the most important in this book.

What is an emergency?

In everyday language, an emergency is an event or set of circumstances that requires urgent action. The United Nations High Commissioner for Refugees

(UNHCR) considers an emergency a situation which 'demands an extraordinary response and exceptional measures' to be resolved. Emergencies are generally associated with disasters, which are synonymous with tragedies and catastrophes and result in casualties and destruction of property. Precise definitions are debated, but for the purposes of this book, an emergency is a situation where the lives of a population are threatened or in danger to a point that exceeds the local capacity to respond or cope. From this standpoint, emergencies are often thought about in one of two ways.

First, emergencies that occur quickly, such as an earthquake and most wars, are known as 'sudden onset' disasters, while emergencies that take time to develop, such as droughts and some wars, are called 'slow onset' disasters. One of the defining factors of emergencies is that vulnerability, often associated with certain groups (e.g. the elderly, children and the extreme poor) can be quickly expanded to include everyone.

A second way is by dividing emergencies into two categories. Natural disasters are familiar to most people as they occur in all parts of the world. Natural disasters can combine, such as an earthquake that causes fires, flooding, landslides, tsunami, displacement of landmines or unexploded ordnance (UXO) and volcanic activity. But humanitarian emergencies are caused by people and typically involve armed conflict, which happens most often in the transitional and developing world. International war, inter-communal violence and civil war and genocide contribute to humanitarian emergencies. The distinction between these two categories is made in Table 1.1.

Probably the greatest challenge faced by the humanitarian community are complex emergencies as have been found in countries such as Afghanistan, Democratic Republic of the Congo, Sudan and Somalia. The UN Inter-Agency Standing Committee (IASC) (1994) defines a complex emergency as:

> A multifaceted humanitarian crisis in a country, region or society where there is total or considerable breakdown of authority resulting from internal or external conflict and which requires a multi-sectoral, international response that goes beyond the mandate or capacity of any single agency.

Put another way, a complex emergency is caused by more than one event or condition such as political and economic failure and a breakdown of social support systems leading to war. The usefulness of describing emergencies as complex can be seen as problematic because it implies that some emergencies are 'simple' and caused by one factor such as economic or political failure. The phrase 'situations of chronic political instability' has also been created to describe better the political, cyclical and long-term nature of complex emergencies.

During the 1990s, humanitarian emergencies became a fixture in many parts of the world where political, social, economic, and often, environmental failures led to widespread human suffering. In December 2001, according to OCHA, there were thirty-seven active complex emergencies in thirty-two locations worldwide. Complex emergencies continue after decades in countries such as Sudan and the Democratic Republic of the Congo.

Table 1.1 Natural disasters compared with humanitarian emergencies

	Natural disasters	Humanitarian emergencies
Causes	Natural origin: floods, landslides earthquakes, tsunami and drought	Manmade events may be exacerbated by natural causes: war (including conflict and ethnic cleansing) and acute political crisis (including revolution)
Typical locations	Anywhere globally but focused on areas where geographic fault-lines (earthquakes), arid regions (drought), volcanic areas and flooding are most prevalent	Areas of high underdevelopment, political transition, social exclusion and/or presence of inter-communal conflict
Scope of emergency	Differs by disaster. Often includes disruption and destruction of social services usually limited to disaster zone. Immediate threats to survivors posed by increased public health risks, shortages of food (except earthquakes), contaminated (especially floods) or lack of (especially drought) water, as well as political, economic and social instability	Destruction of social infrastructure, massive human displacement and state failure usually countrywide. Immediate and long-term threats to all but the most advantaged people
Time-frame	Weeks to months (although reconstruction can take much longer): Short-term focus on response phases of (in order) rescuing of victims, relief for survivors and rehabilitation. Usually possible to link relief to development	Years to decades: Usual medium- and long-term nature of emergency situation makes linking relief to development unrealistic. Different approaches needed such as developmental relief, discussed below
Safety and security	Limited safety concerns such as after-shocks or further flooding. Pillaging/looting possible depending on severity and disruption to government structures	Range of security problems including gunfire, shelling, landmines and increased crime
Typical response	Local government and voluntary sector the first to respond, where they exist, followed by inter-national assistance where agreed upon. Incident Command System (ICS) used in locations with well-developed emergency response systems	Periods of high insecurity can delay and/or hamstring response. While local government and voluntary sector may respond, they may contribute to the causes of the emergency. International organizations may respond where and when possible

cont.

cont.

	Natural disasters	Humanitarian emergencies
Role of NGOs	Supporting existing system in phases of response. Specific sector projects that compliment or fill gaps in response. NGOs may raise significant private funds outside official assistance. NGOs may take on a limited disaster preparedness and mitigation role	Range of possible roles from supporting (as an implementing partner of a donor agency, including the UN system) to acting as the sole mechanism for alleviating and mitigating suffering

Note: Manmade disasters also include industrial accidents such as the Chernobyl nuclear meltdown and transportation disasters such as plane and train crashes. However, NGOs rarely respond to such disasters.

In many cases, a situation involving human suffering may appear 'bad' but it may not classify as a humanitarian emergency. In an attempt to quantify what is an emergency and what is not, clear indicators have been established for categorizing emergencies. Typical indicators are shown in Table 1.2.

Humanitarian response is but a part of a larger international response which typically includes political, diplomatic and military response on various levels. These levels also roughly correspond to the phases of an emergency, typically labelled acute emergency, post-emergency and rehabilitation phases. Together, these phases and levels are shown in Figure 1.1.

In this book, the term 'acute emergency' is used to represent the lowest point in this model. An acute emergency can represent a brief point in time or occur in wave-like episodes where insecurity, human suffering and other conditions reach their worst.

Since there are different ways of looking at emergencies, it is helpful to review several important elements of emergencies: conflict, vulnerability and poverty.

Figure 1.1 Conflict and development continuum

Table 1.2 Emergency indicators

Cause	Category	Rate/Indicator
Crude mortality rate (CMR)	Normal rate among a settled population	0.3–0.5/10,000/day
	Emergency programme under control	<1/10,000/day
	Emergency programme in serious trouble	>1/10,000/day
	Emergency: out of control Major catastrophe	>2/10,000/day
Mortality rate among children under 5 years old (U5MR)	Normal rate among a settled population	1.0/10,000/day
	Emergency programme under control	<2.0/10,000/day
	Emergency programme in serious trouble	>2.0/10,000/day
	Emergency: out of control	>4.0/10,000/day
Lack of clean water	Survival need	7 litres/person/day
	Maintenance allocation	15–20 litres/person/day
	Waterborne disease	25% people with diarrhoea
Lack of food	Survival need	1,900 kcal/person/day
	Maintenance	2,100 kcal/person/day
Malnutrition of children	Severely malnourished	>1% population <5 years old
	Moderately malnourished	>10% population <5 years old
	Nutrition-related disease	Presence of oedema, pellagra, scurvy, beriberi and vitamin A deficiency
Poor shelter	Minimum shelter area	3.5 sq.m/person
	Minimum total site area	30.0 sq.m/person
Lack of sanitation	Latrines	<1 latrine cubicle per 100 persons
Disease	Measles	Any reported cases
	Hemorrhagic-related fevers	Any reported cases
	Acute respiratory infections (ARI)	Pattern of severe cases

Source: Data from Noji and Burkholder (1999); UNHCR (2000). Basic standards are also presented in the Sphere Standards section (pp. 377–80).

Understanding conflict

Conflict is a common element of emergencies. There are many ways to define conflict, ranging from some sort of unequal human relationship, usually called structural violence, to violent conflict over disagreement, usually considered war. Organized violent conflict occurs at different levels of intensity, ranging from low, characterized by guerrilla operations and insurgency, to high, which involves total societal mobilization to becoming field militaries battling similar foes. Violent conflict manifests itself in many different ways, from endemic levels of violent crime to highly organized military violence. In modern conflict civilians are deliberately targeted for military objectives, resulting in high numbers of casualties. These situations present multiple threats to beneficiaries of relief, including the cessation of development, deprivation of social services such as health, the military recruitment of children, gender-based violence (GBV), forced displacement and massacres.

Conflict and the resulting insecurity are features that set emergency relief apart from the rest of the development industry. NGO staff should be knowledgeable about the conflict in which they are working, including its historical context (such as territorial claims), power relations, political and economic dynamics, and cultural perceptions (including religion and ethnicity). Chapter 5 discusses ways to examine conflict at an operational level; see also Chapter 18 for threats to NGO staff.

Understanding vulnerability

Vulnerability can be thought of in different ways but is generally understood to mean the likelihood people can be affected by a hazard such as a violent conflict or natural event including earthquakes and severe storms.

Poverty is a major constituent of vulnerability. Of course, emergencies do not happen only in the poorest of countries, but the least developed countries are also the least able to cope with disasters and more prone to suffer from protracted social conflict.

Understanding how these components are linked and progress from their causes to their outcomes is a necessary first step in designing and implementing effective programmes. All emergencies are part of complex contexts and are not easily understood by staff who parachute in when called upon. Understanding can be engendered throughout an NGO in the way it manages and approaches each emergency. Post-conflict and post-disaster situations allow different measures and activities that address vulnerability and risk along the chain of causality shown in Table 1.3.

Box 1.1 Analysing conflict

There are a number of methods for analysing the fluid conflicts associated with emergencies. Those designed for NGOs providing humanitarian relief include the 'Do No Harm' approach, the 'Benefit/Harms' approach developed by CARE, the 'Making Sense of Turbulent Context' tool created by World Vision and the 'Better Programming Initiative' of the International Federation of the Red Cross (IFRC).

Table 1.3 Vulnerability and risk

Root causes	Dynamic pressures	Unsafe conditions	Disaster	Hazards
Limited access to: power, structures and resources **Ideologies:** political and economic systems	**Lack of** • Local institutions • Training • Appropriate skills • Local investments • Local markets • Press freedom • Ethical standards in public life **Macro-forces** • Rapid population change • Rapid urbanization • Arms expenditure • Debt repayment schedules • Deforestation • Decline in soil productivity	**Physical environment:** Dangerous locations and unprotected buildings and infrastructure **Local economy:** Livelihoods at risk and low income levels **Social relations:** Special groups at risk and lack of local institutions **Public actions and institutions:** Lack of disaster preparedness, prevalence of epidemic disease	**Risk =** **Hazard** **X** **Vulnerability**	Earthquake High winds (cyclone/hurricane/typhoon) Flooding Volcanic eruption Landslide Drought Virus and pests Conflict

Source: Wisner et al. (2004: 51)

Understanding poverty

Poverty is a set of conditions that comprises a number of related elements, such as poor physical status (poor health), powerlessness, isolation and marginalization, as well as material insecurity. As a major contributing element of vulnerability, poverty can exacerbate the consequences of emergencies, yet the relationship between poverty and emergencies is complex. Issues of class, the access to resources and services, the ability to evacuate one's home area and cope with the impacts of disaster all come into play. With this in mind, it is useful to examine poverty through its dichotomous relationship with wealth, as shown in Table 1.4.

At first glance, it may seem that those trapped in a cycle of poverty have nothing on which to create a pathway towards reducing their vulnerability. But a closer look will show that even the destitute have capacities on which to build. By understanding poverty this way, emergency programmes can incorporate elements of sustainable livelihoods and reduce the problems associated with the relief–development continuum.

The role of NGOs

The response to emergencies has become an industry, with a cadre of professionals, educational and training programmes, budgets, media attention, books, journals and conferences. As a field study and practice, emergency relief is actually a sub-field of a sub-field as shown in Figure 1.2.

Table 1.4 Understanding poverty

Wealth	Category	Poverty
Predominantly urban	**Location**	Typically rural but spots of urban
Formal sector	**Economy**	Informal sector (often 80–90%)
'Have' and create	**Jobs**	'Do' (occasional, seasonal or itinerant work)
Professional, increasingly based on information	**Type of labour**	Physical
Property, livestock, business, information	**Ownership**	None to little
Access to credit credit	**Credit**	None or limited access to micro-
Motor vehicles bicycle	**Transport**	None or limited to an animal or
Educated and literate	**Education**	Illiterate
Some voice and influence (e.g. protest or voting)	**Politics**	No voice or participation in CBOs and self-help groups
Many	**Choice**	Little to none

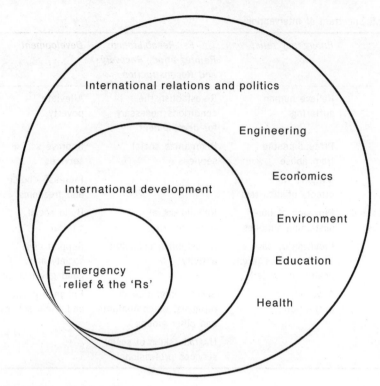

Figure 1.2 The relief industry

In many instances, the main principles, methods and approaches of development are applicable to emergencies. The main differences are time constraints and the objectives of the activities. One way to think of these is as a spectrum of intervention, as shown in Table 1.5, although the lines between the two are often blurred.

NGOs providing humanitarian assistance typically work in two ways. The main approach has been to work at the grassroots level, directly implementing activities. The second method, more common among international non-governmental organizations (INGOs), is to work through partners such as community-based organizations (CBOs) and local NGOs (LNGOs). Multi-sectoral programmes that involve activities from more than one sector are a strategy to bring some holism to what can otherwise be boxed into unconnected sector projects.

Despite the size of the industry and the level of response, it is easy to assume that it has a greater impact than it does. In most emergencies, the affected people find their own solutions themselves. Refugee camps spontaneously appear, children find their parents on their own, most people naturally recover from their psychological wounds and people find ways to adapt, rebuild and restart their livelihoods. External assistance is important, but this importance can be overestimated. The external response to emergencies has developed into a global

Table 1.5 Spectrum of interventions

	Emergency relief	The Rs: Rehabilitation, Reintegration, Recovery and Reconstruction	Development
Goals	Relieve human suffering	Re-establish the conditions necessary for development	Alleviate poverty
	Protect people from abuse	Reorganize social services	Improve social services
	Mitigate the effects of disasters		Increase choice and freedoms
Methods and examples	Provision of life-sustaining supplies	Rebuild social infrastructure	Build social capital
	Provision of basic social services (e.g. health and water)	Re-establish economic activity	Support civil society and good governance
	Advocacy of protection	Social integration of refugees, ex-combatants and other groups	Enhance economic and fiscal activity
		Upgrade skills of social services professionals	

industry with annual governmental budgets of US$78.6 billion in 2004 (OECD figures).

Humanitarian principles

Humanitarian principles are fundamental to giving direction and purpose to emergency programmes. The 'Fundamental Principles of the Red Cross/ Crescent' provide a foundation on which the NGO community operates or at least basically subscribes to. Elements of these principles can be found in individual NGO mission statements and in the Code of Conduct (see pp. 381– 83). Before discussing some of their implications, the key principles are summarized here.

Humanity   NGOs seek 'to prevent and alleviate human suffering wherever it may be found'.

Impartiality   NGO activity 'makes no discrimination as to nationality, race, religious beliefs, class, or political opinions', and gives priority to the most urgent cases.

Independence   NGOs rely on their own organizations' autonomy especially from government. Independence is seen as necessary to fulfil the other principles.

As the first and most basic principle, humanity receives probably the most wide-ranging application and is rarely if ever contested. Impartiality, too, is widely accepted and forms the basis of most NGOs' work, even many with a religious leaning. Because it is much more difficult to preserve in emergencies, neutrality presents more of a dilemma for many relief workers. On a basic level, most organizations do not have a problem with impartiality or neutrality, but many organizations experience difficulty implementing them. Selecting one group as beneficiaries (e.g. working in rebel-held areas but not in government-controlled areas or vice versa) can leave another group out and thus not be neutral. Independence too can be seen as controversial. If an NGO receives the vast majority of its operating budget from a single government or other single source, some feel it cannot claim genuine autonomy. Close association with military forces, by arriving at the same time and coordinating activities, is also seen as a major dilemma (see Chapter 20).

While noble in purpose, adherence to these principles is not absolute nor always easy in practice. Two schools of practice have developed, which can be characterized as classical humanitarianism and neo-humanitarianism. Classical humanitarianism was first advocated by Henri Dunant, a founder of the Red Cross movement, and stresses neutrality and meeting basic needs even in the face of human rights abuses. As an organization, the Red Cross typifies the classical approach.

In contrast, neo-humanitarianism stresses humanity over neutrality. With its emphasis on human rights, however, comes the dilemma of speaking out and jeopardizing access to people in need. Human rights aspects of programming can be difficult to operationalize and may quickly result in suspension of activities: either voluntarily or because local powers no longer tolerate an NGO's outspokenness. Neo-humanitarianism depends on an astute understanding of the situation and readiness to handle its consequences.

Although technically an international organization, the Red Cross has a strongly neutral operating policy and it has at times drawn sharp criticism for this (e.g. by not speaking out more forcefully about war crimes). Some organizations can be highly outspoken about political issues but others feel that these organizations overstep the bounds of neutrality. Still other organizations may adopt a clear partisanship based on their core beliefs. This may often be the case with NGOs established to help particular groups or causes. At times, an NGO may face few options and its hand may be forced. Insecurity in particular can be a determining factor, when an NGO may change its stance from one of involvement to one of withdrawal.

Another way to look at humanitarian principles is by different options for intervention as summarized in Table 1.6. With the difficult situations faced by NGOs having alternatives is critical. Under different circumstances, NGOs managers decide between these difficult courses of action. For this reason, relief workers need to be politically aware of these problems and dilemmas and be able to navigate through them as they arise. While the humanitarian principles have been around since the start of modern humanitarianism and considerable

Table 1.6 Options for intervention

Withdrawal	Neutrality	Active humanitarianism	Clear partnership
NGO work does more harm than good	Someone must try to work operationally on behalf of the victims	Operational NGOs can work to reduce suffering with actions that also help reduce conflict and build the conditions for peace	Operational NGOs should take sides depending on their values (e.g. human rights, ethnicity, religion or politics
It is better to refrain from operational responses and to work on conflict resolution, advocacy, or long-term development	NGOs can best help by negotiating with the belligerents on behalf of victims while maintaining a neutral position on the conflict	Key principles include a comprehensive long-term view, understanding social dynamics and considering how each action could contribute to conflict resolution	It is possible to mix advocacy with conflict resolution and operations
Some principles include tough love and work on the root causes of conflict only	Role specified in the Geneva Conventions		In appropriate conditions sound alliances with military and security forces can be made
	Separation from alliances with military humanitarian operations and human rights groups because division of labour is necessary		

Source: Lindenberg (1999: 219).

ink has been spilled on refining them, as discussed below (pp. 13–15), major problems have arisen for those managing emergency relief. Before discussing this, it is important to briefly mention the legal aspects of humanitarian relief.

International humanitarian law (IHL), the set of rules, treaties and customs intended to protect civilians in times of armed conflict, provides a means by which relief workers can carry out activities in emergencies. While many treaties constitute IHL, the main parts are found in the Geneva Conventions of 1949 and its two Additional Protocols of 1977. IHL extends to all parties of conflict and holds special protection for humanitarian relief workers and free access for relief supplies (when there are blockades). Additionally, the Rome Statute for the International Criminal Court in 1998 makes it a war crime to intentionally direct attacks against civilians in an internal armed conflict, including the staff, offices, supplies or vehicles used in providing humanitarian assistance.

Like IHL, human rights law is founded in rules, treaties and customs including the UN Universal Declaration of Human Rights of 1948 that places obligations on governments to respect the dignity and worth of each person. Human rights law extends to times of both war and peace. Because of their unique status, refugees have additional legal coverage found in several conventions and protocols. Internally displaced people (IDPs) are also covered in the UN Secretary General's Guiding Principles on Internal Displacement of 1998. Summaries of relevant international humanitarian, human rights and refugee law are provided on pp. 384–85.

Problems and dilemmas of the international response system

A traditional view of the development industry was that because of its strong focus on humanitarianism it was inherently ethical and its outputs naturally beneficial. Recent decades have left many countries worse off and evidence pointing towards development aid efforts contributing to violent conflict has turned this traditional view on its head. In this section, some of the specific dilemmas are presented. In the following section on standardized approaches (pp. 15–20), some of the remedies to these dilemmas are discussed.

A small library can now be filled with books that highlight the development industry's failures. The titles alone – *Condemned to Repeat?* (2002), *Famine Crimes* (1998) and *The Road to Hell* (2002) – tell how international aid has been misused, wasted and at times even exacerbated conflict. According to many critics, NGOs have been at times unaccountable, ineffective, dishonest and beholden to major donors who push the political agendas of a few countries. This is a situation that continues to the present. Among the 10 prevalent problems described by Prendergast (1996) and others are the following:

1. **Relief causing harm:** In certain cases, the provision of emergency can have unintended negative consequences. Examples include the diversion of food aid to fighting factions and projects that reinforce divisions between ethnic groups. The reasons for this include a poor understanding of the local context ('it's just like other disasters'), a disregard or a failure to account for the adverse results of aid ('these

---

Box 1.2 Organizations' names

In mainstream development and relief NGOs, it might appear that there is a typical NGO. Common acronyms include local NGOs (LNGOs), international NGOs (INGOS) and 'big' international NGOs (BINGOs). In the US, locally based NGOs that work overseas are called private voluntary organizations (PVOs). But as Fowler (1997) explains it, there are many NGO labels. There are, for example, organizations that are quasi-NGOs established by the government, known as QUANGOs, commercial NGOs called CONGOs and criminally-run NGOs called CRINGOs.

supplies must go through') or being unaware or inflexible about taking advantage of benefits.

2. **Competition:** Every industry experiences competition between organizations and emergency relief is no different. There are several reasons for this, including staff personalities, pressure to perform, resource scarcity or the perception that there are limited funds or areas to implement projects and even survive as an organization. This problem is not just prevalent among NGOs but also other organizations like the UN agencies, that perceive pressure to show that they are operational in an emergency.

3. **Flawed programme design:** Programmes may foster dependency instead of promoting recovery and self-reliance. Programmes may not be holistic (created and run as 'silos'), take into account relationships found in the host community or have a planned handover strategy. Development principles are based on governmental legitimacy and this may be absent during an emergency. Programmes may be based on linear patterns such as the relief–development continuum but emergencies are complex. It is normally unclear when an emergency is over and development begins. As a result, international assistance can be seen in different ways by many people.

4. **Accountability:** Accountability is the responsibility to report to stakeholders regarding plans, the use of resources and the results (i.e. outputs and outcomes) of activities. In relation to the commercial sector, NGOs are thought to have no bottom line (or too many bottom lines), making accountability difficult. Typically, most or all information is reported to the financial donor. In many situations, beneficiaries (i.e. local people) have often not been involved enough.

5. **Lack of creativity:** All too often complex humanitarian emergencies are approached using the same sets of tools and programmes. The old maxim, 'To a hammer, every problem looks like a nail,' more often than not applies. A closely related problem has been too much emphasis on quantitative outputs and not enough on qualitative outcomes.

6. **Lack of clarity:** Some NGOs have a poor understanding of the local context. There may be little usable information from assessments which may not, moreover, be shared between organizations. There may not be any way of knowing when a project can be deemed a success because of a lack of suitable measurements or codes.

7. **Humanitarian access:** Putting a stress on reaching those in need, regardless of the consequences, has had negative consequences in some contexts. Following the mantra, 'the aid must get through', some assistance efforts have proceeded without preserving human rights or taking into account unintended results.

8. **Using aid instead of political action:** As many have said, 'There are no humanitarian solutions to political problems,' yet emergency

programmes have often been the primary response to complex political problems and have been used as a substitute for political action. It is now widely understood, though still poorly implemented, that comprehensive and integrated solutions need to be found in which NGOs only play a part.

9. **Poor funding:** Ironically, despite the high political spotlight emergencies often find themselves in, responses rarely receive the funding sought. The need for publicity and funds has often led to distortion of facts on the ground, such as calling limited but chronic food shortages famine. Also, many NGOs work in so-called forgotten emergencies, where media attention is low, making fundraising difficult.

10. **Poor management:** Perhaps because NGOs rely on such a disparate recruitment pool, good management practices are often lacking. Although the situation is improving, recruitment of poorly qualified people has been widespread. Some NGOs rely heavily on volunteers who have little more to offer than good intentions and sympathy. Emergency programmes typically suffer from a high turnover of staff and other human resource problems.

Standardized initiatives and approaches

In response to the problems and dilemmas described above, the development industry has been actively seeking remedies. Although many emergencies are political in nature, in which case relief programming can realistically only address symptoms (or fallout), programming can be politically sophisticated enough to take root causes into account.

Box 1.3 Should I go to school for this?

As the humanitarian industry becomes more professionalized, there are more training and educational opportunities. Good training is available from a number of organizations based in the UK, including RedR and Intrac. Specialized training in project management can be found in Brussels through PCM and for accounting from Mango. Education is available from a number of universities in the US, including Columbia, Harvard and Tufts, among others, as well as in the UK, including the LSE, Manchester, Sussex and York, and in France at Paris Université VII. These schools tend to have a theoretical slant and will not necessarily give the skills needed to effectively manage programmes, but they will provide a firm grounding in the issues discussed in this chapter. The question then becomes whether it is worth paying for expensive tuition and spending time away from the field. That question needs to be answered at the individual level, taking long-term personal goals into consideration. There are programmes that split the difference between training and education, of which the month-long International Diploma in Humanitarian Affairs administered jointly by the University of Geneva and Fordham University in New York is notable. The UN's Reliefweb has probably the most comprehensive database of training and educational opportunities in the humanitarian industry. See pp. 395–7 for relevant websites.

Over time, the approach to responding to humanitarian emergencies has followed trends that have become popular and then fallen out of favour. Buzzwords develop. These initiatives and approaches represent current conventional wisdom and are in need of further research and development.

Most of the initiatives and approaches presented here have developed from significant research in many parts of the world. As a relatively new field, it is important to be aware of poorly supported fads and trends. Other chapters of this book discuss many of the elements discussed here, so what appears here are summaries of some of the more popular and substantive standardized methods.

Initiatives

Code of Conduct

Originally created by five international NGOs and the Red Cross in 1994, the Code of Conduct is described thus in the Sphere Code:

> This Code of Conduct seeks to guard our standards of behaviour. As such, it is not about operational details, such as how one should calculate food rations or set up a refugee camp. Rather, it seeks to maintain the high standards of independence, effectiveness and impact to which disaster response NGOs and the International Red Cross and Red Crescent Movement aspire. It is a voluntary code, enforced by the will of the organization accepting it to maintain the standards laid down in the Code. (Sphere Project, 2004)

The Sphere Project

The Sphere Project is a multi-organizational effort that developed the Humanitarian Charter and Minimum Standards in which organizations commit to quality and accountability. Until the Sphere Project, there were few concrete standards with which to guide assistance, set values and measure performance. As the Sphere Project describes it:

> The initiative was launched in 1997 by a group of humanitarian NGOs and the Red Cross and Red Crescent movement, who framed a Humanitarian Charter and identified Minimum Standards to be attained in disaster assistance, in each of five key sectors (water supply and sanitation, nutrition, food aid, shelter and health services). This process led to the publication of the first Sphere handbook in 2000. Taken together, the Humanitarian Charter and the Minimum Standards contribute to an operational framework for accountability in disaster assistance efforts. (Sphere Project, 2004)

The Sphere Project produces a book of standards which are summarized on pp. 375–80.

Inter-Agency Standing Committee (IASC)

The IASC was established in 1992 following a UN resolution designed to improve inter-agency coordination. The IASC is made up of the heads of UN specialized agencies involved in emergencies, the ICRC and two NGO umbrella organizations (the International Council of Voluntary Agencies, ICVA, and Interaction). The IASC meets regularly to develop policy, divide responsibilities, identify gaps in humanitarian response and advocate. Specific sub-committees work on issues such as education, psychosocial and GBV initiatives and accompanying guidelines. The IASC is also responsible for the development of the cluster approach discussed further in Chapter 20.

Humanitarian Accountability Project (HAP)

HAP is an inter-agency initiative to strengthen the accountability of organizations to those affected and to facilitate improved performance in the humanitarian sector. The HAP's operational framework is based on the following questions:

1. **Who is accountable?** Duty-bearers (e.g. NGOs, UN, donors, government and militaries).
2. **To whom?** Affected individuals or communities and other stakeholders.
3. **For what?** To meet commitments as defined by standards and benchmarks.
4. **How?** Monitoring: listening, reviewing, evaluating; responding; informing and reporting; identifying duty-holders; self-regulation and independent mechanisms.
5. **For which outcome?** Changes in programmes and operations, awards, redress, sanctions.

Recommendations for an accountable organization are provided on pp. 385–6.

Compas Qualité *(Quality COMPAS)*

The Quality COMPAS (Criteria and Tools for the Management and Piloting of humanitarian ASsistance) is an initiative by the Groupe Urgence Réhabilitation et Développement. As an alternative approach to Sphere and HAP, the main thrust is that quality cannot be based simply on technical indicators but on a realistic and comprehensive understanding all aspects of an intervention. The quality approach takes into account different stakeholders and the relationships between them, and issues such as short-term projects dealing with long-term problems, a focus on contracts and human resources. To achieve this end, the Quality COMPAS has developed tools and processes in order to support effective action in emergencies. This includes tools for analysis, diagnosis, design, action and evaluation, as well as processes that build on experience, creating technical reports, making institutional changes and training staff for emergencies.

People in Aid Code

The People in Aid Code was first drawn up organizations involved in humanitarian relief in the UK between 1995 and 1997, to address the widely acknowledged deficiencies in human resources management (HRM) among NGOs. The code has undergone revisions and consists of seven guiding principles supported by specific indicators (see pp. 386–9 for the text of the code). The People in Aid organization is working to deepen the code and make it more operational as well as providing support to NGOs in implementing it.

Do No Harm

Recognizing that humanitarian relief was no longer an exclusively neutral and beneficial tool, Mary Anderson (1999) and others sought to devise a means of ensuring that assistance does not cause more harm than good. Their project, called Local Capacities for Peace through Aid, became known as Do No Harm, following its adaptation of the Hippocratic oath. The principles of Do No Harm are that once an understanding has been gained of how aid might have an adverse impact on peace, such as the diversion of aid to warring factions or sending messages that (even inadvertently) bestow legitimacy on warriors or reinforce animosity, there are three categories of ways aid may help local people who want to disengage from conflict. Such aid provides a safe space for non-war actors, a voice for peace (or non-war) and incentives to disengage from conflict.

Global Humanitarian Platform

The Global Humanitarian Platform (GHP) initiative seeks to improve humanitarian response by strengthening partnerships at the global and field levels. Created in 2006 following consultations with a large group of NGOs, the Red Cross/Red Crescent movement, and UN agencies and other intergovernmental organizations, the GHP was formed with an aim to enhance cooperation between organizations. Specific issues of mutual concern include accountability to the beneficiary populations, capacity building of local partners, staff safety and security; and organizational roles in transitional situations. An output of the GHP is the 'Principles of Partnership', which cover issues such as equality, transparency, result-oriented approaches, responsibility and complementarity. Partners in the GHP try to ensure that these principles are present in their operations and activities.

Approaches

Participation

Participation is the process of involving stakeholders, particularly beneficiaries, in planning, carrying out and evaluating a project or programme. The philosophy of participation is summed up in this parable: 'Give a man a fish and you feed

> **Box 1.4** Principles of relief delivery
>
> The late Fred Cuny (1999) set out several principles of relief delivery:
> * The context of the emergency is crucial; local politics, economics and other conditions cannot be separated from an intervention.
> * Traditional responses by international agencies can cause more harm than good.
> * International aid is a drop in the bucket compared with local aid.
> * The key to success in relief aid is involving local people directly.
> * Relief and development are intricately linked.
> * Relief aid is not a logistical exercise – it is a process to accelerate recovery.
> * Relief intervention teaches us lessons; we should heed the lessons learned from the past.

him for a day; teach a man to fish and you feed him for a lifetime.' Participation's key strengths include its ability to engender buy-in and ownership of an NGO's activities and objectives by beneficiaries. True participatory projects will include the views of the traditionally marginalized, such as women, children and the elderly.

Livelihoods approaches

Livelihoods are the capacities, resources and activities that generate an income. Traditional emergency relief focused on immediate needs and left long-term economic concerns to locally led initiatives and development-oriented activities, which left people without the means to reduce their own vulnerability. A disaster-resistant sustainable livelihoods approach (see Chapter 2), is especially helpful in areas where there is a basis for economic activity and a likelihood of recurring shocks such as cyclones and low-intensity conflict. One of the key strengths of this approach is its ability to create durable solutions to vulnerability (especially poverty) and linkages at the macro and micro levels. For this reason, a thorough understanding of the context in which emergencies occur and how activities may positively and negatively affect the situation is critical. Not all emergencies are suitable to livelihood interventions and, if conditions are right, the timing is especially important.

Peace building

While not traditionally part of humanitarian relief, the reduction of tension through peace building is now considered by many to be critical for the prevention of conflict. Peace building is typically thought of as measures that are undertaken to address the root causes of conflict and promote reconciliation between groups. In this way, it is something that can be added to programmes, depending on the context. Water projects, for example, can involve inter-ethnic interaction at the planning and implementation stages, where elements of the projects may physically be present in geographic areas containing different ethnic groups. Similarly, trading developed out of microfinance activities might involve different ethnic groups exchanging goods and services across former front-lines. Peace education courses are important. Women and children in particular are often targeted for such training to help break the cycle of violence from one generation to the next.

Rights-based approaches

Rights-based approaches seek for duty-holders (e.g. donors, NGOs and government) to be accountable and respect, protect and realize the human rights of beneficiaries. In this way, programming plans, policies and processes focus not simply on the needs of beneficiaries, as in a traditional needs-based approach. Its strength is in its emphasis on the moral and legal rights of beneficiaries through humanitarian principles and the analysis and addressing of root causes. A problem is the practical application of a rights-based approach, especially in conflict areas. A rights-based approach is not incompatible with a needs-based approach, but the two are different and not always easily articulated on the ground.

Developmental relief

Developmental relief is an approach which takes into account normal and long-term coping strategies and the community structures through which these strategies are implemented. The approach seeks to support and strengthen community resources to withstand the shock of emergencies. Developmental relief centres on a number of basic operating features, including those outlined by the IFRC (1996: 50–1):

1. Participation
2. Accountability
3. Decentralized control
4. Demonstrating concern for sustaining livelihoods
5. Basing strategies on the reality of a disaster
6. Identifying the needs and capacities of diverse disaster survivors
7. Building on survivors' capacities
8. Building on local institutions
9. Setting sustainable standards for services

Although developmental-relief contains many elements that may be useful in implementing emergency programmes, the continuum in which it is based is open to debate. Some feel that scaling up project-oriented relief to policy-oriented development is difficult, if not impossible, and blurring the distinction between war and peace may cause further problems.

CHAPTER 2
Understanding disaster-affected populations and programme sectors

The core business of NGOs is implementing activities in programme sectors and thus a basic awareness of the different sectors is an important aspect of being an effective relief worker. The purpose of this chapter is to provide an overview of the programme sectors and describe some of the issues and common approaches. The humanitarian sectors are often divided into several areas including activities that address immediate survival needs, protection, rehabilitation and development and several cross-cutting themes. Following this division, this chapter covers the following topics.

- Essential sectors: food and nutrition, health, water and sanitation, and shelter
- Protection: refugees and the internally displaced, psychosocial projects and specifically targeted programmes
- Rehabilitation and development: infrastructure rehabilitation, education and microfinance development
- Cross-cutting themes: community participation, gender-based violence, sustainable livelihoods, demobilization of ex-combatants and disaster preparedness and mitigation

While providing or improving a technical project is relatively straightforward, breaking bad habits that relate to them is more difficult. In other words, improving health is about changing practices as much as building clinics, and often more so. In each case, additional resources and specialists in each sector will be needed to implement programmes effectively.

Food and nutrition

Public nutrition basics

Lack of access to food, leading to malnutrition, is a major contributing factor to morbidity and mortality during emergencies. Public nutrition focuses on providing food security to an entire population. Food security relates to people's access to the food needed at any time to achieve an active and healthy life. Lack of knowledge and information, poor health care and other factors also contribute to food insecurity. An average adult's intake of food is thought to average 2,100 kcal per day and includes a healthy mix of energy, protein, fat and nutrients, known as a person's food basket. If people receive less than this, and undergo health problems such as failure to grow, they do not have food security and will experience malnutrition.

Malnutrition encompasses a range of medical conditions in which a person cannot achieve normal functions such as growth, pregnancy, lactation, and resisting and recovering from disease as a result from a lack of one or more nutrients. In emergencies, particularly armed conflict, malnutrition tends to afflict young children less than 5 years of age. The reasons for this can be explained in a causal chain from a lack of food and poor health (especially relating to infectious disease) and the shocks found in emergencies. A conceptual framework for understanding the linkages starts with basic causes such as lack of resources, exclusion, political failure and conflict. These are linked to underlying causes such as food insecurity, poor environmental conditions and lack of access to health care. There are also immediate causes such as inadequate food intake and increased morbidity (illness). Together, these result in malnutrition and mortality (death).

In this way, malnutrition results from a variety of basic, underlying and immediate causes. During emergencies, especially since the 1990s, women and children are more open to attack. Under long-term emergencies a spiral of hunger forms that continues from one generation to the next. For example, inadequate eating during a women's pregnancy leads to a baby with low weight. The baby will typically not have enough to eat as he or she grows into a child so will have poor physical development, which is closely linked to lower resistance to disease (morbidity).

Access is the key component of food security and lack of access causes the extreme cases of food insecurity characterized by famine. Famine results when some people do not have access to food, usually as a result of manmade causes. Rather than caused simply by a shock such as drought, food insecurity occurs when the entitlement system breaks down or is manipulated in times of emergency, and it is these conditions that cause malnutrition. Even in stable conditions, underweight children are very common in many countries and may make up 10–60 per cent of the population.

When the situation is grave enough for the coping mechanisms to be inadequate, malnutrition is the result. Malnutrition includes a range of medical conditions in which people do not receive enough nutrients and where normal physical and mental development and function is impaired. Famine, extreme cases of food insecurity, is often an outcome of conflict in one of several ways, as follows:

- Armies take or requisition food including international supplies.
- Military forces destroy crops, silos and livestock, and they may cause farmers to flee from their land.
- Government budgets shift from social support to military operations.
- Large areas are lost to landmines or military infrastructure such as trenches and encampments.
- Conflict disrupts normal patterns that permit the pursuit of livelihoods.
- Control of trade may contribute to localized famines.
- Social disintegration.

In emergencies, access to food can be cut off or controlled by the powerful. Yet people everywhere have a strong ability to survive by relying on coping mechanisms that may be positively or negatively impacted by the types of programmes carried out by NGOs. As conditions worsen, people commit more of their resources to coping with crisis conditions and as options dwindle, so does their ability to recover, until few options are left besides selling their last assets and migrating to other areas which may put them in greater dangers.

The most common form of malnutrition especially among infants and young children is protein energy malnutrition (PEM). The type of PEM depends on the diet and whether they have access to a balance of proteins. There are three clinical forms of PEM: marasmus, kwashiorkor and a combined form of marasmic kwashiorkor.

Acute malnutrition Typically found in acute emergencies as a result of recent rapid weight loss or a failure to gain weight. If treated promptly, effects are reversible once conditions are improved. Acute malnutrition is usually measured using weight-for-height. Symptoms include rapid weight loss resulting in marasmus (see Figure 2.1).

Chronic malnutrition Typically found in situations of long-term underdevelopment and permanent emergencies. Children may appear normal but younger than their actual age. This is usually measured using a height-for-age tool. Symptoms of chronic malnutrition include weight loss over a long period, resulting in kwashiorkor (see Figure 2.2).

Other forms of malnutrition In addition to PEM, here are other types of malnutrition resulting from disease and deficiency of micro-nutrients (MDD). Lack of micro-nutrients can result in iron deficiency anaemia, vitamin A xerophthalmia (which leads to night blindness), iodine deficiency disorders (such as goitre), vitamin C scurvy, niacin pellagra and thiamin beriberi (both vitamin B deficiencies).

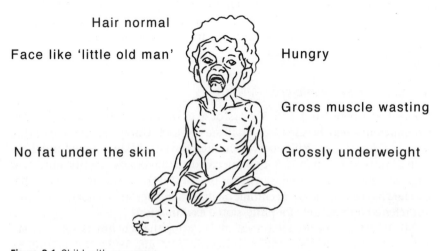

Figure 2.1 Child with marasmus

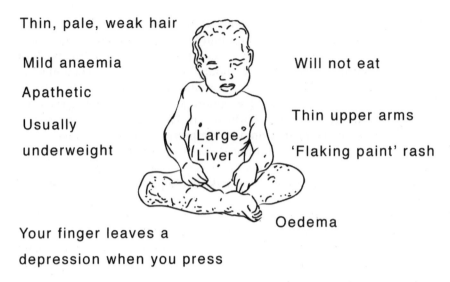

Thin, pale, weak hair

Mild anaemia

Apathetic

Usually

underweight

Will not eat

Thin upper arms

'Flaking paint' rash

Oedema

Your finger leaves a

depression when you press

Figure 2.2 Child with kwashiorkor

Nutritional monitoring

There are a number of ways of monitoring the growth of malnourished people, using what are known as anthropometric measurements. Nutritional monitoring is done using age, sex, height/length and weight as indices. Malnourished adults can be measured using body mass index (BMI = [weight (kg)/height (m)]^2); however, there is no standard method for measuring the elderly or those unable to stand up straight. There is a number of ways to monitor the nutritional status of children, the main victims of malnutrition. Here, four of the most common methods of growth monitoring are presented, starting with the most commonly used in emergencies.

Mid-upper arm circumference (MUAC)

For children between 1 and 5 years of age, measuring the mid-upper arm circumference may be used as a rapid survey tool. Using a simple measuring tape, in Figure 2.3, large numbers of children can be quickly screened and those with a MUAC of less than 12.5–13.5 cm, based on the colour-coded measurement strip, are referred for further weight-for-height (WFH) measurement. Note that if a child has oedema, a sign of chronic malnutrition, they should not be measured but referred immediately for professional examination.

   MUAC can also be used to screen adults, using the benchmarks of less than 185 mm for moderate malnutrition and less than 160 mm for severe malnutrition.

Figure 2.3 MUAC

Weight-for-height (WFH)

The standard measurement used in emergencies, WFH is used to show recent weight loss or gain and is useful when the age is of a child is unknown. This measurement is used for both nutritional surveys and as a selection method for selective feeding programmes. For infants that cannot stand, 'weight-for-length' is used, whereby children are laid flat and measured lengthwise.

Height-for-age (HFA)

HFA is used to measure skeletal growth and is the best measurement for past under-nutrition and chronic malnutrition. For children who cannot stand, usually under 2 years of age, 'length-for-age' is used. HFA is generally not used in acute emergencies because it cannot measure short-term growth changes.

Weight-for-age (WFA)

WFA is generally used to measure under-nourishment and can reflect a combination of acute and chronic malnutrition. In stable situations, children up to 35 months are monitored using what are known as 'Road-to-Health' charts. Carried out at least every three months, a child's growth is plotted, giving a useful picture that can show if a child begins to falter as a result of malnutrition or disease.

Calculating measurement scores

Once measured, a child's anthropometric measurement is compared with the expected value or reference of children of the same height or age from a reference population (available to nutritionists). The measurement can be expressed as either a percentage of the median or a standard deviation (often called SD score or Z-score). Children with less than 80 per cent (a Z-score of –2) weight-for-height than the median are considered malnourished and those with less than 70 per cent (a Z-score of –3) are considered severely malnourished. A summary of the anthropometric benchmarks are provided in Table 2.1.

Nutritionists usually use computer software, such as Epi Info™ (available free from the CDC and WHO websites on pp. 395 and 397), to calculate a surveyed population and the Z-scores of the malnourished. Regardless of the methods used, it is important to analyse the results of a nutrition survey in a particular context. In some situations, for example, a relatively low incidence of global malnutrition may mask conditions where coping mechanisms have been exhausted.

To address food and nutrition in emergencies, there is a range of possible remedies, depending on the situation. Here, feeding programmes, agriculture and livestock projects are presented.

Feeding programmes

Feeding programmes are carried out in several ways usually as general food distribution, where all beneficiaries receive rations such as at a refugee camp or at selective feeding programmes. There are two types of these programmes: supplementary (SFP) or therapeutic. The objectives, selection criteria and common provisions are summarized in Table 2.2.

Table 2.1 Anthropometric benchmarks

	Well-nourished	Mild malnutrition	Moderate malnutrition	Severe malnutrition
Oedema	No	No	No	Yes (oedematous malnutrition)
MUAC	>13.5 cm		12.5–13.5 cm	<12.5 cm
Weight-for-height	90–120% or +2 to –1 Z-score	80–89% or –1 to –2 Z-score	70–79% or –2 to –3 Z-score	<70% or +2 to –1 Z-score (severe wasting)
Height-for-age	95–110% or +2 to –1 Z-score	90–94% or –1 to –2 Z-score	85–89% or –2 to –3 Z-score	<85% or < –3 Z-score (severe stunting)
Weight-for-age			60–80% or –2 to –3 Z-score	<60% or –3 Z-score (severe underweight)

Source: Modified from WFP (2002: 143).

Table 2.2 Feeding programmes

Programme	Objectives	Criteria for selection and target group	Provision/treatment
Blanket SFP	Prevent deterioration of nutritional situation	Children under 3 years or under 5 years	Usually consists of dry rations such as blended foods (e.g. CSB) with additional supplements such as oil and salt
	Reduce prevalence of acute malnutrition in children under 5 years	All pregnant women (from date of confirmed pregnancy) and nursing mothers (until maximum 6 months after delivery)	Dry rations, consisting of 1,000–1,200 kcal per meal, are often provided on a weekly basis
	Ensure safety net measures	Other at-risk groups	
	Reduce mortality and morbidity risk		
Targeted SFP	Correct moderate malnutrition	Children under 5 years moderately malnourished:	Typically 500–700 kcal meals provided at one time in wet feedings
	Prevent the moderately malnourished from becoming severely malnourished	70–80% of median weight-for height or:	
	Reduce mortality and morbidity risk in children under 5 years of age	between −3 and −2 Z-scores weight-for height	
	Provide nutritional support to selected pregnant women and nursing mothers	Malnourished individuals (based on weight-for-height, body mass indicator, MUAC or clinic signs): older children (5–10 years), adolescents,	
	Provide follow-up services to those discharged from therapeutic feeding programmes:	adults and elderly persons, or:	
		Medical referrals Selected pregnant women (from date of confirmed pregnancy) and nursing mothers (until 6 months after delivery), for instance	

cont.

cont.

Programme objectives	Criteria for selection and target group	Provision/treatment
	using MUAC <22 cm as a cut-off indicator for pregnant women	
	Referrals from TFP	
TFP	Reduce excess mortality and morbidity risk usually in children under 5 years	Children under 5 years severely malnourished:	Three weeks of 24-hour medical treatment at a TFC
	Provide medical/ nutritional treatment for the severely malnourished:	<70% of the median weight-for-height and/ or oedema or:	Immediate medical concerns include sudden death from dehydration, electrolyte disturbance, hypoglycaemia and infection
		<−3 Z-scores weight-for-height and/or oedema	Initially, small and frequent liquid feeding is done orally or by nasogastric tube
		Severely malnourished children older than 5 years, adolescents and adults admitted based on available weight-for-height standards or presence of oedema	After 4–7 days, special diets can begin
		Low birth-weight babies	After two weeks, resumption of normal diet
		Orphans <1 year (only when traditional care practices are inadequate	Psychosocial activities become increasingly important as medical concerns improve
		Mothers of children younger than 1 year with breast feeding failure (only in exceptional cases where relactation through counselling and traditional alternative feeding has failed	

Source: Modified from UNHCR/WFP (2002). Note that this is for informational purposes only. Current guidelines should be referenced by trained staff.

The aim of SFPs is to provide nutrition (food) in addition to the general ration or what is locally available. The aim is to rehabilitate moderately malnourished persons or to prevent deterioration in the nutritional status of those most at risk by meeting their additional needs, usually focusing on children, pregnant women and nursing mothers.

Because of the gravity of severe malnourishment, people need urgent specialized medical care through therapeutic feeding programmes (TFP) in therapeutic feeding centres where children spend three weeks undergoing treatment. TFCs are often established next to health facilities (a hospital) and are designed to care for between 50 and 100 people. Once admitted to a TFC, a person receives 24-hour care, consisting of treatment of infection, rehydration, immunization, 6–12 small meals a day of high-energy milk, supplemented by vitamins, especially Vitamin A. If the mother is lactating, infants are typically breast-fed as well. Following treatment, children are expected to return to SFP if it is still needed and available. In some cases therapeutic feeding can done through a community-based outreach programme, recognized by WHO as Community Therapeutic Care (CTC), where the community handles its own malnutrition issues and only severe medical conditions are referred to medical treatment.

There are two types of food distributions: wet and dry. Wet rations are prepared meals which can be given directly to beneficiaries. Typically, wet rations are provided at camps, schools or other facilities and require cooking and eating facilities, as well as good attendance by beneficiaries which may be disrupted by insecurity. In some cases, distribution of wet rations may be preferred because of the low risk of loss or diversion. Dry rations are less labour-intensive to distribute but in insecure situations they may be lost (stolen or sold) or diverted to away from the intended beneficiaries (e.g. from children to adults) and require cooking which may be difficult in some circumstances.

Food consumption is highly dependent on local culture. Traditional habits and ethno-religious factors play a significant role in what people eat. All rations should be acceptable to beneficiaries. There are a number of foods commonly available, such as maize, wheat and rice. For targeted interventions, commercial nutritional foods include UNIMIX, BP5, Corn-Soya Based (CSB) and Plumpy'nut.

Food distributions need to be well planned and coordinated. Exit criteria for people in feeding programmes should be clearly established and phase-out plans should be developed early on (see Chapter 21). The conditions which contribute to the abuse of food distributions include prolonged conflict, a weak state or absent law enforcement, economic crisis or collapse and the presence of armed rebel groups that lack financial support. In such cases, increased precautions may be necessary, such as registration, monitoring, coordination and consideration of rations given (e.g. wet or dry, or direct distribution to households). Distributions are discussed further in Chapter 12.

Agriculture in emergencies

Emergencies, as mentioned, can adversely affect agricultural production in a number of ways, including the looting of supplies, killing or stealing livestock and the disruption of agricultural work that would normally continue from one season to the next. Agricultural development involves a complex variety of considerations from crop variety, water availability and pest control to gender and land rights (FAO, 1998). As with projects in other sectors, it is vital that any proposed agriculture project be fully approved and in line with any existing regulations and larger plans.

Typical interventions involve the distribution of seeds and tools (Johnson, 1998), but to be effective should also include some training and extension (supervision) activities as well. Indicators for this type of project include the amount of land planted and cultivated per household, the amount of harvest and a drop in malnutrition rates. Some general considerations include the following.

Seeds

- Follow the advice of local farmers. They rely on experience passed down for generations. In emergencies, experimenting with crops and other programme aspects may do more harm than good.
- Locally available seeds are usually better than imported seeds as they are known by farmers and suited to local conditions. However, they may be of poor quality and dealing with local suppliers may be problematic because buying large sums may also disrupt or cause damage to local markets. Distribution of fertilizers, especially in emergencies, is generally not a good idea because of sustainability and the impact on the environment.
- Potential suppliers should also be reviewed by knowledge organizations (e.g. local agronomists, Ministry of Agriculture, UN or other NGOs). If seeds are imported, they should be accompanied by a certificate ensuring their quality.
- Common crops, including grains (sorghum, millet, maize and rice), root crops (cassava), legumes (groundnuts and beans) and vegetables come in a great variety. Following local custom in terms of a typical food basket is critical and should involve farmers and both gender groups.
- To ease implementation, crop variety should be limited to no more than several seed varieties. Small gardens are easier to manage and can allow for a varied food basket.

Tools

- Following an assessment, make sure that the different tools needed for planting, crop maintenance and harvesting tools are planned for during the project design.

- Even in emergencies, farmers usually manage to retain some tools, but the quantity may not be sufficient to be productive. Depending on the country, standard items like axes, hoes, picks, rakes and shovels are widely available in markets but perhaps not in a disaster affected area.
- The main issue when procuring tools is quality, for which price is a good indicator. If the government is functioning, standards may be regulated, but the range between poor and good tools can be significant.
- Make sure local farmers are consulted before selecting and procuring tools. Tool specifications (e.g. size and materials) can vary from one region to the next.
- Make sure that a means of repairing tools, for example files, is also supplied during tool distributions.

Livestock

Livestock, such as camels, cattle, fowl, goats, pigs and sheep, provides people with a number of key resources. For full-time pastoralists, livestock gives the bulk of their food, labour, power and income. Agriculturalists rely primarily on the crops they grow, but many also raise livestock to supplement what they grow. Agro-pastoralists mix both methods depending on the seasons. There are a number of considerations when working with livestock, including:

- When planning a livestock project, the local context, people, crops, livestock and natural resources need to be taken into account. Depending on the area and local familiarity, there is usually a range of good animals to be used in emergency interventions, including goat, cattle, chickens and sheep.
- The decision to start a livestock project may be difficult and cause tension, especially when livestock needs may compete with human needs (such as continuing drought). Providing livestock should only be done after a careful analysis of the situation and where people are dependent on animals which have been reduced as a result of an emergency. Other types of intervention may be more developmentally sustainable.
- Semi-urban and urban areas as well as rural areas may be targeted. In certain cases, rabbits, fowl and others may be appropriate.
- The balance between livestock, people and natural resources (e.g. water and pasture) need to be maintained, so if livestock is provided it should be as 'seeds' in which to re-grow herds. Usually, targeting marginalized groups such as returnees or female-headed households is more effective than blanket interventions.
- If veterinary services are provided or supplemented, they should be combined with local knowledge, which will likely be well informed of breeding, diseases and specific needs.

Health

Health is perhaps the most essential of the sectors. According to WHO, health is a state of complete physical, mental and social wellbeing, and not merely the absence of disease or infirmity. Health is a fundamental human right and the attainment of the highest possible level of health requires the action of many other social and economic sectors, including nutrition, shelter, water and sanitation. Because of its importance, the health sector was where the first modern humanitarians, such as Henri Dunant and Clara Barton, began their interventions.

Emergencies negatively affect health, resulting in increased mortality and morbidity. Events or conditions harmful to health include:

- decline in access to health services because of disaster or insecurity;
- rise in emergency-related health needs, such as trauma wounds and other life-threatening cases, at a time when the ability to meet these needs is reduced;
- increased sexual violence, including rape;
- inadequate or non-existent social services infrastructure, including health facilities that are damaged or destroyed in fighting;
- health workers being forced to flee or working under intimidation;
- inability to follow schedule-related health care such as immunizations and directly observed therapy (e.g. for tuberculosis);
- supplies and equipment looted or destroyed;
- reduction in or inability to carry out public health measures such as education and promotion.

Incorporating public health, medicine and many overlapping sectors, the health sector is also perhaps the largest sector; therefore, what appears here is a brief overview of issues related to the provision of health programming in emergencies. The differences between primary health in stable situations and emergencies are summarized in Table 2.3.

Given these differences, the most serious issue is the proper use of scarce resources. Public health in transitional countries, and even more in emergencies, is characterized by a planned utilization of resources and establishing priority. Health programming should support and seek to improve, or transform, existing services. In limited cases, such as when no health services exist or when existing facilities are overwhelmed (e.g. as a result of an influx of displaced people) and health authorities request assistance, establishing additional health services may be necessary. When a parallel system is developed, a number of problems may arise, including inequities in the quality of care and tension between those who have access to such care and those do not, such as refugees and host populations. Such problems should be addressed early and mitigated against by developing a phase-out plan and by working with health authorities and community leaders.

Table 2.3 Health programming

Health in stable situations	Health in emergencies
Fostering education on common health problems, their prevention, and control measures	Immunization against measles and meningitis
Treating common diseases and injuries	Maternal and child clinics; reproductive health programmes with family planning
Access to essential drugs	Control of communicable disease outbreaks including control of vectors and surveillance
Immunizing against major infectious diseases	Provision of food rations and selective feeding programmes
Improving maternal and child health care including family planning	First-level health services and referral system
Preventing and controlling locally endemic diseases	Provision of essential drugs
Promoting good nutrition	Access to potable water and waste disposal systems
Access to safe water and basic sanitation	Protection against cold (shelter, blanket, clothes)
	Health education based on community health workers' programme

Source: Modified from Saade and Burnham (2000: 8–10).

Infectious diseases

Infectious or communicable diseases pose one of the greatest threats to human life in emergencies (WHO, 2005). As shown in Figure 2.4, there is a natural equilibrium between a host population, an agent (e.g. parasites, bacteria and viruses) and the environment. In emergencies, however, where the balance between the environment, the population and agents may be disrupted, the risk of infectious disease greatly increases. The risk of epidemics, outbreaks that exceed typically expected number of cases, is particularly significant where health services are disrupted or people live in crowded circumstances (e.g. refugee camps). This leads to an increased likelihood that agents will be spread through the air, faecal matter, vectors such as mosquitoes and sexual transmission.

To address this imbalance that leads to greater morbidity and mortality is the aim of many emergency programmes where the largest threats are measles, diarrhoeal diseases, acute respiratory infections (ARI), malaria and malnutrition. Emergencies, where population displacement and the disruption of social services are common, increase the likelihood of infectious diseases outbreaks. For all NGO staff, it is useful to have basic information about common diseases

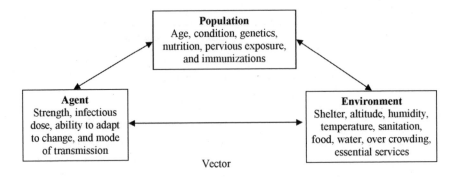

Figure 2.4 Population, agent and environment
Source: Saade and Burnham (2000: 7–5).

that commonly affect people in emergencies, including how they are caused and how they may be prevented, as summarized in Table 2.4.

HIV/AIDS in emergencies

Because of the seriousness of the HIV/AIDS pandemic, additional conditions are needed in emergencies. While still under research, HIV/AIDS prevalence seems to be exacerbated by emergencies, where there is an increase in gender-based violence (GBV), such as rape, and little or no access to a means of safe sex. Groups at risk include women, adolescents, mobile populations and the extremely poor. According to the IASC Task Force on HIV/AIDS in emergencies settings, the following actions should be undertaken:
- Establish coordination mechanisms, assess baseline data and set-up and manage a shared database.
- Prevent and respond to sexual violence and exploitation and protect orphaned and separated children. Manage the consequences of sexual violence.
- Include HIV/AIDS considerations in the planning and implementation of all sectors including food and nutrition, health, protection, and water and sanitation. Promote appropriate care and feeding practices for people living with HIV/AIDS (PLWH/A).
- Ensure access to condoms for peacekeepers, military and humanitarian staff, as well as the general population. Education campaigns should provide information on HIV/AIDS prevention and care.
- Establish the treatment of syndromic sexually transmitted infections (STIs), ensure a safe blood supply and safe deliveries.
- Prevent discrimination by HIV/AIDS status in staff management, ensure universal precautions are followed by health staff and provide post-exposure prophylaxis (PEP) for humanitarian staff.

Table 2.4 Infectious diseases

Disease	Description	Preventive measures
Acute respiratory infection (ARI)	Different causes including influenza (viral) and pneumonia (bacterial)	Health education
	Contributing factors are poor housing, lack of blankets and clothing, and smoke in living areas	Minimum living space standards and proper ventilation in shelters
	Leads to aches, cough, fever and other symptoms especially among children and older persons	Adequate clothing and blankets
Diarrhoeal diseases (DD)	Defined as 3 or more liquid stools a day, watery diarrhoea (e.g. bacillary dysentery/shigellosis) is caused by bacteria, viruses, fungi or parasites and bloody diarrhoea (e.g. cholera) is caused by bacteria or parasites	Adequate living space
	Contributing factors are overcrowding, water, food contamination and poor hygiene	Public health education
	Treated with rehydration (using ORT) and, when appropriate, antibiotics	Distribution of soap
		Good hygiene (personal and food preparation)
		Safe water supply
		Adequate sanitation
Hepatitis	Caused by homonymous viruses with different transmissions and manifestations	Health education
	Contributing factors for Hepatitis A and E are poor hygiene and contamination of food and water	Safe water supply
		Effective sanitation
		Safe blood transfusions
Malaria	Caused by one of four parasites (*Plasmodium vivax, P. ovale, P. malariae* and *P. falciparum;* the last is the largest killer) transmitted to humans by the vector Anopheles mosquito.	Destroying mosquito breeding places, larvae and adult mosquitoes by spraying. However, the success of vector control is dependent on particular mosquito habits and local experts must be consulted
	Contributing factors include new environment for displaced persons, stagnant water, apathy on part of	Provision of chemically treated mosquito bed nets and awareness

cont.

Disease	Description	Preventive measures
	local populace and public health officials	raising on their importance
	Previous exposure (having the disease) does not provide immunization	Drug prophylaxis (e.g. pregnant women and young children according to national protocols)
Measles	Viral infection spread through the air (via droplets) and direct contact	Minimum living space standards
	Contributing factors are over-crowding, inadequate living space and low vaccination coverage	Immunization of children with distribution of Vitamin A
	If unaddressed, a significant threat in emergencies	Immunization from 6 months up to 15 years of age (rather than the standard 5 years) is recommended because of the increased risks from living conditions
Meningitis	Caused by a either a virus or bacteria	Minimum living space standards
	Contributing factors include over-crowding in areas where meningitis disease is endemic (often has local seasonal pattern)	Immunization only after expert advice when surveys suggest necessity
Micro-nutrient disorders (non-infectious but common among popu-lations in emergencies)	Lack of Vitamin A (xerophthamia) results in night blindness	
	Lack of thiamin results in different types of beriberi	Health education on dietary needs and possible introduction of change in cooking and eating habits
	Lack of niacin results in pellagra	Prevention/treatment of contributory disease
	Lack of Vitamin C results in scurvy	Adequate dietary intake of appropriate vitamins through changed diet
	Lack of iron and folate results in anaemia	If diet change is not possible, provision of vitamin fortified food. If this is not possible, vitamin supplements
	Lack of iodine results in a number of conditions including goitre	Immunization against measles and systematic prophylaxis (Vit. A) for children, every 4–6 months

cont.

Disease	Description	Preventive measures
	These disorders often follow acute prolonged deficiency infections, malaria, measles and other diseases	
Scabies	Caused by a parasite transmitted by mites	Public education and coordination to bring under control
	Contributing factors are over-crowding and poor personal hygiene	Minimum living space standards
	Leads to intense itching and lesions found on certain parts of the body such as skin folds	Enough water and soap for washing
STIs/HIV	Caused by a host of viruses and bacteria through sexual and blood transmissions	Health and sexual education
	Contributing factors are loss of social organization, poor trans-fusion practices and lack of information	Test for syphilis during pregnancy
		Test all blood before transfusion
		Ensure adherence to universal precautions
		Availability of condoms
		Treat partners
Tetanus (lockjaw)	Caused by a bacteria that is transmitted through the air into the site of an injury	Good first aid
	Contributing factors are injuries to unimmunized people and poor obstetrical practice leading to neo-natal tetanus	Immunization of pregnant women and subsequently as part of EPI
		Training of midwives and clean ligatures scissors, razors and other sharps
Tuberculosis (TB)	Caused by a bacterial and trans-mitted through the air especially to people with weakened immune systems	Systematic public health interventions needed following directly observed therapy, short-course (DOTS) for patients
	Contributing factors are over-crowding minimum living space standards, malnutrition, and high HIV prevalence	Minimum living space standards (but where it is endemic it will remain a problem)

cont.

Disease	Description	Preventive measures
	Short-term contact normally does not pose a threat to healthy individuals	Immunization (BCG)
Typhus	Transmitted through lice (louse borne)	Vector (lice) control including the use of insecticide
	Contributing factors include overcrowding and unhygienic conditions where lice thrive	Improved hygiene including washing bed linen and clothing
	Marked by headache, chills and fever	
Typhoid	Obtained through faecal-oral transmission and caused by the bacteria *salmonella typhi*	Minimum living space standards
	Contributing factors include overcrowding, poor personal hygiene, contaminated water supply and inadequate sanitation public	Health education
	Although one of the leading causes of persistent fever in warm climates, laboratory tests are needed to confirm the disease as many cases are asymptomatic	Safe water and proper sanitation
		Good personal, food and public hygiene. WHO does not recommend vaccination as it offers only low, short-term individual protection and little or no protection against the spread of the disease
Worms	Parasitic disease transmitted through different means (e.g. hookworms through the soil into skin and schistosomiasis/bilharzias from snails in stagnant water)	Health education
	Contributing factors are overcrowding and poor sanitation	Minimum living space standards
		Proper sanitation to avoid soil contamination
		Wearing shoes
		Good personal hygiene

Source: Modified from Chin (2000) and UNHCR (2000: 370).
Note: The focus here is on prevention, not treatment, which should be left to medical professionals.

- Ensure appropriate care, provide condoms and establish condom supplies.
- As with all sectors and areas, follow the most recent evidence-based recommendations. Official policies change (e.g. recommendations on infant breast-feeding has flip-flopped a number of times), so it is important that staff are up to date.

Mass casualty incidents (MCIs)

When a particular event, such as earthquakes, floods or a bout of intense fighting, occurs that exceeds the capacity of locally available health care service, it is considered to be a mass casualty incident (MCI). While MCIs are unusual, NGOs may be involved in the response. If this occurs, it is helpful to be familiar with considerations such as the following.

Search and rescue (SAR) Immediately following an incident, there may be a need to find the victims and provide initial care. Specialists should be in charge of search and rescue, but volunteers and support staff may be needed, especially those with skills in medicine, logistics, communications and certain types of engineers. Safety concerns should be highlighted, especially in built-up areas where shifting or falling rubble can injure search staff. Knowledgeable engineers should oversee digging, cutting and other search activities and shoring up of dangerous structures. Depending on the situation, the SAR phase rarely exceeds more than a few days to a week.

Casualty identification To help speed triage (sorting) of casualties, a widely recognized four-level colour-code scheme has been developed. The key, however, is the rapid transport of casualties to qualified healthcare providers. A typical system involves triaging victims into one of these four categories:

Priority 1 (red) Treat immediately: treatable life-threatening illness or injuries

Priority 2 (yellow) Delay: Serious but not life-threatening illness or injuries (e.g. burns or broken bones)

Priority 3 (green) Hold: Walking wounded (minor injuries)

Priority 4 or 'zero' (black): Dead or fatally injured (e.g. exposed brain matter or decapitation)

Logistics During MCIs, existing social structures become overwhelmed and access to victims may be blocked. The need for stock items, such as medical supplies, will likely become acute. There will also likely be a need for items, such as information and communication technology (ICT) equipment and vehicles that are already in the possession of NGOs. Follow-up in the days and weeks following an MCI become especially important as the number of deaths may continue to rise.

Incident management system (IMS) To manage and coordinate the different actors involved in the response to MCIs, an IMS or similar structure is often established. If involved in an MCI, NGOs will provide a supporting role to whatever response is launched, whether by local government or an international body such as the UN. If in charge, the local government may be faced with considerable challenges in which NGOs can provide assistance. NGOs can bolster existing health care and recovery systems in preparation, response and mitigation of MCIs. Issues to consider include:

- Contingency planning: before an MCI, NGOs can help at various levels, but especially in the communities in which they work, to develop disaster plans that outline what should happen in the event of specific emergencies. These plans should be written, well known, realistic and rehearsed (see pp. 192–3).
- Coordination: ideally established before an MCI, this is needed with relevant government authorities, the UN, other international organizations and NGOs. Information sharing can be an especially important element, as MCIs change rapidly and decision-makers do not always have the best information.
- Making resources available: should take place as soon as an MCI occurs. In some countries, government healthcare workers and volunteers do not have basic resources available such as transportation, communications and commodities. NGOs can help provide skilled volunteers and technical expertise, medical supplies, ICT equipment, food, non-food items (NFIs) and vehicle transport.
- Following up with recovery and rehabilitation: after many disasters, the immediate international and local response is adequate, but the follow-up is poor. NGOs have a significant role in the rehabilitation of social infrastructure and other activities that help communities recover from and prepare for future shocks.

Disposal of dead bodies Following an emergency, particularly an MCI, there is a likelihood that the capacity of morgues will be surpassed (PAHO, 2004). Issues to consider include:

- Decent and respectful burial is a priority over quick disposal: bodies should be disposed of according to local, especially religious, customs. Certain religions, for example, dictate how soon corpses need to be buried, while other religions specify cremation. However, some traditional practices, such as touching corpses of people who died of a communicable disease such as cholera or hemorrhagic fever may spread the disease.
- While exposed corpses are likely hosts of diseases, evidence suggests that dead bodies do not pose an immediate health risk as long as they do not directly pollute drinking water sources directly. According to the Sphere Standards, graveyards should be at least 30 m from sources of potable water and the bottom of any grave at least 1.5 m above the water table (although 10 times this amount is safer). Corpses should be disinfected with an appropriate substance such as quicklime.
- Local laws must be respected and if inquests are required it may make sense to do these as a group in cases of mass casualties. Graves should be properly identified and legal authorities should be fully informed where possible. Mass graves should be avoided.

- Accurate record-keeping is essential: in certain disasters, where mutilation is common, identification of bodies may be impossible and specialists may be required. In most countries, hospital staff are normally responsible for the funeral rites of unidentified bodies. Photographing every body, although a gruesome task, may be particularly important for identification.
- Identification of bodies may be needed for familial obligations for final respects, but there are usually legal requirements such as for widows, orphans, pension funds and insurance claims.
- Deploying personnel to dispose of bodies is important for social and moral reasons, just as deploying health personnel is important for the living,.

If handling corpses, use standard ('universal') precautions such as wearing gloves and face protection and thoroughly cleaning after exposure to infectious pathogens. In particular, cuts or other skin lesions of the care-taker need to be promptly treated and completely covered as this is the main pathway for the transmission of diseases.

Possible interventions

Health surveillance and information

Epidemiology is the study of disease transmission and evolution in human populations. The information learnt from epidemiology can be especially important for decision-makers during epidemics that accompany emergencies. Information collected during emergencies usually falls into several categories: environment, demography including history, mortality and morbidity rates, basic needs, and the ongoing and planned activities of implementing organizations. Additional information may be collected and analysed during the later phases of an emergency. Sources of epidemiological information include the affected population, government health authorities, health facilities and other organizations (i.e. NGOs, the UN and donors). From these sources, interviews are held and observations are carried out (e.g. at graveyards or going from house to house), using records including birth registrations, censuses and camp registration information. Specialists are needed to examine data properly.

Provision of curative care

Provision of curative care may take many different forms and take place at different locations depending on the level of need and assets in a location or country. At the tertiary and secondary levels, it may mean seconding specialized health professionals or establishing wards or even hospitals. In such cases, extensive resources including technical expertise will be needed. At the primary health care (PHC) level, supporting health posts is common, as is running mobile health clinics in remote or underserved areas. In all cases, good organization, logistics and adequate technical knowledge are needed.

Mobile clinics usually consist of a medical doctor and a health worker, such as a physician's assistant or nurse, who travel to one or more locations in a day to provide on-the-spot medical care. The capacity of each mobile clinic depends on the distance travelled to each site, and the amount of supplies and medical staff available. In many cases, mobile clinics become community events where large crowds may gather. Information sharing is important, as is the assistance of local leaders to manage crowds. The needs of pregnant and lactating mothers, children under 5 years of age and case-specific morbidity need to be prioritized.

Capacity building through training is also an important element of curative care. It can take place in a number of ways, ranging from formal classroom lectures to on-the-job demonstrations. Gearing such training to the needs and capabilities of the participants is vital.

While it is a classic image of relief workers, provision of curative care is also unsustainable and it is often difficult to phase out once it has begun. The short-term nature makes this suited for emergencies but problematic during periods of transition such as post-conflict situations. The needs of health staff, supplies and transportation make it difficult for local health structures to support. Alternatives need to be found early so that effective phase-outs can be realized.

Reproductive health

This important area focuses on safe sexual practices and assisting mothers (and fathers) before, during and after their pregnancies. Reproductive health generally includes two main components: first, the prevention of and response to GBV and the prevention of STIs, including HIV/AIDS. This may involve education, awareness raising and the distribution of contraceptives.

Second, reproductive health includes family planning to encourage activities such as birth spacing, and assistance with safe motherhood, antenatal and postnatal care, and care during deliveries. Obstetrical emergencies, which lead to maternal and child morbidity and mortality, increase in emergencies where mothers may be malnourished, complications may be undetected, conditions are unhygienic and there is little or no opportunity for referral. To help meet reproductive health needs in emergencies, a Minimum Initial Service Package (MISP) has been developed (see pp. 390 and 396).

Provision of health supplies

Often in emergencies, the most important missing element is the right supplies. NGOs often play a role in providing logistical support with warehousing, transport and distribution of medical supplies and maintenance of cold-chains. An important part of health supplies includes the provision of essential drugs (commonly used pharmaceuticals that are provided from a reliable and cost-effective source). To help jump-start and supplement the provision of health care during an emergency, the UN often makes available standardized health kits.

The sophistication of medical supplies increases with each level of a health system, but even health posts and clinics should possess basic laboratory equipment and supplies. Health staff should work closely with programme support staff to ensure that the right supplies are provided when and where needed.

Immunization

Immunization prevents disease by injecting a vaccine, a chemical of micro-organisms or toxoids, in which the human creates a resistance. When available, immunization is the most cost-effective way of preventing diseases such as measles and meningitis. Emergencies present unstable situations that make meeting immunization schedules difficult, if not impossible, to meet.

During an emergency, the most pressing health threat to children is measles. The goal should be to immunize everyone (100% coverage). Records are often lost, but when in doubt the best practice is to vaccinate, as there is no danger in receiving two immunizations.

As a situation stabilizes, NGOs are often involved in helping implement an Expanded Programme of Immunization (EPI). An EPI requires coordinated efforts at the national level of a particular country, resources including human, financial and logistics, and a stable population for at least between three and six months. Typical EPI coverage is provided in Table 2.5.

Table 2.5 EPI coverage

Vaccine	Target age group
Bacillus of Calmette-Guerin (BCG) for tuberculosis	Birth
Oral polio	Birth to 14 weeks but up to 5 years or older if outbreak or if missed in eradication efforts
Diphtheria, pertussis and tetanus (DPT)	6–14 weeks or up to 5 years if needed
Measles	9 months or up to 5 years or older as preventive in case of outbreak
Yellow fever	9 months
Hepatitis B	6–14 weeks

Note that EPI varies from country to country, depending on a number of local factors such as high incidence of disease and government policies. Where the risk is high, for example, measles immunization may be recommended twice, at 6 and 9 months. Different types (schemes) of the hepatitis vaccine are recommended for different countries. The unproven efficacy of some vaccines, such as cholera, means that policies and practices vary widely.

Vector control

Vectors are animals, such as rats and insects, which carry disease from a reservoir (a carrier of disease) to a human. Vectors are normally endemic to human settlement, but emergencies can cause their numbers to swell and contribute to the spread of disease. Vector control can be especially effective in rolling back certain diseases such as malaria (mosquitoes), sleeping sickness (tsetse flies) and several diseases for which rats are vectors.

In emergencies, vector control strategies should be relatively simple and easy to implement, although in certain circumstances, such as epidemics in camps, specialists may be needed to carry out aggressive control programmes. Strategies include chemicals such as insecticides, mechanical devices such as traps, containers for food and bed nets, and environmental measures including the draining of stagnant water and reducing the amount of waste present. To be successful, each of these strategies will need to involve significant amounts of public education and participation.

Health education and promotion

Health promotion and education are a critical part of health, and water and sanitation programming (Oxfam, n.d.). Without people actively taking part in their own health, many initiatives will likely become undone. Health promotion and education are also responsible for reducing morbidity and mortality by improving people's knowledge and influencing their behaviour.

According to WHO, health promotion is the process of enabling people to increase control over, and improve, their health. For this reason, the responsibility for health promotion extends beyond the health sector and includes aspects that contribute to wellbeing. Hygiene promotion seeks to develop the right behaviours that lead to better health. Examples include hand washing and other activities that lead to improved hygiene. In this way, hygiene is a more specific aspect of health promotion.

Examples of health education include teaching parents to maintain clean water and cooking areas and holding child-to-child classes on safety around the household. Health promotion examples include a campaign to drain stagnant water in public places and ensuring children do not play in dangerous areas (e.g. suspected landmine/UXO areas or near military operations). Provision of soap at latrines, information campaigns encouraging mothers to properly dispose of their infant's faeces and encouraging children to wash their hands are examples of hygiene promotion. However, health promotion, and hygiene promotion in particular, is not a substitute for the provision of water and sanitation.

Rehabilitation of the health infrastructure

Emergencies, as has been pointed out, often leave the health infrastructure damaged and destroyed. Although health workers are not entirely dependent on this infrastructure, they cannot do an effective job without proper facilities. With the exception of home visits, each level of health care will need a physical structure. Depending on the purpose of the health structure, concerns will include safety and security, water and sanitation facilities, electrical power, waiting areas, administrative office space and storage. Access by road is also important.

The higher the level of health care provided, the more complex and resource-intensive the rehabilitation and follow-on maintenance will become. A health post for 5,000 people, for example, may consist of several rooms for screening and treatment and a lockable closet for supplies. A secondary health clinic for 20,000 people may need space for treatment rooms, a lab, an adult outpatient room, a mother and child room, in-patient wards, including maternity, and a space for a dispensary, in addition to administrative and storage space. Adequate space, neither too small nor too big, will be needed depending on the plans of the government health authority, the level of care provided and the size of the local population.

Shelter

People need shelter to survive. Shelter is a priority sector, especially in inclement weather and during mass population displacement situations that witness massive destruction of housing, such as earthquakes and certain kinds of conflict, are likely to see extensive shelter programmes.

Providing shelter is more than a supplying a roof; for a shelter to be inhabitable, it must protect against the elements, accommodate sleeping materials, clothing and other supplies, be able to provide heat if necessary and have access to cooking facilities, water and sanitation. Harsh temperatures and heavy precipitation can accelerate the need for adequate shelter. Finally, shelter must also be culturally appropriate, preserve the health of the inhabitants and provide privacy, dignity and security. In cases where people have not been displaced, it is important that they are supported because property and land are often the most valuable asset a family can possess.

Shelter units are based on the extended or nuclear family unit. In emergencies, shelters are often temporary because of displacement or total destruction of former housing but people frequently live in semi-destroyed dwellings. While this section focuses on basic technical aspects of the shelter sector it is critical that shelter be approached comprehensively and holistically. Shelter projects should take into account project management, security and other programme aspects such as distributions, nutrition, health and especially water and sanitation (wat/san).

Types of shelter

Available resources and the climate will be the major determining factors in the sheltering process, with the aim to keep people covered and dry at an appropriate temperature. Priorities should be based on climatic and environmental considerations:

In hot climates, the main purpose of shelters is to provide shade and a place to get out of the rain. Desert areas are often cold at night and, depending on the altitude, may experience harsh winters with sub-zero temperatures.

Cold or freezing winter conditions require insulated and robust shelters, therefore tents should be avoided. Even when they are insulated, tents are poor at retaining heat. It is important to protect against the conduction of heat into the ground, radiation of heat through walls and, critically, drafts of wind pushing heat out through the door, windows and seams.

There are three types of temporary shelter typically used in emergency settings, as follows.

Tents

In emergencies, tents can be used as family dwellings as well as for community services and warehouse space. Typically, however, they should be a last option. A summary of the different types are provided in Table 2.6.

Table 2.6 Temporary shelter options

Type of shelter	Uses	Disadvantages
Plastic sheeting and poles (made for humanitarian purposes)	Works well in the initial stages of an emergency Adaptable and flexible	Not always as easy to set up as a tent
		Less coverage than other types of shelter
Ridge tent: traditional relief tent	Ease of use	Limited headroom at sides
Centre-pole tent	Good headroom	Heavy
		Not good in strong winds
Hoop tent: tunnel-shaped	Good headroom Small footprint	Requires many poles Technology in development
Frame tent: rigid frame with tent covering	Good headroom throughout	Requires many poles
		Can be complex to set up
		Often expensive
Nomadic/traditional shelter: various designs such as yurt	Well adapted to local climates, materials and traditions	Usually very heavy
		Large-scale production in short period not possible

Source: Modified from Ashmore (2004: 38).

According to Corsellis and Vitale (2004), there are a number of considerations concerning using tents as shelter. These include:

- Whether the design considered meets international standards, such as the covered area required per person (see Sphere Project, 2004; UNHCR, 2000).
- Flexibility of the outside space around the tent for activities such as child care, cooking and making surface water drainage, all of which can be constrained by entry points and guy ropes.
- Ease of adaptability by the users.
- Ease of assembly and whether there are clear instructions.
- Whether there is a repair kit, with spare materials.
- What the tent will be used for.
- How long the tent should last.
- In what climatic range the tent will be used, and whether there are any winterization measures.
- The range of household-shelter NFIs the tent will be used in conjunction with.
- Weight and packing volume
- Lead-time to delivery and production capacity of the supplier.
- National and international stockpiles of aid organizations and suppliers.
- Fire-retardance measures, such as flame spread across materials.
- The ease of opening doors.
- Whether there are valences or mud-flaps around the bottom of the tent, sufficient in size to be buried to add to stability in high winds, and whether they are made from a material that does not rot.

Semi-permanent shelter

Depending on country and context, where the local population has the knowledge and skills, beneficiaries may be expected to build shelters themselves. This approach saves time and contributes to self-reliance, empowerment and community participation. However, the ability of local communities to build effectively with complex designs and non-traditional materials (such as reinforcing bars in concrete), where they have not been previously used, should be considered. In such cases, more supervision and quality control may be needed. Often, temporary accommodation needs to be provided to accommodate new arrivals while family dwellings are being constructed. Tents and public buildings can also be used as short-term accommodation.

Buildings

Semi-destroyed and abandoned buildings are often the best source of shelter available in emergencies and these may be the best option available. There are, however, several serious concerns regarding safety, including:

- The cause of the original damage and the extent of unseen damage or weakening.

- The structure itself, including its walls and, if there is more than one floor, its storeys, must be declared safe by an engineer experienced in structural design and safety.
- Booby traps and landmines.

Shelter site selection

Site selection happens at two interrelated levels. At the micro-level, individual shelters should be sited to optimize health and wellbeing.

- Orientation for wind and sun: in areas with high winds, doors should not face prevailing wind directions.
- Drainage: because rain runoff can be especially large in the tropics and stagnant water quickly becomes a breeding ground for vectors, drainage can be especially important. Good site planning and shelter construction (e.g. with guttering) is critical. Water supplies need to be protected as well. According to the Sphere Standards, the slope should not be more than 6 per cent and not less than 1 per cent.
- Firebreaks and means of escape: cooking and heating flues, if unattended or not carefully watched, can become superheated and ignite the shelter itself.
- Space: shelter space must be culturally appropriate and adequate. Shelter space is generally 3.5 sq.m per person (except for short-term situations) and various authorities suggest not less than 18 sq.m for families, which-ever may be greater. For a camp, the Sphere Standards indicate a mini-mum of 45 sq.m per person, including space for roads and public areas (e.g. recreation and markets) but not agricultural space. Under ideal con-ditions there should be adequate ventilation and shade in hot climates.
- Health considerations: shelters should be well ventilated and located away from areas where vectors breed. For individuals, chemically impregnated bed nets are considered a priority in malaria-endemic areas. Overcrowding is another significant risk and should be avoided by providing enough space.

Site planning considerations for displaced persons camps is discussed below (see pp. 62–5). An accurate, verifiable and well coordinated shelter survey should be carried out (more information on assessments is provided in Chapter 4). In acute phases of an emergency, meeting needs will occupy significant time, but during other phases, rights and vulnerability must be more skilfully handled. In many cases, sites are self-selected (i.e. set up spontaneously) or selected by host government authorities.

Shelter considerations in hazard resistance

Improvements in design and construction are usually carried out to save lives. It may not be possible to render a shelter or structure disaster-proof from dangers following the initial hazard such as earthquake aftershocks. Although the quality of construction may not be strong, it is a good idea to examine the traditional structure which will have been engineered through experience. These considerations are summarized in Table 2.7.

Table 2.7 Shelter and hazard resistance

Hazard	Consideration
Earthquakes	Low buildings with few storeys are safer than tall multi-storey buildings
	Building design should be symmetrical and uniform (not 'T'- or 'L' shaped)
	Separating building components into structurally separate buildings may be more resistant to shaking
	Long walls should be supported and without many openings
	Structure should be strongly tied together (e.g. roof to walls and walls to foundation)
	If masonry is used, it should be supported with timber or concrete belts
	Danger from falling objects (e.g. large trees and heavy roof tiles) should be removed or secured in the event of heavy shaking
	Windows and doors should be located away from corners and wall joints, not oversized and symmetrical where possible
Fires	Always ensure suitable and safe access routes. Site planning should include breaks between shelters to prevent fires spreading from one shelter to another. According to UNHCR (2000), buildings should be twice as far apart as they are tall, or more, if shelters are made from flammable materials such as thatch
	Cooking and heating fires in shelters pose a considerable hazard through poorly designed fire places, careless inhabitants (from cigarettes, candles and faulty electrical wires) and smoke leading to disease (respiratory infections). Improving stove design, awareness raising and ventilation can help reduce this hazard
	Community structures should have designated fire-fighting people, fire assembly points and a formal means of fire fighting including training
	Fire-fighting items such as blankets and pots of water should be readily available anywhere where there are open flames, especially cooking areas
Floods	Local knowledge is especially important in site planning as many flood-prone areas depend on seasonal changes
	In flood-prone areas buildings may be built on higher ground or stilts as multi-storeyed structures. Adequate foundations are essential against scour
Storms	Site planning can take advantage of topographical barriers and vegetation against strong winds
	Roofs can be reinforced against high winds in a number of ways, including straps and other connections tied directly to the foundation, construction with a higher number of nails, hipped roofs instead of gabled roofs and roof angles of 30° (which are more structurally safe than greater or lesser angles). Building orientation to prevailing winds can also reduce damage caused by high winds although this may have to be balanced with the possibility of snow loadings
	Having a detached veranda and other roof components will lessen the opportunity that damage to one part of the structure will damage other parts if blown apart by high winds

Source: Information adopted from Corellis and Vitale (2004).

Shelter-related items

Shelters are, as mentioned, not simply the structure themselves. Once erected, people will likely need household items, including mattresses, blankets, clothing, lamps, buckets/water containers, cooking and eating sets, a means of cooking and controlling vectors and, if necessary, a way to stay warm. Chapter 12 discusses these items in further detail. Here, stoves and fuel are briefly presented.

Stoves

Stoves should be selected according to their ease of use and efficiency, fuel cost and availability and safety and reparability. According to Corsellis and Vitale (2004), stove efficiency can be improved by controlling the burn rate and ventilation, cutting wood, putting lids on cooking pots and pre-soaking hard foods such as pulses. Communal cooking is also more efficient than single families cooking for themselves.

Most stoves are designated by the type of fuel they use and some stoves can serve as both heaters and cookers. While prefabricated stoves made of steel or other material may be the most expeditious means of meeting emergency need, at times mud or earthen stoves may be more sustainable and appropriate. In some situations, such as with long-term displacement, it may be possible to have populations fabricate their own stoves (or mattresses, clothing or household items) which can then be purchased as an income generating activity.

Fuel

Providing fuel for stoves is a major concern in supporting displaced populations. Fuel can represent a considerable recurrent cost, logistical need and a negative environmental impact (especially where wood is aggressively collected in ecologically fragile areas). Inappropriate fuel and inefficient stoves are a leading cause of ARI among children. There are many different types of fuel. These include, from least to most efficient, biomass (such as peat moss or animal dung), wood, charcoal and liquid or gas fuel.

Water and sanitation

Water resources and environmental sanitation (wat/san) are a priority sector. During the acute phases of an emergency, priority should be given to supplying adequate water supplies to sustain health and maintain environmental sanitation to prevent disease. Wat/san is more than solving engineering problems: looked at holistically, wat/san involves health activities, community development and hygiene promotion as well as project management. Like the other survival sectors, there is a strong link between water and sanitation on the one hand and health, nutrition and shelter on the other. Clean water and hygiene contribute significantly to good health. At the individual level, the transmission of infectious disease is discussed on pp. 33–9.

For the purposes of wat/san programming, there are two main sources of water: groundwater found underground and from springs, and surface water from lakes, ponds, reservoirs, streams and rivers. Groundwater is an excellent source of water, especially when supplied by springs, because it is usually filtered naturally and thus does not normally require treatment. Where available, surface water may also be a reliable source of potable water, but it normally requires treatment because of the high potential for contamination.

Water can also be collected from rain (e.g. by collecting rain runoff into barrels), although this may not be reliable. Where available, sea water may also be used to supplement non-drinking requirements such as cleaning cooking utensils.

Water requirements: quantity

The first wat/san priority is meeting sufficient water quantity, followed by improving the quality. Minimum survival drinking-water requirements for an individual are 3–5 litres per day, but larger amounts of drinking water and water for cooking and cleaning are needed. The typical water planning figure is 15 litres per person per day, but usage will vary depending on the situation and cultural context, as suggested by Table 2.8.

Table 2.8 Water quantities

Type of service	Water requirement (litres/day)
People	
Basic need including (per person):	
Drinking	3–4
Food preparation and clean-up	2–3
Personal hygiene	6–7
Hygiene	4–6
Total	15–20
Water-flushed toilets:	
Pour-flush latrines 1–4 litres/flush	2–8
Conventional flush 10–20 litres/flush	20–50
Health facilities (per patient)	
In-patient facilities	50
Surgery or maternity wards	100
Consultation or dressing	5
TFC	20–30
Kitchen	10
Livestock	
Cattle	20–40
Donkeys, mules, horses	10–40
Sheep, goats	1–5
Camels	40–90
Irrigation	
Wide variation, typical values	3,000–6,000

Sources: Davis and Lambert (2002); MSF (1997); USAID/OFDA (2005). Note that Sphere standards may be slightly lower than the figures provided here.

Meeting the water needs of large groups of people can pose a major challenge. To help the planning process, essential water needs for different-sized populations is provided in Table 2.9.

The priority should be providing drinking and cooking water, with excess going to other needs until there is sufficient to meet all needs. In most cases, and although people should not be provided with dirty water, the quantity of water is thought to be more important than quality. Because of the link with disease, the water availability for sanitation is also an important priority. Unless kitchen areas, hands and eating utensils are cleaned, waterborne diseases will increase and dirty clothes and linen will result in increased skin-related diseases. As a preventative health measure, wash points and soap should be made available as soon as possible and included in all programmes that focus on the provision of water. Recently displaced persons may be unfamiliar with how to maintain sanitation in their new living conditions, so hygiene education is an important element of wat/san activities.

According to Sphere standards, the maximum number of people per water source depends on the yield and the availability at each source, which usually fluctuate according to the time of day and overall usage. It is recommended 250 people can use one water tap based on a flow of 7.5 litres per minute, up to 400 people can use a single-user open well based on a flow of 12.5 litres per minute and 500 people can use a hand-pump based on a flow of 16.6 litres per minute.

Water requirements: quality

People prefer to drink clear (not turbid), odour-free and good tasting water. While these are superficial indicators, water quality is critical for potable water. Water contamination can happen at the source or during transportation, resulting in waterborne infections, for example dysentery, cholera, giardia and typhoid, and waterborne diseases resulting from chemicals and metals. In emergencies, the

Table 2.9 Population water needs

Population	Time (days)						
	1	30	60	90	120	180	365
500	0.0075	0.225	0.45	0.675	0.91	1.350	2.738
1,000	0.0150	0.450	0.90	1.350	1.80	2.70	5.475
5,000	0.0750	2.250	4.50	6.750	9.00	13.50	27.38
10,000	0.150	4.50	9.00	13.50	18.00	27.00	54.75
20,000	0.30	9.00	18.00	27.00	36.00	54.00	108.60
50,000	0.750	22.50	45.00	67.50	90.00	135.00	237.75
100,000	1.500	45.00	90.00	135.00	180.00	270.00	547.50
500,000	7.500	225.00	450.00	675.00	900.00	1,350.00	2,737.50
1,000,000	15.00	450.00	900.00	1,350.00	1,800.00	2,700.00	5,475.00

Source: USAID/OFDA (2005: III-12). The formula used is 15 litres × number of people × days = litres/day (1 million litre increments).

most prominent risk is from infections, although the risk of waterborne disease should not be overlooked, especially in industrial and formerly industrial areas.

The minimum quality for protection from waterborne infections is usually determined by measuring the amount of faecal coliforms per 100 millilitres (mL). Faecal coliforms measuring 0–10 mL are considered of reasonable quality; 11–100 mL is polluted; and over 100 mL is very polluted. Water testing usually takes about 24 hours and requires training on one of the available field testing kits such as that made by Delagua/Oxfam, which tests for bacteriological contamination, chlorine, pH balance, turbidity and temperature.

To increase water quality, several means of treatment are available. Most treatment methods, when combined, aim to remove or destroy organic matter to bring water to a potable quality. These include the following.

Flocculation and sedimentation: when water supplies are heavily silted or contaminated, flocculation clumps together and sinks solid matter, usually using a coagulant such as aluminium sulphate. Sedimentation separates solid matter over time by leaving water supplies motionless. Normally, the top layer of water is removed for use. These methods are time-consuming and difficult to do for large amounts of water, in comparison with filtration and disinfection.

Filtration Once large matter is removed from water, it can be filtered to remove small particulates and pathogenic organisms. Common filters using gravel and sand, what is call slow sand filtration, can often bring water to a potable quality, but it too is time-consuming.

Disinfection When large amounts of water are needed quickly, disinfection is standard practice. For household use, boiling water is perhaps the most common method. For larger water quantities, chlorine compounds (mostly calcium hypochlorite) are the most effective treatment method in emergencies (see Box 2.1). Depending on a number of factors, water should be treated for at least one hour but up to six hours before it is ready for use (e.g. in cold weather). Distributed water should always contain residual chlorine to deal with further

---

Box 2.1 Water chlorination at home

If calcium hypochlorite powder (a chlorine compound) is available, a concentrate solution can be prepared adding three teaspoonfuls (33 g) of powder to 1 litre of water: 1 cc of such a solution will contain 3.3 g % cc or 0.33 g per 10 cc or 0.033 g per cc. To make the water safe for drinking, three drops of the above described concentrated chlorine solution are to be added to 1 litre of water and used after 30 minutes to allow for bacterial killing. Assuming one drop is about 1/30 cc, three drops will be 3/30 cc. This method will prepare a calcium hypochlorite concentration of 3 mg per litre. However, because calcium hypochlorite only gives about 70% of free chlorine by weight, 70% of 3 mg = 2.1 mg, or 2.1 ppm. This is the amount suggested by the Sphere project. It is quite high and will make water safe for sure, though with some taste of chlorine. Alternatively, commercial bleach can be used in a concentration of around 4.5% or 5%. At these concentrations of bleach, 0.01 cc of bleach per 1 litre of water will give a concentration of 0.5 ppm, which should be enough for limpid water in storage tanks. The chlorination should be repeated if water is not used in the following few weeks, particularly at very high summer temperatures.

contamination. Leaving water in the sun can provide some measure of disinfection through radiation (UV rays) and increased temperature.

Possible interventions

Water

There are a number of immediate needs that need to be undertaken in emergencies. Because each situation will differ significantly, possible actions are summarized in Table 2.10.

Table 2.10 Water interventions

Possible action	Comment
Protect and monitor source	Protection and monitoring of source is both an immediate and long-term priority. This may involve site planning, protective measures (such as fencing and guards) and education of people in the area.
Organize tankering	Costly and unsustainable but necessary in cases where no or insufficient source of water exist. The logistics involved in tinkering water are considerable; for example, to supply 10,000 people who have no other source of water, six tankers of 5,000-litre capacity will be needed to make six deliveries a day including distribution and travel time.
Organize distribution	Good water distributions depend on a number of factors: easy access, equity to beneficiaries, good drainage, storage of 24-hour reserve, enough space for increased demand and improvements. If people are unaccustomed to it, water rationing may be difficult. Goal should be to minimize wastage and waiting times (Sphere <15 minutes), while meeting basic needs especially for those with special needs (e.g. EVIs).
Provide containers	Water containers need to be of a high standard. Buckets are useful but prone to contamination, whereas jerry cans are more difficult to clean and use. According to Sphere, two vessels of 10–20 litres each, with narrow necks and covers, are required for collecting, plus one vessel of 20 litres for water storage.
Establish water storage	Static tanks, bladders and other means of storage are necessary for distribution and as reserve. Storage requires protection and monitoring but can improve water quality through sedimentation and heating (from the sun).
Water treatment	To improve quality, treatment may be needed (see pp. 52–4)
Develop current or alternative sources	Once immediate needs are met, existing and alternative water sources will need to be developed. Surface water flow can be diverted, collected through infiltration or gathered directly from a source (e.g. lake or river). Groundwater can be collected in storage tanks and spring boxes.
People move to a better source	If no new water source can be found or the existing sources cannot be improved, people will need to relocate. Political or security reasons may make this is a difficult option.

Source: Information from Davis and Lambert (2002).

Wells

There are a variety of wells that may be used depending on the depth of the water table, the availability of equipment, the type of soil and the expertise available. Wells work by extracting (through abstraction) groundwater from the water table. As water is removed, it is replenished by water seeping through porous soil or fissures back into the well hollow. The length of time depends on soil composition, the height of the water table and the rate of abstraction. (See Figure 2.5.)

A well's depth usually depends on the depth of the water table. Shallow wells are generally 1–15 m in depth and the water can be undrinkable because of bacteria if sources of contamination (e.g. latrines) are too close. Deep wells, usually 40–150 m deep, are generally not subject to bacterial contamination. In emergencies, people may deliberately poison or dump corpses in wells to cause contamination.

The site selection of wells will typically need to be made by a trained specialist. Putting wells too close together can lower the yield by reducing the water table. During well construction, rocks or other obstructions may be encountered, making it necessary to sink other well holes. The types of well construction used in emergencies include hand-dug and borehole wells.

Hand-dug wells are very common as they are simple to make, but they still require skilled workers. However, they may become easily contaminated and are prone to drying if not dug properly. A small group of labourers can dig down

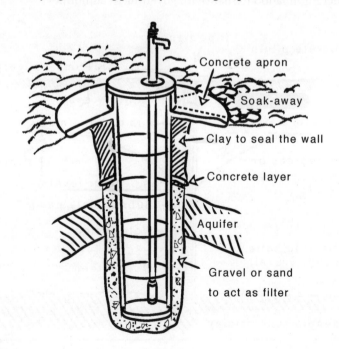

Figure 2.5 Standard well

30–40 m in a couple of days, depending on soil conditions. During construction, safety procedures are important because of the danger of soil collapse, objects falling into the pit and the build-up of noxious gases.

Borehole construction is usually done using a mechanized drilling rig which represents a more complicated but efficient means of well construction. Boreholes are normally lined with PVC casing. Drilling rigs may be expensive and it requires skilled staff, logistical support including a vehicle and additional supplies for their operation. Depending on its design capacity, a mechanical drilling rig can reach depths of 100 m or more in a few days of operation. (See Figure 2.6.)

The driven tube well can be constructed using a small-tipped pipe which is hammered into the ground. Although this type of well can be constructed quickly in a day or two, it requires a special filter well point at the top of the pipe. This type of well is only used when the water table is very close to the surface, with a maximum depth of 10–15 m. The similar augur-bored tube well can be dug to a maximum of 25 m of soil and usually takes two or three days to complete.

When working on wells, the following points need consideration.

- The location of wells should be decided by qualified specialists. Tools used for locating wells include burring apparatus, hydro-geological maps and a terrameter resistivity device. Even with good planning, obstacles (such as rocks) still might be struck, requiring the digging of a new well hole.
- Wat/san staff should maintain a log of well location, type, water level and other information to share with government authorities.

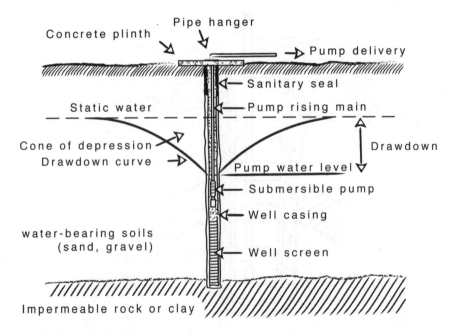

Figure 2.6 Borehole well

- Wells should be tested for yield (volume per time) for the intended use. Once disinfected through chlorination, new wells should be protected, either sealed or capped, until a pump or final covering is installed.
- Well deepening and cleaning is a common task in and following emergencies. Well deepening may be needed as a result of drought. There needs to be more research regarding lowering the water table in terms of long-term environmental impact.
- Well cleaning is done through emptying and disinfection. If flooded, wells can be cleaned by slowly pumping out half the water, disinfecting the well hole and repeating the process after the well is full again (recharged). Flooded wells should not be pumped out quickly or completely and wells in close proximity (closer than 50 m) should not be cleaned out together.
- Well heads should normally be protected with fences, especially in rural areas where animals are present. People should not be allowed to wash clothes or bathe near wells.
- In many situations, well pumps may be overused, damaged by corrosive groundwater and the lack of a system for maintenance and repair. Pumps should conform to village-level operation and maintenance (VLOM), with parts that are easy to access and replaceable by beneficiaries, be of a good quality and have theft-resistant parts. There are many types of well hand-pumps available and makes and models vary from region to region.
- Mechanized submersible pumps are generally not suited for community or similar water projects because of their complexity and maintenance. Buckets that are lowered into wells are usually not recommended because of the risk of contamination.
- Community members (usually part of a wat/san or well committee) should be trained to maintain wells and repair pumps.

Sanitation

As with water-related activities, there are a number of immediate sanitation needs to be addressed in emergencies are summarized in Table 2.11.

Latrines

In situations where there are no working sanitation systems, people will require latrines, either as a standard sanitation system or until normal services as can be restored. Latrines should be comfortable, clean and hygienic, safe (accessible day and night), the right distance away from living areas and of the right quantity. There are three main types of latrines: pit, ventilated pit latrine (VIP) and pour-flush. The most basic type is simply a dug hole (pit' or, in temporary situations where large numbers of latrines are needed, large trenches are made. If there are enough time and resources, toilet stalls or screens can be erected. The next higher level is the VIP, which greatly reduces the presence of flies and

Table 2.11 Sanitation interventions

Possible action	Comment
Control defecation	In some situations and contexts, uncontrolled defecation may quickly become a problem. In such cases, formation of sanitation committees will become an important forum which can be used to establish hygiene education and a means of excreta disposal
Provide fuel and utensils	Particularly in situations of displacement, providing cooking fuel allows a means to improve water quality (if this is an issue) and clean utensils help hygienic practices if they are being disregarded (see pp. 231 and 380 for a list of different utensils provided as a minimum standard)
Provide hygiene education	Beginning hygiene education early is beneficial for preventing disease. Hygiene education should be tailored to the local context and address cultural and gender aspects of both water and sanitation practices. Examples include training parents to boil water and wash the hands of their children
Establish means of excreta disposal, depending on what is currently available	1. If no means of excreta disposal exist (if people are defecating indiscriminately), a defecation field may need to be established. This consists of a designated area, often fenced, where defecation occurs in an organized way
1.Establish defecation field	2. If a designated defecation field already exists, trenches can be dug as a further temporary measure. Trench latrines can be separated by privacy screens or partitions using plastic sheeting or local materials (such as mats)
2.Create trench latrines	3. If trench latrines exist, formal latrines should be built. The level of sophistication will depend on available resources and time. Basic pit latrines with screens can be built in a number of hours but these will not last as long as other models discussed further below
3.Build latrines	
Provide follow-up	A key sanitation activity is ensuring the maintenance of sanitation systems and that people carry out hygienic practices. Dedicated resources will be needed to maintain healthy conditions

Source: Information from Davis and Lambert (2002).

odours. Using a mesh-covered tube (see Figure 2.7), airflow is routed through the latrine stall (which must be kept dark) and the latrine hole, attracting flies and trapping them inside the tube. Finally, where water is plentiful, there is the pour-flush latrine which uses a toilet-type basin.

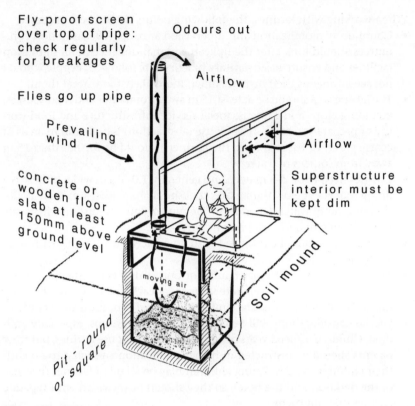

Fly-proof screen over top of pipe: check regularly for breakages

Odours out

Airflow

Flies go up pipe

Prevailing wind

Airflow

concrete or wooden floor slab at least 150mm above ground level

Superstructure interior must be kept dim

moving air

Soil mound

Pit - round or square

Figure 2.7a VIP latrine

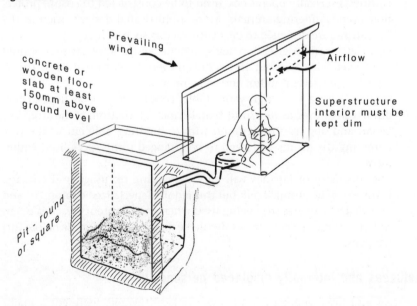

Prevailing wind

Airflow

concrete or wooden floor slab at least 150mm above ground level

Superstructure interior must be kept dim

Pit - round or square

Figure 2.7b Pour-flush latrine

When working with latrines, the following points should be considered.

- Community mobilization and supervision are essential. Sanitation committees should look after the upkeep and maintenance of all sanitation facilities and ensure basic sanitary practices are followed. People who do not see latrines as their own are much more likely to mistreat them.
- The latrine area should be at least 15 m away from water and food sources, including crops and gardens, social service infrastructure and food storage or preparation areas. If water use (abstraction) is high and in areas of coarse gravel or fissured rock, the latrine(s) should be further than 15 m away from sources of water.
- Latrines need to be 2–3 m deep and generally 1.0–1.5 m wide. If there is a lining that goes below the surface, that should be at least 1 m deep. Pollution of ground water depends on the type of soil and distance from the source or height above the water table.
- Each latrine should be provided with an adjacent wash point with soap and water.
- The ideal is one latrine per family, or one latrine per 20 people. If not arranged by the family, separate latrines for each gender should be organized. The latrines should be similar in terms of condition and standard.
- Special considerations will be needed for certain groups, especially children. Children under 3 years of age generally do not use latrines, but their parents should be instructed in hygiene education and what to do with their children's faeces. Young children may be afraid of latrines (because of the darkness and the hole), so they should be provided with separate latrines that suit them.
- Latrines, especially open ones, need to be constructed to ensure protection from wandering animals. More sophisticated designs, such as the VIP latrine, are designed to deal with vectors such as flies.
- Open latrines (i.e. defecation fields, trenches and basic pit latrines) should be covered with at about 10 cm of soil every two or three days. This is especially important in hot and wet climates.
- In areas with a very high water table, containers such as disused fuel drums can be used as very short-term latrines. The bottom of the drum can be cut and dug into the ground with a squatting hole cut in the top. Emptying the drums will need to be arranged using specialized equipment.
- The longevity of latrines will vary depending on usage and climate. Latrines can be pumped out, but this requires specialized equipment and knowledge. Latrines stop being used when their contents reaches 0.5 m from the surface. New latrines should be dug and ready for use before this happens.

Refugees and internally displaced persons (IDPs)

Refugees and IDPs, generally known as displaced people, represent a major concern in preparing for and responding to emergencies. With more than 30 million estimated worldwide, the number of displaced people is staggering. A single emergency may generate millions of displaced people, and, in most situations, their lasting settlement (a durable solution) takes years to achieve. While many of the approaches and methods are the same for displaced people as others affected by emergencies, they typically receive additional consideration in emergencies as a result of their specific protection needs.

According to UNHCR, a refugee is defined as any person who is outside his/her country of origin and who is unwilling or unable to return there or to avail him/herself of its protection because of first, a well-founded fear of being persecuted for reasons of race, religion, nationality, membership of a particular social group or political opinion; or second, a threat to life or security as a result of armed conflict and other forms of widespread violence which seriously disturb the public order.

Refugees receive protection of basic rights from refugee law (see pp. 384–5). Ensuring these rights takes effective prevention and response from a number of actors including government, NGOs and the UNHCR, the UN agency responsible for assisting refugees. Refugees' rights include:

- Entitlement to safety and wellbeing away from dangerous frontiers.
- Enjoyment of full legal and civil rights and basic needs such as food, shelter and health facilities as well as access to education, mail, registration (e.g. birth, marriage and death) and the ability to transfer assets.
- Freedom from being penalized or exposed to any unfavourable treatment, including discrimination, nor have their movements restricted expect in the interest of public health and order.
- Access to assistance and be helped to find a durable solution of their status.

At the same time, criminals (except in cases of political offence) may not seek refugee status and legitimate refugees must respect the laws of their country of asylum and refrain from subversive activities against any government.

Status as a refugee depends on a person meeting one of these criteria, not on whether they have been formally recognized as a refugee. Determination as an IDP is more legalistic. In many ways, an IDP is a refugee who has not crossed an internal boundary. There are many instances (e.g. Palestine and Sudan) where IDPs remain in this status for years. There is a distinct difference, in that normally IDPs are not afforded the same legal protection as refugees and are under the jurisdiction of national laws. In practice, this can have significant consequences. National governments are bound by few external laws and thus international standards are much harder to enforce.

Possible interventions

The prevention of situations that cause displacement may be the ideal intervention, but the socio-political issues involved are typically beyond the influence of NGOs involved in emergencies. Yet NGOs can play an important role in information gathering and advocacy. At the programme level, awareness of a possible negative impact is important. If not carefully thought through, programme outputs can create push/pull conditions that may place displaced people in greater harm and maintaining some assistance programmes may degrade self-reliance and make a lasting settlement difficult.

When people are displaced, there are a range of possible solutions for providing assistance. These include camp settlement, repatriation, local integration and resettlement or temporary asylum. Each has distinct perceived advantages and disadvantages as outlined in Table 2.12.

Camp management

While sometimes a necessity, camps where people 'warehoused' and restricted from normal life is the not the best place for displaced people. For this reason, mass displacement requires an in-depth and comprehensive approach beyond the standard assistance activities. Camps are usually headed by a lead NGO for camp management, which is responsible for day-to-day activities. This requires good organization and management. The organization responsible for camp management must work closely with the leadership from the displaced population and representatives from local government, the UN (especially UNHCR) and each NGO carrying out activities in the camp. According to the NRC (2004), this important role includes overseeing, monitoring, mediation and leadership in a range of activities including registration, monitoring and coordination of all activities in the camp, the collection (in a database) and dissemination of information, the enforcement of camp standards and regulation, the prevention of abuse by staff and an equitable distribution of assistance. Camp management considerations include the following:

Assessment and coordination

Determining need is important and discussed further in Chapter 4. Standard information gathered on displaced people includes location, demographic numbers (typically, percentage by gender and age groups 0–4, 5–17, 18–59 and over 60 years), culture and background (including legal status), location and current living arrangements, immediate needs such as health, and assets such as household goods. In some cases, alternatives to camps can be found and this may constitute a significant activity unto itself. It is important to know what assistance is and can be provided. This last step takes coordination with other organizations, including local government and the UN if present. In most instances, a particular NGO will be responsible for camp management, with other organizations assisting with different sectors and issues, making coordination a day-to-day concern.

Site selection and camp planning

The success of a camp starts first with its site selection. In many cases, refugees will spontaneously settle where they find appropriate. Minimum standards are

Table 2.12 Settlement advantages and disadvantages

Solution	Perceived advantages	Disadvantages
Camp settlement	Allows more efficient service delivery	Puts displaced people's lives on hold
	Better accounting of relief distribution	Overcrowding and increased ill health*
	Easier to identify beneficiaries	Duplicates rather than strengthens local capacity and infrastructure
	Greater control of population's activities	Least accessible and poor quality land
	Increases physical access to services	Environmental degradation
	Enhanced security	Breakdown of social structure/ norms and development of new less protective roles
	Cost effectiveness of relief	Idleness and restriction of activities can increase security threat
	Monitoring of programme	May create dependency syndrome which is destructive and difficult to handle
Repatriation	Restores country's economic stability	May lack access to original homes or land
	People regain control over their lives	Root causes of displacement may persist
	Fewer social problems or conflicts	Forceful adjustment from total dependency to relative self-sufficiency
	Voluntary repatriation is the best solution for refugees, host country and donors	Limited external aid for economic rehabilitation and reconstruction
Local integration	Integrates assistance to refugees and locals	Reduces control of population's activities
	Promotes self-sufficiency and minimizes dependency on aid	Too complicated to support, leading to possible exclusion from aid
	Builds morale and self-pride	Conflicts over resources with locals
		Encourages permanent settlement
Resettlement or temporary asylum	Provides protection to selected people facing real threat to personal safety (protection is temporary until safe return to place of origin is possible)	Many asylum restrictions to reduce magnet effect

cont.

cont.

Solution	Perceived advantages	Disadvantages
	May be only option when second country is un-welcoming	May detain asylum seekers for duration of application or as protection
	Puts strong emphasis on preparation for return	Restricted access to work and other benefits until asylum is granted
		Voluntary repatriation when safe return is possible may be difficult

Source: Saade and Burnham (2000: 1–21). * Note that refugees may have better access to social services (e.g. health care) than the local host population.

spelled out by the Sphere project and UNHCR (see pp. 377–80). Additional considerations include:

- Distance from the frontier or danger areas should be enough to provide protection at a safe distance (e.g. out of artillery range) but close enough to facilitate repatriation. The Sphere Project specifies 50 km from the threat. In some cases, refugees may spontaneously settle close to frontiers or a safe location may rapidly deteriorate. Security considerations, such as GBV and military recruitment, should be carefully weighed in planning.
- Access by road, availability of water and sanitation and other concerns such as markets and firewood are priorities.
- According to UNHCR (2000), camps are generally planned for no more than 20,000 people, because in camps with more than this number, management and other concerns (e.g. safety and health) become more problematic. Camps should also allow for population growth rates of 3–4 per cent per year. Modular planning may be organized as shown in Table 2.13.
- In new situations of displacement, the uncertainty of conflict or further disaster may result in the rapid influx of more people seeking shelter and other assistance. If displaced people are staying in shared guest housing or other alternatives, there will be a heavy strain on identifying suitable space. In camps, there must be physical space to accommodate expansion. In long-term situations, conditions will need to meet appropriate international standards and have enough resources for social services and liveli-

Table 2.13 Settlement size

Module	Consisting of:	Rough estimate of persons
Family	1 family	4–6 persons
1 community	16 families	80 persons
1 block	16 communities	1,250 persons
1 sector	4 blocks	5,000 persons
1 camp	4 sectors	20,000 persons

hoods if possible. Even with no new arrivals, according to UNHCR (2000), natural population increase will result in camp growth of 3–4 per cent per year.

- Urban refugee camps are a prominent feature of recent emergencies. People displaced by conflict inhabit high-rise buildings in diverse cities as Kabul, Monrovia and Tbilisi.
- The relationship with the host community is especially important and it should be involved in planning. While a typical image of a refugee camp is an unused rural patch of land, camps might be on fertile farm land or in an urban high-rise building. In most cases, land or property ownership will require negotiations and formal agreements which, ideally, the host government or UNHCR should arrange.
- Consideration should be paid to the cultural features of the refugees. To the extent possible, shelters should meet the local expectations of temporary family housing. Unsuitable clustering of single men, single women and children and ethnic groups should be avoided. Typically, the camp layout arranged in small clusters that fosters a sense of community is preferred to a grid layout.
- Environmental considerations are also particularly important in site selection. To the best extent possible, camps should be in areas safe from areas like flood plains and vector breeding swamps, as well as away from protected and environmentally fragile areas. Providing firewood rations, for example, may be necessary to prevent deforestation or desertification.
- The site should be large enough to allow for distributions, play and activity space, and at the same time accommodate registrations and safety and security concerns. Table 2.14 summarizes the UNHCR (2000) recommendations for camp components and size.

Staff management

The lead camp management NGO will have its own staff to carry out their responsibilities, including a camp manager and an assistant camp manager who supervise a number of programme focused staff (e.g. community service

Table 2.14 Camp components and size

Camp component	Per number of modules (and persons)
1 water tap	1 community (80–100 persons)
1 latrine	1 family (6–10 persons)
1 health centre	1 camp (20,000 persons)
1 referral hospital	10 camps (200,000 persons)
1 school block	1 sector (5,000 persons)
4 distribution points	1 camp (20,000 persons)
1 market	1 camp (20,000 persons)
1 feeding centre	1 camp (20,000 persons)
2 refuse drums	1 community (80–100 persons)

officers, social workers and field monitors) and programme support staff (e.g. logisticians and administrative assistants). Another important element is working with elected representatives from the displaced population who should be in daily contact with the camp management staff. Human resource management is discussed further in Chapter 8.

Provision of basic needs

Although there is, at least initially, an early focus on the basic sectors (e.g. health and nutrition) and protection, every sector and sub-sector (such as education and livelihoods activities) needs to be addressed in a camp setting. In some refugee situations, displaced people live under better conditions than local residents or at least have better access to goods and services. Care should be taken to mitigate this and reach a workable degree of parity. This can be accomplished by either including local residents in the planning and implementation of projects or by setting up separate projects to address their needs.

Safety and security

Safety concerns, such as fire prevention, should be addressed starting during the planning stages. In some cases, the displaced will be unfamiliar with living in such conditions, increasing their exposure to risks. Security issues will also be a significant concern. NRC (2004) outlines a number of steps that can be taken in camp settings, including having elected committees, establishing a system of by-laws, training on civic education and security, creating neighbourhood watch systems, limiting the abuse of alcohol and drugs, working with host governments and having contingency plans, such as good communications and stand-by emergency vehicles. NGOs working in camps should practice good security management as outline in Chapter 18.

Camp closure

Camp closure is an important aspect of camp management. A camp may need to be closed for a number of reasons, such as an improvement or deterioration of a situation, denied or lack of access to the displaced population or lack of funding. In such cases, the activities will either need to be handed over or phased out as described in Chapter 21. In camp closures, especially important is coordinating with government agencies responsible for the safety of displaced people and the safeguarding of records.

Durable solutions

Durable solutions are a range of activities designed to find lasting resolution for the plight of displaced people. Activities to find durable solutions may include providing information about a person's options, legal advice, individual counselling and referral, education and training, and self-help activities. These activities may take place over the course of a number of years and in different countries where refugees are located.

The starting point for durable solutions for refugees is repatriation. This cannot begin unless a refugee is voluntarily ready to go back to his or her country of origin, coordination has been achieved on both sides and a formal (tripartite) agreement has been reached between the two governments and the UN, and conditions are ready (or safe) for the return of refugees, including the access to social services and the absence of widespread violence. Assistance, such as NFI kits, medicine and food, should also be ready to aid in the repatriation process. In most cases, refugees will return on their own (or spontaneously), with a small number receiving official assistance, as shown in Figure 2.8.

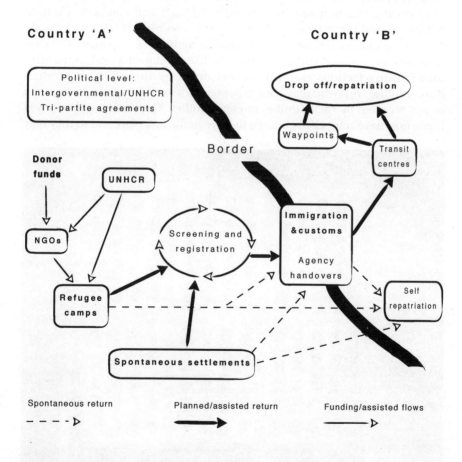

Figure 2.8 Refugee repatriation process
Source: Modified from Interagency Working Group (2004).

Family tracing and reunification

During emergencies, families often become physically separated and typically are unable maintain contact. This can have especially difficult repercussions for vulnerable people, such as children. Tracing is the process of looking for family members for the purpose of reuniting them. This is accomplished using lists, picture boards and staff who actively search for family members. The International Committee of the Red Cross (ICRC), which has particular experience and skills in tracing, often takes the lead in tracing, with NGOs assisting in the follow-up with vulnerable groups, especially children.

UNICEF (2005) distinguishes between the passive and active tracing of children. Passive tracing is done by comparing records of lost children and their parents, and active tracing involves investigating all available information to find a child's family. Children should be regularly informed about the tracing efforts, but they are not usually directly involved in tracing.

Reuniting children can be especially difficult and complex. Cultural differences and the realities of the recent past can make it unique from one situation to another. Insuring wellbeing during transition is important. Children who have experienced particular problems like delinquency and recruitment into fighting factions may not be welcomed by their families or their communities. Girls who may have experienced sexual abuse may be shunned or not accepted by their families or communities. Conversely, difficulties at home may have compelled children to leave in the first place and so they may

Photo 2.1 Picture boards can help trace lost family members

be reluctant to return to a situation where they may be abused. Active case management, including follow-up, is one way to address these concerns.

Psychosocial projects

The impact of emergencies on the psychological wellbeing of the affected people can be pervasive. Only in the last couple of decades has psychosocial intervention to address this impact been recognized as an important sector for humanitarian assistance. In emergencies, a person can experience tremendous stress resulting from events such as witnessing bombings or the killing of their family, participation in violent acts and injuries or starvation resulting in physical handicaps. This is then complicated by the loss of homes or displacement. Extreme situations result in not just individuals but populations being affected. However, most people (usually estimated at 85–90 per cent) will self-cope and recover without outside intervention. A small percentage (10–15 per cent) of people may develop psychological issues that may either worsen or improve on their own. Only a tiny proportion (perhaps 1–2 per cent) of people affected by trauma develop psychological issues that may require outside intervention such as counselling.

Although there is no wide agreement on a psychosocial definition and good practice, psychosocial projects are generally intended to improve a person's wellbeing in both a psychological (e.g. thinking and feelings) and a social (e.g. culture, family and friends) sense. One of the several reasons why psychosocial interventions are criticized is that the concept of trauma may be seen as Western, beneficiaries involved in psychosocial projects may be perceived as having 'mental problems', and the interventions themselves may not be effective in addressing the intended issues.

NGOs may be involved in a number of activities to address psychosocial concerns, including: support to vulnerable groups; tracing and reunification; community support mechanisms: resumption of activities including recreation, education and livelihoods; counselling in extreme cases of GBV and persons who do not respond to less intrusive measures; and protection of vulnerable cases.

Specifically targeted programmes

Child protection

Children, defined as anyone less than 18 years of age, can encounter many problems, including maltreatment, exploitation, separation from family, cruelty, and gender-based and other forms of violence. Child protection is a broad concept that includes not just protection against physical abuse, but also ensuring a child's legal rights, access to social services and maintaining wellbeing. Complex emergencies present a range of problems for children that are related to protection, including displacement, psychosocial distress, GBV and lack of education and health. Long-term emergencies mean that generations of children have failed or are slow to reach developmental milestones in health, education and other sectors. Scores of children may live on the street and resort to violence or other destructive behaviour to survive. In addition to these problems, children in emergencies may experience two unique problems.

First, separation from family, where children are apart from their natural parents but may be cared for by another relative. In emergencies, with displacement and extreme poverty, this may be common but the understanding of a child's status may be confused. Unaccompanied minors (UAMs) are children who have been separated from parents as well as relatives. In this case, children are alone and fending for themselves without the help of a related adult. Orphans are children whose parents have died; however, in some countries, this may not be the case. Children can be sent to receive assistance as orphans when their parents are unable or unwilling to fully care for them. As a result of separation, families may become headed by a child. Many situations of displacement witness older children caring for their families after the departure of adults. As a planning figure, 3–5 per cent of a refugee population may be separated children or UAMs.

Second, children may be recruited as soldiers. The use of children in conflict probably goes back to the origins of warfare itself. What is different more recently is the scale in which children are involved. According to the Coalition to Stop the Use of Child Soldiers 2004 report, child soldiers were active in 28 conflict-affected countries between 2001 and 2004.

While there are many instances of children serving as war fighters (combatants), and sometimes even as commanders, many children are forced to serve in support positions, such as porters, aids, lookouts, cleaners, cooks and, for girls in particular, forced into marriage and for sexual exploitation. In other cases, children become involved with a military simply because to stay at home lacks a future or might be more dangerous.

Possible interventions

Child Protection Agencies (CPAs), NGOs that focus on child protection, are likely to implement a range of activities that are seen to be child-friendly. These may include:

Advocacy and legal protection As a part of the larger protection sector, child protection is well supported by international humanitarian law (IHL). In particular, the UN Convention on the Rights of the Child (CRC) established a universal set of rights for children. The CRC is comprised of 54 articles covering four sets of rights including, but not limited to, the following.

- Survival: all children are entitled to a right to life, non-discrimination, a right to identity, name and nationality, and a right to be with their parents. They also have a right to health services, including rehabilitative care following abuse.
- Development: children have a right to education, expression and association. Parents have joint responsibility for their children's upbringing and governments are obliged to help in this. Children also have a right to

leisure, recreation and cultural activities, as well as a right to a private life and protection against neglect.

- Protection: children have a right to be protected from abuse and exploitation, including labour, drug abuse, sexual abuse, sale, trafficking and abduction, torture and deprivation of liberty. Cases of child prostitution and pornography as well as involvement in armed conflict are also covered. In cases where children have committed crimes, they have a right to legal and other assistance following appropriate juvenile justice.
- Participation: children have a right to voice opinions, become involved in decision making and respect the opinion of others.

Early childhood care and development (ECCD) Encompasses a range of activities designed to engender good care and development for children below 5 years of age. ECCD-related activities are usually pursued as part of wider developmental goals, but they can play an important part in emergencies and

---

Box 2.2 Developmental milestones of children

0–18 months Child recognizes people, can follow simple instructions and verbalize simple words and phrases. Crawls and stands up, begins to talk and walk. Displays of stress, such as crying, largely are dependent on care giver.

18–36 months Toddler stage, where a child can move with greater mobility (e.g. catching a ball and walking up and down stairs). Uses basic sentences and expresses feelings. Begins to use symbols (e.g. pretend play), drawings and short songs.

3–5 years Preschool stage when a child further develops memory, walking and talking skills. Cognitive ability grows with counting, asking why and matching patterns. Plays with others and more willing to share. Until the age of 5, children are generally very vulnerable to infectious disease and malnutrition. Following an emergency, they may re-enact violence in play, have nightmares, act younger than their age and may relate the death of family or others to their own actions. Stress may cause children to become withdrawn.

5–8 years School-age stage, children have full body control and become increasingly independent. Learning and social interaction with other children and adults becomes more sophisticated, with individual decisions made using emotions and rationality. Children may blame stressful events on themselves.

Identification, monitoring and information sharing Documentation provides a child with proof of identity, helps in tracing activities and gives access to social services such as nutrition, health and education. In situations of displacement, registration is especially important and is usually handled by a specialized agency.

Child-friendly spaces The aim of a child-friendly space is a basic protection intervention designed to provide a safe child-friendly environment for children to take part in play, and social and learning opportunities. Research shows that most children will recover from the effects of war when normalizing activities are re-established. The child-friendly space also provides a chance to access health and other social services, including social work, on an as needed basis. Activities may include sports and other recreational activities, creative playing, listening, dancing and singing, and introductory or non-formal learning.

protection. Examples of ECCD include health (including access to EPI) and developmental activities, such as organized play, socialization and opportunities for learning. Training parents to improve the care of their children (e.g. hygiene promotion) and support community initiatives such as sharing child care are also typical ECCD activities.

Typically, psychosocial centres should have a life-span of up to six months after a crisis and before schools are operational. These activities respond to the needs of children that have difficulty concentrating. Structured recreational and learning activities that are less rigorous than those provided at formal schools are suitable for these children in this time frame after a crisis. However, once schools are operational, the child-friendly space needs to phase-out or redefine itself as an after school activity or similar function.

Extremely vulnerable individuals

Social exclusion and marginalization that may be 'normal' in stable times often become exacerbated in emergencies. According to the Sphere Standards, the most regularly identified vulnerable groups are women, children, PLWH/A, ethnic minorities, disabled and older people. When one group is vulnerable, it is almost always the case that other groups are also vulnerable.

In some cases, people may become vulnerable as a result of their ethnicity or other communal traits such as religion, race, political or tribal affiliation, as well as being afflicted by infectious disease (e.g. PLWH/A). In many cases, the projects to assist such individuals are part of larger programming, while in some cases specialized NGOs target them. However, in many cases, nothing is done to address their special needs, so awareness of their concerns is important when designing and implementing programmes.

At times, these groups are identified as extremely vulnerable individuals (EVIs) to distinguish them from a larger group, such as a refugee population, that itself may be considered vulnerable. In these cases, EVIs may be disabled or older people who may require specifically targeted interventions to ensure their wellbeing.

Box 2.3 How to talk to children who have been affected by trauma

Be ready to engage children at their level and on their own terms. Activities such as acting, drawing, games and most forms of play are essential for recovery. Children should be given choice and be allowed to feel some sense of control.

Be constructive and supportive in a way that is culturally appropriate. Usually, the best way is to return gestures and affection that are given.

Be ready to talk about what has happened; do not lie or be afraid to answer questions.

Be aware of negative behaviour such as hyperactivity, re-enactment and avoidance. While often normal, these behaviours may indicate deeper issues.

Be prepared to intervene on a child's behalf if he or she is being adversely affected by play or the actions of others.

Disabled persons

Disabled persons are considered to have one or more impairments relating to individual physical (either from birth or as a result of injury), sensory, neurological, cognitive or psychiatric conditions. A physical impairment is not necessarily an impediment to lifelong achievement and development, but cases in disaster-stricken countries can make this situation especially difficult for people. In developing countries, where only the most advantaged have access to opportunity, disabled persons may be at the end of a long line of marginalized people. In countries that have undergone conflict, there is a higher percentage of disabled persons from war-related trauma, including landmines and UXO. Social stigma is also a considerable impediment to education and obtaining a viable livelihood.

Many countries are yet to become accessible for physically disable people. In emergencies, disabled persons may have difficulty accessing goods and social services. This lack of access may mean they are not able to obtain basic necessities, partake in distributions or have access to information, and thus they may miss out on opportunities. Disabled children may not reach developmental milestones and in some cases they may be ostracized by family and community members. Activities that address these issues include advocacy to improve conditions for the disabled and landmine/UXO awareness training to prevent additional injuries. Provision of rehabilitative services including physical therapy and mobility aids such prostheses, orthoses, crutches and wheelchairs can be provided alongside activities that improve balance, coordination and function. The rehabilitation of the social service infrastructure should provide accessibility for disabled persons.

Older persons

An older or elderly person is defined by the UN as a person over the age of 60, yet in some parts of the world this may be less relevant, with standing in the community and the onset of disease being more important than chronological age (Wells, 2005). Older persons may have difficulty adjusting to the massive changes brought on by emergencies. Older persons may face a number of specific problems stemming from a relative lack of mobility. Older persons may stay in place longer, may not have access to social services and may need daily support in terms of medicine, heating, food and water. Even in warm temperatures, they may need additional clothing and blankets. If faced with new cultures and languages, older persons may find it be difficult to adapt as fast as younger people. If still of working age, their skills may not be in demand in the new environment.

Despite their special needs, older persons can help mitigate the impact of emergencies in a number of ways. In many situations, older people can foster a sense of community and help resolve conflict. They may serve a protection role by looking after children, especially in the absence or separation from parents.

Finally, older persons are good sources of information and cultural wisdom. They may be aware of coping mechanisms that younger generations have forgotten.

Activities which can assist older persons may include understanding the number and location of older persons with needs, inclusion in planning, involvement of those with skills, provision of outreach services and addressing specific needs (such as medicines, clothing, blankets, nutrition and mobility aids), as well as setting aside particular clinic hours, queues in distributions and psychosocial activities geared for older persons.

Infrastructure rehabilitation

During emergencies, the social service infrastructure, such as schools, clinics and roads, are often targeted for destruction, used for military purposes and severely neglected. Schools may be destroyed for their ethnic affiliation, clinics may be turned into military trauma wards and then come under attack, roads may be used for tank movement and bridges blown up or washed out. While engineering projects may take place at any stage of an emergency, it becomes a programme sector in its own right during the post-emergency phases.

The rehabilitation of damaged and destroyed social service infrastructure serves many purposes in recovering from emergencies. Rehabilitation activities help jump-start social services, support a fragile government and generate income through hiring labour and granting contracts, thereby helping economic re-growth.

Engineering projects, depending on their size and complexity, typically take weeks or months to set up. Various elements must come together including stakeholders' agreement, engineering assessments and full agreement on budgeting. These elements include the following.

Government and community relations As part of the planning process, the involvement of government and community members should be initiated from the start. Ownership and buy-in can determine the success or failure of a project, especially those involving infrastructure rehabilitation. Issues relating to maintenance and provision of supplies (e.g. medical equipment, school supplies, desks and chairs) should be cleared up before agreement is reached. Also, all projects should be part of larger plans, so that the relevant ministry will have to be consulted at all levels. Agreements should be formal and in writing.

Box 2.4 Landmines

Landmines and UXO are an especially dangerous threat in many emergencies. Areas where landmines are found should be avoided. NGO staff and beneficiaries ought to undergo risk awareness training, which includes identification and recognizing danger areas, safety principles and emergency procedures, including how to assist a landmine/ UXO victim. Humanitarian de-mining should be left to specialist organizations with the appropriate expertise. For more information see www.mineaction.org

Codes and standards Local standards, codes and specifications for the particular structure must be met. Most countries have specific guidelines for the construction of social service infrastructure. While such guidelines are not always realistic, they may need to be followed unless some compromise can be found.

Appropriateness The infrastructure should meet basic standards and be appropriate for its intended use. There should be, for example, equal sanitation facilities for both genders. Changes and modifications to the infrastructure should be in line with local traditions. In some cases, structures may have been part of previous developmental efforts that failed, so it is important to know the history of the site, including its significance to the community. Sufficient space for an increase in population size, such as returnees adding to the student population, more people requiring health care and more vehicles on roads, should also be taken into account.

Site selection Stakeholders' consensus should be obtained about the site of the infrastructure. Access is often a primary concern, but this should be weighed with other considerations, such as gender. For example, if it is a clinic, school or similar structure, there should be access to water and sanitation. Schools and health facilities should be in an area that children and people needing health care can reasonably reach. Property and land ownership should be formally settled before formal agreement.

Environment Safety and security concerns need to be weighed carefully. When considering the site there are number of considerations, such as the ability to dispose of waste, the presence of landmines/UXO, and the proximity to vectors and pollution. The impact of psychological trauma on beneficiaries should also be considered, as the infrastructure may be a reminder of past events, such as massacres or disaster-related deaths.

Risk analysis Careful consideration should go into weighing different possibilities of failure and the different options available. The infrastructure should not be immediately threatened by national hazards (e.g. flood plains) and resistance to common threats such as floods and high winds. In ideal circumstances, a detailed projection should be made, taking into account population growth, including returning displaced people, government or community budget projections and the commitment to such spending, with written agreement by stakeholders. This usually involves the NGO, donor, local government representatives and national-level line-ministry approval.

Education

Education is a child's right. Unless the level of violence or extent of a disaster simply makes the continuation of education impossible, establishing primary education for every child is an emergency priority. Education serves several important functions in that it:

- Provides a safe place to learn and develop.
- Decreases the chances of children's exploitation. If children are occupied in school, this may prevent or delay their recruitment into military services.

- Serves as a means for children to learn survival and life skills, including health and hygiene and safety issues such as landmine risk awareness (where appropriate) as well as basic skills including literacy and numeracy.
- Education is a gateway to psychosocial activities which can help in the recovery following traumatic events such as recreational and sports.
- Affords parents time to concentrate on family survival needs, such as obtaining food and pursuit of their livelihood.
- Help students reintegrate and develop once the emergency has subsided or conditions have improved.

In emergencies, the goal is to move to a normalized education as soon as possible. According to Nicolai (2003), this process can follow three distinct phases: one, recreational and participatory; two, non-formal schooling; and three, reintroducing a curriculum. While not necessarily linear, each phase may be approached in a number of ways, including the following.

Support to existing education system Because the government is primarily responsible for providing education, assisting the state is vital to providing education. Capacity building can be provided to the Ministry of Education at different levels, including teacher training, providing textbooks and other supplies, and developing the curriculum. School committees can also be supported by assistance with the creation, planning and training and provision of supplies (see UNICEF's 'School-In-A-Box' on p. 390).

Photo 2.2: Talking to children. Communicating effectively with children involves talking at their level and in a way they understand.

Although it helps, education does not require a building. Education is a process that can happen in homes, community buildings, tents, outdoors under a tree or a plastic sheet, as well as at a school. Schools can also be rehabilitated and provided with the appropriate facilities such as heat, wat/san, chairs, shade, places to play, fences and walls, community contributions, electricity and kitchen areas.

Organization of out-of-school alternatives In a variety of situations in emergencies, it is beneficial to begin educational activities in the absence of formal education. Non-formal education or structured learning activities offers a flexible way to engage children with learning. Non-formal education can include literacy and numeracy classes, cultural activities and sports. Targeted learning can be done on specific subjects such as hygiene education and STI information, landmine/UXO awareness and peace-building education. Building social skills is also important through child-led initiatives, such as the organization and support of activity clubs.

Supporting measures to return children to school Because emergencies can significantly disrupt education, assisting the children to re-enter school is important. Advocacy for access can be done through training on child related aspects of IHL and local law, awareness-raising efforts and arranging means to address large-scale enrolment such as double shifts at school. Accelerated learning programmes (ALP) can be organized for those who have fallen behind in school and intend to return at a level appropriate for their age. Following specific courses and exams based on standard school curricula, ALP allows students to achieve their education in shorter times. In some cases, such as where the schools are below capacity because of specific needs, short-term relief, such as the provision of school supplies or targeted teacher training, should be considered.

Coordination of non-school age programmes State schooling normally targets 5–13-year-olds, so many children will not be exposed to education. To reach younger children, ECCD reaches children below 5 years of age. Adolescent education targets youth who do not attend formal education. Activities can include basic education (for those without plans to return to school), recreational clubs, vocational training and sexual and reproductive health education.

Microfinance development

Emergencies tend to destroy livelihoods while increasing poverty and other vulnerabilities. One way to address this is through microfinance development, which provides financial assistance to the poor. It provides a means for those with low incomes to gain access to services normally available to the non-poor through banks and other commercial firms. Microfinance focuses on the provision of credit (funds) for individuals and groups who intend to undertake entrepreneurial projects or business growth. The term 'microcredit' is limited to the provision of loans, and has now been supplanted by the term 'microfinance', which includes savings mobilization, small-scale insurance, money transfers, microleasing and credit.

The beneficiaries of microfinance projects should be relatively stable populations (e.g. long-term refugees) that are or can be economically active in functioning cash-based markets and have the capacity to work and pay back loans. For this reason, microfinance needs to be targeted at specific beneficiaries who meet these criteria. Although local materials can, and probably should, be heavily relied on, sufficient levels of factors that promote market activity within the supply and demand equation must be present. Beneficiary selection is crucial and individuals already involved or with a background and interest in pursuing commercial enterprise should come into the microfinance programme. For this reason, microfinance is not the same as a self-employment programme.

Generally, the credit provided is very small, depending on the country's GDP per head, and must be repaid. For this reason, microfinance does not involve lending in kind or grants. However, this is microfinance's strengths: that by providing loans, people have a vested interested in planning and successfully seeing through their own relief and development. Microfinance's aim is to create a sustainable livelihood for business-oriented individuals in the long term.

A typical project may involve entrepreneurial efforts such as bike repair, bottling of drinking water, small-scale trade, making and selling food items and tool making. In some contexts, tie-dye, tailoring, embroidery, soap making are good skills to know, but do not work as well because these are often common skills without a market. Beneficiaries must find a market niche that needs to be filled ,so there is a large variety of what might be attempted.

Training and sensitization may include women's groups, long-term approaches, sustainability, risk, how agreements work (assets and collateral) and government regulations, combining with other projects. Approaches that involve women in solidarity groups are preferred in order to manage credit risk and the costs involved in the delivery of financial services. As the loans are given without collateral, the solidarity group approach is used to cover the risk. If the groups are trained to manage the funds, as in self-help groups or in village banking, then the cost of service delivery is also reduced, because the programme does not need many credit officers. Even in emergency or post-emergency situations, there should be a plan to continue the financial services, as the clients will require repeat loans to improve their business activity and also to allow the programme to increase outreach. For this reason, sustainability can be an issue for the NGO providing a loan.

Food-for-work

In areas where there is food scarcity and wages are low, food-for-work (FFW) schemes can be incorporated into labour-intensive projects. FFW activities are meant to be short-term, stop-gap or one-off activities. Typical activities include the rehabilitation of roads and community infrastructure, such as repairing meeting spaces and possibly irrigation or schools. FFW normally targets unskilled labour and does not work with skilled labour positions where a cash salary is expected. FFW can also be provided as an incentive or top-up when regular salaries are unsustainably low, such as government-supported health and education positions.

FFW should only be established where there is insufficient food production, prices are unstable or market mechanisms do not work and workers do not possess enough resources to purchase their own food. FFW should also be phased out as soon as an emergency situation is over and should not contribute to activities that require sustainability, such as the maintenance of infrastructure.

Ideally, food should only constitute no more than half of the remuneration to beneficiaries. The likelihood that beneficiaries sell the food is high, especially in changing situations and particularly if the food ration is of an unpopular type (e.g. rice is highly prized in some areas whereas bulgur wheat is not).

Often the UN World Food Programme (WFP) will have a calculated standard ration that can be used as a planning figure. This typically involves determining daily market rates for specific activities needed for a project and deciding the equivalent in food commodities. Before implementing FFW, careful analysis should carried out on local markets to consider the impact FFW will have.

Cash-for-work

In situations where temporary labour is needed, cash-for-work (CFW) schemes can be used to provide cash input for beneficiaries, thereby injecting cash into a local economy and, by the outputs of its projects, materials and community works. CFW works well with the rehabilitation of community infrastructure, including the rehabilitation of schools and clinics.

All people (men and women) should be paid the same wage for the same work and women should be paid directly (i.e. not through their husbands or other relatives). There are two ways to provide CFW: time-based and production-based. The time-based method, done according to hours or days worked, is relatively easy to organize but must be supervised closely. Production-based payment depends on the worker's output. This method is good at maximizing a beneficiary's output, but is more difficult to organize and monitor and may lead to self-exploitation.

CFW works only with short-term projects and not long-term activities that need sustainability, such as regular salaries or maintenance. CFW is an income-generating activity, but it is not a sustainable livelihood. Also, like FFW, local market conditions need to be examined because CFW can cause inflation, thus causing more harm than good. In contrast to FFW, CFW has the benefit of working with unskilled as well as skilled labourers and being logistically relatively easily to implement. When implementing CFW, a basic rate should be established based on local market rates for a particular activity. Table 2.15 summarizes these approaches.

Table 2.15 Microfinance approaches

	Advantages/When to use	Disadvantages/When not to use
FFW	Provides food security	Can create dependency; food is often sold and can be spoiled; cannot always be saved. Distribution problems and costs. Can distort local food production supply and markets
	Can target malnutrition by the type of food	
	Can target children (who otherwise will not get a fair share)	
CFW	Kick-starts the economic life of the area	If not targeted or monitored, can lead to abuse (such as consumption of drugs or alcohol); inflation, distort labour market if rate is above national rate; may preclude women and disabled people as they may not be able to do the work; may prevent an early return to gainful/skilled labour. Should be stopped when people can return to original work/ livelihood
	Cost-effective and logistically easy	
	People have a choice in what to do with the money	
	May encourage saving	
	Encourages investment as economic life and confidence picks up	
Small grants	Kick-starts the economic life	Can create dependency; cash can be stolen or spent on a non-intended purpose
	Promotes investment in business activities	
Microfinance	Recovery phase	Immediately after a major disaster or during conflict with continuous displacement it would be difficult to implement microfinance
	Revitalizes the economic sector of the poor	

Sources: Multiple, including Bryson and Hansch (1993) and Peppiatt et al. (2001).

Gender-based violence (GBV)

GBV often accompanies and is exacerbated by emergencies (UNHCR, 2003). Agricultural development involves a complex variety of considerations from crop variety, water availability and pest control to gender and land rights (FAO, 1998). According to the UN Convention on the Elimination of all forms of Discrimination Against Women (CEDAW), GBV is any physical, mental, or social abuse (including sexual violence) that is attempted or threatened against a person's will, based on his or her gender. In most circumstances of GBV, a person has no choice to refuse or pursue other options without severe physical, psychological or social consequences. In all cases, GBV can adversely affect a person's physical and psychological health, development and identity.

GBV is rooted in power inequities and traditional gender roles that result in women having a lower status in society. Contributing risk factors may include the weakness of the law, discriminatory cultural and traditional beliefs and practices, ignorance, separation, neglect, poverty, and war or conflict, as well as individual risks such as physical and mental disabilities and psychological trauma. GBV may also be a factor in many cultural practices. That said, it is important to note that in many parts of the world, most forms of GBV are not considered criminal acts. In fact, in many countries acts that may be considered as GBV to a Westerner, such as female circumcision (or female genital mutilation), may be part of the traditional cultural fabric, even if we disagree with them. During emergencies, however, these practices can be twisted and expanded to cover acts that would not normally be tolerated, such as incest. Emergencies can crush the positive traditional value systems, which during peacetime allowed for checks and balances on otherwise aberrant behaviours. Types of GBV include:

- **physical** slapping, kicking, hitting and burning;
- **sexual** rape, incest, forced sodomy, abuse, exploitation, forced prostitution, trafficking, harassment and refusing safer sex;
- **emotional** threatened force, controlling behaviour, humiliation, confinement, verbal abuse, shouting, showing extreme jealousy, insulting and extreme criticism;
- **cultural** female genital mutilation (FGM), ritual or honour killings, early or forced marriage, infanticide or neglect and denial of education for women or girls;

Box 2.5 The right to confidentiality

The survivor's right to confidentiality is important for both the survivors' emotional wellbeing and for security reasons. Care should be taken to ensure survivors are not unduly singled out for questioning and intervention by staff. All staff involved in social service projects should be provided with at least an introductory training on GBV and those tasked with case management should receive lengthy instruction. Professional social workers can take up to one year of training before they are competent in properly addressing the needs of survivors.

- **economic** discrimination and/or denial of opportunities or services, social exclusion or ostracism, obstructive legal practice, denying inheritance, taking earnings, controlling money, bride price, refusing ownership of property.

The potential for debilitating long-term effects of GBV is great. The emotional and physical trauma associated with GBV can result in severe health and psychosocial problems. Non-fatal outcomes of GBV can include: disability, chronic infections, gastro-intestinal problems, eating disorders, sleep disorders, alcohol and drug abuse, miscarriage, unwanted pregnancy, STIs (including HIV/AIDS), gynaecological disorders, depression, anxiety, fear and shame. Fatal outcomes include homicide, suicide, maternal and infant mortality, and AIDS-related mortality.

Possible interventions

Addressing GBV should use a multisectoral approach that combines health and psychosocial activities with legal and security protection. Staff involved in social projects should receive specific training on case management and how to handle survivors of GBV. In such projects, the primary function of the staff is to ensure the fair and equal treatment of survivors. This is accomplished through confidentiality, security, respect, patience, empathy, non-judgement and encouragement. This is done by:

- Comprehensively assessing survivors' needs through systematic and confidential intake and information gathering, including conducting a safety planning assessment, as necessary
- Exploring feelings through active listening and therapeutic interaction techniques
- Providing information on choices survivors face, because they should not be given advice
- Providing survivors with access to information; this gives them control over their own choices and shows respect for their opinions
- Discussing options; creating an action plan
- Supporting decisions by using encouraging language and posture
- Referring the survivors to health, psychosocial, legal and police services as necessary and appropriate
- Following up with the survivors to review their progress and discuss next steps. This should be done within several days of the first meeting and at least once per week until the staff have confidence that survivors are on track towards rebuilding their lives

Mainstreaming GBV prevention into emergency programming

In order to prevent or minimize the risk of GBV in emergencies, it is vital to design and implement programmes in a way that considers women's needs throughout. For example, looking at a refugee or IDP camp setting, ask questions such as:

- Have you provided separate housing for female-headed households?
- Have you distributed food and NFIs directly to women?
- Have you ensured that the camp is well lit and that latrines are clearly demarcated as male and female?
- Are women equal participants in camp leadership?
- Is there police protection or other security at the camp?

In general it is important to be informed about the refugees', IDPs' and host community's culture, traditions and gender/power relations. It is also important to identify areas where people may be exposed to GBV, such as at distribution points and border points. Finally, it is important to have strong partners in the community as well as with other agencies in the health, psychosocial, legal and security sectors.

Special approaches

Sustainable livelihoods

During most emergencies, most people find a way of making a living. A person's livelihood is their means of obtaining the basic necessities of life through activities, assets and entitlements, in what is commonly thought of as work. A sustainable livelihood is one that can withstand the shock of a disaster and is economically effective, socially equitable and environmentally sound. Examples are as varied as creativity allows. In rural areas, and in many parts of the world's peri-urban areas, livelihoods tend to focus on farming, herding and animal husbandry, food production and small-scale artisanal work. These activities are directly linked to and rely on markets. FFW and CFW projects are not sustainable livelihoods, but can serve as a stopgap measure between an emergency and the resumption of development.

The sustainable livelihoods approach (SLA) rests on a framework of five principles:

1. **It is centred on people** The first step is an analysis of livelihoods and how they are affected by conflict. This analysis is participatory and continues throughout every activity.
2. **It is holistic** In recognizing that people adopt various strategies to secure their livelihoods, the analysis cuts across sectors, geographic areas and social groups. In doing so, multiple actors are contacted and involved, including the private sector, government, CBOs, local (national) non-governmental organizations (LNGOs) and international bodies.
3. **It is dynamic** Building on strengths, the sustainable livelihoods framework tries to understand the complex nature and dynamic influences of relationships.

4. **It has micro–macro links** The sustainable livelihoods programme looks at the influence of macro-level policy and institutions with the aim of informing their decisions appropriately and giving priority to the poor.
5. **It aims for sustainability** For success to take hold, the impact of the approach must be lasting and continue beyond the period of specific projects.

As presented by the UK Department for International Development (DFID), shown in Figure 2.9, the sustainable livelihood framework outlines the main factors and relationships that affect people's livelihoods. The framework brings attention to fundamental influences and processes, and can be used as a checklist of important issues and the interactions between them.

The SLA approach uses many of the same tools and techniques used in participatory development. In the field, a common critique of SLA is that we already do this. In development circles, this is very probable, but it seems less common in periods of post-conflict and disaster recovery, where this approach is needed.

For assessments, using rapid appraisal, stakeholder analysis, mapping, surveys and vulnerability are common. During implementation and monitoring, participatory planning, institutional capacity building and action research are used. The aim of initiatives can be multi-faceted, but they usually involve the enhancement of livelihood assets. The outputs may include support to a local company that undertakes construction of disaster-resistant social infrastructure, increasing livelihood options in fishery and agriculture sectors through income-generating initiatives, and government policy changes resulting in more favourable microfinance and socially responsible markets.

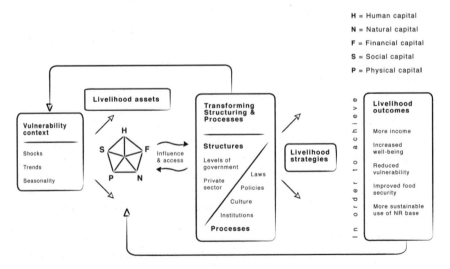

Figure 2.9 Sustainable livelihoods framework
Source: DFID (1999)

Demobilization of ex-combatants

Standing military factions are recognized as an impediment to the resolution of conflict. Disgruntled, jobless and idle soldiers can threaten progress towards the peaceful settlement of conflict and prolong emergency conditions. Working with the factions that were party to the conflict to disarm, demobilize and reintegrate (DDR) their ex-combatants is a critical step following the end of war. Essentially a military recruitment process in reverse, the aim of the DDR is to restore stability and transform a society into one experiencing sustainable peace.

Before the DDR process can begin, a number of requisites need to be in place, including an agreement to which all parties are committed, the availability of sufficient resources, including funding, the cessation of hostilities, some measures of security and a comprehensive approach that incorporates short-, medium- and long-term goals. The DDR process involves all factions, government and peacekeeping forces, with several key areas implemented by NGOs.

Disarmament By necessity, this first stage must be directed by military leaders and overseen by peacekeeping forces. For organized military units, turning in arms may be done within a few months. However, especially where there are irregular military forces, collecting large arms and stockpiles can take much longer and pose a security threat until completed. During this stage, women and children associated with the fighting factions may be identified for protection activities that occur in the later stages of the process.

Demobilization This stage serves to release soldiers from military service and transition them to civilian life. Demobilized soldiers are typically housed at a demobilization site for up to a week where they undergo briefings on the DDR process, receive medical treatment and food. Ex-combatants are usually provided with a relocation package that includes an identification card (used during reintegration) and a stipend, and are transported back to their areas of origin. In some cases, NGOs have organized and run demobilization sites. NGOs may come under criticism for focusing too much on ex-combatants, people who directly contributed to destruction and suffering, and not enough on civilians who did not contribute to the conflict.

Children associated with the fighting forces (CAFF) and armed groups are separated from adults at the start of the demobilization process and are placed in interim care centres (ICCs). At ICCs, boys and girls undergo normalizing activities such as sports and crafts and, for those who require it, counselling is available. Although it varies, CAFF are usually expected to stay in an ICC for no more than a month while they are traced back to their families. On their departure, they should receive the same benefits as adults. If included in this stage, women associated with fighting forces (WAFF) may stay in separate facilities at the demobilization site. For WAFF with children and those who experienced GBV, for example, their protection needs may vary widely, so a flexible response may be needed.

Reintegration To prevent reversal of the gains made up to this point in the DDR, by the demobilization stage it is important that reintegration is funded and put into place. The aim of this stage is the peaceful inclusion of ex-combatants back in society. While many ex-combatants will be eager to return to civilian life and may be readily accepted by their communities, others will not. Short-, medium- and long-term efforts at all levels are needed for ex-combatants to successful reintegrate, such as national awareness and reconciliation campaigns, training and education opportunities, short-term income employment and economic integration programmes, including access to land and credit.

In some instances, the reintegration phase may be further divided into a number of 'Rs', including resettlement, repatriation and rehabilitation.

Disaster preparedness and mitigation

Even the best relief programmes can be quickly undone by further disaster. The old adage 'An ounce of prevention is worth a pound of cure' is instructive. Activities aimed at preparedness and mitigation can make an impact when a catastrophic event occurs. Such activities that address hazards such as earthquakes, flooding or volcanic eruptions, fall into several categories, as described by Twigg (2004):

- **Preparedness** Specific measures taken before disasters strike, usually to forecast or warn against them, take precautions when they threaten and arrange for the appropriate response (such as organizing evacuation, stock-piling food supplies and early warning systems). Preparedness falls within the broader field of mitigation.
- **Prevention** Activities to ensure that the adverse impact of hazards and related disasters is avoided. As this is unrealistic in most cases, the term is not widely used.
- **Mitigation** Any action taken to minimize the extent of a disaster or potential disaster. Mitigation can take place before, during or after a disaster, but the term is most often used to refer to actions against potential disasters. Mitigation measures are physical and/or structural (including flood defences or strengthening buildings) and non-structural (such as training in disaster management, regulating land and crop use, and public education).

Possible interventions

Risk mapping and disaster planning An important first step in disaster preparedness and mitigation is risk mapping, which identifies communities' vulnerabilities and capacities for responding to disasters. This intervention often includes country or area background, the identification of hazards and likely disasters (based on available data) and the drafting of a plan that addresses likely scenarios. A key element is the assessment of vulnerability, probability and risk, with attention to individuals and communities most at risk and weighed with existing assets and capacities.

Local community disaster committee organization The creation and support of community disaster committees (CDCs) are an internationally recognized means of disaster preparedness and mitigation at the community level. CDCs are usually made up of volunteers but should also be closely linked to government disaster management systems. Women are an important element of CDCs, as they are often disproportionately affected by disaster and are generally the last to benefit from assistance activities. Community action planning should be shared with authorities at the district and national levels, as appropriate.

Awareness campaigns and training Along with community mobilization, awareness raising can help lessen the feeling of helplessness and foreboding that accompanies different disasters. This can be done by incorporating local songs and theatre activities, and other approaches, such as contests and games, provide a sense of agency which can be fostered among community members. Training can be organized at several levels such as CDC members, youth groups (e.g. Scouts), teachers and community leaders. Training may consist of steps to prepare for a disaster, information on hazards faced, first aid and responsibilities based on position. Police, fire, local government authorities and public health professionals can be included in awareness campaigns and training, in order to increase collective effectiveness.

Early warning and communication systems Traditionally, for example, people have known that an unusual withdrawing tide might mean an incipient tsunami or that heavy rains in mountains mean flooding in low land areas. When combined with the CDCs and training, communities can be equipped with an effective means of early warning, such as community-based lookouts, sirens and radio warning signs, which are low-cost yet effective early warning systems. In addition to awareness, an effective means of communicating that a disaster is imminent is often lacking. NGOs can help fill gaps at the community-level, such as with radios and IT equipment, so as to get disaster information out as part of early warning and follow-up information sharing. If undertaken, it is important that this activity links to national and international disaster preparedness and mitigation efforts.

Emergency stockpiles The social service infrastructure is often strained, with some hospitals and municipal assets severely damaged or destroyed. During most disasters, people rely on whatever medical and other support that can be found, including that provided by international actors. Pre-positioned kits help communities to self-cope. The contents of the kits, which can include appropriate NFIs as well as water and food, should be developed with communities and should take into account their assets and capacities.

Disaster-resistant infrastructure As a classic mitigation effort, buildings and other structures that comprise homes and social service infrastructure can be designed and constructed to be resistant to local hazards. Examples include watershed management such as erosion prevention using vegetation, reducing flood damage with the use of gabion walls and installing reinforcements to reduce wind damage. Improving general design and construction standards is also a standard mitigation practice.

CHAPTER 3
Managing in emergencies

Management, the act of supervising and controlling activities, plays a critical role in emergencies. Because an organization is only as good as the people who work in it, practising good management remains one of the major dilemmas for NGOs. The potential of insecurity, scarce or non-existent resources, cultural differences, extraordinary time constraints and high stress all present NGO managers with special challenges. To provide an understanding of some basic concepts of management, this chapter focuses on:

- Management fundamentals
- Management methods
- Organizational design
- Team building
- Assessing management

Management is an expansive topic that includes concerns as diverse as accounting, logistics and programme. For this reason, many of the topics often discussed in management are covered elsewhere including human resources management (Chapter 8) and project management (Chapter 9).

Management fundamentals

Most definitions of management centre on the use of an organization's resources to achieve stated aims. Management involves elements of planning, organizing, controlling (i.e. approving or disapproving), representation, leading and role-modelling, coordination, information generation and sharing. The comparison between management and leadership is useful in illustrating the role of a manager and how an organization functions. The management expert Peter Drucker (1967) describes the difference: 'Management is doing things right; leadership is doing the right things.' Managers are usually assigned to formal positions. They focus on the present, ensure the control of and the meeting of objectives, make sure procedures are followed, seek improvement through elimination of errors, and focus on efficiency and process. In contrast, leaders can have an informal position. Leaders are forward-looking, provide vision, inspire staff, set an example, and focus on effectiveness and the end-product. In this way, any staff member can exercise good leadership despite not being part of management. While personality, training and experience can lead people to be either a manager or a leader, people can be both managers and leaders. In emergencies, qualities of both are needed to be effective, especially in times of ambiguity and change.

Key management tasks typically relevant to emergencies include:

- Authority: within organizations, authority is formally granted according to people's positions, as spelled out in the founding documentation, organizational charts and job descriptions.
- Responsibility: like the staff below them, each manager has a set of tasks he or she is required or has the responsibility to do. Managers achieve objectives based on their ability to work with others, so in their way, their primary responsibility is to coach and nurture others.
- Accountability: managers answer to their supervisors (or in the case of the executive, to the board) while supporting their staff. Externally, managers must account for their actions and that of their organization to various stakeholders, especially donors and beneficiaries.
- Delegation: managers have a responsibility to share and organize the work of others in a way that is efficient and effective. When necessary, managers need to play a supporting and advocating role when staff encounter problems with their responsibilities.

NGO management at the field level in emergencies is confronted by a number of key challenges that can combine and lead to poor decision making and ineffective management. These include the following.

Key challenge no. 1: lack of time The amount of work to be done in emergencies can be daunting. Managers of emergency programmes are often faced with tension between expediency, accuracy and effectiveness. Compounded with the lack of time, managers face a very wide scope of tasks that need to be completed. For this reason, managers may face a difficult trade-off between finishing a few tasks while leaving others untouched or having everything less than partially done.

Key challenge no. 2: diversity of skills, experience and culture humanitarian relief brings together people with different skills, experience and culture. While this can be interesting, it can be a significant challenge for a manager. Many professions have conventions or well-established rules which provide a set of norms. This is less common in NGOs, and so field programmes tend to be highly personality-driven, which can result in major problems when a manager is not effective and there is high staff turnover.

Key challenge no. 3: effective systems NGOs tend to have clearly defined organizational aims, yet their systems may be insufficiently developed to respond to emergencies. Without effective systems, an NGO's management might be characterized by a permanent reaction to crisis. The dissimilarity of each disaster makes the creation of case-specific ways of carrying out day-to-day tasks a difficult challenge.

Key challenge no. 4: closeness of work and social life With the close overlap between work and social life, a common comparison with life in the field is that of living and working on a ship at sea. Unlike typical work situations, managers often have to live with the staff they manage, which presents a challenge in which the boundaries between work and social life are ambiguous.

Especially in countries that have strict cultural traditions, rules may need to extend into social areas which staff may normally consider separate and private.

Key challenge no. 5: geographic separateness Emergencies typically occur over large geographic areas and locations that are commonly considered remote. Refugees, for example, often settle along frontiers than may be difficult to travel to and a long journey from the centre of government, trade and transportation. This necessitates multiple offices and staff who work in different locales, thus making management a challenge. Developments in ICT have made this challenge more workable.

Keeping these challenges in mind, effective management in emergencies combines aspects of both management and leadership, following three steps.

Step 1 Managing yourself

Knowledge One of the most important characteristics of being a manager is knowing oneself. In emergencies, stress-inducing situations can stretch people in ways that can adversely affect an organization. Managers ought to be aware of their own personalities, approach to others and limitations. They should also understand their NGO and its culture and how to reach its objectives with little contact from supervisors.

Skills Being fully proficient in basic skills is important for leading by example. Effective managers actively seek improvement and to familiarize themselves with skills and techniques in areas under their responsibility. Specific skills will vary between contexts and organizations; however, verbal and written communication skills, use of ICT equipment and project management are essential. An understanding of the local context, the development industry and breadth of topics discussed throughout this book is also important.

Attitude A large part of managing is filling a role that others can follow. This may change depending on the situation, but includes showing compassion, acting decisively and presenting a professional and positive image externally despite personal opinions. Preparation and training to acquire the right mix of knowledge and skills can make assuming the right attitude easier.

Step 2 Managing others

Managing others can be very challenging. In emergencies, managers have a responsibility to their staff to look beyond standard work issues and consider wider concerns such as staff welfare and other things which may affect their motivation. Many NGO managers find it helpful to meet their staff regularly to discuss welfare, such as the following:

- Staff need outlets such as privacy, exercise and opportunities for down-time, which may be scarce or difficult to obtain in emergency settings
- Some staff may benefit from their hours of work being limited and enforcing holiday vacation schedules

- Sleeping and living quarters should be made separate from office or work space, from the start or as soon as possible
- Providing a balanced diet by bringing in perishable items (e.g. fruits and vegetables) if they are not normally available
- Where possible, security needs should be balanced with freedom and access to normal activities

Relief workers are usually motivated by serving others, but it is nonetheless important for managers to help staff to maintain their enthusiasm. Effective leadership communicates vision and find ways to inspire. Empowerment comes from giving real responsibility, helping others to realize their potential, building on their self-esteem and sense of belonging, and recognizing and rewarding success. However, it is typically a mistake to think that this is enough to maintain motivation. Disingenuous efforts to include others in decision making are likely to be counterproductive. It does no good to ask for opinions which are then ignored or half-heartedly added to decisions that have already been made. Monetary motivation may work for some, but it is generally seen as a short-term measure, and if attached to conditions, the constructive effect intended will be even less.

Step 3 Managing your boss

The concept of managing your boss was first developed by Gabarro and Kotter (1979). Because everyone has a boss in one form or another, and because it is possible to do everything right and still end in failure without getting along with your supervisor, this idea is crucial in considering management. There are several ways to manage a boss, as outlined by Hudson (2002):

- Understand the broader context in which your boss is working.
- Discover your boss's preferred working style (and strengths and weaknesses).
- Use your boss to help with tasks he or she is good at.
- Expect your boss to provide support .
- See the relationship as a learning opportunity.
- Look elsewhere for support when your boss in unable to provide it.

Management methods

There are many management methods, some of which are rather complex. The business world is filled with models and techniques for increasing and measuring performance, but few of these are practised by humanitarian organizations. Perhaps one of the reasons for this is that the models themselves do not easily fit humanitarian relief. At times, there is little inventory, even less machinery, and the mention of control is contrary to the personality and motives of many who started with NGOs to be away from these more staid aspects of the commercial sector. Nonetheless, there are many management methods or tools available to NGOs working in emergencies, such as Gantt charts and logical framework analysis (logframes), discussed in Chapter 9. In this section, management style, innovation and delegation are discussed.

Style

Management style is a manager's approach to the task at hand. Some of the most famous leaders in history are noted for their very distinctive management styles (e.g. Napoleon Bonaparte and Winston Churchill). Different personality types give rise to different roles (discussed further below) in group situations. Although heavily based on an individual's personality, some have put forward the idea that management style is based on different views of staff members' willingness to be productive. McGregor's (1960) classic theory of X and Y established two styles; one authoritarian, which assumes that staff are natural slackers, and another more laissez-faire style where staff are self-motivated and work in pursuit of objectives to which they are fully committed.

Different situations will require distinct approaches to management. Sometimes managers need to be diplomatic and conciliatory, while at other times a situation will require them to be forthright and resolute. In emergency programmes, which are by definition time-bound and may relate to critical issues like security, there is a need for quick decision making. A manager who has a particularly strong personality must avoid alienating fellow staff. A directive style where people are told what to do may be necessary, but such a style is ineffective during most other times. Similarly, a hands-off approach may be effective for self-motivated and competent staff, but this can produce negative results if the person needs a lot of direction. In most cases, it is far easier to go from a strict style to a more relaxed mode of working than to go from a loose to a tight style. People may tend to tolerate this tight style for short periods, such as during a crisis, but more collaborative methods are needed over time.

Innovation and change

Emergencies often present challenges that demand resourcefulness and original problem solving. While many methods have been developed over time and have now become standard practice, there is still much room for improvement. Community-based approaches to mobile health clinics and feeding programmes, for example, represent new and innovative approaches to otherwise standard methodologies. The inclusion of new technologies is another area where innovation can play an important part in improving humanitarian relief.

Effective managers create working environments that foster creativity and continuous improvement. To do this, managers can clear obstacles for their staff, allow for experimentation and permit mistakes to happen. In this way, change is critical innovation. A phased approach can bring about changes in a more manageable way. Some NGOs find it helpful to manage change in a systematic way, like this, for example:

Step 1 Obtain agreement on the need to change (especially between the country director (or CD), HQ and board if required).
Step 2 Begin a review to identify specific problems.
Step 3 Develop options about general principles.
Step 4 Prepare a detailed plan for the new structure, outlining which positions will be changed, added or deleted.
Step 5 Implement changes.

Options for change include changing key staff or the head leadership, creating working groups or similar structures involving staff from different departments, and changing or improving management or other ways of working. Some organizations appoint or identify specific staff as internal change agent who examine organizational issues and help facilitate change.

Delegation

When managing others, delegating has a number of advantages for developing the skills of staff and relieving a manager in order to extend his or her capacity to manage. According to Armstrong (2004), delegation should be put in place when the manager has more work than can effectively be carried out, cannot allocate sufficient time to priority tasks, wants to develop subordinates or the job can be done adequately by subordinate(s). To delegate, a manager must decide when and to whom to delegate, how to inform or brief a subordinate and how to guide and monitor performance.

There are many ways to delegate. One way adopts a traditional management approach in which people are managed through duties or steps in a process (tasks). This facilitates control but leaves little room for staff to exercise creativity, and staff may feel 'micromanaged' and are hence unlikely to take much responsibility for or feel ownership in the work they do. But management by objective occurs when managers communicate the final result (objective) and leave it to the staff to discover their own best route to achieving it. A number of factors may determine which approach is best, including experience and staff competency, cultural differences, trustworthiness and the ability of managers to delegate (Figure 3.1).

The Hersey and Blanchard model (see Figure 3.2) of situational leadership is helpful in understanding what type of style may be the best fit for staff members at different times based on relationships and tasks. The curved line represents a staff member's tenure with an organization. Following recruitment, in the first phase the staff member will need to have a lot of direction without much emphasis on building a relationship. In the second phase, the staff member should begin to become proficient in the tasks and a relationship can be built. In this way, the staff member will need less direction, but without being given full responsibility. In the third phase, the manager will not have to focus on the staff member tasks as much as the relationship, as the staff member seeks greater responsibility. In the final phase, the staff member has more self-reliance and may start to exercise more leadership.

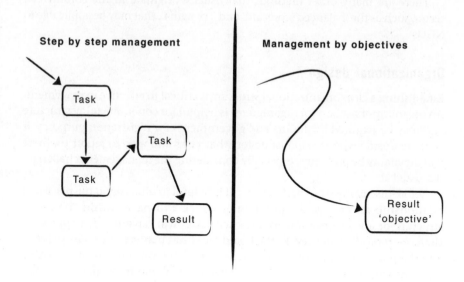

Figure 3.1 Delegation methods

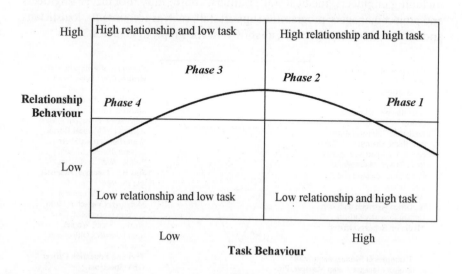

Figure 3.2 Hersey and Blanchard model

There are many other methods that usually originate in the commercial sector, such as the 'balanced scorecard' and 'six sigma', that may be applicable to NGOs.

Organizational design

Establishing a clear organizational structure is critical to effective management. An organizational chart (or organigram) is helpful for communicating structure and may be required by donors and governments for registration purposes. If staff are unsure who is responsible for what tasks and who to report to, there will inevitably be problems, especially considering the management challenges discussed above.

Before discussing structural options, it is helpful to understand the place and relationship an emergency programme office will have within the larger structure of an organization. While each NGO will have its own approach, there are typically three levels: the board and headquarters, the country office and the project site or work place. Generally each level concerns itself with a different view of strategy, time span, level of detail and frequency of dealing with particular issues. The board of an NGO, for example, will have a long-term strategic vision that occasionally looks into the details of particular programmes. Project site staff, in contrast, will have a relatively short-term highly detailed day-to-day view focused on targets.

When discussing organizational design, it is also useful to categorize types of staff typically found in emergency NGOs. These include: programme staff, including engineers, medical staff, trainers, community mobilizers, engineers and project managers; programme support staff, such as accountants, logisticians and drivers; and management, as shown in the graph in Figure 3.3.

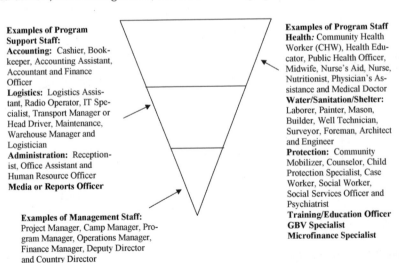

Examples of Program Support Staff:
Accounting: Cashier, Bookkeeper, Accounting Assistant, Accountant and Finance Officer
Logistics: Logistics Assistant, Radio Operator, IT Specialist, Transport Manager or Head Driver, Maintenance, Warehouse Manager and Logistician
Administration: Receptionist, Office Assistant and Human Resource Officer
Media or Reports Officer

Examples of Management Staff:
Project Manager, Camp Manager, Program Manager, Operations Manager, Finance Manager, Deputy Director and Country Director

Examples of Program Staff
Health: Community Health Worker (CHW), Health Educator, Public Health Officer, Midwife, Nurse's Aid, Nurse, Nutritionist, Physician's Assistance and Medical Doctor
Water/Sanitation/Shelter: Laborer, Painter, Mason, Builder, Well Technician, Surveyor, Foreman, Architect and Engineer
Protection: Community Mobilizer, Counselor, Child Protection Specialist, Case Worker, Social Worker, Social Services Officer and Psychiatrist
Training/Education Officer
GBV Specialist
Microfinance Specialist

Figure 3.3 Staff structure

The inverted triangle represents first the higher number of staff in programmes than in programme support and management. Second, and more important, it shows that management has a supportive role in both programmes and programme support. In some parts of the world, this is a controversial arrangement, where management comes with an emphasis on rights and less on responsibilities. In this example, it is upside-down, to show an alternative approach.

Organizational structure can be established along several lines including by function, service users (e.g. children and adults), programme (e.g. shelter and water/sanitation), donor or geography. A typical structure includes both functional and geographical elements at the HQ level. At the country or field level, there are often programme and functional (often called programme support) elements, as in the examples discussed below. In some situations, less hierarchical (i.e. flatter) structures work well when conditions are relatively stable and staff are well trained. In emergencies, a pyramid structure is typical because it eases communications and gives staff clear roles and responsibilities. In response to crisis (a serious or dangerous event or series of events that faces an organization and requires significant resources to resolve, such as the abduction of a staff member), some organizations form a task force or crisis management team. This approach brings together key decision-makers within an organization and allows them to focus on the crisis until it has passed. Because this approach may differ from the formal organizational structure, it is best to identify its membership and specific responsibilities before a crisis occurs.

Ultimately, the best model is the one that works most efficiently and helps an NGO achieve its goals. No organizational structure is ideal or permanent. Organizational charts are important for communicating how relationships and communication function within an organization on paper, but they are rarely adequate nor do they show the team approach in which most organizations work. Organizations typically revisit organizational charts periodically to revise and make changes. It is best to experiment to get the right mix for each situation. The start of a new country programme may look like Figure 3.4.

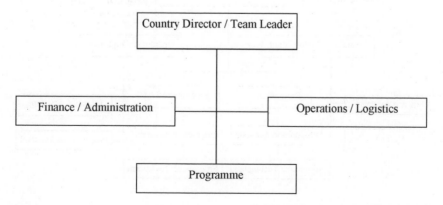

Figure 3.4 Organigram no. 1

As discussed in Chapter 5, an NGO's initial emergency response team may have a number of short-term staff, such as proposal writers, media specialists and others to help establish a programme. Over time, as programme activities expand, more positions can be added to this basic model in a way so that each forms a section or department (Figure 3.5).

As the programme grows further, organizational structures tend to become more vertical with increased levels of managers. Figure 3.6 incorporates one deputy but some NGOs use a dual assistant directorship with one overseeing all programme related activities and a second supervising administration such as finance, logistics and human resources.

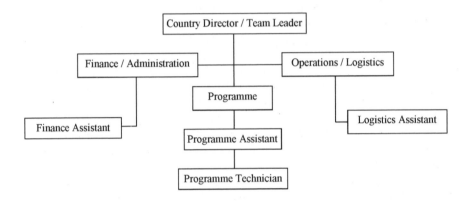

Figure 3.5 Organigram no. 2

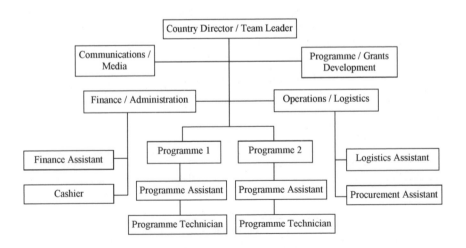

Figure 3.6 Organigram no. 3

As the emergency programme grows or expands, so does the complexity. There are several problems to work out in developing a workable organization. The problems addressed below are presented in ascending order of relevance during programme growth.

1. **Clarity of function** From the beginning, the role and responsibility of each position ought to be known to all staff. Unless explicitly spelled out and enforced, issues relating to responsibility, span of control, oversight and follow-through will become problems. Most responsibilities may seem obvious (e.g. that of drivers or nurses), but some duties, such as procurement, can fall into the spaces between roles.

2. **Centralization or decentralization** As an emergency programme expands, some tasks can be delegated while some responsibilities cannot, in what is called loose-tight organization. Decentralizing as the programme expands is important as not all responsibilities can be controlled from the top by a group – and much less by a single person.

3. **Cross-departmental relationships** Most emergency programmes involve a country-level HQ office (usually in the capital city) and one or more sub-offices. This can lead to a situation where staff report to two people: one at HQ for technical or big-picture issues and another at the sub-office for day-to-day issues such as logistics and coordination. This dual reporting can cause problems between staff. In most cases, having an effective head of the sub-office (or a similar management position) will address this issue by making a single geographic manager responsible.

4. **Deputy directors** As the organization continues to grow, the CD's time will be at a premium and the need for someone else to share the workload of the programme's administration and management will be crucial. According to Hudson (2002), there are essentially four types of deputy: a substitute director for when the CD is physically not present; a deputy who assumes responsibility for an entire part of the programme; a fixer who floats, looking for problems to fix; and a line-manager who manages staff and allows the CD to focus on external relations and strategic issues. Finding the best solution will depend on the personalities and contexts.

When there is an existing development programme, some NGOs form a separate emergency team structure because of the different sorts of programming needed, as distinct from the development activities of the NGO. This can present unique challenges for both the leaders of the distinct development programme, which tends to be stable and long-term, compared with the emergency programme, which is short-term and likely to have a much higher profile. Two steps can help mitigate the friction that accompanies this arrangement. First, having explicit terms of reference (TOR) with clearly delineated areas of responsibility is essential. The TOR should be in writing and shared with all staff to prevent confusion. Second, frequent information and team building measures (whether formal or informal) are important to lessen the effect of the 'them against us' thinking that may develop in dual programmes.

Making substantial changes to the structure of an organization often becomes necessary as the programme advances away from the acute phases of an emergency. Unless specifically needed (e.g. in urgent situations), abrupt changes are best avoided.

Team building

The team-building process can be thought of as comprising four stages, as described by Handy (1985): forming, storming, norming and performing. Each stage will be examined here in sequence.

Stage 1: Forming, or orientation

In forming, the group is identified as a set of individuals who are finding their places in the team. People make and form impressions in establishing their identity within the group and they may test each other. The manager's role in this involves understanding who may be placed on a team and adjusting the team to suit the personalities.

When forming a team, people naturally assume different roles. As outlined by Heller (1998) in Table 3.1, there are several key roles in any team that need to be filled. While a single individual may assume more than one role, it is important to consider these roles against the members of the team.

Stage 2: Storming, or dissatisfaction

In the storming stage, teams experience conflict that develops when personal agendas and idiosyncracies are revealed between members. In most situations, the team will adjust itself (perhaps with the help and prodding of its leadership) with more realistic expectations, as a result. However, if the situation deteriorates, the team may need to split or not begin on its objectives.

Judging the readiness of others to follow is also an important management skill. By knowing staff's skills and perceptions, management decisions can be made and tailored accordingly. This can be thought of in terms of ability and willingness, as follows.

Can do – will do The best candidate for delegation. Has both the right attitude and skills to do the task required.

Will do – can't do This candidate has the right attitude but lacks the skills. Probably needs training and mentoring.

Can do – won't do While this candidate has the skills, he or she has underlying problems that make him/her uncooperative and may not be a team player. He or she may need encouragement or convincing to undertake the task.

Can't do – won't do This candidate lacks both the skills and attitude to undertake a particular task. Altering the position may be the only solution to make him or her a productive staff member (modified from Heller, 1998: 24).

Table 3.1 Team roles

Team role	Responsibilities	Necessary traits
Team leader	Recruits new team members and develops team spirit	Excellent judge of character Able to find way of overcoming weaknesses Good communicator Able to inspire and sustain enthusiasm
Ideas person	Brings innovation to the team and inspires others to do the same	Lively with a zest for new ideas Eager for and receptive to the ideas of others Sees problems as opportunities Never at a loss for a good suggestion
Critic	Guardian and analyst of the team's long-term effectiveness	Satisfied only with the best solution Analyses solutions to find possible weaknesses in them Insists faults be found and corrected Constructive in pointing ways to possible remedies
Implementer	Ensures the momentum and smooth running of the team's actions	Thinks methodically and according to schedules Anticipates conflicts and schedules time for them to be prevented Has a can-do mentality and is a fixer Able to rally support and overcome defeatism
Coordinator	Pulls together the work of the team as a whole into a cohesive plan	Understands how difficult tasks interrelate Has a strong set of priorities Has a mind able to grasp several things at once Good at maintaining internal contacts Skilled at heading off potential trouble
Inspector	Ensures that high standards are sought and maintained	Strict and sometimes even pedantic in enforcing rigorous standards Good judge of performance in others Does not hesitate to bring problems to the surface Able to praise as well as to find fault
External contact	Looks after the team's external relations	Diplomatic and good judge of the needs of others Has a reassuring and authoritative presence Grasps the overall picture of the team's work Discreet when handling confidential information

Source: Modified from Heller (1998: 17).

While dealing with conflict is discussed further in Chapter 10, it is helpful to know what to do when subordinate staff are difficult to manage. Armstrong (2004) offers a number of approaches:

- Anticipate problems.
- Subject your own behaviour to close scrutiny.
- When there are specific issues, discuss them with the individual.
- When dealing with aggressive people, stand your ground by being assertive.
- Always be calm.
- Try to reason with the difficult person.
- Use avoidance tactics only as a short-term solution.
- Think carefully about the words you use.
- Always try to reach agreement that a problem exists.

Stage 3 Norming, or resolution

In this stage, people in the team develop an understanding of others and patterns that can be identified with their particular group. Cooperation and adherence within the group or team can start to increase the organization's performance. There are a number of approaches to help foster team spirit, including all-team meetings, team-building events (social outings), induction (and rituals associated with this), providing timely and useful feedback, giving verbal praise, challenging strengths and addressing weaknesses. To be successful, a mixture of solutions will be needed, while taking into account the local context, staff personalities, organizational realities and external factors such as the degree that the emergency affects the staff.

Stage 4 Performing, or production

In the final stage of team building, the team begins to execute its activities and achieve its objectives. Performing means that time is spent on the task at hand rather than positioning and working against others. A healthy group identity will develop, but over time this may need to be kept in check to prevent the 'us against them' thinking in the organization (e.g. 'us' in the field against 'them' at HQ). At this stage, maintaining performance will become the primary concern. This can be achieved by creating structures, rewards and cohesion, so that the common goal can be concentrated on.

Assessing management

The following tool (Table 3.2) can be used to assess the existing management capacity in an NGO as a self-assessment or as a capacity-building tool when working with partners. While it can be used to measure a manager's performance, it will be less effective to assess a team of managers with such a tool. Each management issue can be given a score following the criteria given in order to identify areas for improvement.

Table 3.2 Assessing management

Management issue	1	2	3
Management	Inconsistency in direction provided. Work place is disorganized and makes it difficult to work. Few objectives and requirements are achieved	Direction is hit or miss. Certain elements of the work place are not in place or are in disarray. Some objectives and requirements are met while others are not	Consistent direction provided. Organized work place. All objectives and requirements met
Leadership	It is unclear where the organization is headed. Change and opportunities for improvement are stifled. Those in charge do little to inspire or cause others to follow.	Vision may have been clear in the past, but it is now muddled. Change is possible but not without considerable difficulty. Staff feel occasional bouts of inspiration but it is not a consistent ethos.	Clear vision established and imparted to staff. A clear path for innovation and improvement is known to all staff and they are inspired to do follow it. Charisma and self-confidence are displayed at all times.
Relationships	Staff duplicate work and waste resources as a result. Conflict is caused when more than one staff member works on a project and it is poorly resolved by management. Few or no major tasks are passed to junior staff	Some tasks are handled through effective teamwork, but not always. Staff do not always feel supported by management. When conflict arises, time is wasted when management is indecisive or takes sides	Roles and responsibilities are clearly defined with the optimal amount of delegation. Staff view management as positive, supportive and compassionate when needed. Conflict is efficiently resolved
Systems	Policies and procedures do not exist. Staff feel they must 'reinvent the wheel' or muddle through. Basic structures such as filing systems are not available	Policies and procedures exist for some positions or functions but not for others. Although some structures might be in place, they are weak or inefficient.	Policies are logical and applied consistently. Procedures are efficient and make best use of resources and technology. Staff have their needs met
Planning	If planning happens, it is only done by the top managers and their decisions are not transparent. Staff learn of plans inconsis-	Planning is done by some staff but rarely with the input of those who will likely have to implement the plans. When plans are	Planning involves all relevant staff (at different levels). Plans are communicated and put in writing. Action planning and

cont.

cont.

Management issue	1	2	3
	tently and usually by rumour. Decisions are arrived at based on whims and not deliberation and the use of widely accepted tools	communicated it is usually done verbally and at the last minute. Planning tools may be used but not in an efficient way	other tools are used for impact and follow-through
Communication	Staff have little idea what they are supposed to be doing beyond a few immediate tasks. Monitoring is carried out in a destructive inspection style. They wait for top-down decisions and feel little room to professionally develop or to learn how the organization functions	Staff know some of the reasons why they work, but not all. Management monitors staff with both positive and negative approaches. Staff have little leeway to learn other aspects of the organization which would improve efficiency and effectiveness	Goals, objectives, activities and processes are known to all staff. Monitoring is a positive process. Learning is encouraged and facilitated

CHAPTER 4
Carrying out an assessment

An assessment is an appraisal or review of an emergency carried out to assist in timely decision making. To best understand a situation, a mixture of quantitative and qualitative information is needed. As the main purpose of an initial assessment is to find out what is going on, and to help decide if a further assessment is needed, external sources of information such as a government, a donor, a UN or research institution report, can be heavily relied on.

The purpose of this chapter is to provide an overview of how assessments are used in emergencies. To do this, this chapter looks at assessments on two levels, general and programme-specific, as well as presenting different methods that are available. It covers:
- Gaining background knowledge of a disaster zone
- Quantitative methods
- Qualitative methods

When a situation is unclear, or lacks specific evidence to justify or support an intervention, an assessment is needed. Each NGO project should be based on specific needs and to support rights. Assessments can help identify needs, the scope of the emergency and specific problems. Examples of information needed in an emergency include mortality and morbidity rates, the extent of the infrastructure destruction and information regarding the knowledge, attitudes and practices of beneficiary populations. Typical examples from an emergency situation include a nutritional assessment of displaced children less than 5 years of age, or an assessment of water use and availability among vulnerable people in a specified location.

To be efficient, assessments often focus on a particular sector and geographic area. What determines the path is discussed in greater detail later and in Chapter 9. An initial assessment aims to gain an appreciation of an emergency or its particular facets. A mixture of quantitative and qualitative information is needed.

Much has been written on assessments and many tools have been developed, seemingly to the point where staff can forget that simply asking a question may reveal the information needed. The purpose of this chapter is to provide an overview of assessments in emergencies.

Gaining information about a disaster zone

Assessments of emergencies should focus on symptomatic or immediate problems and their root causes, so that a response can be generated. The reasons for carrying out an assessment include understanding the situation, identifying needs and matching these with possible interventions. Unless activities, objectives and goals are based on a sound analysis of good data, projects may fail. The need to do something should be balanced against the need to make good decisions. For this reason, considerable effort should go into making sure that staff understand the links between the programmes and the root causes of the problems.

A baseline, an assessment or set of data about a population before an emergency or start of a programme is established when an NGO first begins programming or, if the information needed fits properly, is borrowed from other sources. Political and socio-economic factors need to be taken into account, so that immediate, medium- and long-term needs are identified and balanced with existing capacities among the group of beneficiaries. For example, chronic food shortages should be distinguished from acute famine, because the programmatic approach may differ.

Elements of a successful assessment

1. **Need for an assessment** The first, most important question is whether or not an assessment is needed in the first place. If an assessment will lead to a decision about a programme and there is a not a critical beneficiary need (e.g. immediate provision of food, water or shelter) that would be delayed because of an assessment, then an assessment should go ahead.

2. **Decide on the consumers of the assessment information** Assessments are done to help decision makers determine if there is a need to intervene and if so on what scale and using what approach. These decision makers will be internal to the NGO, but in many cases assessment information is shared externally (e.g. with other NGOs, local government, the UN and donors). In this way, assessment can provide needed evidence to address critical humanitarian needs and advocate for others to act.

3. **Plan information and resources needs** If not designed and planned for properly, assessments can become a waste of time because they do not gather the types of information needed. Before any work is done on the assessment tools themselves, consideration should be given to what types of interventions are possible with the capacity of the NGO (although the process should not go too far in only gathering information that solely supports the position of any particular organization). If staff, vehicles, office space and other resources are needed to carry out the assessment, this should be planned with other staff and managers. Logistical issues such as travel arrangements and authorizations may delay the start and implementation of an assessment.

4. **Consider the place and time** Emergency assessments have to take into account geographic location because of the vastly different conditions that can be created in small areas. Although the location

may experience normality, disaster-stricken areas may be only walking distance away. Further, carrying out an assessment at a feeding centre will distort assessment findings, because all the beneficiaries require food. Timing is also important, both seasonal changes and the considerable difference between one day and another.

5. **Qualified staff** No activity will be possible without qualified staff and assessments are no exception. In fact, assessments can be especially technical and require trained and experienced staff. To carry out an assessment, staff must be literate, numerate and have the ability to pay attention to detail to collect accurate results. Ideally, all staff will have experience in the conditions found in the assessment area and speak the languages of the population being assessed.

6. **Make use of local knowledge** Check sources of information and results with local informants for possible different interpretations and missing information. In particular, be aware that the local context and culture may mean a particularly important aspect of the situation may be hidden or unclear to outsiders. Local staff can help with this aspect.

7. **Coordinate with other organizations** In most cases, others are aware of the same problems. There may be previous assessment information that can negate the need for a new assessment or at least provide valuable baseline information. Or work may be under way by another organization to assess the same area or population. To prevent duplication of efforts, assessments should not be carried out in isolation.

8. **Decide on the format and how the assessment will be presented** Normally, the conclusions of the assessment will have to be shared with managers and decision makers who probably do not have a background in the particular area. A format and style should be easily and quickly understood. For this reason, use standard methods, terminology and approaches so that others can understand and use the information gathered.

9. **Balance needs and vulnerabilities with capacities and assets** Focusing simply on need undermines local capacity, degrades people's confidence in themselves and communities and creates dependency. Addressing need and reducing vulnerabilities while using local capacities is good programming and leads to better long-term results.

10. **Distinguish between types of need** All developing countries have chronic needs which may be very different from emergency needs. The assessment should show what is chronic (or normal in certain contexts) and what is not. Over time, both types of need should be addressed, but during an emergency certain needs will be critical.

11. **Build in triangulation** Triangulation is obtaining information from several sources or perspectives to prevent bias and distortion. Such information gathered should be concrete and specific – not just

anecdotal. If an assessment is planned to rely on one method, information should be gathered from several sources.

12. **Test methods in the local context** Although there are many common assessment tools and approaches, what works in one place may not work in another. Sampling methods should be practical and suited to field conditions. Questionnaires, in particular, may contain questions that are not understood between one culture or context and another. Pre-testing can also provide an opportunity for training staff involved in the assessment to ensure that the right techniques are followed.

13. **Maintain flexibility** Be prepared for abrupt changes (e.g. an influx or outflow of refugees or an abrupt change in the security situation) that may happen during the assessment.

As Table 4.1 shows, there are several issues that may arise during assessments. A common problem worth noting is that beneficiaries may begin to feel that they are being over-assessed. This is the case where there is a high number of organizations working in an area.

Assessment planning

When planning an assessment, sequence and timing are important. As Figure 4.1 shows, each task will take a different amount of time; deciding and planning the assessment may not take much time. However, carrying out the assessment and writing up the findings can take considerable amounts of time, and this should be taken into account. Some of the tasks overlap, but for some types of assessments analysis might need to wait until after collection.

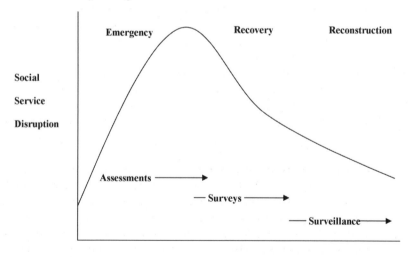

Figure 4.1 Assessment phases
Source: Modified from Burkle in Cahill (2003: 60).

Table 4.1 Assessment errors and preventive action

Common errors	Preventative action
The assessment is poorly coordinated between various NGOs and excludes the host government and the affected community	Appoint a team leader to coordinate the assessment with the host government, the affected community's leaders and other agencies, so results are shared and not duplicated. This helps ensure future support of relief activities
The assessment team lacks the expertise needed	Select members of the team with disaster-specific (prior) experience, site-specific (geography, language, culture), or specialty-specific (epidemiologist, physician, public-health nurse, logistician, environmental engineer) skills
The needs assessment is conducted too late	Strengthen disaster preparedness by establishing an early warning system for detecting humanitarian emergencies. Communication and coordination between organizations about existing knowledge and information about an area prior to a disaster
Collection of information requires a certain amount of time, yet often the time is limited.	
The data collected are often incomplete (due to poor access) or inappropriate (does not cover all the important areas.	Plan the field assessment: define the objectives, the relevant information needed and methods for collecting data. Discuss plans with local authorities, community representatives and other agencies
The data collected are not linked to an ongoing information system. More data are collected than needed or used	Ensure that one of the main outcomes from carrying out the needs assessment is setting up an information system. Collect only data that can be processed
The estimated size of the target population – the critical denominator – is unreliable	Make better estimates by mapping the location and dividing it into sections. Then determine the average family size in selected households of some sections and apply findings to the entire map
The survey sample does not accurately represent the affected population	Follow procedures when carrying out population-based surveys. Ask questions about characteristics of the affected population and be aware that vulnerable people (young, female and elderly) may be underrepresented

cont.

cont.

Common errors	Preventative action
The assessment report does not consider the affected population's perceived needs	Involve representatives from the affected population at every stage of the assessment, including drawing conclusions from the local response and outstanding needs
Causes of death are incorrectly attributed to the disaster even for slow-onset disasters, such as drought and famine	Collect background information: interview former staff, local authorities and the media; review field reports, country profiles or internet
The assessment team does not complete its task, as members are drawn into setting up initial activities. Thus, there is not enough time for accurate assessments, the assessment period is extended and serious delays in vital action may occur	Arrange for a local emergency response team (health, fire, police) to take care of the injured and limit harm from hazards (such as fire or epidemics,) so the assessment proceeds smoothly

Source: Modified from Saade and Burnham (2000: 138).

As with many of the subjects of this book, it is helpful to think through a process of understanding an emergency and where assessments fit into that framework. One way of thinking of this is presented below.

Step 1 Analyse initial sources of information such as local staff, beneficiaries, local government, other NGOs, the UN, donors, journals, books and reports, maps and photos.

Step 2 If further assessment is needed, decide on methods and make preparations.

Step 3 Carry out assessment and analyse findings.

Step 4 Present findings for review and decision making.

Step 5 If needed, take action, including writing a proposal, implementing a project.

This framework is part of the larger project cycle management discussed in Chapter 9.

The amount of time needed to carry out an assessment will vary depending on security, the remoteness of the population and the degree of cooperation. To obtain a reasonably accurate data set, standard practice suggests 30 cluster samples of 30 households. Over a period of two or three days, data can be collected from 600–900 households. Most assessments, including baseline and population surveys, can be carried out within two weeks or less.

Quantitative methods

Quantitative methods gather statistical information or data. They have several advantages and disadvantages, as outlined here in Table 4.2.

Table 4.2 Quantitative methods

Advantages	Disadvantages
Information revealed is usually easily translatable into project design that focuses on outputs	Can be resource-intensive (e.g. time, logistics and well-qualified staff)
Tend to be wide-ranging and a large sample size is possible	Provide data and related information which does not necessarily give a full picture
Techniques are often widely known and easily taught	May take several weeks to complete
Accuracy can be tested and data can be compared	Respondents may be uncooperative and this may lead to poor data
	Questionnaires can be inflexible
	Questions may be misinterpreted
	Do not allow for contextual information which may have important negative effect on interpretation
	Data usually entered and analysed far from the source, so mistakes realized later may be unfixable
	Poor design, collection or analysis may invalidate information gathered

The most common way used to by NGOs gather quantitative data is to carry out a survey. Surveys have the advantage of gathering information from a broad range of sources and are used to gain a broad understanding of a situation. They produce hard evidence to support decisions. Such information can be used to identify differences in population and who is worst affected. Two types of quantitative surveys are discussed here:

Mini-surveys

The purpose of a mini-survey is to obtain either a general picture or information on specific issues when time is limited. Mini-surveys are also useful to develop questions, hypotheses and propositions for further testing or when quantitative data are needed to supplement qualitative information. These surveys use a small sample (usually 25–70 respondents). So the evidence is not statistically reliable nor to be used for wider generalizations.

Knowledge attitudes and practices surveys

The purpose of this type of survey is to collect information about the knowledge, attitudes and practices of a specific group of people. These surveys are useful in that they can be used to establish a baseline against which to measure progress, or they may function as a monitoring tool to determine progress on certain indicators. Usually, these surveys include closed-end (yes/no or multiple choice) questions, adaptable to local populations and purpose. They are easily analysable by hand or computer, involve around 200–300 interviews and are based on a particular group or sample cluster. Because of their relative complexity, these surveys require training and supervision to ensure accuracy in interviewing and selecting area clusters in which to carry out the assessment.

Qualitative methods

Qualitative assessment methods obtain information using comparisons such as camp conditions or health characteristics. They can reveal illustrative evidence, such as personal stories, in a way that is obscured in quantitative data. An important element of qualitative methods is participation among the different stakeholders involved in the assessment. This is important, so that ownership and influence over the project can be gained – in the end strengthening the project.

Most assessments combine methods and, like quantitative methods, rely on temporarily hired staff who have some background in carrying out assessments. Typical qualitative methods are outlined below.

Semi-structured interviews

Semi-structured interviews are the most common type of interview because they can be informal in nature and might reveal information that structured interviews might leave out. Those carrying out assessments rely on interviews to gain an in-depth understanding of the issues involved in an emergency. Semi-structured interviews allow for leeway for the interviewee to respond freely to different open-ended questions while being given some direction. Key informants such as elders, doctors and teachers can be especially helpful in identifying larger problems.

Focus group discussions (FGDs)

A type of interview, FGDs bring together small groups of people based on their knowledge or interests for directed discussions. Typically, potential direct beneficiaries such as mothers or community health workers participate in FGDs to gain an appreciation of a situation. FGDs typically target small groups (4–8 people) who would not normally speak in larger meetings, and so an informal approach is used. Using trained facilitators, FGD meetings usually take between one and two hours, but the results may be difficult and time-consuming to analyse.

Observation

Direct observation involves members of the assessment team spending time viewing people, places and things, and crosscheck this information with what they hear. A typical way to carry out observation is to walk through camps, disaster sites and other programme areas, to see firsthand material that can confirm what has been learned through other methods. Transects, where observations are made along a line through a site, can help to organize this sort of observation.

Auto-diagnosis

Originally designed as a diagnostic tool and community-level problem solving process for women, auto-diagnosis involves a four-stage process: identification of the problem, planning together, implementing and evaluating the results. Like other qualitative methods, auto-diagnosis requires good facilitation skills and a commitment to process. Because it is time-consuming, its application is best suited to the rehabilitation phases of emergencies.

Group activities

There are many good group activities that, when performed well, encourage participation and discussion. They can thus be revealing in terms of the type of information they provide about context, relationships and connections between many different aspects of the situation. This group of approaches works especially well with communities and with groups without literacy skills. However, these activities can be time-consuming and the information produced may not immediately convert into workable projects. With good design and with the goals of the assessment in mind, group activities can be tailored to the needs of an emergency situation. Examples include ranking and scoring, picture drawing ('rich pictures'), timelines such as 'seasonal calendars' and mapping. Many different qualitative methods have been developed. Before looking at one of these methods more closely, a brief survey will be given of a number of approaches.

Participatory methods

Participatory methods are a group of approaches that has been championed by Robert Chambers (1992) and others over the last several decades. Participatory rural appraisal (PRA) represents a break with traditional approaches in its emphasis on community involvement in assessments and focus on non-traditional roles (e.g. women). While not just a rural technique, PRA aims at getting analysis and decision making out of the hands of professionals (e.g. bureaucrats, politicians and consultants) and into the hands of the ultimate beneficiaries.

More recently in development practice, appraisal has shifted from being simply a diagnostic method to one for helping communities plan, in what is called participatory learning and action (PLA). As part of the participatory process, outsiders (e.g. NGOs) learn from the insiders (the beneficiaries). In this way, it is as much a way of thinking as a method for gathering information.

Here a brief overview of PRA is presented because of its wide-ranging application. The full PRA method, it should first be noted, was designed for and is best suited for development, and so its utility in emergencies is limited. Still, by modifying this into rapid rural appraisal (RRA), participatory methods are very helpful in revealing qualitative data. In particular it may help in uncovering aspects of the situation in the area that are not obvious from surveys or direct observation and so might prove important for the success of the programme.

The application of participatory techniques also has a wider scope and can help within and between organizations to facilitate communication and planning. More recently in development practice, appraisal has shifted from being simply a diagnostic method to one for helping communities plan in PLA. There are many positive attributes to participatory approaches, but there are also downsides (Table 4.3).

Participatory methods usually involve a workshop and follow-on activities to gather and confirm information. Community workshops bring together

Table 4.3 Qualitative methods

Advantages	Disadvantages
Enable thorough understanding of local (community) context	Time-consuming, better suited for developmental approaches
Build rapport between people	People desire action but discussion is needed first
Allow community influence and under-standing of their own solutions to problems	Can reveal interventions that the NGO can do little about (e.g. a health NGO finding priorities in shelter and nutrition), although this can be addressed by sharing results with other organizations
Capable of working with different types of people	In postwar situations, where tension remains high, activities may focus too much on the past; better to focus on activities that bring people together rather than rehashing root causes
Can be used with people with low literacy rates and different languages	Results may apply only to local community
Learning throughout process not just at the end after analysis	
Produce tangible products and unexpected information	

community members, not just leaders, and the results are presented by the community to the community, with the facilitating workshop merely observing.

The features of PRA include the triangulation of information, multidisciplinary teams (of professionals as well as members of different organizations), mixed methods (informal community-based, non-detailed and ongoing) and on-the-spot analysis. Generally, a series of open meetings are held in which the purpose of the assessment is explained, participation is sought using a number of different techniques and then follow-up is provided. The main PRA techniques include:

- Direct observation
- Semi-structured interviews, FGD and conversations
- People being asked to give an oral history of a place or situation
- Ranking and scoring (preference, pair-wise or direct scoring)
- Diagram and map making

The difference between PRA and RRA is that PRA seeks ownership of the process and conclusions are produced by the community members themselves. In this way, PRA gives more power to the community and shifts power relations. RRA, on the other hand, can borrow from PRA and be adapted to the needs of emergencies. It is generally not realistic for NGOs involved in emergencies to claim to be able to adequately carry out PRA, which can take 6–12 months to complete. This may be more appropriate in follow-on stages.

CHAPTER 5
Launching in a new country or area

During an emergency, for many there is a natural tendency to intervene – to want to do something. Establishing a new programme can be one of the most critical decisions faced by a NGO because their work can have such a direct impact on the people affected by an emergency. So the decision to respond should not be taken lightly. The purpose of this chapter is to discuss and provide some basic tools in deciding and preparing to launch a new programme. It covers:

- Deciding to enter
- Government relations and registration
- Legal issues
- Levels of involvement
- Dealing with HQ
- The emergency team

As discussed in Chapter 1, a mismanaged, poorly designed or otherwise ill-conceived emergency intervention has serious consequences. There are many considerations – personal, organizational and factors external to both such as security, politics and logistical constraints.

Deciding to enter

Most NGOs, like other organizations involved in emergency response, have some mechanism for deciding if they will respond to an emergency. Key considerations include humanitarian need, security, funding, clear goals, sufficient capacity, the possibility of working with others and coordination. Some NGOs focus on particular geographic areas, while others have a wider reach but try to concentrate on countries with a severe disaster, ongoing conflict or poor development indicators such as UNDP's Human Development Index (HDI).

There are significant ethical issues in providing humanitarian aid. Some NGOs, for example, reserve the right not to enter and to leave as they deem appropriate. Making this decision, assessing or carrying out analysis, includes a number of steps and skills, but it does not have to be too complicated. A simple way might follow these steps.

- **Understand your organization's objectives** Why are you carrying out the analysis?
- **Appreciate what came before** Can a base be established for the conditions or situation before the emergency occurred?
- **Recognize uncertainty** No model or set of tools can adequately account for reality especially in the chaos of emergencies.

- **Collect and interpret information** Devise a means for systematically gathering and thinking about all available data. Be willing to think laterally and consider different options.
- **Record and share** Information that is not shared is not useful.

Before a decision can be made to launch a new programme, a number of factors need to be weighed. Here, four different tools to assess situational factors, stakeholders, risk and the decision to enter are provided.

Assessing situational factors

This tool was developed for businesses to help assess how external factors may affect their objectives. First, brainstorm relevant factors covering socio-economic, technological, ethical, environmental and political factors. Next, identify information that applies to these factors. Finally, draw conclusions and alter actions. This last step is critical in developing meaningful analysis. Table 5.1 provides examples of relevant factors.

Table 5.1 The STEEP tool

Socio-economic	Technological	Ethical	Environmental	Political
Population growth and age profile	Existing infrastructure	Possibility of maintaining humanitarian principles	Impact of disaster	Government type
Infectious diseases	Degree of spread of information technology (e.g. internet)	Unintended consequences and effects	Impact of beneficiaries (e.g. mass displacement)	Types of opposition
Social mobility	Technology transfers		Impact of programming (e.g. wat/san)	Degree of stability
Public opinion and social norms	Appropriateness and impact of emerging technologies		Land distribution	Degree of freedom
Degree of change			Marginalization	Legislation
Degree of intercommunal tension			Level of change present	Donor interest
Economic indicators (e.g. inflation and unemployment)			Likelihood of recovery	Tax, trade and tariffs
Degree of exclusion and deprivation				History of conflict

Possible indicators for socio-political failures leading to impending humanitarian emergency include heightened political activities and movements, shortages of food and water, outbreaks of disease, military setbacks or offensives, natural disasters contributing to crop failure, fuel shortages, seasonal change and deterioration of law and order, including the police forces and judicial system.

Assessing the stakeholders

This is another tool that can be used to analyse different stakeholder interests. Such a tool can be used in planning sessions to gauge views and opinions but also may bring up important issues about decision-making and accountability. Figure 5.1 can be used to generate different courses of action depending on relevant stakeholders. In this example, an NGO's emergency planning team assess different stakeholders and plot their probable power and interest relationships on a matrix. While their regional director has some concerns about launching a new emergency programme, the executive director views it as an important element of achieving wider aims. This example also considers two external groups (donor and an advocacy NGO) and shows that both have a keen interest in their NGO launching a new emergency programme, thus making their decision to enter easier to discuss and reach a conclusion.

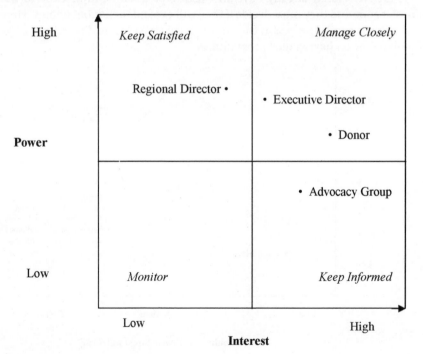

Figure 5.1 Power/interest matrix
Source: Modified from mindtools.com

Assessing risk

This tool can be used to decide to launch an emergency programme. After deciding on key threats, plot points in terms of likelihood and degree of impact. In the process, shown in Figure 5.2, a discussion can then be held to determine what is and what is not acceptable to the organization. This exercise works well with a number of types of risk, including security threats (discussed further in Chapter 18). In this example, the NGO plots three separate threats and, after some debate, decides that it will withdraw or end programming in the area or country if a member of staff is kidnapped. This tool is good for discussing perceived risks at a point in time and reaching consensus on what level of risk could be acceptable to the group.

Assessing the decision to enter

There are a number of specific questions to ask once other factors have been weighed. Figure 5.3 shows the possible decision making involved in establishing a new programme intervention. The two most important questions are at the top and bottom of the diagram.

Careful consideration to closing the programme, either through handover or phase-out, should also be given consideration at this point (see Chapter 21).

Some NGOs may already have an existing programme in or close to the disaster zone and they must decide if they will expand their programmes. They will follow a similar process as the one outlined above. More discussion can be found below on having duel programmes.

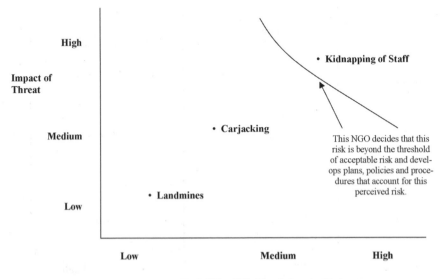

Figure 5.2 Risk assessment

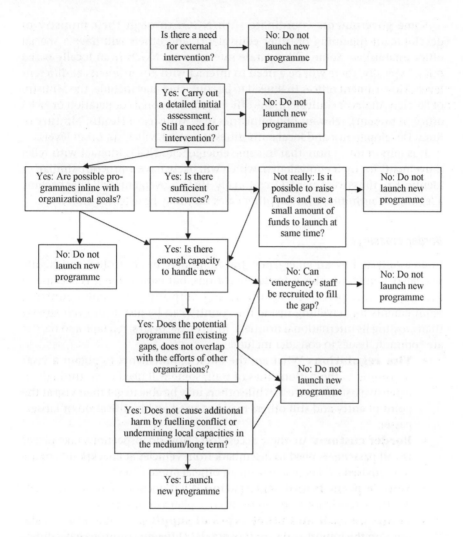

Figure 5.3 Decision-making process for launching an emergency programme

Government and legal issues

As a pro forma or legal obligation, NGOs must be known to the government or ruling authority. Government relations are discussed in Chapter 20, but several points are worth discussing here. Each ruling authority will have its own policy of interacting with NGOs. Despite being non-governmental, NGOs are not exempt from following laws and regulations, paying required fees (although these may be waived), observing standards and following through with commitments.

Some governments coordinate with NGOs through their ministry of development (planning or other equivalent), and others will have a special office established. Some will separate international NGOs from locally based ones. Typically, there will be a need to interact with governments at different levels. Government offices that need to be contacted may include: the Ministry of Foreign Affairs or equivalent; the office of international cooperation or NGO office (if present); relevant line-ministries (e.g. Ministry of Health, Ministry of Rural Development); and local authorities at district, village or other levels.

It is important to note that in some emergencies NGOs interact with rebel movements (or their equivalents), which will likely have a structure similar, or identical, to the government. Occasionally, these movements will later become a legitimate authority, while in other cases they may be defeated entirely.

Border crossings

In areas affected by an emergency, travelling may be controlled and highly regulated. Sometimes this is for safety reasons, but more often it is because of security threats perceived by the ruling authority. In some countries, requirements for travelling inside the country can be just as or even stricter than crossing its international frontiers. In any case, delays, red tape and hassles are common. Issues to consider include:

- **Visa regulations** What are the latest requirements to obtain a visa? According to the nationalities of staff, some will need to go through an extensive issuing process, while others may be able to get their visa at the point of entry and still others may just need an identification or laissez-passer.
- **Border customs** Are there access fees? How do inspections take place? Do all passengers need to disembark from vehicles at checkpoints or are they advised to stay inside until an official approaches?
- **Vehicle permits and registration** What documentation is needed? Are there restrictions on certain licence plates or models?
- **Limits on cash and other types of supplies** What are the regulations on the import and export of goods? Different countries have different regulations for medications, IT equipment and other goods, and these may change over time.

Registration

In some countries, registration may be through a simple application, and in others it may require personal meetings. If appointments are needed, introductions should follow local customs and protocol, so the decision of which staff to send is important. Typically, the most mature and diplomatic staff are the best. For international NGOs, pairing the senior national with expatriate staff members is typically a good idea. During an initial introduction, clarification should be sought of what documents will be needed for formal registration, some of which may only be available from an organization's HQ. For example:

- Original registration or articles of incorporation
- Proof of funds, budget or funding
- Proposals, funded or just submitted
- Staff lists
- Staff qualifications
- Statement of purpose or goals
- Letter of introduction and/or application

As legal entities that manage staff, enter into contracts and own, distribute and occasionally damage property, an NGO will run into legal issues during the course of its activities. For this reason, it is a good idea to have a lawyer or attorney on retainer.

Reporting

A typical requirement is that NGOs report on their ongoing and planned activities. Typically, this involves submitting a quarterly report, which may not differ significantly from regular reporting. Reporting requirements will differ from country to country and may change over time, so it is important to know current requirements. Reporting should be consistent for all NGOs.

Some authorities may require financial or other information, which some NGOs may consider confidential, and some may request information about the background of the staff (e.g. ethnicity, race, religion and gender). Consistency and the use of such information are the important factors. If such requests are viewed as problematic, NGOs tend to band together and seek assistance from legal professionals and organizations such as the UN or donor organizations.

Levels of involvement

An NGO has several options when first establishing an emergency programme, depending on, for example, security, level of funding and capacity. From the least to most operationally involved, there are a range of options.

- **Proxy** This level of involvement is achieved by working with or through a partner. Typically, the partnership can be with a locally based organization or through another international NGO (see Chapter 15). Memorandums of understanding (MOU) are usually created to prevent problems throughout the programme. Apart from providing funds, NGOs using this option should develop a well thought-out plan for monitoring and capacity building. This option presents the lowest physical risk, but also provides the least amount of interaction with beneficiaries and thus has the lowest amount of influence over a programme's objectives.
- **Crossborder** This option usually involves routinely travelling across the frontier or relying on locally based staff to carry on activities while a decision is made whether to phase out or scale up programming. The

NGO may send staff to the programme area for oversight visits and capacity building, but more frequently than in the proxy option above.

- **Full presence** As this implies, this option involves establishing a programme, as described in this book, but it also presents the highest risk to staff.

Dealing with HQ

The manager's responsibility when interacting with HQ is to share information, minimize conflict and prevent misunderstanding.

Suggestions for HQ staff

- Be organized and responsive. A complete answer is not always necessary immediately, but an acknowledgement is.
- Be understanding. When there are genuine obstacles and challenges, give leeway that is appropriate to the emergency context (e.g. lack of electrical power or renewed fighting). Do not expect the immediacy from the field that is present in the HQ.
- Know the organization and be able to communicate the NGO's values, goals, expectations and working ethos.
- Develop action plans based on different scenarios, such as a vehicles being stolen, withdrawal of funding or a major insecurity incident. The risk assessment tool described above (p. 120) can help in this regard. Comparing the results of the exercise between HQ and the field can lead to better understanding.
- Do everything possible to create a strong management and administrative system that supports the field. This should include standard operating procedures, policies and procedures, forms, templates and examples from work of the organization carried out in other emergencies.
- Identify and promote professional development opportunities for field staff who may be too busy to do this themselves. Field staff will need training on organizational systems as well.

Suggestions for existing country offices

Some NGOs have existing development-oriented offices in areas where an emergency occurs. Having dual programmes can create problems leading to tension between the development staff and the emergency staff. Reasons for this include differences in the focus and/or personality of staff (with a higher tendency to use expatriate staff in emergencies), greater media attention, extra funds and more resources. Some ways to mitigate this are as follows.

- Respect the work and perspective of others. Development-focused staff will have a long-range view and will likely have invaluable insight of how things were or ought to be. Relief-focused staff can make an immediate impact that is not possible using purely developmental methods. Together, each can make an important contribution.

- From a management and administrative perspective, establish clear and detailed protocols for cooperation.
- At the start of an emergency, a new organizational chart and TOR may be helpful in reducing any ambiguity of roles and lines of control. Senior management should meet regularly to discuss details and to ensure unity of effort.
- Where feasible, share resources such as logistics and combine public relations efforts.
- Develop plans and act together. Where possible do not separate programmes into arbitrary or theoretical frameworks (like dividing relief and development), which may have little meaning for people on the ground. At the appropriate time, these plans should include handover and phase-out.

Suggestions for field-based staff

- Understanding the organization's approach to emergencies, their values and aims is critical for new field staff. Every field staff member should know their NGO's history and future plans. This should involve knowing who is on the NGO's governing board and how the senior management makes decisions. Knowing from the start its attitude towards humanitarian principles may save misunderstanding later on.
- Understand that the challenges at HQ are different but no less real. In many cases, the desk or programme officer and other staff know that field staff's time is divided between several projects and/or countries. Many NGOs do not have large HQ staff and HQ staff may not have significant field experience.
- Do not assume that HQ staff know the working conditions in the field. If, for example, there has been no power for three days and staff have been sick with dysentery, let the staff HQ know this (without complaining about it).
- Share success stories as well as challenging times. Quantitative data alone do not foster understanding a situation.
- Encourage HQ staff to visit the field and arrange for field-based staff to visit HQ. Communication should happen at a human (face-to-face) level.

The emergency team

Team make-up

Each NGO approaches the emergency team concept in its own way. While some NGOs tend to follow an ad hoc approach ('Who's available right now?'), others have dedicated teams, established along the lines of a fire brigade, who are standing by to go at a moment's notice. As a middle path, most NGOs have rosters of potential staff, and when an emergency occurs, they simply go through the pre-qualified lists of candidates to confirm the availability of potential staff. Well-funded INGOs maintain stocks of emergency supplies and established relationships with specialist donors, such as ECHO, OFDA and the UN specialized agencies. Overall, this approach is a significantly different approach from that of development-oriented organizations.

Most NGOs form teams consisting (with title variations) of a team leader, admin/finance, logistics/security and programme specialists (see Chapter 8). Programme staff may vary in size and composition depending on an organization's specialization and what the initial assessments reveal. With the large presence of media that accompany most emergencies, many NGOs include a communications or media specialist as part of this team. In this way, teams of up to a dozen expatriate staff, augmented by national staff, may respond to an acute emergency. The key indicators for the success of an emergency team include:

- Adherence to a good programmatic approach
- Focus on core vision, values and mission
- Effective leadership from the team leader and support from HQ
- Fostering of a positive image among beneficiaries and donors
- Effective systems, structure, staff and organizational commitment to the programme, including the input of non-grant (private) funds; this is less critical but also important

Personal issues

Successful relief workers find that trying to work out personal issues before departing for an emergency is the best thing to do. For many relief workers, departure includes more mental and emotional activities than logistical ones. The logistical preparations are essential to providing peace of mind while away. Some of the things that may need attention include: packing; arranging for bills to be paid, and property and other expenses to be taken care of during absences; photocopying one's passport, credit cards and other important documents (in case of loss in the field); and, for some, writing a will.

Packing lists

Although guidance can be helpful, the usefulness of packing lists is often fairly limited. The first staff going into a disaster zone should have the wherewithal to take what they need, obtain locally or do without. Follow-on staff should be given guidance, which may be in the form of a list or a description of what might be useful. The problem with lists is that they are invariably incomplete or cause confusion to the uninitiated. People who have not been to a desert before, for example, may not understand how cold it can be especially at night.

Therefore, a descriptive note to incoming staff is more helpful and might include the following information:

- Daily temperatures, climatic conditions and how they are expected to change
- Availability of goods and services
- Staff living arrangements and conditions, including sleeping arrangements
- Eating/cooking and cleaning arrangements
- Presence of any utilities such as electricity, water and heating
- Amount of walking and other physical exercise expected

If local staff are expected to travel to remote areas, they should be given allowances or team equipment in areas where items such as sleeping bags, torches (flashlights) and cooking supplies are needed.

CHAPTER 6
Establishing an office and accommodation

When establishing or expanding an emergency programme, establishing an office and setting up staff accommodation are priorities. While this may seem to be a mundane task, in a developing country during conflict or another emergency, it can be a real challenge. Buildings may be destroyed or entire areas may be unsafe and without basic services such as water and electricity. Regardless of the NGO's size or type, however, its physical presence should be safe, comfortable and provide basic necessities. The purpose of this chapter is to help those responsible for finding work and living space by covering five basic tasks:

- Property rental and purchasing
- Staff accommodation
- Buying office equipment
- Setting up an office and filing systems
- Ordering and maintaining a generator

Property rental and purchasing

An NGO's office and staff accommodation can be anything from a tent to an apartment to a large compound containing several buildings. The key is to have adequate space for office-based staff, such as accountants and managers, and some room to accommodate staff based outside the office (i.e. those who may only need work space for hours or a few days at a time). Security, utilities, a separate conference space and adequate work space should be taken into consideration when looking at new property.

There are several ways to go about finding property and a combination of those mentioned below may be needed, especially when it is urgent:

- **Physical search** Sometimes a drive or walk around an area will reveal property that may be suitable.
- **Other organizations** Most often, there are others looking for property. Staff from other organizations may know about available property if they have looked recently.
- **Influential or powerful persons** Property may be controlled by a few individuals or families, so working with them may be the only way to find and acquire work and living space. In such cases, it may be worth contacting several property owners to ensure a fair deal and put all agreed points in writing.
- **Property rental agents** Where they exist, agents are often the most efficient way to find property. They have the benefit of knowing many

potential locations and can help people new to an area. They should also have template contract agreements. Be watchful for conditions (extra fees) that may be attached to the agreement, such as any ties or favourites that the agents may have.

Once a property has been identified, it should be inspected, considering the following:

- **Location** How far is it from transport, utilities and other organizations? In some cases, the influx of organizations working on an emergency can increase prices for both local people and NGOs.
- **Security** Is it in a dangerous area? Consider the location, the neighbours, and physical features such as the thickness of walls and doors and access to the property (see Chapter 18).
- **Utilities** Sources of water and electricity, secure parking, storage capacity, a place for the guards to be and facilities for a radio antenna.
- **Short- and long-term plans** How long will the organization be present in the country? Look at needs beyond the immediate programme and those needs that need weighing against strategic plans.
- **Additional needs** Is it possible to build on the property? If necessary, have a surveyor or qualified engineer look over it in order to identify potential problems (such as leaks and foundations) and rehabilitation needs.

Contracts

Contracts can be arranged in a variety of ways. The key issue is to have clarity on all points and to be aware of conditions that may cause problems at a later date. It is important to have a *force majeure* clause in contracts that releases the organization from obligations in the event of conflict or other disaster. Other important conditions include the assignment of the responsibility for repairs and how payments and taxation will be handled. At a minimum, contracts should cover the following points:

- Start and end dates
- Contact information for all parties
- Condition of property
- How repairs will be carried out
- Visiting rights of the landlord
- Conditions for extension or withdrawal of the contract
- Cost and how payments will be made
- Cancellation of contract
- Detailed inventory list of movable items left in the property for use by the tenant

Visibility

Careful thought needs to be given to what level of visibility should be assumed by NGOs in insecure countries. In most cases, decals, flags, signboards and notices to other organizations help establish an NGO's presence. In some cases, where NGOs are seen as largely helpful to communities and neutral, high visibility can offer some measure of protection against violence. Where NGOs may be perceived to be biased or representing soft targets, a low profile is a better choice. The difficulty comes when different parts of the same country require different levels of visibility (it may be useful if the visibility of vehicles can change to suit the situation). It is likely that the entire NGO community will follow similar practices in a given area.

Staff accommodation

In many situations, working in emergencies is like being on a ship at sea: staff live, eat, work and socialize together as a group. Generosity, forgiveness and a sense of humour are important to be productive at work and these are significantly affected by living arrangements.

At the beginning of an emergency, there may be several options to consider, such as different types of property, leasing agreement details and staffing needs. It is not uncommon for NGO staff to live and work in the same location, but that situation is not sustainable. In general, the longer people stay in an area the more they require privacy and a separate space between work and accommodation. Depending on security conditions and the availability of living space, adequate living quarters should be a priority.

There are a number of issues involved in living conditions and standards. Is providing a comfortable arrangement for staff in conflict with security arrangements or at such a distance from the local populace that staff will lose touch with who they are meant to be helping? If conditions are crowded or there is high turnover, are house rules needed to help staff get along? Does the community being served, for example, have uninterrupted electrical power? What about recreation such as swimming pools: does having one place the NGO among the category of people who are responsible for the emergency?

Also worth considering is the impact the influx of expatriate staff has on the availability for local residents. Immediately following a disaster, when there is

---

Box 6.1 Door keys

When taking control of a new property, the door key or keys should be labelled and kept in a secure place. Initially, the landlord should be held accountable for supplying or accounting for all keys and their duplicates. If in doubt, and criminality and security are concerns in the area, change the lock(s). New locks usually come with keys in triplicate copies. The spare keys should not be left on the key ring. Ill-intentioned visitors may steal one of the copies and return later to steal things in the property.

a scarcity of available housing, prices can rapidly inflate, which plays into the hands of landlords and outsiders, who may be the only people who can afford accommodation.

Buying office equipment

While procuring office equipment is a routine task, in countries that are experiencing emergencies it can present particular challenges. General recommendations include allowing enough time for procurement (see Chapter 12). In most cases, many NGOs find that procuring used equipment in the end is not worth it and for some items, maintenance can be as costly as the item itself. For electrical items, always consider voltage requirements (220 or 110) and consider the quality of the item in regard its eventual use. Ensure that staff know how to use the equipment that is given to them. Equipment like laptops and radio handsets should be assigned to a specific staff member who signs a responsibility form.

Although staff may be anxious to use new equipment, especially major assets, make sure that before they are assigned to individuals all relevant information (e.g. serial numbers) is recorded in the inventory. Table 6.1 provides information on procuring specific items.

Table 6.2 provides a checklist of standard procurement and office set-up tasks. Some of the items below are action points, and others are goods to purchase. The amounts will depend on how large the office becomes in the first weeks or months.

Office and filing systems

Office arrangements

An effective office consists of the work space and a location that is suitable for each staff position. It includes adequate office furniture, record maintenance systems and other equipment staff will need to carry out their responsibilities (e.g. computers will need an extension cord, UPS and access to printers). Specific suggestions include the following.

Reception and security These staff should be positioned to directly observe entrances and exits. The function should typically have a means of handling visitors, such as visitor badges and sign-in books. Reception and security staff should be instructed how to communicate with visitors and what to do when problems occur.

Logistics Some organizations find it useful to locate this office near doors, vehicles and storage space to monitor other support functions.

Accounting Some organizations prefer this office(s) to be in the most secure area of the office structure. Others will place the cashier in an accessible space to make payments.

Table 6.1 Office procurement

Item	Buying considerations	Usage suggestions
Computers	New computers do not always contain the software needed (e.g. word-processing and spreadsheets), so make sure these are loaded before being shipped to the field	Desktops generally not suited for emergency situations (because of difficulty of transport and electrical requirements)
	New computers may require on-line registration which may be impossible in many areas of the world	Desktops may be used for certain tasks such as for large data entry but they must have an UPS or similar device
	If possible, try to procure computers locally as helps with servicing, avoids difficulties with import, having the right electrical fittings and compatibility with other computers	Always make back-up copies of all files with a CD writer and/or USB Pen/Flash Drive. Floppy disks are prone to failure and are gradually being phased out
	Beware of phoney copies or clones of computers (which often have suspect labels). Full-brand computers may cost more but are worth it in the long run	Always have the latest possible version of virus-protection programs
	Laptops are best for mobile positions (e.g. managers, evaluators)	Do not transport laptops while switched on or 'hibernating' as this may damage the hard disk
	Desktops are best for static positions such as accounting and database entry	Some users prefer older copies of software (e.g. Windows 95 or 98) as these versions are more basic and rely less on interconnectivity
		In dusty areas, consider covering the computer while not in use and having a soft brush (such as an unused paintbrush or camera duster) for cleaning off screens and key pads
Printers	Try to buy one printer per computer to avoid moving them around or, if possible, network office computers.	Laser printers are slightly more expensive but are more reliable and can print documents quickly. Their major downside is size, but it is uncommon to travel with printers
	Cartridges and/or toners are expensive. Monitor staff so that	Beware of dust and humidity. Use a cloth or plastic cover when

cont.

cont.

Item	Buying considerations	Usage suggestions
	they do not overuse or waste printers, especially in colour mode	printer is not in use
Photocopiers	In some areas, it may possible to purchase locally which will help after-sale service and re-supply of accessories.	Especially sensitive to movement, sunlight, dust and overuse
	Prices vary considerably: use a bidding process	Assign one person in the office to operate the copier to avoid incorrect or overuse.
	Be sure to procure the right capacity (usually determined by copies made per minute) for the size of the programme	When the copies start to fade, shake the toner cartridge
	Photocopiers include many 'bells and whistles'. so the more basic the better.	Use only fresh sheets of paper to avoid jamming
		Repairs may take a long time
Television	Obtainable in nearly every capital city; there is little need to import	For use in training programmes
		There are three standards: PAL (western Europe), SECAM (France and eastern Europe) and NTSC (USA)
		Choose the antenna based on local advice
Communications equipment (general)	Choose the type of system (e.g. HF, VHF, satellite) depending on communication needs. Most organizations prefer to have all three	Follow standard use for all electronic. See Chapter 14 for further information
	Typically, such equipment must be ordered from outside a disaster zone.	While most radios designed for field use are rugged, make sure staff treat and maintain equipment appropriately
	Talk to other organizations (including the UN if they have specialists present) to determine the standard (including the frequency range being used) for the area	
	Do not try to get non-standard equipment which will not be compatible with other organizations	

Item	Buying considerations	Usage suggestions
Telephones	The more basic the phone, more often the better (people usually do not use all the functions available)	Few developing countries provide an itemized phone bill, therefore there should be a log-book to account for every call made
Heaters/AC	Describe the room size to the dealer to see if he or she can help determine the right size heater or AC	While for short periods it is possible to tough it out when it becomes hot or cold, regulating the temperature is critical for being productive in the office
	Negotiate with the dealer to be able to return the equipment if it is not the right size or is faulty	Follow all safety precaution, especially with heaters
	Make sure generator can handle electrical load (see pp. 139–42)	Try to economize on use by considering where and how equipment will be used

Source: Adapted and expanded from MSF (1998).

Programme staff There should be enough room to accommodate visiting field staff. If the office is large, it may be helpful to locate programme offices next to or near the conference room space so as to facilitate training and other meetings.

Senior managers Some organizations prefer work space that allows for private meetings.

Most organizations create a post or pigeonhole system arranged by department and for specific senior staff. Often consisting of boxes, this should be in a mutually convenient space in the office. Incoming and outgoing mail can be logged into a book and a staff member (e.g. an administrative assistant or receptionist) is typically responsible for the post system's maintenance.

Filing systems

Having a streamlined system is important for keeping an organized office, but there is no one best way to manage records. A good system is one that:
- Is neat and organized
- Where records can be found when needed
- Is not over-complicated and not dependent on a specific staff member to locate records
- Secures confidential information
- Has a back-up or second copy (e.g. in case of fire or looting)

New staff should be told how the system functions so that they can create their own files. Centralized systems are generally too bureaucratic and difficult to maintain unless there are specific staff charged with such duties. Most NGOs have a decentralized system where individual project managers are responsible

Table 6.2 Procurement and office set-up checklist

	✓		✓
Staff in/out board		Mailing system and/or in- and out-boxes	
Vehicle tracking board (chalk or whiteboard)		Signboard for visibility (depending on security; generally offices – but not residences – should be labelled with NGO sign/logo)	
Visitor sign-in sheets and visitor ID badges		Fans and Heaters	
Office furniture		Waste/trash receptacle for each room	
NGO PR materials		Staff care items as needed (tissues, aspirin, umbrellas)	
Computers (desktop/laptop) and printers (computers and printers should be networked but this can be done later). If available, connections to an ISP should be considered, otherwise some provision should be made using satellite communication (see Chapter 14)		Stationery supplies and stock (e.g. pens, paper (blocks, pads and for printer), tape (different types including for packing), folders, stapler and staples, scissors, adhesive notes, envelopes of different size, calculator/s, permanent and whiteboard markers, highlighters, calendar, push pins, dictionary	
Easel with whiteboard surface and block paper for presentations		Cabinets for storage	
Radio room (see Chapter 14)		Refreshments, including drinking water appropriate for location and cups, spoons, towels	
Telephone and log (if deemed necessary)		Cleaning supplies (broom, mop with bucket, rags, cleaning solution)	
Radio log		First-aid kit	
Maps		Torch (flashlight)	
Safe/cash lock box		Organizational stamp with inkpad	
Filing system, shelves, list of files		Letterhead (or electronic copy)	
Voltage stabilizers/uninterrupted power supply (UPS) as needed		Keyboard or lock-box	
Bulletin board with standard operation procedures (SOPs) and announcements		Board for staff/project pictures	
Toilet supplies (paper, air freshener)		Candles/lanterns/lighters/matches	
Radio AM/FM/Shortwave		Boxes/files for archiving accounting and other records	

for managing their records. This has the highest likelihood of being maintained but is open to sloppiness and the creation of personalized systems in which others will not be able to find records.

Hard copy

Storing documents including paper reports, maps, accounts, books and photographs requires attention. Consider the following points.

- Different types of files exist (e.g. box files and hanging files in cabinets), but availability and preference are the only real differences between them. If using box files, label each file sequentially (i.e. 1, 2, 3...) so that it is easy to see when a file is missing.
- Each file should be categorized and having 'miscellaneous' files should be avoided. For more complex systems, like accounting records, a code system can be established. The category will depend on the department and the type of activities. For documents that are difficult to classify, such as contracts, a simple decision will have to be made about where they will be filed. Table 6.3 provides an example that may be used in logistics.
- Filing should be done in a way that preserves them against damage from moisture, sunlight and pests (e.g. rats and insects).
- A schedule should be made for updating and disposing of records. Donors may have requirements for how long records must be kept on hand should they decide to carry out an audit.
- Have at least two people in each department or section who know where every document can be found.

Table 6.3 Filing codes

Code	File title	Document examples
100	Policies	Policy memos and master copies of all forms
200	Transportation	
210	Vehicles	Vehicle ownership documents and warrantees, mileage and repair logs
220	Air travel	Flight schedules, air travel regulations and manifests
230	Waybills	Copies of all incoming and outgoing waybills
300	Communications	Radio communication authorizations, telephone 'tree', call-sign assignments and training materials
400	Procurement	
410	Vendors	Lists of contacts and prices
420	Requisitions	Requests (duplicates)
430	Invoices	Receipts (duplicates)
500	Security	

Soft copy

Electronic files are extremely important to an NGO's work because they provide the advantage of allowing copies to be transported easily and maintained at another location (see Figure 6.1). Just as with hard copies, each computer should have a folder system for filing each document. Coded document names tend to cause problems later when people have difficulty remembering or deciphering the code, so the fewer abbreviations or acronyms the better. Instead, each document should be saved using the project name, location and date when it was first saved. Many organizations include the document's name somewhere in the document so that when a hard copy is printed, it can be easily found at a later date.

Ordering and maintaining a generator

Disruptions to electrical power are an inevitable consequence of emergencies. In some conflict-affected countries, power outages have been known to last for years, and in some places poverty exacerbated by an emergency has prevented electrification in the first place. Generators are therefore an important consideration when establishing an office, and they remain a constant issue thereafter.

Generators are simply machines that are powered by fuel (either diesel or gasoline) and produce an electrical output. Generators are usually described by the level of output as measured in Watts (W), kVA or Kilowatts (KW) (equal to 1,000 Watts). Generally, only small generators run on gasoline and most

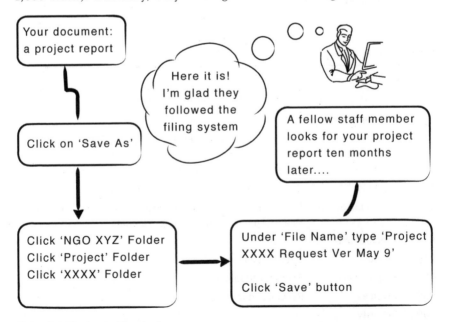

Figure 6.1 Electronic file sharing

generators consume diesel which is a safer and more economical fuel (see Chapter 13). The larger and more expensive generators are of better quality and have more features, such as electric start, monitoring gauges and mufflers.

Size and capacity

There are several ways to determine the capacity of generator needed. Perhaps the best way is to add the power required by every electrical item that will use the generator at the same time. This load is the amount of power drawn from the generator. Although it is possible to measure the amps needed using a meter, most electrical items will list the power needed on the item itself. The difficulty comes with induction motors, which need a higher load to start, found in typical items such as refrigerators, air conditioners and water pumps. Induction motors can draw up to three times their normal electrical need when first turned on (which can cause lights to dim) and if a generator cannot maintain 90 per cent of its output while turning these items on, the motor will fail to start.

As a rough estimate, when planning for instance, Table 6.4 provides a guide (though a specialist needs to be consulted for more precise estimates).

Used generators are like used vehicles: the probability of getting a lemon is high. Unless there is an expert mechanic on the staff, a lot of frustration can be

Table 6.4 Generator sizes

Generator size	Characteristics	Examples of electrical items supported	Typical cost
Up to 2 kVA	Portable gasoline- or diesel-powered. The smallest can be slightly larger than a car battery.	Lights, radio, fans and a maximum of 1 desktop computer and printer	US$100–300
3–5 kVA	Usually diesel-powered that can be started with either electric or pull-cord. Roughly the size of a wheelbarrow	Above items plus a refrigerator, several computers and 2-KW hot-water heater	US$900–1,500
10 kVA	Diesel-powered typically with an electric key start with a pull-cord as a back-up. Size may vary but the larger one may be the size of a small desk	All the above items plus up to 3 2-KW air conditioners	US$2,000–10,000
20 kVA	Diesel-powered typically with an electric key start. Size may only be slightly larger than a 10 kVA	All the above items plus up to 5 2-KW air conditioners	US$15,000–25,000

avoided by purchasing a new generator. Also, like vehicles, there is a number of reputable generator-makers, such as Perkins, Lister and Honda.

Set-up

Safety should be a prime concern with generators. Always follow the generator's instruction manual. There is a real possibility of electrical shock: do not touch wet cords. Harm is caused by carbon monoxide fumes, so run generators outside in well-ventilated areas. Hot generators can burn people: do not refuel or open the radiator of a hot generator.

In areas where generator power is the norm, there is likely to be a special generator house structure. Points to consider when setting up a generator house include:

- The generator house should be located away from areas that need to be quiet, such as offices and bedrooms. It should protect the generator from weather but allow for sufficient cooling through ventilation holes.
- The generator house be protected against theft and ideally be large enough to allow for storage and maintenance.
- Fire extinguishers, capable of dousing both fuel and electrical fires, should also be co-located with generators, because of the high combustion risk.
- Diesel and oil can be kept in the generator house but they should be stored at least 1 m or more away from the generator.
- Vibration can be a problem with some models, leading to mechanical difficulties and annoyance to those working or living nearby. For long-term use on concrete floors, generators should be either placed on rubber pads or secured to the floor. This can also help reduce noise.

Because of the danger of electrical shock, generators must be hooked up properly in one of two ways. For small loads, many generators allow electrical items to be plugged directly into the set. This is typically a temporary set-up or in areas where only a small amount of power is needed close to where the generator lies outdoors.

Another more widely used option is to have a transfer or throw switch which transfers power produced by the generator into the house or other electrical system. This is the only option for powering an entire house or compound and needs to be installed by a qualified person. This type of switch also makes it easy to go back and forth between generator and main-grid power, depending on availability. There is a third option of hooking up a generator directly to an electrical system, but this can be dangerous, carrying the chance of electrocution and fire. It can also send electrical power into the main grid, if it exists, presenting a significant danger to anyone working on those lines.

If the generator is of any size over 5 kVA, it is best to find a qualified person to set it up. Many generators require grounding and dealing with the electrical system may require a level of knowledge not presented here.

Operation

Once the generator is turned on and running, the throw switch which puts a load on the generator should be activated only after several minutes. Activating the throw switch immediately, before the generator has stabilized, can cause mechanical problems. Before plugging in any expensive items, such as computers, ensure that the voltage is compatible. In some developing countries there is a mix of voltage ranges (e.g. 110 and 220) and imported items may be incompatible with the generator output.

Fuel consumption will vary for each generator and will depend on the load. To find out the consumption for a particular generator, it is possible to run the generator for one hour, providing power to its typical load. Alternatively, Table 6.5 can be used as an approximate guide.

In general, 80 per cent load on the generator is ideal; however, in warmer climates the generator should be maintained above 50 per cent load. Long-term operation at lower than 50 per cent load (e.g. running a single house of light-bulbs and fans on a 50 kVA generator) will cause damage to the generator, although this can compensated for by occasionally putting a heavier load on the generator.

If the load is too big for the generator, the generator and items drawing the load may be damaged. Under a heavy load, the voltage will fall, causing circuit breakers to switch, which may or may not protect the electrical items on load. For such cases, voltage regulators (separate shoe-box-sized devices) are necessary for more expensive and sensitive items such as computers, printers and televisions.

Cooling – giving the generator a rest – is critical to effective generator operation. The length of time needed for cooling will depend on the capacity of the generator, the load placed on the generator during operation and the ambient temperature. A typical schedule allows for an hour or longer at midday, but the schedule should be regularized to help staff plan their work activities, especially if people are using computers. The operating manual for the generator should be consulted for optimal use.

Maintenance

The key to a long life for a generator, as with any motor, is preventative maintenance and servicing. A regular maintenance schedule for a generator in

Table 6.5 Generator loads, litres per hour

kVA Rating	25% load	50% load	75% load	100% load
5	1.1	1.2	1.7	2.1
15	1.42	2.50	3.7	4.7
20	2	3.3	4.6	6
50	3.7	6.8	9.2	12.3

daily use is a must. Personnel involved in this must be qualified and ideally should be recommended by someone reputable. If the regular maintenance schedule is disrupted for some reason, it is important to make sure that the oil is sufficient and is being changed as needed.

Alternatives to generators

Generators definitely have drawbacks, not least of which is their reliance on fuel, their unpleasant noise and their upkeep. Consider some of the other options.

- **An inverter** For temporary supplies, a motor vehicle can charge items like radio batteries and laptop computers with the right inverter. Even tractor motors can also be set up for this purpose.
- **Large batteries** can be charged while the generator or main-grid power is on and then provide power for hours afterward. Using a charger, and – once the battery is charged – a DC/AC converter, this option can provide a quiet power scheme.
- **Using locally available fuels** In many developing countries, there is little reliance on electrical appliances, but they can be replaced with gas cookers, kerosene lamps and heating systems that use locally available fuels.
- **Solar and wind options** are not really fully developed for emergencies, but solar options are available for satellite telephone and computers. In some locations, solar power may help to heat water and provide light.

CHAPTER 7
Preparing a proposal and negotiating with donors

The purpose of this chapter is to provide practical information on how to prepare winning proposals and negotiate with donors when the humanitarian need is clear. This chapter covers:
- Fundraising fundamentals
- Sources of funding
- Writing a proposal step by step
- Proposal formatting
- Negotiating with donors

Fundraising is usually a top priority in managing humanitarian relief programmes. There are many ways to fundraise, but the main method used in emergency programmes is to develop an idea for addressing problems, write a description of how the problem will be addressed (i.e. a proposal) and present (or sell) that idea to a donor who may provide funds for a particular project or programme.

Despite the high profile of emergencies, there is often a great deal of pressure to raise funds in the field and this may involve curbing moral goals to meet the interests of donors. In particular, relief workers in areas outside mainstream Western political and media attention, in so-called 'forgotten crisis' areas, may find that the issue is far from easy.

Fundraising fundamentals

Fundraising is an organizational pursuit and staff based in the field are likely to play an important role in mobilizing funds to support activities. Rather than an add-on activity simply when funds are needed, developing opportunities to gain or win grants should be done as part of a larger strategic planning and action process. Just as there is consistent and positive interaction with beneficiaries, a conscious effort is needed to initiate and maintain relationships with donors.

Fundraising involves the relationship between three key actors: donors, NGOs and beneficiaries of particular activities. For this reason, NGOs have a responsibility to balance the interests of those being served and to make sure that they are all included in the process. Under ideal conditions, genuine partnership should exist, which are characterized by joint planning, the exchange of information and mutual agreement about the sustainable solutions to humanitarian emergencies. Often, however, it is seen as a contractual relationship where one actor doles out goods and services to the other.

Of course, there are many issues to take into account when fundraising. The fundamental principles are summarized here.

1. **Know the situation and context** Some NGOs find it helpful to develop written plans that include an analysis of a particular emergency, a review of the current management and programme capacity, matching of grant opportunities and organizational strengths and action planning based on realistic analysis.

2. **Informing donors is an important part of fundraising** In many instances, donors may not be fully aware of particular problems relating to an affected population. Transparency, sharing both positive and negative information, is necessary in fundraising. During a project activity, effective organizations are upfront and do not hide information, even when there are problems.

3. **Fundraising is about addressing need, not just getting money** There are many ways to achieve the objective of alleviating human suffering; a cash fund is just one of them. But while it is important to ask for the right amount, it is often said that 'You don't get what you don't ask for'.

4. **Fundraising is about building relationships** Donors give to people they get to know and in whom they develop trust. Effective NGOs match the right person with the donor, get to know them and always say thank you. Happy donors are more likely to give more.

5. **Getting the grant is only the start** A grant agreement starts project activities. Specific expectations of different donors are discussed further below. Professionalism, meeting deadlines and follow-through will result in effective programming and possibly more funding.

Understanding donors

Donors to emergency programmes come in many different forms. In acute emergencies, there will probably not be enough time to tap the various donors who may contribute to a programme, but as a situation stabilizes, it should be possible to obtain funds from a variety of sources. This can best be done in conjunction with HQ, as many of the different donors are based in developed countries.

While certain governments in the developed world tend to be the largest donors, there are many other possibilities to raise funds. Many NGOs attempt to diversify the source of funds they are granted, in order to operate efficiently and ensure the country-level sustainability of the organization (e.g. a donor may pull out of an emergency) as well as to improve their degree of independence and neutrality. Another consideration is that some donors, notably the ones who themselves rely on other donor funds, can be stingy, and reliance on one of these will invariably lead to problems during the implementation of a project.

Table 7.1 Donor typology

Type	Examples	Characteristics/Giving style
Commercial entities	Procter and Gamble, Coca-Cola	Motivated mainly by business advantage
		Giving ranges from philanthropy to sponsorship
		Non-controversial and safe causes
		Support up to three years
		Decision usually made by key individual
		Seeks recognition for the company
Foundations/ trusts	Soros, Gates, Rotary International	Purpose is to give money
		Private funds
		Policy-driven, so necessary to match their priorities
		Likes to focus on particular issues, up to five years
		Seeks little in return for support
		Large range of foundations
Government	Intergovernmental organizations (such as the UN), national and local governments	Bureaucratic
		Strictly policy-driven
		Can provide large-scale support
		Will fund unpopular causes
		Good reporting required
Individuals	Wealthy individuals	Emotionally driven
		Seek very little in return
		Short-term funding
		Needs to be a good cause
		Often unplanned
		Wide range of ways of support
		Influenced by who asks
Other organizations	Religious bodies, non-profits and service organizations	Similar to individual giving
		Mainly short-term
		Motivated often by individual contact
		May seek increased status for the organization
		May seek little in return

Savvy NGOs can prevent these issues by having a range of donors. The range of donors which an NGO may approach to support its goals are outlined in Table 7.1.

Donors can be found in a variety of ways, including searching the internet or hard-copy resource materials, talking to other NGOs and seeing what grants have been awarded in the past. Typically, in the field, it simply involves scheduling an appointment with the local representative. The NGO's background and capacity will likely have a huge effect on the outcome of any proposal submission. Large, well-known NGOs benefit from their perceived capacity and may already be well-known by donor organizations. In the end, however, the main issue is the perceived level of confidence the donor has in a NGO. NGOs consider carefully the source of the funds vis-à-vis their mandate and approach. Questions they consider with reference to donors include: is it reasonable to accept funding from a government involved in military action? If assisting children or doing health programming, is a tobacco company acceptable, or how about its parent company? What is the potential conflict between beneficiaries' needs and other principles such as 'Do no harm'?

Governments tend to be the largest donors and they will be the focus in this section. These statutory donors are usually present through their embassy and sometimes deploy staff in the field who are expected to process grant documents faster than the normal bureaucratic process typified by their parent organizations.

Each government donor has a different approach to how they operate in emergencies. The UK's DFID is known for its hands-on approach and intellectual contributions to the field. Other donors, such as the Canadian International Development Agency (CIDA) and many bilateral European governments, prefer to channel their funding through multilateral agencies of the UN. Almost all donors have a limited geographic presence, like Australian Aid (AUSAID) in South-east Asia. Japan has a similar geographic focus, and contributes heavily through in-kind donations such as vehicles. New statutory donors are also emerging from among the new EU member states, although they will remain regionally focused for some time to come. The UN is also an important funder of NGOs (see Chapter 20).

In emergencies, there are usually a number of donor organizations present on the ground. Of these, the EU's European Community's Humanitarian Office (ECHO) and the US government's Office for US Foreign Disaster Assistance (OFDA) are among the largest. Understanding how each of these function can help when seeking funds from them.

ECHO

ECHO was established in 1992 to enable a collective European ability to quickly respond to humanitarian emergencies. Although significant in size, ECHO funding has fluctuated considerably. In recent years, the amount has increased significantly, from US$6.8m in 2000, US$441m in 2002, US$771m in 2004 and US$832m in 2006, in response to emergencies worldwide. Geographic priorities have tended to focus on the Balkans (although this has been curtailed recently), central Africa and specific emergencies in countries such as Sierra Leone and Afghanistan.

Organizational make-up

As a multilateral organization, funds come from all EU member states before going to ECHO, as shown in Figure 7.1.

How ECHO works in emergencies

To help preserve its response capacity, ECHO maintains some autonomy from the EU's bureaucracy, depending on the situation and amount of need. Since 1996, oversight has been provided by member states who collectively decide on all expenditures over €2m through the Humanitarian Aid Committee (HAC). ECHO funds organizations through a framework partnership agreement (FPA), which has been revised several times over the years to help expedite funding. In emergencies, ECHO itself can decide on expenditures of up to €10m without consulting the HAC and, since 2001, can commit up to €3m within 72 hours of an emergency. For long-term activities, global plans are developed with decisions made through written procedure within the EU.

ECHO has experimented with different models for fielding personnel. Normally, ECHO staff are based out of one of the 126 EU diplomatic missions around the world. In the Balkans, in 1999, contracted field monitors were used because of the intense level of activity.

Funding patterns

ECHO projects' priorities depend on country strategy papers (CSP) when one has been established. ECHO follows its emergency mandate by funding primary-sector activities, such as health, water and sanitation, feeding and shelter programmes. As situations move from relief towards reconstruction and rehabilitation, there is a handover to the Europe Aid Cooperation Office (AIDCO).

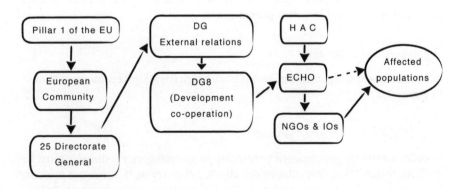

Figure 7.1 ECHO

Established in 2001, AIDCO continues to work with ECHO to determine the best mode of handover.

ECHO seeks to provide funding for NGOs with a proven capacity in both programmes and management (including financial accountability). The mandate and objectives of the NGO are also considered important. Funding caps exist on certain line-items such as personnel salaries, with the expectation that the NGO will share costs. Like the rest of the EU aid system and many bilateral European aid programmes, ECHO will only fund NGOs that have permanently established offices in the EU.

OFDA

OFDA was established in 1964 as part of USAID to coordinate the US government's response to natural and manmade disasters. Since that time, OFDA has undergone little structural change, although its funding has fluctuated considerably over the years, with high points experienced during the early and late 1990s. Because their official funding is determined by the US Congress, donations relate to the purpose of the assistance, namely its linkage to political causes to help bring about change, such as Somalia in the early 1990s. In recent years. OFDA's funding has increased from US$176m in 2000, US$260m in 2002, US$360m in 2004 and US$596m in 2006, in response to emergencies round the world. Of that total, 66 per cent was provided to NGOs and the majority (about 70%) was spent in responding to emergencies in Africa.

While OFDA serves as the primary office for emergency response, there are several other avenues for funding from the US government. The relatively new Office of Transition Initiatives (OTI) was originally set up to help countries shift towards democratic and free-market societies and has worked in a number of post-conflict situations. Under what is known as Public Law 480, the Office of Food for Peace (FFP) makes tonnes of food available each year, with NGOs carrying out distribution in many countries. Finally, the Department of State's Bureau of Population, Refugees and Migration (BPRM) funds primarily international organizations (e.g. UNHCR, ICRC and IOM), but supports NGOs as well in refugee and returnee programmes.

Organizational make-up

As a governmental organization, funds go through the US government, as shown in Figure 7.2.

How OFDA works in emergencies

In order for the US government to respond to an emergency, a disaster must be declared by the US ambassador in the affected country or, if one is not present, the deputy chief of mission or appropriate US assistant secretary of state. During emergencies, OFDA can send a Disaster Assistance Response Team (DART) to

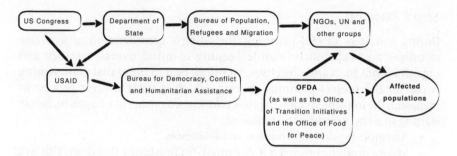

Figure 7.2 OFDA

help coordinate the response, conduct assessments and gather information. The DART is designed to help disburse funds quickly, although final approval on large funds (it varies) is required from their headquarters in Washington, DC. The DART can also provide in-kind supplies such as plastic sheeting and, depending on the team's make-up, carry out some activities such as search and rescue. Most often, however, OFDA is represented by a single staff member assigned regionally or at the country's US embassy.

Funding patterns

As with all donors, there are a plethora of rules and regulations to follow and NGOs are wise to employ staff who are familiar with USAID requirements (available on their website). These requirements, for example, spelling out which sectors are addressed, the inclusion of additional documents such as a 'Safety and Security Plan' and limiting proposals to 20 pages. OFDA is flexible with its funding as long as a proposal is compelling and fits within their mandate. Funding normally includes the primary sectors (i.e. health, nutrition, and water and sanitation), and in the past this has included everything from garbage trucks to information technology.

Once funds are received, OFDA tends to be understanding about the difficulties of implementing an emergency programme. Between budget line-items, there is complete flexibility as long as the grant total is not exceeded. No-cost (time only) extensions of up to three months (90 days) are also nearly automatic as long as they are requested in writing. Still, any funds received from USAID are subject to audits and issues like completed time-sheets, inventories and accurate accounting must be up-to-date to avoid problems.

Writing a proposal step by step

Although each organization will have its own approach to proposal writing, and may have a list of essential pre-proposal actions before starting to write a grant concept or proposal, the typical process may follow a four-step process.

Step 1 Planning

During this step, careful planning, including a consideration of available resources and capabilities, while keeping in mind overall strategy and organizational goals and objectives, is critical. Bear in mind that grant writing is part of the project planning process, which is itself a larger process in managing the implementation of projects (discussed further in Chapter 8). Before starting to write, consider the following:

- Assemble needed information and references.
- Make a deadline (even if it is unwritten) for finishing a first draft. This will help you manage your time. If there is an official donor deadline, it is often a good idea to have an artificially early internal deadline to allow for unforeseen problems.
- Consult previously successful proposals which may be available from the donor.
- Allow enough time if additional help or input is needed.

Discussions with the donor, while often a continual process, are sometimes not a necessary step before beginning work on a concept paper.

Step 2 Analysis

Based on available technical data, identify the problems to be addressed during a potential intervention. Many NGOs find it helpful to hold a discussion or meeting with those who will work on the project to work out the following elements:

- Match identified needs with the available assets of all stakeholders.
- Consider how additional resources will address the problem(s) identified.
- Clarify problems and consider appropriate goals, objectives and activities.
- Weigh donor interest and other considerations.
- Prioritize and allocate available resources.
- Assign tasks for follow-up to specific individuals.

Further details of this process, for example, the tool for stakeholder analysis, and how to carry out an assessment are discussed in Chapter 4.

Step 3 Writing a proposal

When writing a concept or proposal, some NGOs find to helpful to follow the process outlined below.

1. Write a draft of the concept or proposal. Use the approach which helps to quickly and effectively produce the best first draft possible.
2. Double-check the first draft after first doing some other task as a break. It is also important that the proposal makes no unsupported assumptions, is free of jargon and is interesting to read.
3. Have a colleague proofread and edit the first draft.
4. Make revisions as necessary.

5. Submit the revised draft for internal review if this is required by the NGO.
6. Incorporate suggestions and verify any changes.

Length is also an important consideration. When no specific format or guidance is given by the funding source, it is generally safe to assume that the proposal for an emergency should be no more than 20 pages long (single-spaced). Remember that less is often more. In some cases, a five-page proposal can cover all the main points of a project to be funded. Therefore, the shorter and easier to understand a concept or proposal, the easier it is for everyone.

Step 4 Supporting documents

Assemble any supporting documentation (e.g. reports or baseline data) that will be attached as annexes. A covering letter in support of a proposal is often required and time should be allotted for this as well. When writing the cover letter, follow the same process as Step 3 above.

Step 5 Editing and submission

In conjunction with the staff responsible for liaising with the donor, submit the proposal and make sure that any follow-up is done in a timely and professional manner. Make sure that the next step after the submission (i.e. when the response will be) is clearly understood by everyone. Be sure to share this information with the relevant staff.

Proposal formatting

Always try to obtain a copy of the donor's proposal format and, if possible, an example of a previously successful proposal. If there is no specific format available, the following may be useful in developing a proposal. Typically, proposals follow this format, starting with a header or title-page that includes a programme title, contact details, partners (if any) and date.

1. Background, problem statement or needs assessment

This section should include specific data and make a compelling case for justifying the proposed project. Information based on objective research, not subjective impressions, should be provided to justify the need or problem. These data, however, should not be voluminous, but sufficient to demonstrate that a problem or need exists. Information provided might include:

- Description of the target population (beneficiaries).
- Description of the problem to be addressed and the need in the geographical area or catchment area (the problem should be people-focused, solvable and urgent).
- The connection with the purposes and goals of the NGO.

- The problem should be of reasonable dimensions, not trying to solve all the problems of the world.
- Relevant statistical evidence, relevant anecdotal evidence and, where appropriate, statements from authorities on the subject matter.

2. Programme description or strategy

This section should describe the programme clearly, using action verbs (e.g. increase, promote, develop or rehabilitate). If it will be a large programme, there may be a separate description and strategy section. Some attention should be devoted to the methods that will be used to achieve the programme's objectives. If a community-based approach will be a central theme of the programme, this should be explained in this section.

3. The programme's goal, objectives and activities

Goal The overarching purpose or desired impact of a project or programme. Sometimes called 'aim' or 'overall objective', this is a statement of the big picture of the programme, such as reducing suffering in a beneficiary population.

Objectives A verifiable statement describing the end sought in a project or programme. Depending on its size, most programmes have two or three objectives, but more than this may mean that the objectives as a whole are not realistic. There are at least four types of objectives:

- **Behavioural** – A human action is anticipated. Example: Fifty of the seventy children participating will learn basic hygiene.
- **Performance** – A specific timeframe within which an activity will occur, at an expected proficiency level. Example: Fifty of the seventy nurses will learn to train others in health education topics to accepted standards within four months.
- **Process** – The manner in which something occurs is an end in itself. Example: We will document the teaching methods utilized, identifying those with the greatest success.
- **Product** – A tangible item. Example: A manual will be created to be used to teach health and hygiene to this age and proficiency group in the future.

A useful guide for writing objectives is to make them SMART: specific, measurable, achievable, realistic and time-specific. The wording of an objective is an important part of a proposal. A weakly worded objective might be 'To improve the lives of refugee children by providing health care' while a stronger (or SMART) objective would be to 'To improve the quality of health care for 2,000 refugee children below the age of five within six months'.

Activities An activity is any action or work done to achieve an objective. In other words, it is a process of transforming inputs into outputs and outcomes. Activities are usually the easiest element of the concept or proposal to write, since these are what will actually happen once the project is funded. There should be a limited number of objectives, but each one will likely be supported by several or more activities. When writing about activities, it is important that they are as detailed and descriptive as possible. Be sure to include action verbs and quantities where appropriate. As with objectives, vagueness can be eliminated by using numbers and concrete examples. In this section additional information may be included about how the programme will be monitored and evaluated and what indices will be used.

4. Assumptions, inputs and outputs (or outcomes)

Assumption This is something outside the direct influence of the NGO, like the security situation, the likelihood of hazardous events (e.g. earthquakes), the availability of materials and community participation.

Input This is the element that goes into a programme, such as funds or in-kind donations. Typically, donors like to see that they are not providing the only input and therefore matching funds can be an important part of obtaining grant funds.

Output or outcome An output is what is produced by the programme, for example the number of patients treated, people fed or teachers trained. An outcome differs in that it is more general and indicates a change of some sort, such as less disease as a result of cleaner water.

5. Partnerships

Donors like to see partnerships (see also Chapter 15). In a proposal, partnerships can be demonstrated in several ways, including detailed descriptions of the type of partnership and MOU with local authorities, other NGOs, CBOs and research institutions.

6. Organizational capacity

The purpose of this section is to demonstrate that we can pull off what we talk about in the rest of the document. Management should be discussed, in order to show the support structures of the entire organization. This section can be used to elaborate past programmes, especially those that were in the same sector or similar in any way.

7. Budget

The budget should be developed in conjunction with the staff accountant. A budget narrative may be required, detailing each budget line-item and providing a rationale of how costs were estimated. Each budget category (e.g. staff or personnel, travel, programme supplies, office equipment and training) is typically divided into detailed items such as each staff position, quantity and type of travel, and so forth. A budget narrative should address each line-item, as shown in Table 7.2.

Table 7.2 Budget narrative example

Budget item	Narrative description
Programme manager, expatriate	Programme manager, based in Nairobi, Kenya, will devote 100% of his/her time to management of the programme. The responsibilities include personnel, procurement, financial management, coordination and reporting. The salary is in accordance with established compensation plans and NGO salary scales
Regional travel	Regional travel at an average cost of US$150 per trip from Nairobi to the programme sites with six trips (two per month) for oversight, monitoring and consultations between staff

Some larger proposals may require supporting documents such as quantitative data, maps, logical frameworks or reports, which can be added as addendums to the proposal narrative. It is best to have someone independently read over the finalized proposal one last time making sure each element or specific element mentioned is included in the budget. The checklist in Table 7.3 can help make sure that nothing has been forgotten. (See also budgeting in Chapter 11.)

Negotiating with donors

Following the submission of a proposal there is usually a process of negotiation where agreement is reached on specific details of the programme. These details will vary with each donor and may depend on individual personalities. While it is the donors' job to give away money, they have an obligation to maximize the impact the funds have on an emergency. Typically, therefore, the budget occupies the greatest part of the negotiations, as this determines the amount of resources available to achieve the activities detailed in the proposal.

Before beginning a negotiation, it is important to consider the most effective approach. According to Fisher and Ury (1996), successful negotiations have four common elements. First, when the focus is on the personalities of the negotiators little headway can be made, so negotiations should centre on problems of mutual interest. Second, similarly, negotiations should focus on common, not individual, interests. Third, progress can be made by developing different options, and this should be done before any final position is settled. Finally, successful negotiations set objective standards, as opposed to subjective feelings.

When meeting the donor, it is important that NGO staff are very familiar with the organization they represent. Although staff may work for an NGO that is known for expertise in a particular sector, or perhaps the donor representative is familiar with the NGO in another context, it is important to clarify the areas or sectors the NGO already addresses or plans to work in. In the best cases, the donor and the NGO work together, based on needs they have jointly identified, to address issues within their mandates and interests.

Table 7.3 Proposal checklist

Format/style	✓	Content	✓	Finance	✓
Cover letter		Previous contact		Request correct size of grant	
Title (something catchy)		Reader's perspective		Value to donor	
Writing (prose and grammar)		Donor's interests addressed		Detailed income statement	
Appropriate length		Clear project concept		Correct arithmetic, formulae	
Tone		Descriptive, active voice		Takes all costs into account	
Logical flow		Technical details correct		All cost-share included	
Visual (margins and layout)		Supported by facts		Indirect costs explained	
Letterhead		SMART objectives		Budget narrative (if required)	
Follows guidelines		Demonstration of capacity		Inflation taken into account	
Page numbers		Supporting documents			
Contact information					

There is a lot of uncertainty during emergencies. Therefore if it is a new relationship, and if the situation allows it, it may be helpful to suggest a small activity or pilot to start. To help save time, have a short concept paper prepared, even if it is not presented in the meeting. Be prepared to follow up immediately after a meeting. In more stable situations, solicited proposals, which may be made public or announced discreetly, are common among some donors. Successful NGOs maintain positive and regular contact with donors to get advance warning of donors' intentions.

Some donors negotiate from a superior position and pay lip-service to the idea of partnership. To mitigate this, consider the following points:

- Arrive fully prepared. Immediately before meeting the donor, for example, review the latest reports, plan briefings from project managers and visit the site of the work under discussion. Bring maps, photographs and data to support negotiation.

- Be transparent and realistic, but especially in initial meetings consider how much to reveal.
- Know the NGO's history and future plans. The NGO may have done projects or have staff elsewhere that may be called in to boost organizational capacity.
- Ask questions and encourage the donor to be specific. While there should be some give and take, NGOs are entitled to know the donor's goals and plans.
- Bring a technician or programme specialist to answer specific details. These staff usually spend the most time in the field and they can provide a wealth of information, including specific examples and stories, which the donor may not have access to.
- Use evidence to suggest how funds given to the organization will further the donor's objectives and interests.
- Be prepared to say 'no', especially if the donor's expectations are unrealistic. Especially when money is scarce, it may be tempting to pursue any funding opportunity, but do not let the donor cut the budget below the point at which the project can be successfully implemented.

This last point deserves further consideration. NGOs should protect themselves from donor officials who do not follow through with verbal agreements. Two problems, in particular, seem common. One is for the donor to be late in providing funds and, when the project needs an extension for more time, the donor fails to understand why the project is late and has reservations about granting an extension. A second problem is for the donor to promise in-kind assistance, such as materials or technical backing, and then be late or unresponsive in providing it. To address these problems, some NGOs find it helpful to create a well-established paper trail by following every meeting or conversation with a written memo outlining what was agreed upon.

Donors' visits

During the negotiation phase, donors may visit the project office or work site. There are several types of visits made by donors, as follows.

- **Assessment** of an NGO's capacity in one or more of the following areas: management, financial accountability and the programme's technical competence.
- **Monitoring** an ongoing project in order to make sure that objectives will be met and to see if any corrections or amendments are needed.
- **Evaluating** a project that is being finalized to consider its impact and extensions either with or without new funding. One way is called a cost extension where additional funds are granted, and another way is a no-cost extension in which only additional time is given.

Initiation of a visit may be based on a routine schedule or because the donor has heard that something is wrong. Constant good news (or conversely no news) may raise concerns, so it best to be candid and to share information about constraints or mistaken assumptions as the project progresses. There are also a number of other elements that will influence a donor's visit, including time and logistical constraints (such as distance and difficulty in travelling to the site), and visits such as from the head or representative of an agency or government. Regardless of the reason for the visit, however, it is an opportunity to demonstrate a capacity to implement activities. To ensure a successful visit, consider the following:

- **Plan ahead** Make a realistic schedule. Take into account all constraints (e.g. time and logistics) to the best extent possible. If there is no meal planned, for example, make sure that drinking water is available and that the location of toilet facilities is known. If there is time, carry out a pre-visit to make sure the most up-to-date information is available and to see if anything needs correction or adjustment. Although it is the donor's responsibility to share their goals and intentions for the visit, it makes sense to ask to ensure these goals are met.
- **Put on a show** Have staff available during the visit and make sure they have been briefed on what to do and say. Ensure that the visit is run smoothly without excessive waiting or other hiccups. An unprofessionally run visit will likely leave the impression with the donor's representative that the project is also poorly run.
- **Respect local culture** A donor's visit should not be too disruptive. It is one thing to ask community members or other beneficiaries to be available during a visit, but another thing to have them wait all day or spend too much time away from important activities like planting or harvesting. Donors should be made aware of norms and issues such as taking photographs before going or en route to the site.
- **Try to maximize learning** Allow for the exchange of information. Time should be planned for question-and-answer sessions as well as informal exchanges with beneficiaries (e.g. children, patients or workers). It helps to have information on paper, but this should be presented in a way, or at a time, which does not interfere with personal interaction during the trip.

CHAPTER 8
Managing human resources

The purpose of this chapter is to help address these problems at the field level. NGOs can use basic and streamlined systems to help manage and develop their staff. Running emergency programmes can be improved substantially by balancing human resources with organizational needs. Topics this chapter covers in depth are:
• Human resource management (HRM) system
• Recruitment
• Induction
• Performance management
• End of contract
• Assessing HR: a manager's tool

An organization is only as good as its staff and the best NGOs are the ones that treat their staff the best. In this sense, human resources management (HRM) is the most important element in running an emergency programme. HRM is about more than filling positions: it covers each aspect of a staff member's involvement with an organization, from recruitment and induction to promotion and termination. If staff are unmotivated or unsupported or experience other problems, the programme will suffer as a result.

Many different elements of management are included under the title of HRM. In fact, HRM typically encompasses topics as diverse as governmental regulation, unionization and organizational development. Because this book covers some of these areas in depth, key subjects can be found in their own chapters, including general management (Chapter 3), stress and conflict (Chapter 10) and security (Chapter 18).

HRM systems

Basic needs

Discussion of HRM begins with basic human needs. As outlined by Abraham Maslow (1987), each human has basic needs that form a hierarchy:
Self-actualization a need to set and achieve personal goals
Esteem a need for appreciation, recognition and a feeling of value
Belonging a need to be part of a group or team
Safety a need to have a sense of security and freedom from harm
Physiological a need for life-sustaining objects such as food, water and shelter
From this, it is possible to see how professional needs flow from basic needs. At the most basic level, staff need adequate and sheltered work space. They need

time off to take care of their personal issues and breaks to eat and drink. At this level, staff need a secure and safe place to work from, without occupational hazards (e.g. everything from safe construction sites to ergonomic office equipment) and security incidents. Just as every organization has its own threshold for what level of risk it thinks is acceptable, it is important to find out how much risk individual staff members can accept when working in emergency situations.

Staff also need to feel that they belong to the NGO and the team in which they work. For this reason, staff t-shirts and informal gatherings, for example, may help staff to fit in. Sharing good news, even if staff are not directly responsible for a particular aspect of a programme, can help motivate staff and create a sense of team work. Equity and fair treatment before others is also important in this regard.

Routine appreciation and recognition are critical to achieve the next level of Maslow's hierarchy. While being part of a team is important, individuals must feel the value of their contribution, at least from time to time. Monetary awards are important but not sufficient for a well-functioning programme. To maximize staff contributions, managers must show interest and support for their work.

Finally, for individual staff members to achieve optimal performance, they must set and achieve personal goals. For some staff, this may mean becoming more efficient with a particular responsibility or learning new skills, while for others it may be promotion. Self-actualization may also involve passing on skills to others. In areas affected by conflict, it may often involve a return to normal living conditions or realizing a professional standard for which they have previously trained. Management can help reach self-actualization in their staff by creating an environment where staff development and equitable promotions take place.

These basic needs can be addressed throughout the human resource management cycle in Figure 8.1.

Key to this process is supporting staff who can then positively help the organization to better achieve its objectives. Without a system, this will not happen on any level, except for a few haphazard instances. Ideally, HRM will be joined with other management and programme elements to benefit, not just the organization, but the primary beneficiaries the NGO serves. Several key challenges include:

Key challenge no. 1: planning Because emergencies are by definition sudden and overwhelming, planning for HRM can be especially difficult. Abrupt

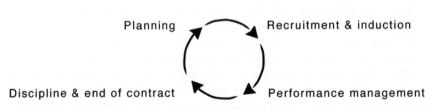

Planning   Recruitment & induction

Discipline & end of contract   Performance management

Figure 8.1 HRM cycle

programme changes (e.g. an influx of refugees or outbreaks of disease) are aggravated by an inability to position resources and the impossibility of knowing exactly what is to come. This issue can be mitigated by having basic standards and systems in place and then trying to be flexible to rapid change. If an influx of refugees is anticipated, for example, the entire recruitment cycle can be carried out up to the point of deploying staff.

Key challenge no. 2: capacity An NGO's lack of capacity can manifest itself in several ways. There can be low local capacity, inexperienced or inappropriate expatriate staff, management unable to provide good supervision and HQ's inability to carry out effective HRM. Staff may be relying on telephone interviews for jobs and may not have the resources to follow up essential tasks like checking references.

Key challenge no. 3: equity Equity can manifest itself in many ways. There can be different levels of stress and exposure to violence for different jobs, inequity between types of staff, professional development opportunities and job security for some positions but not other, lack of opportunities for women and minorities. In some places, a local sub-class develops. In Bosnia, for example, so-called *lokci* have become an upper-income social class employed by the international community involved in reconstructing the country. This separates staff from those they are trying to help and could adversely affect programmes.

Key challenge no. 4: culture Although various writers have considered diversity in the work place, humanitarian relief work embodies a culturally international mix found in almost no other field. NGO staff routinely consists of people from many countries and backgrounds. Considerable managerial resources may be needed to balance needs, expectations and the interests of staff.

Policy and procedures

Record-keeping

Good record-keeping is an important element of HRM. Its function is to maintain order and prevent mistakes like hiring unqualified candidates. The maintenance of records and other specifics can be considered personnel functions (an older name for HRM). It forms the basis for organizational memory and, if done correctly, can save a fair amount of grief as programmes progress. The contents of a basic HRM system are discussed below.

Staff policy manuals

A thorough staff policy manual, or a similar document covering country- or programme-specific HRM, is a must. A staff policy manual will answer staff questions, set a framework for expectations and prevent or mitigate disputes. Only in rare cases can a manual from the NGO's HQ be applied to field programmes, because of different laws, cultures and local conditions. Examples include observances of religious holidays (e.g. Christmas or Eid), holiday leave (vacation) and sick-leave allowances, which are difficult to directly translate from one country to another. The length of the document may vary. Table 8.1 provides the five elements often included in staff policy manuals.

Government regulations

Where government rule exists, HRM is normally a highly regulated area. In many countries the Ministry of Labour is responsible for overseeing how organizations manage staff. Vacancy notices, record-keeping, taxation, work hours, holiday leave and benefits are just some of the things that might be regulated by law. Some governments view the local staff of NGOs as informal or black market because of their failure to pay tax and follow other regulations. NGOs that skirt or ignore the law may be penalized (e.g. by heavy fines) later on.

Pressure driven by urgency may lead to quickly hiring new staff, but this can lead to problems almost from the start. If not done before, laws need to be checked against the NGO's HRM policy. One method used by some NGOs is to offer only daily or short-term contracts (e.g. two weeks), but this may be inconsistent with local labour laws. For this and other reasons (as outlined in Chapter 5), it is best to have a lawyer on retainer (or at least identified) to handle disputes as they arise.

Table 8.1 Staff policy manual

Expectations	Terms	Compensation	Leave	Discipline
NGO standards and proper conduct	Job description	Salary scale and other details	Annual leave	Minor and gross infractions
Applicable laws	Dates of employment	Pay dates	Public holidays	Warning policy
Conflicts of interest including non-affiliation	Probation period	Per diems	Sick leave	Grievance and appeal
Use/misuse of NGO assets including intellectual property	Office hours	Benefits	Bereavement leave	Termination (types and procedures)
		Tax	Maternity and paternity leave	
		Evaluations and raises	Leave of absence	

Types of staff

In an emergency programme there is typically a need for many different types of staff. While some people may be employed on a full-time basis to manage and administer programmes, many others may be employed on a part-time or casual basis. This may included unskilled (e.g. digging, loading, hauling and erecting temporary structures) and skilled tasks (e.g. extra health staff for immunization campaigns or an engineer to monitor a construction activity).

Full contracts may not be needed but this will depend on the donor's auditing requirements. It is best to at least to have a letter of appointment (a simple memo) which spells out the terms of employment, including when the employment will end, and tasks to be performed. It may also help the temporary staff for passing through checkpoints. For more professional staff some sort of written job description, scope of work (SOW), or terms of reference (TOR) may be essential. Determinants of staff are normally based mostly on available funding, but should be based on need. There are three types of staff.

Volunteers What distinguishes volunteers from employees is compensation, especially salary, and sometimes the scope of work or level of responsibility. In the field, however, volunteers can make an especially high impact. They can be either a national or expatriate and hold positions anywhere in the organization from board members to cleaners. Volunteers can help NGOs in a myriad of ways that their labour can be used.

National employees (local staff) There can be different categories, such as long-term national staff or core staff and staff hired temporarily or for specific projects. Some NGOs draw a distinction between core staff and those hired for temporary projects.

As much as possible, local staff should not be hired on the basis of language skills alone. In fact, except in certain cases such as document translation or for short-term needs where an expatriate is essential, NGOs should not maintain a position for a translator, but should actively seek professionally skilled staff who also have language abilities. While there may be a need for translators in a short-term capacity, such as an acute medical situation or for high-level meetings or interviews, in the medium and long term it does nothing to build local capacity and reinforces certain types of negative relationships between internationals and host nationals. NGOs should try to hire staff that are multilingual and, when possible, provide an opportunity to obtain language skills.

International employees (expatriate staff) Reasons for taking on expatriate staff depend on the place. In emergency situations, local nationals may genuinely be absent or unavailable. In East Timor, for example, following the crisis in 1999, there were only a handful of medical doctors in the entire country. NGOs should make every effort to hire locals and, as applicable, people from the region. One half-measure may be to hire people from the region who may understand the local context better, will likely speak the local language and should be less prone to local corruption. Some NGOs hire qualified candidates from countries with a historical or cultural tie, for example, Portuguese-speaking

Brazilians work in Angola or East Timor. The classic image of the white Western relief worker is still prevalent in the field, but not as much as before.

Many NGOs use international employees at the beginning or start-up of an emergency programme. The learning curve for foreigners coming to many emergency situations is very steep. All expatriate staff are managers.

Some say relief workers are one of three types: missionaries, mercenaries and madmen. Others, such as Cross (2001), offer a more considered view, according to which relief workers typically progress through three phases during a career. First there is an altruistic, if naive, phase, usually during the first years. Second comes a phase that is more brash and driven but also possibly dysfunctional and political. Finally, in more mature years, relief workers are more caring and have a fuller understanding of the constraints and reality of the work they do. Understanding the background of staff can help managers to adjust their actions and follow up problems where necessary.

According to Fowler (1997), there are a number of reasons why expatriate staff may be needed in development situations. First, particular skills are not available and a gap needs to be filled while training is provided to a local person. Second, there is a short-term need for confidence building and communication with donors. Third, an exchange of mutual learning and breaking down stereotypical views between North, South and East are required. Fourth, there is a need to speed up learning and spreading specific skills from outside. Finally, there is a recognized, valid need for the challenging inputs expatriates can bring.

There are also less valid reasons for having expatriate staff. Expatriates may act as impartial gatekeepers for resources. They can ensure consistency, interpret organizational goals and policies and make sure donors' and beneficiaries' concerns are respected. They may also be used to promote the organization's national identify (fulfilling a tacit expectation, if not formal condition, of bilateral donors).

One of the main downsides of expatriates is that they consume a lot of resources. Expatriates typically earn many times more than national staff and require far more in benefits, including transport, housing and insurance. Some NGOs get around these issues with pay-outs or reduced benefits. But expatriates also require a lot of support in terms of management at different times during their tenures. Because emergency programmes are so personality-driven, having strong expatriate staff is essential. NGOs could consider the cost–benefit of each expatriate and during the recruitment process look carefully at what they are expected to contribute.

Recruitment step by step

Recruitment is a time-consuming task but it is worth taking the time to do it right. The steps outlined below can be abbreviated and done expeditiously if need be but this will have less good results.

Step 1 Planning

In response to the programme's needs, the responsible hiring manager, in conjunction with the senior management, reviews needs and develops requirements for a new position. To determine specific needs based on each programme:

- Consider the details of the programme throughout its cycle (see Chapter 1), including geographic area. If, for example, a programme will be implemented in three separate districts (or other such area), three separate sets of staff may be needed.
- Decide on the programme's scope. This is based on two factors: beneficiaries' needs and size. For some types of programmes, the complexity of a project can make determining HR needs more difficult, while for others the needs can be fairly straightforward. An example of the estimated HR needs of typical health interventions is provided in Table 8.2.
- List tasks to be performed and categories of staff needed. Specific job descriptions will be needed. For some new or changing positions, periodic review of the tasks listed will be necessary to ensure accuracy, which in turn affects performance and efficiency. Examples of job descriptions are provided in other chapters and discussed further below.
- Verify positions against budget. It is also important to consider current management capacity (i.e. consider whether the organization can manage more staff). If the donor will not fund the positions that are needed to achieve the project's objectives, the donor should be informed and a decision should be made whether to proceed with the proposed project.

Table 8.2 Health HR needs

Immunization campaign	1 vaccination team (20 people including 2 vaccinators and 1 cold-chain technician) to immunize 500–700 people per hour 1 supervisor (e.g. nurse) for every 1-2 teams
Out-patient department	1 health worker/50 consultations/day 1 medical doctor (supervisor) 1-2 non-qualified health workers per main tasks (e.g. dressing, sterilization and oral rehydration 1 security guard/8-hour shift
Therapeutic Feeding Centre (TFC) (typical size 100 beneficiaries)	1 medical doctor (part-time) 2–3 trained nurses for supervision and medical follow-up 10 nutritional assistants (1/10 children) 1 storekeeper 4 cooks plus assistants 4 cleaners 1 security guard/8-hour shift

Source: Modified from MSF (1997: 208).

Step 2 Creating a recruitment file

The recruitment process must be fair and work in such a way that enables the NGO to hire the most qualified staff. Being organized is the only way to do this. If the NGO has not already done so, create a filing system. If there is not enough time, relevant information can be collected in a box or file and sorted out later. A specific set of files should be maintained with the following information.

- Current and former vacancy announcements. These are for the record and to be used as templates.
- Incoming curricula vitae (CVs) sorted by position. Perhaps the easiest way is to develop several broad categories such as administration, operations, programme and management.
- Rejected CVs with a note or memo explaining why the individual was not hired. This is necessary in order to prevent people being contacted again in the future.

Step 3 Issuing vacancy notices

To ensure transparency and accountability, each vacant position should be advertised publicly. Perhaps the easiest way to do this is by pasting a vacancy notice on the gate, at other organizations and/or in a periodical such as a newspaper. The vacancy should be open for a specific period, at least one week and preferably between two and three weeks. Applications can be reviewed and evaluated at the end of that period or, if they are needed urgently, on a rolling basis through the vacancy period.

The vacancy announcement should contain the following information:
- Position name
- Work location
- Brief description of the position
- Position qualifications
- Closing date
- Details of what application materials should be submitted and how
- Contact information

Unless required by law, salary range should not be included, as this is usually private information for the applicants and may encourage people for whom a large salary the sole motivation to apply. An announcement template should be available to recruiting staff to save time and create uniformity. To help with recognition, and unless the security situation dictates otherwise, it should also be on the letterhead or contain the organization's logo.

Step 4 Collecting and assessing applications

Collecting applications can be done in one of two ways. One system is for CVs to be turned in as specified in the vacancy announcement. In some places, it is customary to turn in supporting documents such as letters of recommendation at this time. Another method is to use a standardized application form. An application form creates a way to test for literacy, neatness and other qualities. It also facilitates the collection of standard information such as exact dates of employment, which can help account for apparently blank periods in a person's employment history. For these reasons, an application form is well suited for emergency programmes, which should be simple and as self-explanatory as possible.

Applications should be collected by a designated staff member and maintained in a secure file. Once the closing date is reached, the recruiting staff member, usually a programme manager, along with at least one senior manager outside the department, should review the received applications. Alternatively, if the position is urgent, applications can be reviewed on a rolling basis as they arrive; it is important, however, not to make any decisions before the application period is finished, because a more qualified person may apply later in the period.

Once applications have been initially screened (e.g. for completeness or meeting basic requirements) a shortlist should be developed of the best qualified, typically through a committee and/or supervised by an uninvolved senior staff member. In some places it is customary to post shortlisted names publicly, with no other information, (e.g. on the office gate).

In some countries, the creation of false documents (e.g. licences and diplomas) has virtually become a small industry. Before offering a contract for signature, insist on seeing and closely scrutinize the original documentation from all applicants.

To screen what are often loads of applications, some organizations use expensive computer software which does little more than count key words (e.g. 'project' or 'humanitarian'). The best way to screen for shortlisting is to weigh the applications against the specific criteria of the job description. The position's responsibilities and prerequisites can be rated for each applicant. An example of applications of the post of project manager is provided in Table 8.3.

As is often found in acute emergencies, for a hardship post with a high degree of autonomy, resiliency (discussed in Chapter 10) and creativity, recruiters would consider general and technical experience to be less important than prior emergency experience, with the ability to thrive in difficult and ambiguous circumstances being the most important.

Step 5 Interviews

Recruitment is more than just finding qualified people, it involves selecting qualified people who will fit in with other staff and make a positive contribution to the organization's objectives and activities. The best way to select the most suitable candidate at this stage is through face-to-face interviews. This provides an opportunity to verify the applicant's details, exchange views and experiences and assess other indicators (e.g. non-verbal communication and confidence) that might relate to the applicant's ability to perform as a staff member. Some NGOs rely on telephone interviews with expatriate staff, and although this is less than ideal, the same approach can be used over the phone.

Table 8.3 Position evaluation

Responsibilities or prerequisites	Source
Amount of professional experience	CV/Résumé
Amount of project management experience	CV/Résumé
Specific sectoral experience	CV/Résumé
Experience in managing others	CV/Résumé
Appropriate education/training	CV/Résumé
Country/emergency experience	CV/Résumé
Other relevant skills	CV/Résumé
Values and priorities	Reference
Project management abilities	Reference
Ability to take on additional responsibilities	Reference
Quality of work in previous work	Reference
Ability to follow through	Reference
Organizational and communications skills	Reference
Professionalism	Reference

Note that interviews are a third source of information on candidates (see below).

Interviewing styles can vary greatly by country and cultural differences. For these reasons, it is often a good idea to include both national and expatriate staff in interviews, to ensure that the style that most typifies the organization comes through.

One of the critical issues is maintaining fairness in the recruitment process. Many conflict-stricken countries are heavily stratified. Expatriates can help in this regard by ensuring the process is based on merit. At an early stage, care needs to be given to consider inherited and belief-based characteristics (e.g. ethnicity and religion) and the backgrounds of the staff to ensure balance. General tips for interviews include the following.

- Be open and accommodating.
- Provide details about the position.
- Ask if the candidate has any questions.
- At the end of the interview, do not say that the candidate will be contacted unless there is genuinely a plan to do so; instead tell the candidate that other interviews are being carried out and that successful candidate(s) will be notified within a specified time.

Some organizations prefer to interview candidates by a committee, and consensus should be reached or a second interview scheduled if needed. A checklist of subjective rankings may be helpful. Each interviewer ranks the candidate from poor (1) to excellent (5) on categories such as professional appearance, the ability to communicate effectively, a capacity for representing the organization externally, an appropriate education and professional experience, and leadership or management potential. A key question for interviewers is: do you see them as fellow staff?

The key to an effective interview is asking good questions. They should be linked to the criteria of the job description and be as specific as possible. If hypothetical questions are asked, hypothetical answers will be given. Instead, ask questions based on experience and a good idea of a candidate's background will be gained. Questions should be evidence based and open in nature (as opposed to closed questions which can be answered with a 'yes' or 'no'), although it may be necessary to clarify basic information. Here are some typical interview questions.

Competency-based questions How did you use your education or training in your previous work? What are your strengths and weaknesses? How will your experience help us accomplish our mission? Can you operate the equipment (e.g. computers) necessary for the position you have applied for? Tell me about a time you were successful in your last position, Why did you leave your last position? What do you hope to accomplish in this position? In the past, have you passed on your skills to others? How do you deal with work related stress? There is a delay in the project you are working on, how would you handle it?

Specific technical questions These should be developed for each position to demonstrate professional competency. If, for example, an applicant is sought for a shelter-building project, questions should be asked about local construction materials, building techniques, the sub-contracting process and construction site management. If available, samples of building plans and altered bills of quantities (BOQ) might be used to support the interview.

Conceptual or value-based questions Have you worked for an NGO before? How do NGOs differ from other organizations? What do you know about this NGO? Why do you want to work for this NGO? Describe a situation in which you were an effective team member. How can you contribute to a happy work place? What kind of work environment do you work best in?

Potential managers might be asked the following questions. What is your management style? How many people have you managed before? What are your three most important leadership and management qualities?) What do you see yourself doing in five years? When are you available?

Do not ask about family, religious, political (or similar) beliefs.

Step 6 Selection

Once an application is decided upon, action should be taken as soon as possible to contact the applicant. This keeps the applicant from being in limbo as well as preventing them being lost to another organization, especially during a time of influx of international money, when NGOs, the UN, journalists and others compete for qualified workers. Decide with the successful applicant on a start date and time and specify what will be done on the first day. It is also critical at this stage to be clear about compensation.

When making an offer, negotiate by offering material benefits (if in line with the salary scale) and non-material benefits, such as the possibility that this NGO will be in the country longer than others. Establishing and updating a pay scale is a key task in HRM. The longer time goes without doing so, the larger the problem will be later on as new staff are hired.

Creating an appropriate scale should be based on a survey of existing pay rates of other NGOs – neither the government nor UN pay scales are appropriate for NGOs – and weighed to account for local costs of living. Accurate surveys can be complex and time-consuming, as they take into account not just salary payments but different types of compensation, such as transport, per diems, child care, lunches and professional development opportunities. Consideration should be given to whether staff should be paid in the local or foreign currency. Often there may be an existing survey available although it may have been carried out before the most recent crisis, when the corresponding influx of foreign actors alters the local economy.

A simple working scale, subject to regular updating, can be created using grades based on the position and steps (or levels) based on experience both inside and outside the organization. An example, for illustrative purposes only, is provided in Table 8.4.

As is evident from the examples provided, additional levels or a further delineation of staff levels may be needed for real-world situations. Most NGOs only review/change a pay scale yearly and then only in small increments. For the organization and staff that come later, the longer the duration the pay scale the better.

Induction

Each newly recruited staff member should undergo a process that involves contact with each key person or department, including administration, finance, operations and logistics, the programme and, possibly, the country director. At this point the new staff member should be provided with the basic information that he or she needs to function in their job. It is important that the staff take

Table 8.4 Pay scale example

Position	Step 1	Step 2	Step 3	Step 4	Step 5
Senior manager: programme manager	425	450	475	500	525
Manager: project manager (various types), doctor	320	355	380	410	435
Skilled: Project assistant, nurse, engineer, trainer, logistician, accountant	225	250	275	300	330
Semi-skilled: cashier, driver, maintenance, community health worker	120	150	185	210	240
Unskilled: labourer, cook, cleaner, guard	50	65	85	110	140

time to work with new staff. If this is only done for senior staff or expatriates, less senior and national staff cannot be expected to fully function and respond to issues as they arise. If possible, information should be provided in a written form to supplement what is explained verbally, covering the following topics.

- Mission, goals, objectives, vision and values
- NGO history (both worldwide and at the country level)
- Programme overview
- Policies and procedures (e.g. benefits, holiday requests, sick/maternity/ bereavement leave, office hours, office attire and finance/accounting)
- Office structure and contact/telephone lists
- Job description
- Reporting and filing (including computer files)
- Safety
- Staff introductions
- Office and programme area tour

It is very important that each newly recruited staff member should know their responsibilities fully, including who to report to and how, as explained in their job description. They can also be provided with an identification card, t-shirt and other work-related items during this initial induction orientation.

If your NGO is large enough, a mentor or buddy system can be put in place to help new staff members through their induction and first few months on the job. Although few NGOs do it, this can positively affect office morale because the new staff feel welcomed, and it enforces team work, sharing skills and experiences.

Personnel files

Ideally, a file should be created for each staff member that includes the following information:

- CV/Résumé
- Employee's application form with emergency contact information and home address/telephone
- References (and documentation of the recommendation by the referee)
- Copy of all employee's evaluations
- Job description
- Contract
- Promotion form (as appropriate)

In many NGOs, the senior manager who oversees HRM will designate a records custodian who maintains and secures these files. In some cases, depending on the office arrangements, a member of senior staff will maintain these records him/herself because of their confidential nature.

Job descriptions

Job descriptions are one of the most important HRM documents because they clarify objectives, separate work responsibilities and provide a means for measuring performance. While it may seem like just another donor requirement, job descriptions will help nearly all phases of HRM work. For accuracy and reinforcement, job descriptions should be reviewed from time to time. Job descriptions for senior people or positions that frequently change, in particular, should be open to reworking and fine-tuning. Job descriptions typically contain:

- Position title
- Who the post holder reports to
- Who reports to the post holder (if anyone)
- Work location
- General description of position
- Specific responsibilities
- Position requirements
- Place for the staff member's signature for acknowledgement of post holder of duties assigned

It is also very helpful if the phrase 'All other duties assigned' is included at the end of the specific responsibilities section, for new tasks that may be needed.

Employment contracts

Employment contracts formalize the relationship between the staff member and the NGO. Like other HRM methods and tools, contracts should be tailored to fit the local context. For this reason, boilerplate templates from HQ rarely work without major revisions. Both national and international staff should prepare and review the employment contract (as appropriate) and the final draft should be evaluated by a lawyer familiar with local labour laws. Under certain circumstances different types of contracts may be applicable, such as for labourers and professional staff, but, again, this may depend on local laws. In some countries, for example, titles such as 'employee' and 'contractor' entitle the post holder to different compensation and benefits, which may change over time (e.g. after 12 months).

In general, although it will depend on how detailed and pertinent the staff policy manual is at the time, most contracts include:

- Position name and responsibilities
- Reporting structure
- Contract dates
- Governing laws
- Compensation and expenses
- Asset protection and confidentiality
- Code of conduct
- Benefits including breaks and holidays
- End of contract

Performance management

Good management practices encompass staff development and good HRM systems reward staff in transparent and accountable ways. When people are compensated well, not just with money, and are valued as staff members, they will develop a sense of loyalty to the organization. To engender this, the organization itself, through its managers, should make a commitment to developing its staff through learning. This will be shown by plans and budgets and improved through feedback from staff. Managers will need to monitor and encourage this process. This part of the chapter starts with evaluating a staff member's performance and then covers different means of development.

Staff appraisal

Promotion is one of the benefits of hard work and good performance. Promotion should be systematic, in terms of a procedure with which staff are familiar; transparent in the way staff receive promotions; and accountable, in that a record is made as evidence to support the promotion. Following this, most NGO staff receive promotions following a formal evaluation.

Appraisals, or performance reviews, are one of the most feared – for both the staff as well as the evaluator – and thus one of the most put-off HRM tasks. Some feel that formal evaluations over-simplify performance, serve to label people and only focus on the past. Systems that rely on forms can be viewed as bureaucratic and a distraction. In some cultures, evaluations that involve completing forms feels like reporting on someone, unless it is done in an open and transparent manner with the employee fully knowledgeable about what has been written about him or her. Nonetheless, evaluations are important for letting staff members know where they stand, allowing for an exchange of views, and when done properly they may serve as an action plan for the future.

The most important element of appraisals is making time to talk to staff. In emergencies, however, tools such as forms can be important as formal records, especially to national staff, because management turnover tends to be high. From the point of view of transparency and organizational memory, formal evaluations are best done in writing, but they can also be done more often through informal feedback. Written evaluations are also important because they document development and promotion as well as problems.

To objectify the evaluation process, feedback should be a regular part of managing, as discussed in Chapter 3. The key to constructive feedback is more about creating a relationship where people improve rather than avoiding personally descriptive adjectives and focusing on work-related verbs. Formal evaluations are simply times where feedback is recorded.

Most NGOs have devised some means of formal evaluation. In many cases, however, these systems are often cumbersome (e.g. multi-phased forms that are 5–10 pages long) and more geared to evaluating staff at HQ. To streamline formal evaluations, many evaluation systems incorporate a matrix similar to the one below. This one is short (less than one-page) and is designed to be used for all field staff members.

To use the tool, the topics of the form should be discussed with the employee and some consensus reached. Some managers may ask staff to fill out the form before meeting (as a self-assessment), whereas others may want to avoid tension if differences arise. In either case, a discussion of what follow-on is most appropriate depending on the individual staff member will be necessary. In this way, feedback and a way forward are integral to the evaluation process. An appraisal form often uses a scale (e.g. 1 to 5 from 'does not meet expectations' to 'superior performance'), covering a range of competency and value performance measures, as outlined in Table 8.5.

To help facilitate and provide a record of such discussions, a personnel evaluation and development form can be used covering these points. This form will record:

- Positive/strong qualities of employee during evaluation period
- Negative/weak qualities of employee during evaluation period
- Recommended development or corrective measures

Such a tool is designed to facilitate discussion and provide a path for reinforcing or developing positive behaviour, skills and attitude. For example, if a driver is evaluated, it might be possible to say that his or her strengths are punctuality and hard work. To reinforce these traits, it may be possible to recommend the employee for monetary promotion or assign additional responsibilities. But perhaps several times in the last month, this employee may have had difficulty in maintaining the vehicle, because of not paying attention to detail or another reason. This should be noted, as it may be part of a trend, which later leads to bad performance. To correct the issue (because in this case,

Table 8.5 Staff appraisal categories

Organizational skills: Maintains a neat work area, is able to access assets or information when needed	**Improvement**: Seeks ways to cut costs, increase efficiency, and enhance productivity
Helpfulness and initiative: Shows willingness to help others without being asked, suggests ideas, contributes to team building and volunteers when needed	**Quality of work**: Completes work/tasks to a high standard, demonstrates effort to exceed standard expectations
Timeliness: Completes assigned work by deadlines, exhibits punctuality at all times	**Quantity of work**: Keeps pace with assigned work, is able to increase output as required
Judgement: Makes sound decisions, uses commonsense, follows policies and procedures consistently	**Professionalism**: Has a neat and clean appearance, projects a professional image, sets examples, exhibits leadership commensurate with position
Job skills: Possesses ample expertise to perform job, shows willingness to improve those skills, displays willingness to transfer those skills to others	**Overall performance**: Average of the above ratings (can be weighted in the judgement of the evaluator based on observations of the employee's work and output)

it may or may not be that person's fault), it may be possible to offer training or allocate more money to maintaining a vehicle.

Staff development

One of the most common methods of staff development is through training (see Chapter 16), but there is a variety of other pathways, as outlined in Table 8.6.

As may be evident, staff development may focus on a number of different topics. These should be based on actual needs which the staff identify themselves. Training, whether internal courses or package courses, can be considered elementary – computer literacy, first aid, driving for non-drivers, foreign language – or job-specific, such as project management, report and proposal writing, human rights, or familiarization with specific software (e.g. EPI Info, SPSS, and accounting packages).

Discipline and end of contract

Although not every employee will undergo disciplinary procedures, it is an important element of HRM. For most staff, simply knowing the parameters which guide their professional work is enough to prevent problems. Still, every manager is confronted with situations in which unsuitable behaviour must be dealt with. Although it is not always linked to discipline, termination is discussed here and is used specifically in its negative connotation of being fired, as discussed below.

Discipline

Like other elements of a good HRM system, disciplinary procedures should be clearly spelled out, available to all staff and carried out in a transparent and accountable way so that staff can present their own perspective. Before considering any disciplinary measure, however, managers should consider their own state of mind, given the stresses of working in an emergency, to ensure that disciplinary steps are proportionate to the offence. In some circumstances, an on-the-spot correction may be called for if it is likely that the staff member will correct the matter himself or herself and not create a pattern either individually or among other staff.

There are many views on how to handle punishment, but in an emergency setting it should be handled with some care, including taking into account local culture and the context of the emergency. In some cultures, where saving face may be very important, handling disciplinary problems publicly may be counter-productive, whereas in other cultures it may be highly effective.

In emergencies, managers may be confronted with issues that are particularly complex to handle. Three prevalent examples include: gender boundary violation and exploitation, risk taking and danger seeking behaviour, and alcohol and drug use. For these and similar issues, good managers will be familiar

Table 8.6 Staff development methods

Method/staff type	Internal courses	Package courses	Workshops	Seminars/conferences	On-the-job training	Exchanges (visits)	Secondments	Self-study
Programme	Usually cost effective, highly recommended	Suited for technical areas, useful but relevance may be an issue	Team-building, for experienced staff, skilled facilitator important, good to generate knowledge from experience	Good for local level inter-agency sharing	Practical orientation, suited to induction, good for special skill development	Suited to local level inter-agency	Case-by-case decision	Requires motivation and commitment, may help identify performer, needs organizational policy
Technical specialists	Specialty courses as available	Same as above	Good for problem solving, to develop internal linkages and strengthen staff	Highly recommended	Limited application	Useful and relevant, recommended	Recommended where suitable opportunities exist	Same as above, helps keep staff aware of specialist knowledge
Programme support	Relevant but normally of limited application	Relevant for professional development	Useful within departments	Important for internal information sharing	Same as above	Useful within country programmes	Limited application	Same as above
Junior–middle managers	Good for specific	Same as above	Good for problem	Helpful for exposure and	Same as above	Usually relevant and	Use only very selectively	Same as Programme

	organizational systems, high cost if numbers are low, adaptation of external courses recommended	solving, to develop internal linkages and strengthen staff	broadening perspectives, less so for junior managers than for middle		useful, recommended	staff above
Senior/top managers	Same as above; Limited application	Same as above, highly recommended	Good for building networks and those areas helpful for less senior managers, also important for policy development and conceptual issues	Same as above	Useful policy exchange and strategic development	Same as for technical specialists; Only for areas of weakness

Source: Adapted from Fowler (1997: 91). Fowler was writing specifically for development NGOs, but the idea applies nearly as much to those NGOs working in emergencies.

with organizational requirements and make sure that staff are thoroughly briefed from the induction period onward, thoroughly investigate each incident as they occur and follow up fairly and consistently.

End of contract

Ending a staff member's contract needs to be done in a transparent way and according to established procedures, to avoid creating a case that can be taken to a labour court or the local equivalent. Because losing a job can have a significant consequence on the person and their family, each incident should be looked into before invoking the disciplinary procedure. For example, if a staff member has been stealing, an investigation should take place to collect evidence rather than a simple dismissal.

There are two views of staff termination. First, it can be considered a failure of the employee, who performs poorly in the job as a result of family problems, poor motivation or dedication, substance abuse or apathy. The second view is that it can be an organization's failure to support the employee through mismanagement, unrealistic or poorly communicated expectations, or other management failures. Good management tends toward the second view. Still there are times when it will become necessary to let people go.

A traditional disciplinary procedure follows a system of verbal and written warnings depending on the type of offence committed (see Table 8.7).

Grievances

In some instances, problems may arise between a manager and a staff member as a result of disciplinary procedures. Having a known procedure can mitigate or prevent issues altogether. Generally, issues are best handled as close as possible to the point of origin, as shown in Figure 8.2.

A staff council may be formed to look after specific issues of staff welfare. On large staffs, this mechanism can work to improve conditions and raise issues that senior staff may have otherwise not been aware of.

Box 8.1 Whistle blowing

As a means to address genuine concerns of criminal activities, corruption, breach of legal obligations, health and safety violations and cover-ups of these concerns, a whistle-blowing policy is helpful. All staff, especially in areas that are unfamiliar with whistle blowing, should be briefed on the policy. Key points may include:
- How to raise a concern (as distinguished from a grievance procedure)
- Confidential and anonymous disclosure and protection
- Path of enquiry and what happens before and after an investigation
- Raising false allegations with malicious intent will be treated as a disciplinary matter

Table 8.7 Staff disciplinary measures

Type	Examples	1st offence	2nd offence	3rd offence	4th offence
Minor offence	Tardiness or loafing	Verbal	Written warning	Final written warning	Dismissal
Misconduct	Poor performance, absenteeism or abusing benefits	Written	Final written warning	Dismissal	
Gross misconduct	Falsifying records, using drugs or alcohol on duty	Final written warning	Dismissal		
Dismissible offence	Theft, security violations, fighting or damaging property	Dismissal			

Source: Modified from De Beer and Rossouw (2005: 117).

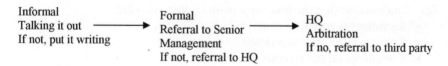

Figure 8.2 Handling a staff grievance

Alternatives to termination

In many circumstances, there are several options a manager can try before firing an employee. These are summarized below (McCurley, 1993).

- **Re-supervise** In emergency and/or programme start-ups, it is possible that a staff member is unaware of policies and procedures, so review or reiteration may be a step towards addressing the problem.
- **Re-assign** In some cases, especially larger programmes, it may be possible to transfer the staff member to another position. Care should taken that this will not mean just transferring the problem.
- **Re-train** Poor performance may be the result of an inadequate understanding of key aspects of the post.
- **Re-vitalize** Sometimes a break can do wonders.

- **Refer** If there is a clear opening and a good match, it may be possible to transfer the staff member to another organization.
- **Retire** Some staff members have simply reached their limit and this method may be a viable in a long established NGO. Dismissing them through retirement helps preserve dignity and acknowledge the work they have contributed.

In some developing countries, especially where violent conflict is widespread, firing an employee can pose a significant security threat. While rare, violent reactions to termination have occurred in emergency situations. To mitigate the chances of former employees seeking revenge, try to:

- Follow policy by putting disciplinary action in writing.
- Give a public second chance to the staff member.
- Make it clear that it was their actions (not other staff members') that have caused their termination.
- As a last resort, cushion the termination by offering a severance package, recommendation, hiring a relative or friend, or other unusual step.

When firing people, be clear, quick and make sure the decision is supported by appropriate evidence. In the ideal case, the employee should feel that, in effect, they have fired themselves. This has importance both for security and legal reasons.

For most positions, especially staff who leave under normal circumstances (e.g. the end of their contract), it is useful for management if they complete an exit evaluation which allows them to comment on different aspects and the organization in general. While it may be helpful to have a standard form for this, a memo covering the following points is just as useful:

- Recruitment and induction
- Comments on staff supervised
- Comments on management
- Relations with HQ
- NGO's image and programme development
- Lessons learned

Assessing HR systems: a manager's tool

This tool can be used to assess the existing HRM capacity within an NGO. Sometimes the problems are obvious, but it is usually best to fine-tune issues. As shown in Table 8.8, each issue can be given a score, following the criteria provided, to identify areas for improvement.

Table 8.8 HRM assessment tool

HRM issue	1	2	3
Planning and structure	Quantity and quality of staff do not meet workload. Organizational structure and/or job design are unclear and work is often duplicated or skipped as a result	Quantity and/or quality of staff sometimes meets workload. Organizational structure and/or job design are not always clear and work is sometimes duplicated or skipped as a result	Quantity and quality of staff meet workload. Meeting objectives is facilitated by the organizational structure and job design
Record-keeping	No coherent files exist. Individual staff records are not available	Files exist but are ill-kept or not centralized. No rules in place for access. Unclear responsibility for maintenance among staff	Information is easily available and up to date. Files are organized and secure
Policy	Non-existent or unclear policies. No job descriptions, employee manual or other essential documents. Staff are uncertain of rules and regulations	Policies are formalized but are not comprehensive or specific to context. Policies are not easily accessible to all staff	Formalized and comprehensive policies are in writing and available to all staff. Policies are pragmatic and tailored to local context
Recruitment	Recruitment is haphazard and informal. Some perceive the system as being nepotistic based on informal contact	HRM recruitment system, incorporating planning and programming requirements, exists but is not always followed	Recruitment is done efficiently and transparently according to established systems. Announcements are posted publicly and more than one staff member is involved in interviewing and hiring
Induction	No orientation programme or induction period is carried out for new staff who are expected to just start working	Programme and/or induction period exists, but is carried out inconsistently or leaves out important elements like performance expectations or organizational goals	Programme and induction period is done for all staff, making them feel welcomed and valued. Expectations, goals and contextual issues (e.g. security) are emphasized

cont.

cont.

HRM issue	1	2	3
Performance management	Management sets poor examples and inadequate supervision. Safety and security issues are rarely addressed. Staff are promoted, or offered professional development opportunities, based on personal feelings of managers.	Management provides inconsistent examples and supervision. An informal safety and security plan and follow-up exists. A system for evaluating performance and promotion is in place but is not always followed or is not participatory	Management consistently sets good examples and provides constructive and supportive supervision. Safety and security issues are fully integrated into all aspects of management and programming. Staff and managers work together to determine top performance. Promotions and professional development decisions are based on transparent reviews
End of contract	Grievance and discipline are handled informally. Staff can be fired without warning or not according to a standard system	System for handing grievances, disciplinary procedures and termination is in place but is not always followed or is unclear to staff	Formal procedures exist, are consistently followed and are known to staff

CHAPTER 9
Planning, managing and reporting on a project

A project can be defined as work that is done within stated parameters (e.g. time, location and budget) to achieve a specific objective. Examples include fixing a well, and conducting a mobile health clinic or a training workshop. The purpose of this chapter is to provide relief workers with the knowledge and a set of tools to implement projects effectively and efficiently at the country level. Specifically, this chapter discusses:

- Project cycle management basics
- Project design
- Planning and management tools
- Project launch
- Reporting
- Holding meetings
- Basic problem solving

For better or for worse, the response to emergencies is done through the project framework. 'Better' because projects can be planned and managed properly. Funding can be raised for projects which meet specifically identified needs, have start and finish dates and accountable resources. 'Worse' because projects can be short-term and may not address the underlying causes of a problem. The episodic nature of the project cycle can freeze thinking and action. This 'projectisis', the negative side of the project framework, leads to inflexibility and short-sightedness. But many projects without set parameters use resources without any real results.

Although sometimes used interchangeably, a programme normally comprises several projects or sets of services. In either case, many of the methods for handling projects and programmes are the same.

Project cycle management basics

Project cycle management provides a framework for thinking about, planning and carrying out projects. It is a good starting point for discussing project management and a useful means where no other guidelines or instructions otherwise exist. Figure 9.1 shows a typical project cycle.

Widely used by NGOs, this model is borrowed from the business sector. As may be apparent, this is model is somewhat flat and is not necessarily an accurate reflection of how projects are truly managed. Similar models stress the cyclical nature of project management. For example, monitoring and planning, in

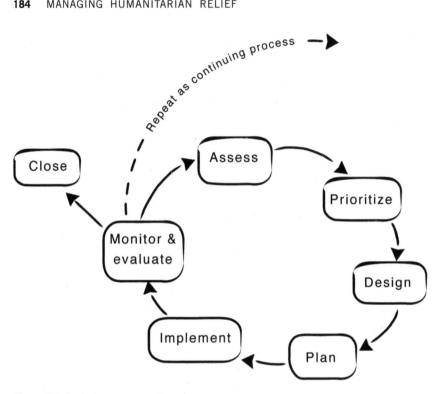

Figure 9.1 Project management cycle

particular, need to occur throughout the cycle if a project is to be effective. Resources not shown in the cycle are also needed at different parts of the cycle, especially if funding is used in the assessing, implementing and evaluating stages.

Because different parts of the project cycle will be encountered at different periods during running an emergency programme, different parts of the project cycle are discussed in depth in different chapters of this book. These are:

Assess Covered in Chapter 4, assessing involves understanding the situation at a basic level using different approaches and tools.

Prioritize Discussed in the section on the decision to launch an emergency programme (see pp. 117–21), prioritizing involves deciding what is most important on a variety of levels and how a project can be accomplished with constraints and resources.

Design In this chapter, determining the course of action, setting goals and objectives and designing project activities are covered.

Plan Also in this chapter, tools and methods for planning and managing projects are presented.

Implement In Chapter 2, the breadth of humanitarian activities is presented.

Monitor and evaluate Controlling and ensuring the progress of a project are covered in Chapter 19.

Close Chapter 21 covers exit strategies and other factors in closing an emergency programme.

Project design

Careful consideration needs to be given to developing a concept before anything is written in a concept or proposal format. The aim is to present (or package) these documents in a way that can be quickly and coherently understood by the various stakeholders who will read them.

Because international development is not a science, there is no single or correct way to successfully conceive, package and implement a project. At the same time, it is also necessary to adhere to certain norms and standards. On the most basic level, every project undertaken should follow a thematic structure which is based on a clearly defined goal, objectives and activities. These terms can be defined as:

- **Goal** The overarching, broad and long-term purpose of the project. This might include alleviating suffering, improving wellbeing or facilitating peaceful coexistence. The term 'goal' is identical to and often used interchangeably with terms like 'overall or wider aim'.
- **Objective** The specific and targeted purpose of the project. Objectives must clearly articulate the key purposes of the project because they say what the project is trying to achieve. A concept or proposal, and thus a project itself, cannot be considered to be good or strong without clearly defined objectives. How to develop effective objectives is discussed further below. 'Objective' is identical to and often used interchangeably with 'immediate or specific objectives' or 'purpose'.
- **Activity** The actual work to be undertaken (or implemented) to achieve the objectives. Examples include training social workers, rehabilitating day-care centres, developing curricula, disseminating health information and organizing a two-day conference on the community's sensitization. Everyone knows what activities are, but it is critically important to remember that activities are not the purpose of the project, but simply the way to reach our objectives. 'Activities' are often used interchangeably with 'inputs'.

Figure 9.2 is an example of what might be a typical health project. It is best to make the elements fit as tightly together as possible. In other words, the internal logic must be solid and all the parts of the project should be connected into a coherent whole. This example shows that activities reasonably contribute to achieving the objectives and the objectives support the goal. The goal can also be easily shaped into a project title.

The example in Figure 9.2 may be a somewhat simplified project an NGO might implement, but it organizes the project in a coherent way that lends itself to be quickly and easily understood, its internal logic can be checked and it creates a path to straightforward and effective monitoring and evaluation.

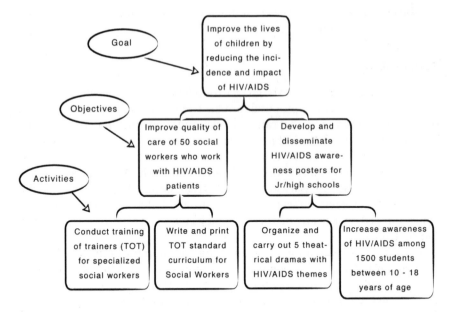

Figure 9.2 Goal, objectives and activities

Indicators

Once the goal, objectives and activities have been established, indicators are needed to show the progress of the project. Although indicators do not prove that the project is successful, if carefully used they can be evidence. The key is to have objectively verifiable ways to measure activities in line with the objectives and goals of the project. ('Objectively verifiable' means that project management tools such as attendance lists, reports, statistics, observation and surveys can be used to confirm indicators.)

There are different types of indicators and different organizations look at them differently. Some look at projects as containing inputs (such as financial and human resources), outputs (the tangible elements of a project), outcomes (the result of the project) and impacts (what has changed). These are presented in Table 9.1.

Others distinguish between process indicators which show whether and how the activities of a project are carried out, and impact indicators which show progress towards objectives. Quantitative indicators, using numbers, and qualitative indicators, using comparisons, can also be used. Several public health examples are shown in Table 9.2.

As may be apparent from Table 9.2, qualitative indicators are more difficult to demonstrate. This may be further complicated when concepts such as participation and wellbeing are part of the indicator. In those cases, pre- and post-tests or surveys may be needed. Proxy indicators, which assess changes that cannot be directly measured, may need to be substituted for direct impact.

Table 9.1 Indicators

Point of measurement	What is measured	Indicator	Example: high prevalence of waterborne disease
Output	Effort	Implementation of activities	Number of wells dug or rehabilitated Number of health education classes carried out
Outcome	Effectiveness	Use of output and production of benefits	Sustained availability of clean water with proper efficient domestic use
Impact	Change	Difference from original situation (baseline)	Reduction of morbidity and mortality

Source: Adapted from Fowler (1997: 164).

Table 9.2 Quantitative and qualitative indicators

	Process	Impact
Quantitative	20 nurses trained	Reduction of children's morbidity and mortality by 25%
Qualitative	Nurses learned how to care for children with acute malnutrition better	Parents and children gain confidence in nurses' ability to look after malnourished children

Different people will need different types of indicators. For project managers, process indicators help to demonstrate that activities are being accomplished, whereas donors will likely insist on impact indicators to show that the objectives they have given support for are being achieved. In designing projects, process indicators should be used sparingly or not at all because they do not demonstrate a positive effect on suffering, protection from abuse and mitigation of disasters.

When developing a strategy in project design, there should be a logical progression and linkage between projects. Interim indicators, or benchmarks, can be used to measure the progression of a project. Aside from the issues of linking relief and development discussed in Chapter 1, typical project design follows a phased approach. Examples of nutrition, education, health and water activities are provided in Table 9.3.

Depending on the emergency itself, the phases shown in Table 9.3 may happen over a period of weeks or months or longer. It is also common for emergency-type activities (such as those in phase 1) to take place in one part of a country while development-type activities (phase 3) to take place in another. In most cases, activities such as distribution should be carried out concurrently with encouraging behaviour that promotes the wellbeing of the beneficiaries

Table 9.3 Programme phases

Phase 1	Phase 2	Phase 3
Therapeutic feeding Centres	Supplementary feeding Programmes	Agriculture extension activities
Distribution of school supplies in camps	Rehabilitation of schools	Training of teachers and updating of curricula
Mobile health clinics	Rehabilitation of clinics	Training of health workers and supplies distribution
Distribution of water by filling water bladders and tanks	Digging of new and repair of existing wells	Hygiene promotion and repair of water systems

such as better hygiene or eating the right diet (balanced meals). While it may not be possible, from a funding, security or programmatic point of view, to launch or maintain all phases together or in congruence with each other, there should be considered thought during the project design stage of how goals and objectives can be met over time, combined with the appropriate activities.

Planning and management tools

Planning can happen in several ways and at different levels. Strategic planning involves all aspects of an emergency or country programme, often combining programme concerns and programme support issues. Programme planning looks at groups of projects, while project planning looks at the smallest detail. All levels of detail should look at impacts and coordination with stakeholders and others active in the area. The tools discussed here can be used at any level.

There are many different methods for planning and managing projects. Theoretically, in emergencies there are two ways to plan, depending on what information is available. In front-to-back planning, the dependent variable is known. For example, there are roughly 2,000 displaced persons in five areas, therefore plans should be made for 10,000 people. Second, back to front, the independent viable is known. For example, there are an estimated 10,000 people displaced; if there are five areas, each will consist of roughly 2,000 people. Plans for activities, budgets and logistics can be thought of in the same way.

In a more practical way, much of planning can be managed by using lists, project-specific calendars and, for coordination and control, memos. Dry-erase whiteboards are especially useful for developing and sharing ideas as well as just keeping on top of things. Several of the most common planning tools used by NGOs are presented below.

Logical framework analysis

During the design and planning stages of project cycle management, some find logical framework analysis (logframes) very useful. The idea for logframes originated in the 1960s as a result of using scientific approaches to management, including management by objectives. By the 1970s, USAID had adopted it as a tool and it has become increasingly used in the last couple of decades. Inclusion of a logframe, or a variation of the matrix, as part of a project proposal is a requirement of some donors.

Logframes are meant to be used at the initial design stage of project cycle management. It is especially useful in checking how project activities (typically labelled outputs) will support and help achieve a project's objectives (outcomes) and ultimately the project goal itself. As such, it can be used to test the logic of a project and helps identify implications and indicators before a project is launched. As a tool, however, it has a wider application, including during the monitoring and evaluation phases of a project.

A logframe presents the elements of a project in a matrix. There are different versions or modifications, but the classic logframe is typically shown, as in Table 9.4, in an abridged public health example.

To check the logic of the logframe, 'if...then....' statements can be used going from bottom to top. In the example in Table 9.4, 'If grant funds are awarded,

Table 9.4 Logframe

Project structure	Indicators	Means of verification	Assumptions
Goal (aim)	Percentage of total population to have access to high-quality PHC by end of project	Baseline and post-activity surveys	Stable political and security situation
Reduced morbidity and mortality among community members			
Objectives (outcome)	Number of community health workers proficient in new skills	Supervision records and site visits	MOU signed with Ministry of Health
Strengthen capacity of community structures to deliver PHC			
Output (activities)	Improved understanding of PHC among community health workers	Progress reports and training examinations of training participants	Good cooperation of community health workers
Training of health workers and skills upgrades			
Input	Grant award and community contribution	Documentation of grant award and contribution	Outside funding delivered on time
Grant funds			

then community health workers can receive training. If community health workers are trained, then the health system will be strengthened. If the health system is strengthened, then the morbidity and mortality of community members should drop.' Nothing is guaranteed, of course, so realistic thought should be given to the assumptions, those situations or events that may hinder any part of the project.

As may be apparent, logframes have drawbacks. First, as it was designed for engineering projects, complex problems must be expressed in simple phrases and in linear fashion. Second, logframes are needs-focused rather than focused on existing assets found within a group of beneficiaries. Third, they stress quantifiable outputs rather than qualitative outcomes. Finally, the logframe structure tends to make it rigid and not particularly flexible in the face of change or new needs.

Objectives-oriented project planning

Often known in its German translation, *Zielorientierte Projekplanung* (ZOPP), this approach analyses a project using a series of stakeholder workshops to set priorities within a planning matrix, similar to a logframe, as its main output. In the workshops, problems are examined, looking at objectives, options and assumptions, and weighing the different interests and expectations of each stakeholder. The planning workshops consist of the following steps.

- Report and analysis of past programme activities
- Creating a vision: defining overall and programme goals
- Who will be involved: stakeholder analysis
- Creating scenarios: assumptions analysis
- Who can we deal with the constraints: problem and solution analysis
- What to do: Defining outputs and activities
- How do we know about success: Defining indicators

During the workshop visual methods are used such as paper cards, pin-boards and flip charts. The material produced in the different steps is continuously updated and used as an information base for the subsequent steps until the participants find the results acceptable.

Action planning

Action planning is little more than putting on paper what is discussed in meetings or written in proposals. In a sense, any meeting that does not have an action plan as an output – even if it is merely jotted in personal notebooks – is a social gathering and not a productive meeting. Although some may feel that this and other tools are too simplistic, this tool can make difficult tasks achievable. The genius of action planning is found in that it provides a time limit and specifically names a person who can be held accountable when a task is or is not completed. For this reason, developing an action plan in a staff meeting can be intimidating for staff who are not especially proactive or tend not to follow through.

Developing an action plan is a straightforward task. The key point is to make it as realistic and specific as possible. The tasks should be clearly spelled out, the due date a specific date (as opposed to a general period of time such as a month) and the name of the person responsible should appear in the action plan, to help keep up accountability, as seen in the example in Table 9.5.

Timeline (Gantt charts)

An effective and simple way of planning the time needed to carry out projects is to create a timeline. Originating from business production scheduling of the late 1800s, Henry Gantt created a matrix that became known as the Gantt chart, as a way to show how projects progress over time. The basic example in Table 9.6 is for a six-month school rehabilitation project.

Table 9.5 Project action plan

Objective/task	Expected output	Staff responsible	Due date	Comment
Project launch meeting	Meeting agenda and minutes	Sarah, Project Manager	3 December	Meeting postponed until 10 December
Procurement of shelter kits	Delivery note (waybill) of requested building items	Jamal, Logistics Manager	20 December	Funding liquidity may cause delay

Table 9.6 Project timeline

Task/Month	January	February	March	April	May	June
Recruitment of staff	▓					
Staff orientation	▓					
Sub-contracting bidding process	▓					
Procurement of supplies	▓	▓				
Coordination with school board and Ministry of Education	▓					
School site cleaning and preparation	▓	▓				
Repair of exteriors including roof		▓	▓			
Repair of interior including electrical and plumbing works			▓	▓		
Painting				▓	▓	
Emplacement of new windows/doors					▓	
Signing over ceremony						▓
Formal monitoring and reporting			▓			▓

One of the most overlooked points to remember when planning a project – and thus creating a Gantt chart – is to factor in adequate time for establishing the project at the initial phases, including tasks such as bringing new staff on board and procurement, and the final phases such as final touch-ups and verification trips to ensure that all the work has been completed.

In the example in Table 9.6, preparation and follow-up are major time consumers. The actual school rehabilitation, the meat of the project, will only take a couple of months, but the complete project is estimated to take a whole six months. Unless the staff have worked together for a considerable period (and hence their capacities and limitations are well known), the amount of time needed to complete relatively simple tasks must be generous. Also important is that all project-related activities should be completed within the time first proposed to a donor.

Other tools of this sort exist, building on the basic idea of the Gantt chart, including the Critical Path Method (CPM) and the Programme Evaluation and Review Technique (PERT), which focus on potential tasks or activities that might hold up a project. However, as these tools were created for production and other complex business activities, they are too complicated and time-consuming for use by NGOs in emergency programmes.

There are a number of software packages that help manage projects. Probably the most ubiquitous and thus compatible is Microsoft's *Project*. Microsoft's *Visio* is a diagramming programme, enabling novices to draw floor plans and other pictures, but also has project management tools, so it can be especially useful.

Contingency planning

When situations are unclear, contingency planning, where plans are developed for probable specific situations, may be needed. Contingency planning is necessary in situations where rapid change is expected. It is based on assumptions, prioritization and preparedness to suit the most likely scenarios. Table 9.7 shows a five-step process and relevant issues to consider. A written plan should be developed outlining different contingencies and likely scenarios. The plan should discuss different hazards, likely triggers, potential beneficiaries and programme strategy, including the basics of potential programmes as well as logistics, HRM and budgets. Consider emergency indicators (see p. 5) and issues relating to disaster preparedness (pp. 86–7). Coordination should also be carried out with other organizations. Perhaps the most challenging issue will be mobilizing resources, especially if there is already difficulty meeting basic needs.

Project launch

Many NGOs find it helpful to hold a formal meeting soon after the signing of any grant agreement and before any activities start under the project. The purpose of such a meeting is to: inform all relevant staff about the goals, objectives,

Table 9.7 Steps in contingency planning

1	2	3	4	5
Analysis of hazards and risks	Contingency prioritization	Scenario building	Preparation of contingency plan	Preparedness actions and plan updating
What hazards and risk exist?	According to analysis what risks and hazards should be planned for?	How might the selected contingencies affect the humanitarian situation?	What is needed to respond in case the scenario occurs?	What actions need to be taken as the situation changes and how will the plan change?
Natural disaster	Drought	Worst case	Massive programme needed	Improved drought conditions, famine less than expected
Violent conflict	Border conflict	Probable case	Sector and project size needed	Negotiated settlement reached and border conflict less likely
		Optimistic case	Specific actions	

Source: WFP (2002: 13).

activities and resources of a specific upcoming project and plan and strategize to ensure the project has every chance of success. Typically, all project-related and supporting staff (according to the organizational chart) should be present, in other words, management, finance and operations as well as direct programme staff. To successfully carry out a project launch, prepare and hand out an agenda of the meeting, which can form part of the invitation to outside stakeholders (if invited). An appropriate meeting space will be needed with flip charts and paper, refreshments and a facilitator/planner and minutes/note taker. The agenda may look something like this.

1. **Introduction: the meeting's purpose and agenda** It is important to start the meeting right. This serves to clarify the purpose and provides an opportunity to give a brief background and set forth the vision for the new project. The meeting facilitator and the senior staff member present may share this responsibility. Participants should also be informed about break times and the opportunity for refreshment, safety issues and the location of toilets facilities. An ice-breaker or warm-up activity sets the tone of the meeting and helps staff to get to know each other (see Chapter 16). If the meeting is long, additional energizers or team-building activities will be needed during the meeting.

2. **Presentation of the project** The project manager, or equivalent, should thoroughly present the goal, objectives and activities of the new project and put them into context. New terms and acronyms should be carefully explained. In some instances, a new type of project will have ramifications for both programme and programme support staff. To foster understanding among the staff, an element of project-specific capacity building is helpful. In some cases, an outside expert such as a UN or donor technical expert may be invited to present this element of the launch meeting (this can also help the donor feel confident the project is getting off to the right start). A display of project hardware such as seeds or tools, recreational equipment and computer software is also a good idea.

3. **Presentation of new staff and changes to the organizational chart** If new staff are present, they should be introduced and welcomed. Their role and responsibilities should be clearly explained. If it has not been done yet as part of the staff members' induction, existing staff present should present themselves and say what role they fill. Both the old and new organizational chart should be available to show how the new project will affect the other projects and activities.

4. **Discussion of timelines** Staff need to know how the project is going to progress from one phase to the next. In-depth discussion of activities may be needed. Holidays, days off and seasonal or climatic concerns should be taken into account. A Gantt chart might be the output for this agenda item or (to save time) prepared beforehand for discussion and modification. This time can also be used for other programme-related action planning.

5. **Presentation of budget, procurement and other logistical arrangements** Key support staff such as the finance manager and logistician, or their equivalents, should discuss financial, procurement and logistical arrangements and give their point of view. A modified budget may be prepared for sharing with all staff. The support staff may wish to raise questions about lessons learned and/or reiterate policies and procedures. If needed to better implement the new project, changes to these policies and procedures may be raised, but should be tabled to a working group so as not to sidetrack the meeting's purpose.

6. **Capacity-building session** Staff may need bolstering of specific skills which will make them more efficient in their work. Bringing them together in this type of forum is an opportunity that should be capitalized on. For these reasons, some capacity-building element, such as radio communications, policies and procedures or community interaction skills, is useful.

7. **Conclusion** The meeting should end on a good note and staff should feel motivated and empowered. A recap of what has been discussed should be done while highlighting the path forward. If the timeline and action plan and other information are felt to be insufficient, an

additional immediate action plan should be drawn up so that staff walk away knowing exactly what to do.

Narrative reporting

Reporting is not complicated but many people find it either intimidating or drudge work. Senior managers should try to ease the process by providing realistic expectations, examples and formats and, if needed, training.

To help streamline and provide uniform reporting (important when compiling reports at a later date), many NGOs find it helpful to have written guidelines to be used for reporting, unless a particular donor specifies different requirements. The guidelines should outline or include who should write the report, who should edit it and who should submit it – if they are different staff. The guidelines should also provide a standard deadline (e.g. the last working day of every month), expected length, types of information to be included and whether the report should be turned in as either hard copy or an electronic soft copy. A simple format may look like Box 9.1.

NGOs often have staff of different backgrounds (i.e. different language abilities, professional backgrounds with different types of reporting, and different educational levels) which can make the task of reporting a challenge. Staff responsible for writing reports should know, preferably in writing, what is expected in terms of style and grammar. Typically, the English used in reports should be formal and of a report standard (e.g. active language, short sentences, concise paragraphs and logical flow). Staff with good writing skills should set aside to time to review and edit reports, and if there is time, pass their skills on to others.

Holding meetings

As much as some people dislike them, meetings are an essential part of managing anything involving more than one person. For individual issues, people can meet one on one but anything that involves information sharing, decision making or consensus building will require some form of meeting. There are many types of team meetings, focus groups (focusing on specific issues, people know the issue and do not really need a leader), progress meetings, one-on-one meetings, reporting and information sharing meetings and meetings for decision-making. For NGOs, meetings are typically are based on one of the following:

- Sector or project team
- Senior management staff
- Staff

Coordination meetings are also important, but they are discussed in Chapter 20.

Box 9.1 Activity Report

NGO XYZ

Monthly Report for XXX project

Prepared by:

Date submitted:

I. Summary

Summarizing what is written in the rest of the report, this section should normally be no longer than several paragraphs, in which project highlights are clearly noted.

II. Results by objective

This is the body of the proposal. This section is best arranged according to, and following the same order as, the objectives spelled out in the project proposal. It should clearly and concisely explain what has been achieved in the reporting period. This section is weakened if non-result-focused activities such as meetings, travel and reports are discussed, unless they are a specific element of meeting the project's objectives. To the greatest extent possible, there should be quantifiable information. Ideally, there should be a table, as shown in Table 9.8, that is backed up by qualitative information, including a success story or two.

Table 9.8 Results

Expected result	Progress to date	Percentage achieved
30 water points rehabbed or constructed	15 water points rendered functional	50
100 trainers trained	75 trainers trained	75

III. Major constraints

The aim of this section is to objectively identify genuine obstacles, normally external, that presented themselves during the reporting period, as a record and creating a means for the issues to be addressed. As such, this section should not disparage or blame others. Examples of constraints may include insecurity, inclement weather, difficulty in recruiting qualified staff, poor road conditions and the unavailability of logistical supplies.

IV. Future plans

A brief paragraph or two about what can be expected in the future reporting period, such as aspects of new or expanded project phases or the project's closure.

There are several strategies for making meetings effective, such as organizing the meeting, holding the meeting in different locations or while standing. In the context of working in developing countries, it is important to consider local norms and traditions. In many countries, etiquette and protocol are critical and meetings that do not conform to these often unstated customs may have little weight. If, for example, the substance of meetings do not start until after a drink, prayer or lengthy salutations, skipping those steps may cause offence.

Box 9.2 Six meeting stoppers

1. **Hogging:** one person, or a small group of people, dominating the meeting by talking too much.
2. **Bogging:** too much focus on a single issue.
3. **Fogging:** being vague or talking about one topic to avoid another.
4. **Frogging:** leaping from one topic to another without a firm conclusion.
5. **Flogging:** not recognizing someone's contribution or attacking them.
6. **Clogging:** Adding more items without accomplishing agreed action points.

Source: Bounds and Woods (1998: 89–90).

There may also be cultural differences that may surface during meetings. Holding general staff meetings in some countries gives 'power to the masses', where pressure can be put on managers for previously unstated grievances (e.g. holiday bonuses). In this way, staff members may feel that if they mention the issue as a group they can leverage a decision that is favourable to them. To give direction to meetings, try the following:

- Let people know about the meeting well in advance and do not be shy in giving reminders. Although genuine emergency meetings arise, if people find out about a meeting two minutes before it starts, they will unlikely to be physically or mentally prepared.
- Prepare an agenda, either given as hand-outs before or at the start of meetings or write it on a white/blackboard (or similar medium).
- During the meeting, establish ground rules and outline objectives. Although there should be room for flexibility, the agenda should be followed as much as possible.
- Make some record or document of the decision and action items (see 'Action planning' above, pp. 190–91).
- If the meeting is formal, make sure that the minutes (or equivalent record) are distributed to all invitees, not just those who attended the meeting.

Basic problem solving

Many people become good problem solvers without conscious effort. But in groups or unique situations, such as humanitarian emergencies, having tools and techniques can be helpful. Many traditional problem-solving approaches are based on the ideas of the German philosopher Georg Hegel, who described a three-stage process of logic – thesis, antithesis and synthesis. More recently, Edward de Bono (2000) has promoted a variety of methods and tools that release creative thinking, including the idea of lateral thinking.

Here, a number of different tools are briefly presented in increasing levels of complexity. Any analysis of problems must be tempered by commonsense and avoiding ineffective approaches such as overreacting, running around putting out fires, blaming others and denying there is a problem in the first place. All these have serious downsides and is the result of poor management. Effective approaches to problem solving involving groups include:

- **Brainstorming** Ordinary brainstorming is rarely effective in emergency situations where staff come from vastly different backgrounds (especially local and international staff) and usually do not know each other well. Typically, dominant personalities will lead the discussion and others will refrain from saying what is on their minds. Variations of brainstorming such as pro-con lists or force field analysis (where supporting and detracting elements are identified) may work where small groups present their findings to larger groups.
- **Research** Specific staff can be assigned to carry out assessments, such as questionnaires, conducting interviews and holding workshops with stakeholders.
- **Cause-and-effect diagrams** While there are several ways to examine cause and effect, a great way is promoted by Werner and Bower (1982). This method looks at the effect and then traces the causes, using symbolic links in a chain. For example, a child's health condition can be traced back to root causes of inequity and marginalization.
- **Nominal-group technique** This involves getting individual opinions in a group setting (thus the name nominal, as a group consensus is not sought). The full approach has group members write down their individual ideas, which are then shared among the group and recorded on a flip chart (or equivalent), after which questions can be asked about clarity, but without substantive discussion. Individuals then award points anonymously to the most convincing solution. The session ends with discussion and action planning.
- **Delphi technique** Using questionnaires, staff are asked to identify solutions to given problems. The results of the questionnaires are shared with staff and they are asked to complete a new questionnaire. Again, the results are reviewed and staff are asked to provide additional information, until consensus is reached. However, this technique is open to manipulation by the facilitator (sometimes called 'facipilation').
- **'Six thinking hats'** Created by Edward de Bono (2000), this technique uses six different perspectives (symbolized by different-coloured hats) to understand the implications and consequences of different decisions. The problems can be addressed using a mixture of angles rather than simply the most rational viewpoint. The six coloured hats are:
  Blue: used by the facilitator, who keeps the group moving, prevents criticism and stops switching styles (hats)
  Yellow: looks at benefits and thinks positively
  White: uses available data to fill knowledge gaps or take them into account
  Green: depends on creativity and free thinking
  Red: based on reaction, emotion and intuition
  Black: looks at bad points and thinks cautiously

CHAPTER 10
Dealing with stress

Because of the adverse consequences of stress and personal conflict, relief workers should be familiar with what stress they may encounter and what to do about it. This chapter covers:
- Understanding stress
- Managing stress
- Conflict resolution between individuals
- Working in different cultures

Stress is an everyday occurrence (IFRC, 2001). It can prepare an individual for a challenging situation and thus it often has motivating and creative power. But excessive levels of stress can be harmful. Unfortunately, humanitarian workers are exposed to high amounts of potentially dangerous stress. Living in difficult conditions can have an accumulative toll, including fatigue and physiological changes. The experience of traumatic events, such as being shot at and witnessing children or co-workers die, can cause psychological reactions. For this reason, understanding and dealing with different types of stress are critical to running an emergency programme.

The problem of stress in emergency programmes is large enough to warrant considerable attention by NGOs and research organizations. A 1998 WHO study found that about half of relief workers surveyed felt they were unable to function well on the day they were interviewed. Of the same group roughly 60 per cent reported general fatigue, while one-half of those interviewed had frequent headaches. Sleeping difficulties, irritability and anger were also common.

Understanding stress

Stress is an evolutionary development found in all animals, an individual's response to arousal or stimulus in their environment. When someone encounters a real or imagined threat or difficult situation, (pre-)historically they were presented with two choices, to confront the challenge (i.e. fight) or to run away (i.e. flee). During an unexpected sight of a large dangerous animal, for example, our ancestors' hearts would have begun to beat fast and their mouths would become dry, while their sense of awareness and physical abilities would temporarily improve, as shown in Figure 10.1. At first, a person's reaction to stress helps them to improve their performance, but over time, being human, a person's performance decreases. Today, although we perceive our world to be more complex, we are faced with a similar choice and our bodies react in essentially the same way.

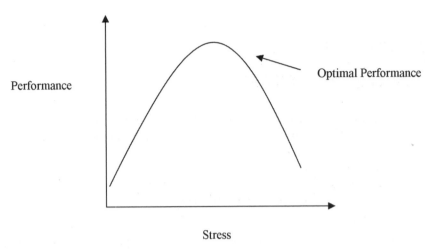

Figure 10.1 Stress and performance
Source: Armstrong (2004: 179).

Traumatic stress may result from sudden or unexpected events which may be life-threatening or represent a dramatic change in a person's life. Over time, cumulative stress may build up if the same threat or environment is encountered.

Causes of stress

In many work environments, stress is produced by a number of factors, such as deadlines, job uncertainty or a feeling of being undervalued, having demanding bosses and difficult colleagues. For relief workers, there are additional stresses associated with dealing with living in hard environments, being apart from family and friends and, sometimes, encountering acute poverty and the effects of disasters and physical violence. There may be acute incidents of stress, but it is equally common to experience ongoing stress that whose effects accumulate. As with all aspects of life, individuals have different thresholds of stress they are able to handle and they may cope in different ways based on their prior experiences, personality and culture.

Stress can originate on several different levels and from a wide range of causes. Examples include:

- **Individual** including self-imposed or unrealistic expectations, feeling of powerlessness, excessive workload, family separation and family pressures.
- **Group** other staff and team members, travel difficulties (including culture shock), poor living conditions, inadequate communications and a high number of vehicle or other accidents.
- **External to the group** for example, the political or humanitarian situation and a difficult environment including physical (insecurity) and emotional threats.

Types of stress

Stress that has a negative impact can be classified into two types: traumatic and cumulative.

Traumatic stress

Traumatic stress follows a life-threatening or near-death event. Acute stress can occur immediately following a traumatic event and can last a few hours or days. People handle this level of stress differently; some people may show few outward signs until well after the event.

Post-traumatic stress disorder (PTSD) can occur months or even years after an event. PTSD is a psychiatric diagnosis that applies to people who have experienced a specific, extraordinarily traumatic event such as a life-threatening experience (or especially repeated exposure to such), being assaulted or held hostage, the death of someone close or witnessing multiple deaths. There are three primary symptoms: nightmares and flashbacks; psychological problems, like jittery nerves and sleeping difficulties; avoidance, where a person withdraws from relationships or becomes emotionally numb.

Cumulative stress

Events like divorce or job loss can cause emotional distress, may speed up ageing and lead to greater health problems. For a relief worker, stresses may come from losing fellow team-mates, being in the presence of the wounded or sick and handling dead bodies. Cumulative stress may come from prolonged exposure to bad weather without modern conveniences, travel difficulties, excessive amounts of work with few breaks or outlets, and living in a chronically violent place. A feeling of powerlessness to change situations in disasters can also be highly stressful for people who have dedicated themselves to helping others. Organizational problems, such as poor communication or lack of resources, also contribute to staff stress.

Research has linked chronic psychological stress to a weakened immune function and thus an increased risk of catching colds and other illnesses. There is little precise information, as medical researchers are trying to understand how stress or tension damages or weakens tissue, leading to ageing. According to the ICRC, during emergencies a type of cumulative stress can develop that may lead to burn-out. This physical or emotional exhaustion commonly affects relief workers resulting from stress of work and living conditions. The symptoms include emotional exhaustion, a diminished sense of personal accomplishment, cynicism and a feeling of drudgery about work that was previously found rewarding.

Managing stress

Once the stress has been identified, the question is what a relief worker or manager should do. Here three possible steps are briefly outlined.

Step 1 Selection and deployment of staff

Forming a successful team through effective recruitment probably has the greatest impact on how stressful situations will be handled in the field. Resilient staff members are more likely to adapt to deteriorating situations and, in times of traumatic stress, be more likely to maintain balance and perspective. This balance and perspective help the individual to focus on the danger at hand and thus serves as a survival mechanism. While nearly everyone can be greatly affected by traumatic events, certain personalities are quicker to return to a normal (pre-stress) level and these people are more likely to have a positive impact on those around them.

Not that all stress can be avoided or handled by good staff, but NGOs that have resilient and effective staff prevent many of the causes of staff stress before they occur. Understanding a potential staff member's motivation, personality and range of experiences is critical to this process. When doing recruitment selection, mental toughness, flexibility and the ability to bounce back from stressful situations should be identified in each candidate. This resiliency comes from a person's experience and development. According to Henderson (2007), these characteristics typically determine resiliency and reduce stress:

Relationships the ability to be a friend and to form positive relationships
Humour having a good sense of humour
Inner direction bases choices and decisions on internal evaluation (internal locus of control)
Perceptiveness insightful understanding of people and situations
Independence adaptive distancing from unhealthy (negative, harmful or destructive) people and situations
Positive view of personal future optimism
Flexibility can adjust to change; can bend as necessary to positively cope with situations
Love of learning capacity for and connection to learning
Self-motivation internal initiative and positive motivation from within
Competence is good at things, good at their job
Self-worth feelings of self-worth and self-confidence
Spirituality personal faith in something greater
Perseverance keeps on despite difficulty, does not give up
Creativity expresses self through artistic endeavour

Once staff are selected, how they are sent to the field is equally critical. In keeping with good HR management practice, staff should receive a thorough briefing, including documents and information to help them prepare for their posting. Chapter 8 on HRM discusses how to go about this in more detail.

Step 2 Diagnosis

Part of managing stress consists of evaluating the situation in which people live and work. The signs and symptoms of stress will depend on the situation and the individual, but general indicators include:

Emotional General or unexplained fatigue, sleep disturbance including insomnia, flashbacks or intrusive recollections, changeable moods, hyper-vigilance, easy startling, poor concentration, anxiety and depression, psychosomatic symptoms (especially headaches, body pains, dizziness and heart palpitations).

Behavioural Changed behaviour is important, not necessarily the behaviour itself. Increased or sometimes decreased alcohol or drug consumption, increased expressions of abusive statements (e.g. racist, sexist), increased involvement in or sanctioning of incidents involving personal or sexual violence, increased complaints of minor health problems, self-neglect, inappropriate sexual behaviour and over-reacting, especially to small issues.

Work-specific Depending on normal behaviour and past performance, lack of punctuality, days off sick, inconsistent reporting, arbitrary and unpredictable decision making and general decline in work standards or output.

For diagnosing serious cases, professional advice should be sought.

Step 3 Action

Managers need to be understanding about stress in their staff because stress is an inherent part of working in emergencies. Once it is understood as a normal reaction, stress should be monitored. Generally, managing stress may include understanding signs and symptoms, taking preventive steps and possible measures to take in response. Specific actions are listed in Table 10.1.

Obviously, some of these measures are easier said than done. A characteristic of good managers is how they deal with stress in themselves as well as others. In difficult situations, a good manager will dig deeper inside himself or herself and set an example for others; conversely a not-so-good manager displays negative behaviour in the same way as those under stress.

Debriefing and defusing a critical incident

Following a traumatic event, it may be helpful to hold a meeting with staff to discuss what has happened, in order to understand and review it. Research has shown that those who decline to participate in such briefings suffer greater long-term problems than those who do. Important considerations include the following:

- A trained specialist should facilitate debriefing or defusing sessions. However, because it is best to hold the session within 24–72 hours, the task may fall to the senior manager in the field. Talk privately with each individual staff member after the incident and ask about the events and what

Table 10.1 Stress management

Stress symptom	Signs and symptoms	Possible preventative steps	Possible measures
Emotional	Fatigue and sleeplessness	Ensure staff work appropriate hours (e.g. do not routinely skip meals) and take scheduled breaks including holiday/R&R	Fast recognition and appropriate responses (e.g. debriefing and professional counselling) to incidents
	Flashbacks	Ensure access to different means of relaxation such as a break room, watching movies, physical exercise and other normal activities	Allow time for re-establishment of personal and professional relationships
	Changeable moods and/or appetite	Create clear plans for emergencies (e.g. following violent incidents and medical problems) and communicate them to staff	
	Hyper-vigilance		
	Easy startling		
	Poor concentration		
	Anxiety and depression		
	Psychosomatic symptoms		
Behaviour	Increased or sometimes decreased alcohol/drug consumption	Brief and train staff to understand stress and ways to deal with its consequences, including awareness of post-incident follow-up measures	Allow for appropriate medical/psychological treatment as needed
	Increasing abusive statements	Ensure that each staff member is fully aware of expectations and parameters governing personal behaviour	Remind staff of Code of Conduct and other ethical standards of behaviour
	Lack of interest or social withdrawal	Engage staff in team-building activities and maintain a sense of humour	Depending on severity, consider referral of problem or transfer or dismissal of staff

	Increased complaints of minor health problems (e.g. neck, stomach or back pain)	Designate co-workers to monitor each others wellbeing	
	Self-neglect		
	Over-reacting especially to small issues (including being rude to others		
Work-specific	Lack of punctuality and too many sick days	Appropriate feedback and sharing information	Depending on the situation, informal or formal counselling
	Inconsistent reporting	Be an active listener	Review policies and management practices
	Arbitrary/unpredictable decision making	Encourage staff to share their concerns in a constructive way	
	Overall decline in work standards and output	Develop a clear a vision and communicate realistic expectations	
		Foster a team spirit among staff	

they feel would have been an appropriate management response, who they feel is most affected and what they would do to ensure safety. Mass meetings may cause mass panic if not handled well.

- Most people do not experience the effects until afterwards, or they experience the effects differently at different times, depending on the significance of the events to their personality and history.
- Staff morale will be negatively affected by having a debriefing meeting in 24 hours and then having management believe that the situation is finalized. Often responses and follow-up action need to be ongoing.
- If a mass debriefing meeting is decided as the best action at the time, the debriefing should have as an endpoint a section on advice from the group about what they would like to see in the way of change and a plan for follow up.

Conflict resolution between individuals

In an emergency, conflict between people can be a major cause of stress. This is unfortunate because it distracts from the task in hand. Conflict can be said to arise from any relationship that is asymmetrical or unequal. In practice, there are many causes of conflict between individuals which may be aggravated when stress levels are high. Within a team, conflict can arise from five different reasons:

1. Similar or overlapping objectives leading to competition, or needless duplication, which can be complicated by a lack of clarity about roles and responsibilities.
2. Tight living quarters or inadequate separation between duty and off-duty time (work-life balance).
3. Competition over resources such as vehicles or the attention (recognition) of others.
4. Personal differences relating from dissimilar views or idiosyncracies which can be based on political or moral positions, culture, gender or organizational position.
5. Communication problems leading to frustration, stress and sometimes a downward spiral leading towards conflict, for instance over problems like resource waste.

There are a number of ways to handle conflict between people. Successful managers will set constructive examples and frame issues (e.g. win-win) so that solutions can be found. Perhaps one of the best ways to handle conflict is to understand the roles people can adopt during a conflict and, based on these roles, adjust interaction. People may assume different roles based on their willingness to sacrifice their own interests and satisfy others. Five possible roles are shown in Figure 10.2.

It is important to understand how these five roles can be used by managers to help reduce conflict. For example, if staff members are in conflict about a values problem, a manager may want to adopt an 'accommodator' or 'collaborator' role, whereas if two staff are quibbling over a minor issue a manager may want to become an 'avoider'. These roles are summarized in the Table 10.2.

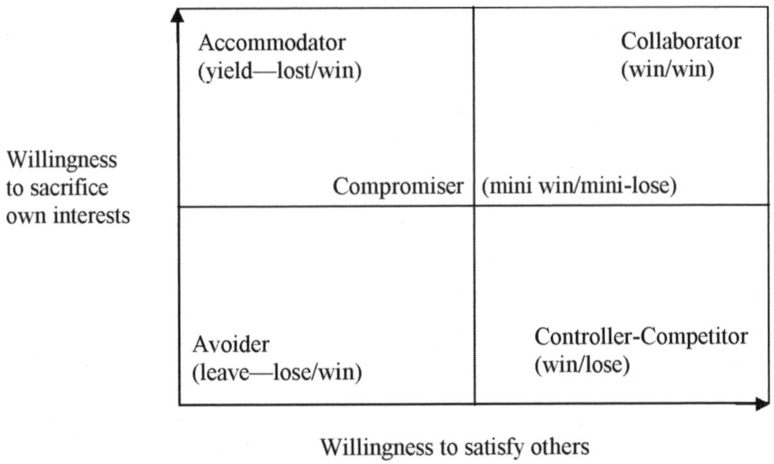

Figure 10.2 Conflict resolution positions
Source: Blake and Mouton (1968).

Table 10.2 Conflict resolution group roles

Uses	Advantages	Disadvantages
Accommodator (generous, neglects own concerns for concerns of others)	Useful when person realizes s/he is wrong	May cause discipline problems
	To show reasonableness	Sacrifices person's point of view
	When an issue is more important to the other person	Limits creative resolution
	When maintaining relationships are important	
	To build up social credits	
	To preserve harmony and avoid division	
Collaborator (win-win or problem-solving behaviour)	When both sets of concerns are too important to be compromised	Lengthy and time-consuming
	To learn by exploring the disagreement	High stress involved in developing trust between parties in conflict
	To work through hard feelings and re-establish interpersonal relationships	
Compromiser (giving up something, but not everything)	When competing behaviour disrupts personal relationships	Sets up climate for gamesmanship
	When other parties have equal power	Can lose sight of large issue due to concentration on strategies
	When person cannot win When the concerns of both parties are too important	Amounts to denial Temporary solution
	When others can better resolve the conflict	
	To achieve a temporary solution to a complex issue	
Avoider (sidestepping issues; doing nothing)	When issue is trivial	Restricts input on problem
	When more important issues are pressing	Decisions on important issues made default
	When no chance of winning	Solution is temporary
	Relieves tension	

cont.

cont.

Uses	Advantages	Disadvantages
	When others can better resolve the conflict	
	Postpones action to gather more information	
Controller-competitor (win-lose behaviour with power being the main prize)	Use when quick, decisive action is vital	Creation of 'yes' men and women
	Helpful with taking action against those who take advantage of non-competitive behaviour	Stops exploration of new approaches
		Damages personal relationships (goals are achieved at the expense of others)
		Temporary solution

Source: Thomas (1976).

Working in different cultures

Working with people from other cultures is a central part of responding to emergencies. For this reason, understanding culture shock is an important element of managing stress. Culture shock is a process of adapting to a new culture that involves a feeling of unease or nervousness. Although common for those outside their own countries, it can occur when people adjust to new environments (e.g. from urban to rural areas) within their own countries. While the symptoms vary from one person to another, culture shock often involves considerable levels of stress. Managers need to help people through their culture shock (and reaction to change and crisis) and intervene where staff are stuck in particular points in their adjustment.

Culture shock can be understood by imagining that there are two ways people encounter or experience a new culture. One is to be open to the new environment, while the other is to be closed. After the initial period of discovery, sometimes called the honeymoon phase, a period of stress follows when people try to adjust. Most people make simple adjustments and they continue to live and work normally. But some people react negatively by feeling or expressing excessive levels frustration, criticism, alienation and isolation from others. Here are some of the considerations.

- People who are open, respect others and find balance tend to do better in different cultures. Knowing more about an area and people (not directly related to work or the emergency) contributes to good adjustment.

- Cultural understanding is a two-way process. Sometimes dealing with stress and culture as a group is helpful. When appropriate, meet and discuss differences and decide on group values (e.g. respect for others, ground rules if needed). Managers should facilitate this.
- For relief workers, language can make even basic communication a challenge. Words may be understood but the meaning can be missed. For example, assuming that common language equals common understanding can lead to a mistakes and misunderstandings.
- Non-verbal communications can also be significantly different. Some examples such as hand gestures can be interesting to compare, but other examples (e.g. eye contact) may be more difficult to work out.
- Signs, symbols and colours which might be considered universally understood in one context may be poorly understood in other places. The colour red (e.g. found on dials and MUAC strips) may not mean 'caution' or 'warning' in certain countries. For this reason, the meaning of clothing or organizational logos should be investigated before the decision to launch a new emergency programme.
- Cultures differ in terms of their emphasis on personal relationships and context. Western culture, for example, tends to be more linear, individualistic and less hierarchical than some other cultures. Visiting expatriates might expect a procedure to be followed in sequence (e.g. A, B, C...) and then will help staff achieve the task. Such an approach may not work in a country where a different sequence (i.e. A, C, B...) is commonly followed and managers are expected to watch (i.e. not 'get their hands dirty').
- It is important to share information that may be considered sensitive, such as power, gender and taboos between staff. Staff living arrangements, socializing and staff behaviour can have meanings that should be investigated. Training and consensus building should include both national and international staff, in order to reach agreement and understanding.
- For some, re-entry shock, when they return to their indigenous culture, can be more challenging than their exposure to a new culture. For this reason, it is best not to assume that going home will be easy.

CHAPTER 11
Overseeing finance and accounting

A strong financial accounting system is an imperative. The purpose of this chapter is to provide enough grounding in finance and accounting to help manage an emergency programme. This chapter covers:
- An overview of NGO accounting
- Budgeting
- Getting funds in a disaster zone
- Petty cash
- Financial audit: a manager's tool

NGOs need to demonstrate accountability in an effective, efficient and transparent way. Without it, an NGO can face criticism, withdrawal of grants and ending of programmes. Because almost all NGOs have accounting policies and procedures, this chapter is written for non-financial specialists, managers who oversee accountants and work with budgets as well as staff who are called upon to account for petty cash.

Overview of NGO accounting

Every NGO has a responsibility to be accountable for its financial support. In fact, the level of detail required of NGOs is generally higher than in most businesses. Like the commercial sector, NGOs typically follow what are known as generally accepted accounting practices (GAAP). Included in this is budgeting, record-keeping, working with banks, accounting for expenses and general concepts such as revenue, credit and debt. There are five terms and concepts NGO managers need to be familiar with.

1. **Chart of accounts** A list of accounting codes, several letters and/ or numbers that cover a specific type of transaction, which classifies the transaction. Accounting codes correspond to specific budget line-items such as personnel, fuel, office supplies or rent. In addition to the budget, the chart of accounts also aligns with the cashbook which is a book or spreadsheet that lists all the transaction made for an individual account.

2. **Segregation of funds** To ensure accountability, different donor funds are normally separated by project. Separate cashbooks and bank accounts can help maintain fund segregation. When funds are taken from different budgets and used together, this is called co-mingling of funds and may be prohibited by donors. A challenge comes when certain expenditures are allocable to several different projects (such as

fuel usage or property rent). In this case, sound record-keeping and reconciliation, where information from two sets of records are compared and straightened out, are needed.

Internal controls A system of checks on a finance system to ensure accountability. Examples of controls include physical security measures, division of responsibility among staff, and review and authorization by senior staff.

Restricted funds These are funds that are dedicated for specific purposes or projects. Nearly all statutory donors provide restricted funds only. Private donors may provide funds openly, which then may be used for supporting the organization, or they may allocate funds to any programmes (see Chapter 7).

Direct and indirect costs Direct costs are allocable to specific budget line-items of a project. Most budgets have a line-item for indirect costs to cover expenditures that help support the project. In other words, an indirect cost is one that is not directly identifiable to any one final cost objective such as extra personnel, office support and contingencies that were not fully identified during the budget preparation. Indirect costs are sometimes called overheads, but that term's negative connotation is somewhat of a misnomer. While some donors understand that there are many costs that go into supporting a project, others are weary of indirect costs and see them as an extra slush fund or waste of funding. This difference is discussed further below.

Budgeting

Budgets are an estimated spending plan for a given period of time, project or activity. There are several types of budgets, such as capital, revenue, project or operating, although the exact definition may differ significantly from one organization or country to the next. For this reason, it is easier to think in terms of the different levels of an organization. At the HQ level, money donated to an NGO is usually allocated to a revenue budget. This budget usually covers a year or longer and supports all HQ expenses including public relations, salaries and other support costs. Many NGOs also use these funds to support capacity building and for responding to new emergencies. Because these funds rarely exceed 20 per cent of the NGOs total yearly revenue, and usually much less, emergency preparedness and expansion can be especially challenging.

At the country or field level, one or more project (or programme) budgets funded through donors are used to cover expenses. Some NGOs, especially the larger ones, will also have an operating budget that is generated from HQ using privately donated funds to support operations in the field that are not covered by project budgets. In many cases, the project and operating budgets will be prepared in the same way and appear to be similar; the only difference is their funding source. The remainder of this section will focus on these field-level budgets.

There are four elements to budgeting: planning, preparation, monitoring and reviewing.

Step 1 Planning

Planning involves thinking ahead in order to be prepared. Although planning is challenging in emergencies, budget planning should still be possible. At an organizational level, NGOs will prepare different budgets according to programme and operations (although these will have different names depending on the organization). At the field level, NGOs typically plan according to specific projects. In planning, programme, logistical and other costs will have to be realistically estimated. Standard lists of prices help this process, but in general planning and preparing budgets can be a time-consuming task. When multiple grants are being implemented, the budget gap analysis discussed below can be helpful.

Step 2 Preparation

The key to an effective budget is to estimate the costs as realistically as possible and to include every expense that can be legitimately allocable to the project. In practice, this can be a significant challenge, especially in emergency situations where change is difficult to plan for and the unexpected can occur, such as rapid inflation or the loss of resources. There are several methods for preparing a budget.

Top-down method Estimates the grant amount and is basically a planning limit. It is the fastest method, but can be the least accurate.

Estimate Provides a rough breakdown based on an estimate of past costs or a 'guesstimate' of expenditures.

Bottom-up or detailed budget estimate Details planned expenditures by category or item, supported by documents, including quotations and a narrative. This is a time-consuming method but is often required by donors.

If possible, use best estimates and averages based on previous experience and cost data collected from other organizations and potential service providers. It is best to obtain the donor's written guidelines or ask what costs are allowable and what will not be paid for.

Preparing budgets are aided by having a ready-made template. Budgets are made up of line-items that detail each category of planned expenditure. Figure 11.1 shows some of the many potential line-items to consider. Costs shown are simply illustrative.

Donors will likely have preferences about the inclusion or exclusion of particular details. Donors maybe unlikely to agree to all costs and so they are shared, described as cost-share or matching funds, in certain line-items. In the example shown in Figure 11.1, the costs for certain line-items or categories (e.g. vehicles) may be especially high and it may be helpful to trim these costs based on percentages of the total, although this may make it difficult to implement the project. The shared costs are split evenly (i.e. 50:50) for simplicity's sake, or the NGO simply covers the cost completely (e.g. HQ staff and certain 'other direct costs'). Three other considerations are important when preparing a budget.

Figure 11.1 Budget template

Budget Line Items	QTY	Duration Months	COST Per Unit	TOTAL DONOR	TOTAL NGO	GRAND TOTAL
Personnel						
Project Coordinator	1	12	300	1,800	1,800	3,600
Project Assistant (One per location)	2	12	250	3,000	3,000	6,000
Project Technical Staff	6	12	200	7,200	7,200	14,400
Community Workers (stipends)	10	12	100	6,000	6,000	12,000
Administrative Assistant	1	12	150	900	900	1,800
Secretary/Cashier	1	12	125	750	750	1,500
Logistician	1	12	175	1,050	1,050	2,100
Drivers	3	12	100	1,800	1,800	3,600
Security Guards	6	12	75	2,700	2,700	5,400
Cleaner	2	12	65	780	780	1,560
TOTAL FIELD SALARIES				**25,980**	**25,980**	**51,960**
NGO Headquarters						
Program/Desk Officer	15%	12	3,000		5,400	5,400
Finance Accounting Officer	15%	12	3,250		5,850	5,850
TOTAL NGO HEADQUARTERS				**0**	**11,250**	**11,250**
Benefits						
Health Insurance and taxes @ 20%				5,196	5,196	**10,392**
NGO HQ Health insurance and taxes @ 35%				0	3,938	**3,938**
TOTAL PERSONNEL BENEFITS				**5,196**	**9,134**	**14,330**
Training						
Training (Specify Type)	3		500	750		750
Refresher courses	2		500	500		500
Training Community groups	8		200	800		800
Workshops	2		250	250		250
Training supplies	4		300	1,200		1,200
TOTAL TRAINING				**3,500**	**0**	**3,500**
Program Costs						
Infrastructure Rehabilitation	15		13,000	195,000		195,000
Community Sensitization & Mobilization	1		1000	1,000		1,000
Community Projects	10		500	5,000		5,000
Materials (specify, e.g. nutritional supplements)	1		20000	20,000		20,000
TOTAL PROGRAMME				**221,000**	**0**	**221,000**

Budget Line Items	QTY	Duration Months	COST Per Unit	TOTAL DONOR	TOTAL NGO	GRAND TOTAL
Office Supplies & Equipment						
Office Stationery (non-programme supplies)	1	12	200	1,200	1,200	2,400
Office Furniture (chairs, desks, cabinets, lamps)	1		2500	1,250	1,250	2,500
Fans, A/C, Heaters	10		100	500	500	1,000
Security Upgrades (Wire, Lights, Locks, etc)	1		250	125	125	250
Photocopier (specify model)	3		800	1,200	1,200	2,400
Photocopier, toner and paper	3	12	50	900	900	1,800
Personal Computer - Desktop	3		700	1,050	1,050	2,100
Personal Computer - Laptop	2		1,000	1,000	1,000	2,000
Printer	5		200	500	500	1,000
Generators (Indicate size in kVA)	2		2,000	2,000	2,000	4,000
Satellite Phones	3		500	750	750	1,500
Mobile Phones	9		100	450	450	900
HF Base Station Radio w/installation	3		1,000	1,500	1,500	3,000
HF Mobile Radio w/installation	3		1,200	1,800	1,800	3,600
VHF Base Satation w/installation	3		800	1,200	1,200	2,400
VHF Handsets w/chargers, extra battery	10		500	2,500	2,500	5,000
UPS, Voltage Stabilizer, etc.	3		100	150	150	300
Battery (back-up) w/charger	3		75	113	113	225
TOTAL SUPPLIES/EQUIPMENT				**18,188**	**18,188**	**26,025**
Contract Services						
Technical assistance	2		2500	2,500		2,500
Mid-term and final evaluation	2		5000	5,000		5,000
Baseline and Final surveys	2		3000	3,000		3,000
TOTAL CONTRACT SERVICES				**10,500**	**0**	**10,500**
Travel & Per Diem						
International Travel	2		2,500		5,000	5,000
Regional Travel	1		1,000		1,000	1,000
Domestic Travel	10		100	1,000		1,000
TOTAL TRAVEL				**1,000**	**6,000**	**7,000**
Vehicles						
Vehicle Purchase	3		35,000	105,000		105,000
Vehicle Rental	2	12	1,000	24,000		24,000
Truck Rental	2	12	2,000	48,000		48,000
Motor bikes w/helmets	5		450	2,250		2,250
Bicycles w/helmets	10		100	1,000		1,000
Vehicle maintenance (at least	1		10,500	10,500		10,500

cont.

cont.

Budget Line Items	QTY	Duration Months	COST Per Unit	TOTAL DONOR	TOTAL NGO	GRAND TOTAL
10%/value/vehicle)						
Motorbike maintenance	5		100	500		500
Generator maintenance	2		300	600		600
Vehicle Insurance	8		100	800		800
Diesel - Vehicle (per project/ litre)	1000	12	3	18,000	18,000	36,000
Diesel - Generator (per project/ litre)	800	12	3	14,400	14,400	28,800
Gasoline - Motorbike	150	12	4	3,600	3,600	7,200
Oil & Lubricants	50	12	5	1,500	1,500	3,000
TOTAL VEHICLES				**230,150**	**37,500**	**267,650**
Other Direct Costs						
Office Rentals	3	12	500	9,000	9,000	18,000
Residence Rental	1	12	400	2,400	2,400	4,800
E-mail Access	1	12	200	1,200	1,200	2,400
Network supplies, installation & maintenance	1	1	500	250	250	500
Computer Software (Anti-Virus, etc.)	1		400	200	200	400
Telephone/fax - Landline	3	12	75	1,350	1,350	2,700
Telephone - Mobile Credit	9	12	25	1,350	1,350	2,700
Postage & shipping	1	12	100	600	600	1,200
Printing & publications	1	2	500	500	500	1,000
ID/Business Cards	1		200		200	200
Visibility: T-shirts, Decals and Flags	1		500		250	250
Advertising	1		200		100	100
Registration Fee (Coordination Bodies, etc.)	1		150		75	75
Visas & Permits	5		500		1,250	1,250
Government Fees	1		250		250	250
Legal Fees (Lawyer retainer, etc.)	1	12	200		2,400	2,400
Office Maintenance	3	12	100	1,800	1,800	3,600
Utilities (Electric, Water, Garbage Disposal)	3	12	75	1,350	1,350	2,700
Drinking water/Coffee/Tea	3	12	25		900	900
Warehouse Rental	3	12	300	5,400	5,400	10,800
TOTAL OTHER OPERATING COST				**25,400**	**30,825**	**56,225**
Total Direct Costs				**540,914**	**138,876**	**679,790**
Indirect Charges (Percentage, in this case 10%)				54,091	13,888	67,979
Totals				**595,005**	**152,764**	**747,768**

First, there are two schools of thought to maximize indirect costs in the budget. First is creating as many line-items as possible listing, every conceivable but realistic costs that will be incurred by the project. Second is using general terms for expenses such as transport, which may be used to cover a variety of expenses.

Second, from a reporting point of view – and perhaps other views as well – a small grant takes about as much time to do as a large grant. In other words, a US$15,000 grant requires nearly the same amount of paperwork as one that is worth US$150,000 or even US$ 1.5m (well, maybe not exactly, but the point should be clear). The difference is like cooking many small meals of different recipes compared with one large meal containing the same ingredients. If possible, to avoid administrative headaches, obtain one grant from one donor at a time.

Finally, there is an impression among some that NGOs make claims that they cannot deliver on, so be sure to under-promise and over-deliver. There is pressure, both from donors and internal stakeholders, to deliver a lot and be cost-effective. Smart NGOs try to resist this, since small projects that make a definitive impact are better than large unwieldy projects that may miss their intended mark.

Step 3 Monitoring

Budget monitoring allows managers to see how closely an organization is achieving its objectives from a financial point of view and take corrective steps when needed. A monitoring report measures budget line-items against spending. Such reports, often called budget and actual statements or variance reports, are usually produced on a monthly (or quarterly) basis. Some organizations may

---

Box 11.1 Accounting software

At a field level, for accounting for petty cash and drafting budgets, Excel is the most widely used programme. For the country and organizational level, some NGOs use off-the-shelf accounting packages, such as QuickBooks or Peachtree, to save costs and training time. In some cases, incoming staff may already be competent in its use. Other NGOs, often those with larger operating budgets, use systems such as ACCPAC series and Sun Systems, which have greater flexibility and complexity. Such accounting packages were designed for small and medium-sized companies with up to US$250m revenue a year. The keys to adopting the right software are budget and staff size, training and implementation costs and ease of use, including the ability to send data.

In some cases, it will be important to provide persuasive justification for the details provided and negotiate on behalf of the project. Budget narratives, which provide a worded description of each budget line-item are sometimes required by donors and are discussed in Chapter 7. Still, it is not altogether uncommon for donor representatives to question project supplies and other direct costs (while sitting in air-conditioned offices with 24-hour utilities).

find it helpful to create a spreadsheet that compares estimates planned costs with what has been spent, to determine the gap (if any).

Budget gap analysis

Using the information from the budget template example in Figure 11.1, a gap analysis can be created to monitor and estimate costs. In Figure 11.2, the NGO has determined the costs incurred for the first eight months of the project (i.e. from January to August), what remains as of September and what expenditures they intend to make for the last four months of the project (i.e. September through December).

By analysing spending and what remains in the budget, it is possible to make important programme and management decisions. In the example in Figure 11.2, it is common that some budget lines are on track and others are either under- or over-spent. Several categories, including salaries, office supplies, equipment, contract services and travel appear to be acceptable, but programme and other direct costs are over-spent. Generally, such expenditures would be justifiable and the over-expenditure (US\$ 6,518 of the total budget) will either be found elsewhere or be allocated to indirect costs. Donor and organizational regulations will determine what might be shifted between budget line-items. Some donors allow a good deal of flexibility, and others insist on being informed before any changes are made.

Step 4 Reviewing

Reviewing budgets involves an analysis of expected expenditures and comparison between multiple grants, including those awarded but not yet started (said to be in the pipeline).

Budget pipeline analysis

The pipeline analysis tool is useful when there are two or more grant budgets. The combined spreadsheet in Figure 11.3 compares different budgets line-items and totals, providing a view of how projects can fit together from an accounting perspective.

In this example in Figure 11.3, the project details used in the budget template (as 'Project A') with the addition of three new project budgets. 'Project B' appears to be a rather small project, 'Project C' may supplement 'Project A' and 'Project D' seems to be a moderate-sized project with new activities. If there were budget expenditure differences discovered during the first project, it may be possible to plan costs (budget) in the subsequent projects. If there were over-runs in certain line-items (e.g. maintenance), the other grants may not be able to cover it and other funds will be needed. Timing, not revealed in this example for the sake of brevity, is important because rarely will multiple projects start and end at the same time.

Figure 11.2 Budget gap analysis

Item	Budget	January–August	Remaining Sept	Projected Expenditure				Total Expenses	Remaining budget
				Sept	Oct	Nov	Dec		
Salaries									
Programme Management	51,960	40,100	11,860	3,953	3,953	3,953		51,960	0
Programme Support	11,250	7,500	3,750	938	938	938	938	11,250	0
Benefits	14,330	9,553	4,777	1,194	1,194	1,194	1,194	14,329	1
Total Salaries	**77,540**	**57,153**	**20,387**	**6,085**	**6,085**	**6,085**	**2,132**	**77,539**	**1**
Training & Programme									
Training	3,500	4,000	-500					4,000	(500)
Program	221,000	222,509	-1,509	840	840	700	550	225,439	(4,439)
Total Training & Programme	**224,500**	**226,509**	**-2,009**	**840**	**840**	**700**	**550**	**229,439**	**(4,939)**
Office Supplies & Equipment									
Office Supplies & Equipment	26,025	24,821	1,204	0	0	0		24,821	1,204
Total Supplies & Equipment	**36,375**	**24,821**	**11,554**	**0**	**0**	**0**	**0**	**24,821**	**1,204**
Contract Services & Travel									
Contract Services	10,500	8,700	1,800				1,000	9,700	800
Travel & Per Diem	7,000	6,750	250			250		7,000	0
Total Contract/Travel	**17,500**	**15,450**	**2,050**	**0**	**0**	**250**	**1,000**	**16,700**	**800**
Vehicles									
Vehicles & Fuel	267,650	252,400	15,250	1,900	1,900	1,900	1,900	260,000	7,650
Total Vehicles	**267,650**	**252,400**	**15,250**	**1,900**	**1,900**	**1,900**	**1,900**	**260,000**	**7,650**
Other Direct Costs									
Other Direct Costs	56,225	57,859	-1,634	2,200	2,200	2,200	2,200	66,659	(10,434)
TOTAL Other	**56,225**	**57,859**	**-1,634**	**2,200**	**2,200**	**2,200**	**2,200**	**66,659**	**(10,434)**
TOTAL	**679,790**	**618,742**	**61,048**	**11,025**	**11,025**	**10,885**	**6,782**	**701,840**	**(6,518)**

Figure 11.3 Budget pipeline analysis

Budget Line Items	Project A	Project B	Project C	Project D
Personnel				
Country Director/Team Leader				9,000
Project Coordinator	3,600	3,600	2,700	3,600
Project Assistant	6,000	1,800		
Project Technical Staff	14,400			8,200
Community Workers	12,000		2,000	
Administrative Assistant	1,800			1,800
Secretary/Cashier	1,500		1,500	1,500
Logistician	2,100		2,000	
Drivers	3,600	1,200	1,200	3,000
Security Guards	5,400			2,700
Cleaner	1,560			500
TOTAL FIELD SALARIES	**51,960**	**6,600**	**9,400**	**30,300**
NGO Headquarters				
Programme/Desk Officer	5,400			3,500
Finance Accounting Officer	5,850			
TOTAL NGO HEADQUARTERS	**11,250**	**0**	**0**	**3,500**
Benefits				
Health Insurance and taxes @ 20%	10,392		1,200	2,800
NGO HQ Health insurance and taxes @ 35%	3,938		0	0
TOTAL PERSONNEL BENEFITS	**14,330**	**0**	**1,200**	**2,800**
Training				
Training (Specify Type)	750	1,500		
Refresher courses	500			
Training Community groups	800		250	
Workshops	250			
Training supplies	1,200			
TOTAL TRAINING	**3,500**	**1,500**	**250**	**0**
Program Costs				
Infrastructure Rehabilitation	195,000		58,000	
Community Sensitization & Mobilization	1,000			
Community Projects	5,000			128,000
Materials (specify, e.g. nutritional supplements)	20,000	5,000		
TOTAL PROGRAMME	**195,000**	**5,000**	**58,000**	**128,000**
Office Supplies & Equipment				
Office Stationery (non-programme supplies)	2,400	300	500	950
Office Furniture (chairs, desks, cabinets, lamps)	2,500			450
Fans, A/C, Heaters	1,000			
Security Upgrades (Wire, Lights, Locks, etc)	250			
Photocopier (specify model)	2,400			
Photocopier, toner and paper	1,800			
Personal Computer - Desktop	2,100	700		

Budget Line Items	Project A	Project B	Project C	Project D
Personal Computer - Laptop	2,000			950
Printer	1,000	200		
Generators (Indicate size in kVA)	4,000			
Satellite Phones	1,500			
Mobile Phones	900	100		200
HF Base Station Radio w/installation	3,000			
HF Mobile Radio w/installation	3,600			
VHF Base Satation w/installation	2,400			
VHF Handsets w/chargers, extra battery	5,000		1,000	
UPS, Voltage Stabilizer, etc.	300			
Battery (back-up) w/charger	225			
TOTAL SUPPLIES/EQUIPMENT	**36,375**	**1,300**	**1,500**	**2,550**
Contract Services				
Technical assistance	2,500		850	
Mid-term and final evaluation	5,000			
Baseline and Final surveys	3,000			
TOTAL CONTRACT SERVICES	**10,500**	**0**	**850**	**0**
Travel & Per Diem				
International Travel	5,000			1,000
Regional Travel	1,000			450
Domestic Travel	6,000		800	250
TOTAL TRAVEL	**12,000**	**0**	**800**	**1,700**
Vehicles				
Vehicle Purchase	105,000			38,000
Vehicle Rental	24,000	10,000	18,000	
Truck Rental	48,000			15,000
Motor bikes w/helmets	2,250			
Bicycles w/helmets	1,000		500	
Vehicle maintenance (at least 10%/ value/vehicle)	10,500			
Motorbike maintenance	500			
Generator maintenance	600			
Vehicle Insurance	800			
Diesel - Vehicle	36,000			8,000
Diesel - Generator	28,800			5,000
Gasoline - Motorbike	7,200			
Oil & Lubricants	3,000			
TOTAL VEHICLES	**267,650**	**10,000**	**18,500**	**66,000**
Other Direct Costs				
Office Rentals	18,000	500	2,000	6,000
Residence Rental	4,800			
E-mail Access	2,400		600	
Network supplies, installation & maintenance	500			
Computer Software (Anti-Virus, etc.)	400		100	
Telephone/fax - Landline	2,700			800
Telephone - Mobile Credit	2,700			

Budget Line Items	Project A	Project B	Project C	Project D
Postage & shipping	1,200			
Printing & publications	1,000			550
ID/Business Cards	200			
Visibility: T-shirts, Decals and Flags	250			
Advertising	100			
Registration Fee (Coordination Bodies, etc.)	75			50
Visas & Permits	1,250			
Government Fees	250			
Legal Fees (Lawyer retainer, etc.)	2,400			
Office Maintenance	3,600			600
Utilities (Electric, Water, Garbage Disposal)	2,700			600
Drinking water/Coffee/Tea	900			
Warehouse Rental	10,800		4,500	
TOTAL OTHER OPERATING COST	56,225	500	7,200	8,600
Total Direct Costs	679,790	24,900	97,700	243,450
Indirect Charges (Percentage, in this case 10%)	67,979	2,490	9,770	24,345
Totals	747,768	27,390	107,470	267,795

Getting funds in a disaster zone

There are four methods of obtaining funds in a country which has been affected by an emergency, as follows.

1. **Bank transfer** This method may rarely be possible in an acute emergency. If banks are operating and connected to international markets, then they may only work in capital cities, and then the next method will have to be used to send funds to sub-offices or other field locations. An open account and all the details will be needed. In some cases, money transfer companies (e.g. Western Union) may be operating.

2. **Hand carry** When infrastructure is lacking, this method is probably the most common way NGOs get money in the field. While it is fairly easy, it can also be unsafe. Commonsense precautions should be taken to safeguard cash. It will also be important to check on laws and customs regulating the export and import of cash (many countries have a US$10,000 limit as well as controls on trading funds into local currency). (Also see p. 343.)

3. **Traditional systems** In some parts of the world, there are informal ways to transfer money. The *hawala* system, available in parts of the Middle East and South Asia, allows funds to be transferred informally from one broker to another wherever they might be. The system is based on simple trust and it can be an effective way of getting money to areas where no formal system exists. Before using the *hawala* system, it is worth checking if donors have regulations prohibiting this.

4. **Using other organizations** In some cases, it may be possible to transfer funds through another organization that has a well-developed system for obtaining funds. To help account for the funds, a formal partnering agreement may be necessary for the transfer.

Petty cash

Petty cash is normally considered a small amount of cash that is not part of the main accounting system or cashbook. Petty cash is meant for small purchases and is usually maintained by one staff member. For many NGOs operating in emergencies, petty cash is often issued to project managers and other staff to allow them to carry out activities without cumbersome accounting.

From an accounting point of view, petty cash is normally handled as a cash advance (or float) and placed against the name of the staff member who accepts it. A typical petty cash amount is US$500 with single purchases authorized of US$50–100. The accounting for petty cash is mostly like an organization's accounting system in miniature, discussed below in Box 11.2.

Physical security In some cases petty cash can be hidden or locked in a drawer or locked box. However, it should be counted on a regular basis, usually at the end of each day.

Petty cash ledger This can be used for recording daily credits and debts. The ledger should accurately record the liquid cash in the cashbox, as shown in Table 11.1. In many cases, the cashbook ledger can maintain in handwritten form where computers and/or electricity is not available.

Following the cashbook ledger, if the petty cash box were to be looked into on the evening of 8 September, there should be exactly US$402 physically present ('on hand').

Collection of receipts and invoices Most NGOs on some level integrate logistics with accounting because the interface with procurement. Some organizations have strict guidelines for what is expected in a proof of purchase (see Box 11.2).

Box 11.2 The 'dodgy' receipt book

A receipt is typically needed for all expenditures. Donors may be very specific in what they require to consider a receipt valid. This usually includes the vendor's name and a reachable address, date, cash amount spelled out and in numbers, the transaction's purpose and a stamp with signature. In capital cities and major towns, this financial requirement is rarely a problem. But in rural areas, such conditions may be impossible to meet. For example, purchasing bananas in support of training, procuring a motorcycle spare part from a farmer and buying rope in a flea market are everyday transactions for relief workers, but not the sort that comes with a valid receipt. It may not be recommended, but many NGOs are forced to use blank receipt books that are then filled out by informal vendors (if they can write).

Table 11.1 Petty cash ledger

No.	Date	Item description	Credit	Debit	Balance
001	7/9	Cash advance	$500		$500
002	7/9	Stationery (A4 paper and markers)		$18	$482
003	7/9	Motor oil (SAE 40)		$14	$468
004	8/9	Cement (3 bags for clinic)		$66	$402

Statement Used for reporting, the petty-cash statement should be based on the cashbook ledger, but the statement is more formal and is often turned provided to accounting staff on a monthly or bi-monthly basis.

Cash requests Planning is needed to replenish cash. Many accounting systems will allow permit replenishment of petty cash only after all cash has been accounted for with receipts and an accurate statement.

Financial audit: a manager's tool

A financial audit is an independent assessment of an organization's finances by an independent person, an auditor, or an organization such as an accounting firm. Audits are a normal process where accounting records are checked at random (often 60 records in a single audit) for authenticity and completeness. Staff may be interviewed and management tools like timesheets and organizational charts may also be checked.

Table 11.2 provides a basic financial audit. While not a technical financial audit, this tool is called an audit in the sense that it can be used to check or review major financial control issues. In the left column, major issues, are listed with key questions that a manager can use to verify the standards at which the NGO is operating and, perhaps, prepare it for an external audit.

Table 11.2 Financial audit tool

Financial control issue	Key questions
Organizational structure	Is there a division of responsibility where financial duties are split between different members of staff? Are there written policies and procedures? Are staff adequately trained? Are there enough finance staff to reasonably handle all financial responsibilities? Does management review operations and day-to-day activities?
Budgetary controls	Is there an annual budget for the whole organization? Are actual expenditures compared with budget on a regular basis? Is variance between expenditures and budget amounts explained in writing? Has the organization run out of money before? What is done to ensure that there is enough cash on hand to cover immediate expenses as well as a reserve for emergencies?

Donor funds	Is there a report prepared showing which donor is funding which costs? Are there enough funds to cover expenditures necessary to run the organization and projects? Are any costs covered by more than one donor for the same project (i.e. is there justified and documented cost-sharing or prohibited overlap, known as double-funding?) Can the emergency programme operate even if a single donor stops providing funding? What will happen in that case?
Accounting records	Are accounting records (e.g. invoices and receipts, bank statements, vouchers, salary records, ledgers and cashbooks) accurate and up-to-date? Do they indicate the payment's purpose? Are quarterly or annual statements prepared? Are statements subject to an external audit? Are audit recommendations implemented? Are financial data used for planning purposes? Is sufficient information available to report back to each donor in the way requested?
Accounting codes	Is a standard chart of accounts used to code all the financial transactions in the cashbooks? Is the same chart of accounts used to write budget and financial reports? Are transactions classified by project activity, using a standard list of cost centres?
Incoming funds	How is mail secured and is it opened in front of more than one staff member? Are incoming cash and cheques entered in the cashbook immediately and put in the bank regularly? Is an acknowledge of incoming funds provided to donors? Are cheques written by someone other than the person originally recording the funds, to ensure income records are accurate?
Expenditure controls	Are all expenditures authorized by a senior staff member? Are there written authority levels for spending? Do different staff authorize payments from those who prepare and sign cheques? Are payments made only with an original invoice?
Purchase controls	Is there an adequate system for procurement? Are several quotes obtained? Who is responsible? Are invoices matched against orders? Are the quality and quantity of goods received checked? Is there a regular inventory of goods?
Bank accounts	If the banking system is functioning, are all accounts registered in the name of the NGO? Are there at least two signatories responsible for signing cheques on each bank account? Are blank cheques ever pre-signed or how is this avoided? Are bank transactions recorded in the cashbook immediately? Are cheques written for as many payments as possible? Are bank accounts reconciled regularly after the statement is received? What happens to cancelled cheques?
Cash transactions	Is cash kept securely? Who holds the keys or knows the combination? Are transactions recorded in the cashbook immediately? Is a numbered receipt issued for cash received? Does someone other than the cashier authorize large

cont.

cont.

Financial control issue	Key questions
	payments? Does the cashier monitor the cash balance? Is the cash counted regularly by a senior member of staff in the cashier's presence?
Physical controls	Is there an updated inventory? Do all the fixed assets shown in the accounts actually exist? Is there insurance coverage? Are all items kept securely? Do vehicles and generators have logbooks? Are staff charged for personal use of telephones? Is all financial stationery (e.g. receipt books and order forms) numbered and held securely? How are salaries paid and who authorizes the payroll? Are all names on the payroll currently on staff?
Debtor controls	Are invoices issued promptly? Are unpaid invoices followed up? Is the outstanding debtors figure regularly reviewed?

Source: Modified from Cammack (1999) and Mango (2003).

CHAPTER 12
Setting up a logistics and procurement system

Logistics involves the acquisition, control, handling, transport, storage and removal of goods or supplies. The purpose of this chapter is to outline the basic elements of an NGO's logistics and procurement system. This chapter covers:
- Logistics fundamentals
- Procurement
- Shipping
- Storage and warehousing
- Distribution
- Maintenance and disposal

The challenges of NGO logistics come from the urgency, inherent constraints and locations where emergencies typically happen, since they are remote, resource-poor and often insecure. Good logistics are rarely praised, while poor logistics are quickly criticized. Poor logistics result in other staff being unable to work effectively and activities will be carried out at a reduced capacity because supplies and other services will be unavailable. While not an end in itself, good logistics are a precondition for those running emergency programmes to ensure that their programmes are successful.

NGO logistics normally involve a number of topics covered in other parts of this book, including establishing an office and accommodation (Chapter 6), vehicles (Chapter 13), telecommunications (Chapter 14) and security (Chapter 18).

Logistics fundamentals

NGO logistics activities consist of procurement, ships, stores, distribution, maintenance and disposal of goods and supplies for humanitarian aims. Collectively, these logistical activities can be thought of as a chain that brings needed supplies to staff and beneficiaries. At every point along an NGO's supply chain, there are unique constraints that make logistics in emergency contexts especially challenging. These include urgency, insecurity, remote locations, scarce resources and overwhelming needs. To help address these challenges, consider the 10 golden rules of logistics.

1. **Plan ahead** Spend time to determine future needs and make allocations. In logistics, anticipation is often more important than reaction. Consider the seasons (e.g. monsoon floods), periods of higher

likelihood of conflict (e.g. intensified fighting at times of elections and spring weather) and the time needed to put supplies in the hands – not just the warehouse – of those who need it, where they need it.

2. **Follow procedures** Establishing and implementing procedures makes managing activities more streamlined and efficient. Procedures may have to be established in the first case, so be prepared for this or improve an existing system. Training and enforcement are an important part of this and may be complicated by staff turnover.

3. **Document everything** Doing things verbally without a paper-trail may be attractive in terms of speed, but it will only cause problems later on. Many donors require records to be kept at every step along the supply chain to ensure that their donations are being correctly used; and in any event, it is good practice. There are many ways to do this, including waybills (see p. 241), inventories (pp. 243–4) and tracking sheets (p. 248).

4. **Communicate** Make a habit of proactively communicating with your staff, and be prepared at any time to inform other people about the status of items, since staff members will need reassurances that something is happening. Distance and limited communication means can make this difficult.

5. **Standardize** The more uniform a system, the more efficient it is. Having a standard computer, vehicle or radio, for example, can make ordering spares and replacements that much easier. Identical kits or packages are simpler to send through the supply chain and maintain than single or distinctive items. The standard paper work (i.e. forms) should also be simple and as few in number as possible.

6. **Test** Never send anything to the field that has not been checked to make sure it is fully functional and that it has complete parts and accessories. This includes turning electronic items on, testing batteries and inventorying the item before putting it back in its box for shipping to the field.

7. **Maintain** Once an item is fielded, maintenance must be planned for. Regardless of the reason – neglect, poor conditions, overuse – even the sturdiest items need to be cared for. This means ensuring that spare parts for equipment are still available and that sufficient budgetary funds have been allocated for repairs.

8. **Buy locally** Although it is sometimes costlier, procuring locally is usually cheaper, faster and easier. It also helps the local economy and builds relations with reliable local suppliers. However, it is not always possible or practical and a few exceptions might include technology items such as vehicles, water-testing kits, computers, some medical equipment and radios.

9. **Have a backup** Not necessarily two of everything, but encourage a mindset that allows you to deal with obstacles before they happen. If a satellite telephone is the primary means of communication, what

happens if it is stolen or broken? What if all supplies are sent by a single road and that road becomes too insecure or one of its bridges gets washed out or destroyed?

10. **Follow-up** At each step along a supply chain, there are potential problems and constant attention is needed to clear bottlenecks and other obstacles. For this reason, regular communication is needed between the field, offices and HQ.

According to Saade and Burnham (2000), there are two types of logistics. First, in a push logistics system, standard quantities of equipment and supplies are estimated, and stored, ready to be quickly pushed to the scene. Second, in a pull logistics system, equipment and supplies are ordered after the need is determined. A response to humanitarian emergencies often begins with push logistics. Pull logistics are essential in events of a long duration, but totally ineffective in the early minutes or hours of a sudden-onset humanitarian emergency.

As NGOs have limited resources, a pull system is far more common. In some cases, a stock can be established if there is an expected or impending emergency situation. This allows for a push system to meet initial needs and then be followed up by a pull system over time. Regardless of the type of initial system, there can be numerous problems. The supply chain, which can be thought of as different stages, is shown in Figure 12.1.

Many problems can arise as items pass through the supply chain. Cuny (1999) suggested several ways to address delays and problems, including cutting out intermediary phases, improving monitoring and repositioning the locations of warehouses. Certain types of logistical items cause more problems than others. For example, food pipelines, the food supply chain that includes different

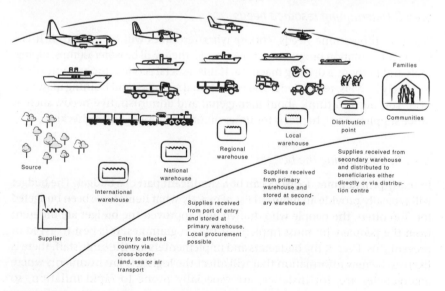

Figure 12.1 Logistics cycle

logistical points such as ports and warehouses, in particular, WFP (2002) suggests drafting written agreements among stakeholders, working through community members, doing smaller distributions more often (although more frequently than weekly is not practical) and labelling food for particular groups to deter theft.

Determining logistical needs

There are many ways to go about deciding logistic requirements. When deciding, here is one, not necessarily sequential, approach:

Step 1 Examining programme and programme support needs

First, coordinate with staff to confirm precise needs and priorities, in order to make informed choices based on sound planning. For determining supplies for staff and programme support needs, it is usually best for logisticians to brainstorm with programme managers to decide what is needed and decide on priorities. Any programme will involve difficult financial trade-offs, so copies of budgets, programme plans and other documents can help make these meetings effective by providing consistent information. This will likely bring some consensus and awareness of what needs to be done. Programme needs may be more difficult to work out, but determining basic supplies for beneficiaries is made easier by the Minimum Standards of the Sphere Project, which identifies the following requirements for displaced people, as shown in Table 12.1. Once the basic requirements are known, more specific plans can be drawn up.

Step 2 Determining resource needs

Based on programme needs, choose what resources will be needed. If it is a water and sanitation programme, for example, there will be water-pumps, piping, tools and perhaps a drilling machine. If it is a social services programme, there will likely be NFIs, recreational and educational supplies, and training materials. Also, you need to think about managerial and administrative needs, such as office supplies. See Chapter 6 for notes on office supplies and a checklist.

Step 3: Considering the budget

In many programmes, logistics can be a significant part of a budget. The budget will typically provide an itemized list of exactly what items have been budgeted for. Too often, the people who drafted and approved the budget are different from the people who must implement the programmes. It is best to avoid or prevent this. Even if the budgeters and implementers are the same staff, there is likely to be new information that will affect the logistics. Environments where emergencies are, for instance, are especially prone to rapid inflation, so adjustments will certainly be needed.

Table 12.1 Logistical needs

Programme sector	Examples of supplies	Comments
Health (1/10,000 population for 3 months)	WHO Emergency Health Kits	Provision of drugs and other medical supplies are needed to supplement these kits
	MISP initially for people's reproductive health needs (see p. 390)	If there are large amounts of war-related trauma wounds, additional supplies may be needed
Water and sanitation	Water for drinking, cooking and bathing (at least 15 litres/person/day)	Additional water may be needed in certain climates and if animals are present
	Clean functioning latrines (1 latrine/20 persons or family) Access to 250 g of soap/month	
Nutrition	Steady and adequate supply of sufficient quality food to sustain life (an average 2,100 kcal/person/day)	Distributions of food may be carried out in different ways, including wet and dry feeding, as well as selective and therapeutic feeding
		Wet distributions require specialists for proper distribution
Shelter	Appropriate shelter material and sufficient blankets per family	Items must be geographically and culturally appropriate
	At least one full set of clothing per person	
	Household items and cooking fuel (1 cooking pot with lid, 1 basin, 1 kitchen knife, 2 wooden spoons, 2 water collection and water storage vessels/family; 1 plate, 1 metal spoon, 1 mug per person)	

Step 4 Weighing the constraints

While the budget may be the largest limitation, there will also be many other constraints, including market availability, the quality and quantity of the items available, shipment time, as well as difficulties arising from customs clearance, testing and (if needed) training. In some emergencies, security too may be a significant constraint because it delays or prevents the logistics chain from working.

Procurement

Procurement is the acquisition of supplies, goods and services. It involves internal request, obtaining pro-forma bids (quotations), selecting an external vendor, pick-up and transport of goods and settling of receipts.

More than any other logistics function, procurement requires a straightforward document system. Procurement should be closely linked with financial accounting and audit because funds are involved. Because it is possible that there may be corruption involved with procurement, as with finance accounting, managers need to closely monitor procurement staff. Corruption is discussed further below (pp. 234–6), but it typically involves conflict of interest, where staff steer business to family and friends, and ordinary kickbacks. To help address the problem, a good system with adequate control measures needs to be in place. Typical procurement documents include the following.

- **Requisition** Form used by staff to request supplies at the start of the procurement process. If the items are already present in a warehouse or can be obtained in kind from another organization, there will be no need to seek the item from commercial vendors (i.e. a store, shop, retailer or a wholesale supplier).

- **Purchase order** Based on a staff requisition, logistics staff usually generate a purchase order to submit to a commercial vendor. Based on a purchase order, vendors will supply the items or provide a pro forma invoice (or quotation) to help organizations through their bidding process.

- **Pro-forma quotations** If the order is likely to be more than a pre-established amount (such as US$500), many NGO require logistics staff to submit the purchase order to at least three different commercial vendors to ensure that the most competitive price and best quality are obtained. The vendors should supply a pro-forma quotation or bid their best estimate of what the request item(s) will cost the NGO. This information should remain confidential between logistics staff and a particular vendor, to avoid price fixing and favouritism. The results may be summarized on an internal form which provides space to explain why a particular commercial vendor was chosen.

- **Invoice** The proof of purchase when money has been exchanged for goods or supplies. While there are ways to establish credit with particular vendors, the invoice provides evidence that the sale has been made. Later delivery can be made, which should be followed up with a delivery note or similar documentation.

Given the amount of paperwork and time needed to go to different vendors, the larger a programme becomes, the greater the need there is to have a separate staff member or section handling procurement.

NGOs typically have procurement carried out by local staff, but verified either regularly or randomly (depending on the amount of time or the system) by expatriate staff. Local staff know the markets, can skilfully negotiate and are

> **Box 12.1** The '7 Rs' of procurement
>
> Some logisticians look for seven qualities in procurement:
>
> Right person
>
> Right supplier
>
> Right quality
>
> Right value
>
> Right cost
>
> Right quantity
>
> Right beneficiary

less likely to be given high prices for routine supplies. Some NGOs have staff approach vendors on foot, rather than stepping out of a luxury 4×4 vehicle, and without pieces of kit like hand-held radios.

Quality is often one of the most pressing concerns. If there will be large quantities of supplies procured, ask for samples before placing an order. The sample should be shared with the staff who originally requested the item. Donations of some supplies, and drugs in particular, are fraught with problems:

- **Shipping and customs fees** Costs will likely far exceed the value of the goods.
- **Time** The time it takes to receive donated goods may be prohibitive and certain items, especially pharmaceuticals, have expiration dates that require verification by trained staff.
- **Appropriateness** There are many famous stories of winter clothing having been sent to tropical countries and toys arriving when there was not enough to eat. Cultural issues also need to be taken into account (e.g. sending inappropriate clothing to culturally conservative areas).

Regardless of the sources of the supplies, some of items are standard and may be available in kind from the UN and donor organizations. Examples of typical NFIs include:

- **Blankets** Usually come in woollen blends depending on the climate (higher wool content for colder climates). Bales usually consist of 30 pieces. Several blankets may be needed by people and are required even in tropical or desert areas. Sphere Standards specify babies under 2 years of age should have a blanket at least 100 × 70 cm.
- **Jerry cans** Different sizes available. Those supplied by UNHCR are normally 10-litre semi-collapsible and are shipped in boxes of 100. Requesting staff should indicate their intended use, to help determine the size needed.

Tarpaulins and plastic sheeting Although there is cotton tarpaulin, plastic sheeting is a standard relief supply item commonly available through some organizations (e.g. UNHCR, ICRC and USAID/OFDA). There are a variety of uses for plastic sheeting (see p. 46).

Some commercial logistics companies have been established specifically to cater for the needs of humanitarian organizations. While the cost of dealing through these companies is often prohibitive for NGOs, if pressed they can often negotiate better prices. Other international commercial firms specialize in relief commodities and can provide a good service, although deliveries (e.g. vehicle orders) originating outside disaster zones have been known to take months to arrive. The large procurement companies, however, remain profit-driven and cannot be expected to bow to NGOs when the media, UN and international militaries are deployed in the same areas.

Theft, fraud and corruption prevention

No discussion about logistics in general and procurement specifically is complete without mentioning theft and corruption. Every endeavour is subject to fraud and international assistance is no exception. Given the difficult circumstances in which many NGOs work, it is logical that the attractions of theft, fraud and corruption are much greater. NGO managers, as the main persons responsible for preventing theft and corruption (and assuming for a moment that they are not part of the problem), are often preoccupied with other tasks such as assessments and reporting. This situation is normal, but opens the NGO to exploitation. Apart from physical infrastructure such as doors and locks, documentation is the primary means of preventing theft and corruption. Several tricks are as follows.

- Staff receiving kickbacks from suppliers for awarding purchase bids and contracts
- Deviation from intended staff or beneficiaries
- Claiming theft that is difficult or impossible to verify
- Phoney documentation, including receipts and waybills
- Price exaggeration

The control system made up of the documents explained above should be strict, well-known (staff require training on how to follow procedures) and frequently checked. Specific potential problems and ways to pre-empt these scams are outlined in Table 12.2.

Kickback, baksheesh, greasing palms, a little extra or gratuity?

Whatever its name, bribery is a common reality when dealing with logistics. The rights and wrongs of it are open to debate. While large-scale graft and corruption are widely seen to be impediments to development, small-scale handouts that amount to unofficial user fees are somewhat understandable given the remuneration rates for many jobs in the developing world. Ethical issues aside, for the uninitiated it is worth understanding how to deal practically with bribery. While it is possible to avoid many of the problems associated with bribery through the use of documentation, there may be times (such as when corrupt officials threaten arrest) when there may be little choice but to comply.

Table 12.2 Fraud prevention

Activity	Fraud type	Preventative action
Procurement	Kickbacks	Quotations collected separately
	Exaggerated invoice amounts (and splitting the difference)	Independent review of documentation
	Diversion of part or whole of a consignment	Verification of deliveries by physical count, inspection, waybills and inventories
Building and repair	Stealing supplies and material	Independent verification of works and supplies against plans, bids and invoices
	Forged bills and invoices	Quality control and random inspections
	Swapping high-quality expensive items for ones of poor quality (and selling the better items)	
HR and labour management	Phoney payroll ('ghost staff')	Verification of staff by identification checks, staff lists and timesheets
	Salary skimming by managers	Random counts
	Exaggerated or fake hours worked	Off-site interview of staff (who are assured of no retribution)
Selection of and activities with partners	Kickbacks and favouritism	Background checks
	Pretend projects	Funding NGO site visits and procurement
	Social events beyond those related to work	Independent verification of invoices

The challenge is to limit the number of times and amounts that it happens. Be polite but aloof and:

- **Reject** In cases where there are 'gifts' made available to staff (with the implicit expectation that these gifts will be rewarded in kind), there should be an explicit policy forbidding staff from accepting gifts over a (low) dollar amount. Even if the policy does not exist, it is possible to claim there is while politely turning it down. Another tactic is to politely suggest that the offering should be given directly to a local organization that has nothing to do with your organization's work (e.g. a CBO). In any case, it is best to maintain transparency and decline to accept anything that is out of the ordinary.
- **Pass** As the final option, discretion is usually important. Monetary gifts are usually the best, as they cannot be traced back to the giver, but some-

thing that is widely available is also effective, as the gift might have been give by anyone. Perhaps the best tactic is to ask for a receipt. This may deter the person from pursuing a bribe, and if not, the payment becomes 'official', with a receipt.

Shipping

Shipping supplies can be a frustrating process especially when items are needed urgently. It pays to do it right in the first place. Four factors should determine the type of shipping used: urgency, reliability, availability and cost.

Once these four factors are decided, the mode of transport can be considered – land, sea or air. Each mode of transport has its advantages. For example, to satisfy urgent requirements, airfreight is faster than any other mode of transport, yet the cost is considerably more – planes usually carry a fraction of what is possible with other modes of transport.

Land transport

In some contexts, rail transport may be a viable option for the first two stages along the supply chain. Rail is especially useful if there is a large amount of supplies and where time is not a major constraint. A standard railway car has 30,000 kg of carrying capacity. Normally, the rail carrier will have cargo regulations and instructions, forms to be completed, schedules and costs specific to their line.

Trucking

Of the modes of land transport, trucking (using lorries) is the most commonly used. While NGOs usually have one or more trucks, the costs, time and annoyance involved in maintaining a trucking fleet are prohibitive. In addition to avoiding these problems, contracting trucks also supports the local economy and shifts liability to a third party. In most circumstances, contracting is the best option for NGOs.

Truck contracting cost rates are based on fixed, variable and mixed costs, as well as factors including weight and distance. In developing countries especially, the road surface and conditions of transit (such as insecurity) are likely to also significantly affect the price. See pp. 293–8 for more information on contracting.

Truck drivers in developing countries notoriously overstretch the capacity of their vehicles. If overseeing loading, ensure that it is done in a way that is safe and protects the cargo. Make sure that if tarps are used they fully cover the goods and are secure enough to last the journey. Unless specifically stated in contracts, trucks are unlikely to have tarps and ropes. In any case, NGOs should be prepared to provide extra or better-quality support supplies.

Although drivers may have their own assistant crews, it is usually best to insist that a NGO staff member travels with the truck to make sure that items are not pilfered along the way. If the resources exist, the best way to do this is with a separate vehicle that has communication equipment and mechanical tools to deal with breakdowns. This staff should also monitor the driving of the truck, making sure it drives safely, especially in areas where there are pedestrians. If logos or flags are provided to a contracted truck for visibility, make sure these are retrieved at the end of the trip or contract.

If the organization is using its own trucks, use better or more robust trucks for long-distance or remote trips. Try to send vehicles in convoy to help deal with breakdowns and security. Trucks usually travel much slower than 4x4 vehicles, so make sure that trucks leave enough time to travel before established curfews.

Pack animals

In remote areas, where roads have withered or were never built in the first place, transporting goods by animal may be the only available means. Like vehicles, each type of animal has advantages and disadvantages. Camels, for example, are excellent in arid regions, but they tend to be slower than other animals. Camels can travel 32–40 km a day carrying roughly 250 kg, and can live for up to two weeks without food or water. Robust and good in mountainous terrain, donkeys can walk 16–24 km a day and carry approximately 100 kg. Local knowledge and experience is essential when using pack animals, especially as the handler is also likely to be the owner. The same, or very similar, contractual arrangements should be made with animals as with other types of shipping. The consequences of loss need to be seriously thought out because of the remoteness involved. Packing should be supervised carefully, especially for items like medicines and fragile equipment. If possible, important items should be spread among different animal trains. Based on load and distance, extra animals might be needed or multiple trips may be necessary.

Sea transport

Like rail transport, transport by sea is a well-established mode of transport. Also like rail transport, sea transport is limited in its capacity and slow, but it does have the advantages being able to transport large quantities. A standard 20 ft/ 6.1 m container has a 30 m³ or 18,000 kg capacity, and a standard 40ft/12.2 m container has a 65 m³ or 26,000 kg capacity. A more likely possibility may be small ships and boats for transport inside the country itself. Similar conditions should then be followed, as discussed under 'Trucking' (in previous section). For working with boats see pp. 266–7.

Air transport

Transport by air is an expensive and unsustainable luxury. It is only used when lives are threatened and there is no other safe means of delivering supplies. A typical cargo plane can carry only about 20 tonnes of cargo (the equivalent of about one truck), at a cost of over US$1,000/tonne on an average flight, whereas by sea or land the same cargo will be a tenth or less of that price. What air transport offers is speed, range and usually security. Capacity varies widely depending on the type of aircraft (see UNHCR, 2000 or USAID/OFDA, 2005 for further details). Of the large aircraft typically present in emergencies, the Russian Ilyushian 76 (Candid) and Antonov 12 (Cub) and the American Hercules (C-130) are the real workhorses. The Cub and Hercules are especially prized for their ability to land on unpaved and short airstrips.

As soon as the road and security situation improves, ground transport needs to be relied on. As commercial carriers rarely operate in areas with ongoing emergencies, NGOs must rely on other organizations, such as the UN Humanitarian Air Service, the ICRC and specialty NGOs like Air Serv, MAF and PacTec. Depending on the situation, the military may also offer to transport humanitarian resources.

Regardless of whether the craft is an airplane or helicopter, using air transport for NGOs is usually a straightforward process of being registered with one of the air service providers (which often involves little more than writing a request and filling out a form by the CD or designated senior staff) and then requesting space on a particular flight. Often, each request must be signed by a specific designee and include the NGO's official stamp. For UN flights in particular, normally a hierarchical pecking order places NGOs in the low-middle below UN and diplomatic staff but above journalists. If possible, try to check the flight manifest in person to confirm reservations are correct.

Other shipping considerations

Unfortunately, sending something that is cheap in one part of the world will not be so cheap once shipping costs are added. Unless the item is truly needed, the resources used to ship a good may cost twice the item itself. Shipping costs include:

- Packing (it should be strong enough)
- Labelling (it should clearly indicate that is humanitarian goods)
- Delivery from point of sale or storage to point of transport (e.g. airport)
- Freight
- Airway bill and documentation charges
- Insurance
- Communications

Considering the above fees and costs that may be faced when sending between locations, normally only critically needed items should be shipped this way. Costs can be calculated by either weight (tonnage), where the costs are fixed once the size of goods is determined, but the goods may be transported with other goods, which may be problematic during transport; or by vehicle per journey per day, where although the vehicle will be dedicated to the NGO for the trip the transport company has an incentive to be slow and/or fill the vehicle to less than capacity knowing that it will be paid extra.

Contingencies for both time and cost should be added to every order. According to Davis and Lambert (2002), there are three main questions to ask when calculating the logistics of transportation.

1. How many tonnes must be moved? By when?
2. How long will the vehicles take to take a load from the delivery point to the reception point and return? (Do not overestimate the speed and include loading and unloading.)
3. What load capacity does the vehicle have?

> Number of possible trips per vehicle = duration of round trip
> Number of loads = total number of tonnes or vehicle capacity
> Number of vehicles = number of loads or number of possible trips or vehicles

Customs clearance

Customs clearance, and its procedures and fees, varies from one country to another. Unfortunately, in some countries, clearing customs may be more about connections than following a set of procedures. One effective way to deal with this is to use an agent to pay 'extras' that may occur. Shop around for these agents, as costs and reliability may vary considerably. Agents can provide information on costs and give updates on the goods or supplies in the customs system. Try to obtain duty-free or similar status, as this should, but will not necessarily, save costs. It is not unheard of to have to pay for documentation marked gratis.

Many NGOs try to avoid these problems altogether, by transporting small but crucial amounts of supplies as the personal baggage of arriving staff. Doing this may cost excess baggage fees, but this will be made up with the speed and safety in which the supplies will travel. Transporting staff should claim such material as personal goods, carry the necessary documents for this status and remove the supplies from their original boxes, otherwise they may be charged for import or encounter other problems when entering the country.

Shipping contracts

Contracts are necessary when transporting supplies using an external service provider. Well-established companies may have a standard contract, but a transport contract should cover the following points.

- **Price and means of payment** Payment can be made in stages, but full payment should not be made until final delivery has been verified.
- **Conditions in which the supplies must be kept** Include specifics if the items need special care such as a specific temperature, watertightness or fragility.
- If dangerous materials are being transported, including fuel, the contract should specify that the materials will be kept separate from other

supplies. Food should be sent in its own vehicle or only with non-hazardous items.

- **Reporting and status updates** The consequences of delay should be fully spelled out in the shipping contract if possible.
- Acceptance of liability for the goods and supplies that are being transported. Clarification can be put in the contract regarding the means of reimbursement (i.e. whether in case or in kind).
- All changes to the contract should be made in writing.

When working with shipping contractors, consider the following:

- **Check references** Ask other NGOs or organizations they have worked for in the past.
- Follow up verbal conversations with written documents. Get verbal reassurances in writing.
- In some areas, cartels that artificially inflate prices can be a problem, so NGOs should adopt standard pricing scales.
- Do not rely solely on the shipper's information (or claim) that the goods or supplies have been fully delivered; it is important to have a reporting mechanism of your own to verify their information. Visual inspection of all claims by the NGO's own staff is crucial to avoid unforeseen problems.

Box 12.2 International cargo abbreviations and terms (INCOMTERMS)

AWB (Air waybill)	A document serving as a guide to a carrier's staff for handling, dispatching and delivering the consignment. It is a non-negotiable document.
Bill of lading	A receipt for goods, contract for their carriage, and documentary evidence of title to goods. It is a bill of exchange and a negotiable document of title.
C and F	Cost and freight. The shipper pays for freight to the named destination port.
CIF	Cost, insurance and freight.
COD	Cash on delivery.
DWT	(dead weight) A ship's dead weight in the number of tonnes (2,240 lb) required to sink the vessel in the water to its load line. DWT cargo capacity is the weight available for cargo after all other allowances have been made.
DDP	Delivery duty paid.
DDU	Delivery duty unpaid.
ExW	Ex-works. Buyer pays for preparation and shipping of goods.
FAS	Free alongside ship. Price of goods at dockside in port of discharge.
FOB	Free on board. The price of goods covers transportation to the port of shipment, loading, and stowage, not transportation costs to final destination.

- If regularly using contract shippers, meet them regularly to ensure smooth operations and to clear up issues.
- Try to use the same tracking numbers, if used, as the shipper, to facilitate reporting and verification.

Inspection

Make sure an inspection, and if necessary reporting, is carried out by a member of staff at each point along the supply chain. The inspection should be as thorough as time will allow and should be standardized to avoid staff taking shortcuts.

Waybills

Waybills are the primary way for maintaining control of shipping. Ideally, the waybill form should be made in at least four carbonless copies: the top original being retained by the sender, the second with the transporter, the third by the receiver and, once receipt can be confirmed by the receiver, the fourth copy returned to the sender.

Staff handling waybills should be trained to verify all listed items against what they are able to account for visually. If there is a difference or discrepancy due to loss or damage, the waybill will help narrow down who may be held accountable. For managers, it is important to review copies of waybills as soon as they are returned. If there is a discrepancy, it should be looked into straight away as the longer time goes by the harder it will be to find out what happened to the missing goods.

Storage and warehousing

Finding storage space

Finding storage space and warehousing can be a challenge, especially when there is little time. If there is a need to store large quantities of supplies, one option is to arrange for other organizations to store the items until the moment they are needed or are ready for shipping. If WFP is to supply food, for example, it may have been funded to store the rations and should not rely on NGOs to handle its warehousing.

Another option is to find existing warehouse space. Many NGOs prefer this as it is better to control and manage their own stocks. Usually a contract has to be drawn up just as with any property rental. In rare cases, it may be possible to appeal to a business or industry to provide storage space. If working in an undeveloped area, it may be likely that a temporary structure may be set up. This may consist of simple tents, large 'Rubb Halls' or prefabricated structures. Care should be taken to ensure that the structures will withstand local conditions, as the case may be, such as torrential downpours, freezing or furnace-like temperatures and gale-force winds.

In terms of size, consider the type of programming that will be supported. Health-oriented programmes may deal with large amount of donated medical supplies and their warehousing needs may fluctuate. Water and sanitation programmes will need, among other things, warehousing space to handle pumps, pipes, water containers, cement for casting water wells and latrine parts. Food distribution programmes tend to require the most space, but calculating space is straightforward. For example, 1 tonne of grain takes up a space of 1 m^2 and a volumetric space of 1 m^3. See Table 12.3.

Security, accountability and convenience need to be balanced. The context and situation need to be considered carefully. In many cases, a single warehouse, as opposed to several small storage spaces, may be best, especially if it can be in the same place as other facilities like vehicle workshops and maintenance areas. This can help control assets, lessen travel time and help prevent small-scale pilfering.

Table 12.3 Warehouse selection and maintenance checklist

✓	✓
Size (i.e. room for expansion of stock, sufficient ventilation around all supplies)	Loading area (i.e. large enough for parking largest vehicle and carrying out counts and inspections). Covered space is ideal
Soundness of warehouse structure (e.g. leak- and pest-free, and good floor with adequate drainage)	Access to extra supplies such as pallets, plastic covering and water
Sufficiently secure doors, windows, and fences and walls	Adequate utilities (e.g. electricity, lighting, ventilation and toilets)
Adequate office space. The office space should at a minimum be sufficient for compiling and storing documentation	Space for workers (i.e. loaders, sorters, security) appropriate to location. At least protecting workers from inclement weather
Availability of labour including causal workers and security guards	Allowance for special items (e.g. such as fuel, medical items and food products) that may need regulated temperatures, protection from strong light or safety considerations

Managing a warehouse

Unloading and loading

Enough staff are needed to count the number of units being loaded into and unloaded out of storage. Casual labour is often available for this purpose and so in most cases there needs to be enough cash on hand to pay them immediately after they have finished work. (See p. 245 for stacking information.)

Packed boxes should be marked on the outside with any special instructions (e.g. temperature requirements or 'fragile') clearly visible. A contents list should be placed inside the top of the package or box to facilitate accountability.

Make sure that the number of units unloaded is accurately reflected on the waybill. A manager should not sign for a waybill or delivery note unless staff are sure of the amount. When receiving the goods, note all shortages and damages on the waybill before signing.

Inventories

Inventories are important for several reasons. First, they are used for planning and determining priorities. Second, an inventory can help keep track of expiration dates. Third, inventories can help managers share resources. Fourth, the value of inventories can be added to the revenue of the NGO; indeed, some donor agencies require them. Finally, and most importantly, they can help control and maintain accountability of an organization's resources. Inventories, such as shown in Table 12.4, are fairly easy to do but should be updated regularly.

For typical NGO supply systems, a simple computer spreadsheet is sufficient for maintaining an adequate inventory. In fact, anything more complicated may overwhelm those who have to work on this system. Still, it helps to be aware of other systems. The Pan-American Health organization (PAHO) (2001) has created for its own use a computer application called SUMA (SUpply and MAnagement system) that is available free from the internet (www.disaster-info.net/SUMA). The system tracks goods and supplies along the supply chain, allowing for tracking and inventorying at a centralized level. Commercial software applications (e.g. see www.intellitrack.net) that are linked with barcode technology have the capability of printing barcode labels for almost any device, vehicle, package or other relief item.

Inventories should not be done just for warehouse commodities but for all assets owned or controlled by a NGO. Typically, there are several types of

Table 12.4 Inventory example

Item no.	Description	Serial no.	Location	Donor	Date of acquisition
001	Radio, VHF handset, Motorola	710-89-192B	Central office	ECHO	10 May
002	Radio, HF base station, Codan	D2C098-4459907	Central office	UN	17 June

inventories. NGOs typically define capital assets as more than a predetermined amount of money (e.g. NGOs funded by USAID use the figure US$5,000), or of a normal service life longer than 12 months. These assets can be provided with a tracking number on a heavy-duty tag or physically imprinted on the item. If required by a donor or it is necessary to maintain control and accountability for supplies, another inventory can be maintained for other items such as desks and chairs. These items may be given a common number that is simply written somewhere on the item. A third inventory can be maintained for programme supplies that would typically be stored in a warehouse or some other storage space.

Inventories should be carried out at regular intervals, depending on the programme and situation, and if possibly before and after a significant shipment, which may have disrupted supplies and resulted in loss. Spot checks should be done periodically to identify discrepancies, whether by mistake or by theft. Train staff how to carry out an inventory, including even seemingly self-explanatory tasks such as how items are to be counted.

Storage

There are a number of ways to organize and maintain supplies to maintain their condition, shown in Figure 12.2. First, a numbering system should be instituted to classify items. Many different methods work, and usually the simpler the better (such as cardboard signs on walls designating different project sectors or dates of arrival or expiration), but the important thing is that there is a system.

Second, goods and supplies should be placed on wooden pallets or similar, to prevent moisture from spoiling the bottoms of stacks. Ventilation is important but protection from sunlight and rain should be maintained. There should also be a way to deal with rodents and other pests. Poisons and traps should be available before trouble starts, and cats also help, but they deserve a long-term commitment.

Finally, it is normal practice to stack items so that the first items in are the first items taken out ('first in first out', or FIFO) which is needed for items with expiration dates. In practice, it is possible that items will arrive with expiry dates earlier than items that are already in storage, so warehouse staff will need to be aware of the date status of all incoming items to decide when they can be shipped out to the next stage in the supply chain.

Stacking must be supervised. Loading staff may be anxious to finish the job and likely to take short cuts, especially if it is at the end of a day or before a break. They may stack goods too high, resulting in damage. If there are shelves, they may also create dangerous loads. They may also mix items, causing inventory problems later on. Close supervision will also help prevent theft. Table 12.5 provides details on stacking.

Some suggestions for handling damaged goods include: establish procedures for recording and handling damaged goods and those that are short in weight. Suspected spoiled items should be separated according to problem. A manager (or a knowledgeable staff member if it is a special item like food or medical equipment) should inspect the damaged item and decide if any of it can be

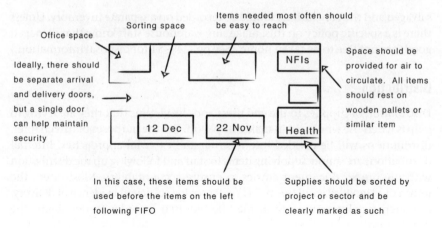

Office space

Sorting space

Items needed most often should be easy to reach

Ideally, there should be separate arrival and delivery doors, but a single door can help maintain security

NFIs

Space should be provided for air to circulate. All items should rest on wooden pallets or similar item

12 Dec   22 Nov   Health

In this case, these items should be used before the items on the left following FIFO

Supplies should be sorted by project or sector and be clearly marked as such

Figure 12.2 Warehouse layout

Table 12.5 Warehouse stacking

Commodity	Approximate volume per tonne ($m^3/1,000$ kg)	Standard package	Typical maximum stacking height
Water	1	None	n/a
Food grains/beans	2	50-kg bag	20–40 bags
Flour and blended foods	2	2-kg bag	20–30 bags
DSM in bags	2.4	25-kg bag	20–30 bags
DSM in tins inside cartons	4	20-kg/carton 4 tins/carton	8 individual cartons or 20 if palletized
Edible oil in tins inside cartons	2	25-kg/carton 6 tins/carton	8 individual cartons or 20 if palletized
Oil in drums	1.4	200-litre or 55-gallon drum	2 drums upright with wood between the rims or 3 drums on their sides
ORS	2.4	35-kg carton	3–4 m
Mixed drugs	3.5	45-kg carton	3–4 m
Clinic equipment and teaching aids	4.5	35–50 kg	3–4 m
Kitchen utensils	5	35–40-kg cartons	3–4 m
Family tents	4.5	35–60 kg/unit	4.5 m*
Compressed blankets	4.5	70 units/bale	4.5 m*
Loose blankets	9	85 kg/bale	3-4 m

Source: UNHCR (2000: 374).
*Where equipment for stacking allows.

salvaged and the conclusions should be recorded on a separate inventory. Unless there is a specific policy on this, make sure warehouse staff know that damaged goods are not free to be taken home. (See pp. 249–51 for disposal information.)

Distribution

Distribution of supplies to the end users and the victims that they are trying to help is when the whole chain makes its payoff. For the purposes of this chapter, distributions will be divided into internal and external approaches. Internal distributions are simply supplying items to staff and following up the distribution with the proper document entries to ensure accountability. Most often, the return of a signed waybill (see p. 241) will provide sufficient evidence of delivery, although a delivery note form may be required in order to document the distribution.

External distributions are more complicated, but they offer a good opportunity to interact with beneficiaries. There are several types of external distributions, as follows.

- **Targeted** This type of distribution is probably the most common and allows specific assessed needs to be addressed (e.g. such as children under 5 years of age). Distributions to selected groups require good assessment and monitoring.
- **Blanket** This type of distribution targets everyone in a particular area (e.g. a camp). Blanket distributions can be done quickly and are easy to monitor. In general, to reduce the possibility of people taking from others, it should not be done where the social system is rigidly stratified, certain types of people are structurally marginalized or insurgents operate in the area with impunity.
- **Area** The goal of this type of distribution, which may be done by air drop, has more to do with public relations than with addressing humanitarian need. Because it is essentially unaccountable and open to widespread redistribution, NGOs typically do not involve themselves with this type of distribution.

There are several types of targeted distributions, each with different advantages and disadvantages, as summarized in Table 12.6.

Box 12.3 Vaccine logistics

Most vaccines, both in tablet and injectable form, must be kept at a consistent cold temperature (neither below freezing nor above 15 degrees centigrade). Cold-chain management refers to the cold-storage refrigerators and cold boxes used for storing and transporting vaccines. Once the vaccines are in the cold chain, it should not be for more than 72 hours. This system requires special equipment, but is made easier with single-unit refrigerators that can be run with either fuel or solar energy depending on the availability of each. Generally, the main problem with cold chains is that staff use the equipment for storing food and drinks, which may destroy vaccines. Managers need to monitor closely the use of this equipment.

Table 12.6 Distributions

Means of distribution	Advantages	Disadvantages
Local government	Quick and efficient when local infrastructure is adequate	Government capacity may be limited
Builds local capacity	High cost when local infrastructure needs to be reinforced	Government (or officials) may have financial or political motives for controlling food distributions
Traditional leaders	The social and cultural values of the population are respected	Knowledge of social structures and power relations is essential
	Easy in the initial stages of emergency and for dispersed populations*	Effective only in small intact communities
Low-cost and quick	Risk of abuse if social structures are broken down or replaced by abusive leadership	
	No external registration or ration cards are needed	Difficult to monitor
New groups or committees	Undermines abusive power relations and has a lower risk of abuse	External registration and ration cards are needed in some cases
	Agency understanding of the local society	Appropriate in stable situations only
	Some community participation, particularly women's representation, occurs	Groups must be elected so that they truly represent communities
	Self-monitoring	Resentment from traditional leadership
	Low-cost	Extensive information campaigns are needed
Households (in groups or individually*)	Efficient for large unstructured population	High cost (staff, materials, time).
	Initial control over beneficiary numbers	Little beneficiary participation
	Undermines abusive power relations and leadership	Registration and ration cards necessary
	Less risk of unequal distribution	
	Easy to monitor	
Individuals (cooked food)	No scope for manipulation or discrimination	Extremely high cost (staff, materials
	Self-targeting	Time-consuming

cont.

cont.

Means of distribution	Advantages	Disadvantages
	No registration or ration cards are needed	Possible only for small groups (1,000 per kitchen)
	Easy to monitor	No possibility for beneficiaries to exchange ration items so all nutritional needs have to be met
	Overcomes problems of limited fuel, utensils and water	Risk of creating population concentrations
		Health risks

Source: WFP (2002: 88–9)
*Distribution to representatives of individual households ensures more direct agency control but requires considerable resources; whereas distribution to pre-defined groups of households is less resource-intensive and less demeaning for beneficiaries. However, it is feasible only where there is good registration and homogeneous groups can be identified.

According to NRC (2004), an effective external distribution includes:
- **Good communication with beneficiaries and others involved in distributions** At a basic level, people need to know when distributions will occur so they can allocate their time. A distribution may take time away from other important activities (such as planting and water collection), so informing people enough in advance is important. There is also a need to understand cultural norms and social structures. The supplies being distributed, of course, should be locally appropriate. Distributions to families or households are the norm, but sometimes this may leave people out.
- **Effective registration and monitoring** Selection and documentation of the beneficiaries are critical. At times, it may be possible to verify a recipient's identity by using existing systems such as that established by the UN. An effective monitoring system that incorporates regular reporting and independent verification is important. At other times, it may be necessary to develop a ration card scheme. A monitoring system should consist of staff dedicated to monitoring, along with occasional checks to verify the staff's findings, cooperation from beneficiaries' leaders and an effective documentation system. A form, such as that shown in Table 12.7, can be used so as to ensure uniform monitoring.

Table 12.7 Distribution monitoring form

Community/Area	Supply type	Amount distributed	Amount received	Remaining balance
Camp 'A'	Hygiene kits	805	778	27

- **Adequate supplies** Before considering a distribution, ensure there are enough supplies to distribute in the first place. Not having enough on a distribution day can cause significant security problems. Even targeted distributions need to be done with enough information sharing and consensus building to avoid a feeling of unfairness among those who will not receive supplies. What to do if there is not enough? There are three main options: target selected groups, reduce amounts given out, or delay distribution until there is enough for everyone.
- **Adequate resources** There needs to be, for example, enough vehicles and registration materials to carry out the distribution. There should be enough staff to organize and control receipts, check records and issue seeds or tools. Although it depends on a number of factors, a team of seven can reasonably do a distribution to 400–500 people in a day.
- **Good site selection** Distributions can become uncontrolled unless an appropriate physical site for the distribution is selected. A number of factors, including accessibility (to both transport and recipients), appropriate size, the ability to control crowds and infrastructure are important considerations. In some places, the beneficiary population may be accustomed to receiving distributions and it is important to learn about the standard practice and expectations for the area.

Maintenance and disposal

Maintenance and disposal are too often an afterthought in logistics. Even if a programme starts with all new equipment of the best standard, it will not take long for dust, heat and cold, moisture, poor treatment and overuse to take effect. Logistics staff should consider the need for maintenance from the start and put in a system that handles items that no longer function. Many NGOs use a form that can be attached to broken items and some tracking sheet or similar to record where items have been taken for repair.

There are several options for dealing with broken items. These include:

- **Hiring full-time maintenance staff** Depending on the size of the programme's resources, this may be an option for camps or other projects (e.g. displaced persons' camps) or for special items like vehicles or IT equipment. The skill level of the maintenance staff should be tested before hiring. Unless there is no better option, the staff should not open items that may be covered under warrantee.
- **Outsourcing** This will most likely be the primary means of repair for most equipment, as the level of sophistication of even basic items is too complex for a repair generalist.
- **Return to supplier or factory** In some cases, this option may be the only one, especially for items like radios. Shipping times and difficulties make this a problematic option for those running emergency programmes. It is worth checking to see if there is an active warrantee on the item and if it is possible to repair the item at a regional service centre.

- **Disposal** There are several options for disposing of items, such as donating or cannibalizing the item for parts. Certain sensitive items (e.g. batteries and medical items) require special attention. In any case, to maintain accountability, a record should be made of the item's disposal; organizations often have a specific policy about how this should be handled.

In practice, each one of these options will be used at one time or another. The key is to track and follow up routinely, so that items are accounted for and can be put back into service or replaced as quickly as possible. If an item becomes obsolete or otherwise unusable, there are several options: sale, scrap, trade, transfer, or donating the item to a person or group that believes they can salvage the item.

Sorting must first be done which may time-consuming, so the task must be planned and well organized. If none of the options is workable, it may be necessary to junk the items or materials. In emergencies, where the breakdown of public services can be expected, logistics staff may have to create a private landfill or find some means of disposal. Certain types of items require different disposal methods, such as medical waste, as summarized in Table 12.8.

Table 12.8 Summary of disposal methods

Item type	Disposal method	Comment
Solids	Landfill placed in sealed drum or similar container	No more than 1% of the daily disposal should be untreated
Semi-solids	Medium- and high-temperature incineration (cement kiln incinerator)	
Powders		
Batteries	Recycle, return to manufacturer, or landfill	An environmental hazard, should be disposed of professionally, which may mean transporting to capital city if not possible locally
Fuels	Recycle or waste encapsulation	Do not put in sewer or open water source. Where possible, try to recycle motor oil through vendors. Spoiled fuel can often be used for other purposes such as cleaning solvents or starting cooking fires
Oils		
Pharmaceutical ampoules	Crush ampoules and flush diluted fluid into sewer	Certain substances (e.g. antineoplastics) should not be put in a sewer or open water source. Ampoules should not be put in an incinerator

cont.

cont.

Item type	Disposal method	Comment
IT equipment	Recycle, return to manufacturer, or landfill	Most computer parts are inert and can be refurbished for reuse. Certain components, especially CPUs, contain environmentally harmful compounds which should be disposed of like batteries
Controlled drugs	Landfill placed in sealed drum or similar container	Do not send to landfills unless encapsulated professionally. Health officials should be contacted regarding expired drugs
	Medium- and high-temperature incineration (cement kiln incinerator)	
Aerosol canisters	Landfill	Do not burn as they may explode
	Waste encapsulation	
Disinfectants	Put in sewer or fast-flowing watercourse: small quantities of diluted disinfectants (maximum 50 litres per day under supervision)	Do not put undiluted disinfectants in sewers or watercourses
		Maximum 50 l per day diluted to sewer or fast-flowing watercourse. Do not put disinfectants at all in slow-moving or stagnant watercourses
PVC plastic, glass	Landfill	Not for burning in open containers
Paper, cardboard	Recycle, burn, landfill	Paper containing sensitive or private information, such as accounting and personnel information, should be shredded or burned

Source: Adapted from WHO (1999).

CHAPTER 13

Handling transport and maintaining vehicles

Transport represents one of the highest expenditures in emergency programmes and managing it can be one of the most time-consuming tasks. The purpose of this chapter is to introduce some of the basic issues, specifically:
- Buying and renting vehicles
- Fleet management
- Driving safely
- Drivers
- Other modes of transport

Procuring, importing and establishing a system for maintenance and the accountable use of vehicles are a major logistical responsibility. Although medium- and large-scale relief programmes usually have separate staff and considerable resources to handle transport, managers of organizations of all sizes should be familiar with fleet management.

Road travel also represents the most dangerous threat to relief workers. Violence and disease are considerable risks, but road accidents happen with alarming frequency in disaster-prone countries. Bad road conditions and poorly trained drivers are only part of the problem. Even experienced drivers can be overworked, leading to wasted time and accidents. To help address these issues, relief workers should be familiar with how to manage vehicles and other forms of transport.

Buying and renting road vehicles

There are several constraints on buying and renting vehicles, such as programme location and budget, which present different options for acquiring vehicles. Here are some of the considerations.

Choosing the vehicle

When assembling a fleet of vehicles, the type of project should be considered first. A variety of vehicles offers the best flexibility. Jeep-style vehicles, for example, are good at transporting people but are poor for hauling supplies and materials. Long-bed pick-ups are good for hauling supplies and materials but can only accommodate two or three people. Double-cabin pick-ups are a good middle choice in many cases, but they tend not to be as ruggedly built as other vehicles and do not have the carrying capacity of a standard long-bed pick-up.

- Ordering a vehicle should take into consideration the features of the local terrain the use the vehicle will be put to. Most NGOs look for rugged features, durability, ability to be serviced locally, high ground clearance and appropriate features, such as air-conditioning for hot climates, high-altitude compensators and self-recovery equipment for poor roads.
- Where possible, NGOs should try to use automobiles (cars) for towns to save costs and help project a frugal image.
- Extra equipment should be considered based on where the vehicle will operate, such as a front-mounted winch, a fording air-intake snorkel, snow chains, ropes and tarps, field kit (e.g. axes and saws) and spare part kits.
- Features such as turbo engines, computerized control systems and power windows may malfunction or breakdown and so doing without may be better.
- Colour is important. White is an almost universal colour for NGO and UN vehicles, but other neutral colours such as light blue work equally well. Dark colours and those associated with military forces, especially green, tan and black, should be avoided.
- Security should also be considered, since expensive vehicles are more likely to be stolen and project an image of wealth. Stickers with 'No Weapons/No Riders' logos should be acquired before vehicles are delivered.
- Some donors, particularly the UN specialized agencies, give vehicles in kind to NGOs as part of a grant agreement. Typically, the NGO must agree to look after the vehicle for the life of the grant. An inspection of the vehicle should be carried out before signing any vehicle agreement.

Buying

- Budget at least 20 per cent of the cost of the vehicle for maintenance, including for the vehicle's first year of use.
- Obtain comprehensive insurance or ensure there is significant money set aside for accidents and pay-outs that would normally be paid by an insurance company.
- Vehicle dealerships can be found in the capitals of most countries. While they might not offer the most competitive prices, this can be made up for in services. Vehicles can also be ordered through commercial firms such as Bukkhave (www.bukkhave.com) or Kjaer & Kjaer (www.kjaer.com).
- Work with local dealers if they exists and do a pre-delivery inspection as detailed by the manufacturer. Typically, this must be done before the vehicle is driven or warrantees may be voided.

Renting

- Try to have a clear idea of who the owner of the vehicle is and how the vehicle was used before it was for rental.

- Insist on inspecting the vehicle's original documents.
- Check the vehicle thoroughly, make sure everything works (including, for example, rear windows) and that a spare tyre is present). Take it for a test drive, making sure gears and brakes are effective, and that the vehicle performs and handles as it should.
- Clear and realistic contracts are the important. In most cases, the owner will be responsible for maintenance, except for minor faults like flat tyres and changing the oil. Payment details should be worked out at a rate that is consistent with what other NGOs pay.

Fleet management

This section covers four topics relating to managing a fleet of vehicles: basic trip planning, maintenance, fuel use and accountability. (See pp. 260–65 for driving and drivers.)

An NGO fleet can consist of three or more vehicles. More than a half-dozen vehicles will likely need a transport manager and more than a dozen vehicles will require a dedicated facility (or designated garage if available) for maintenance and servicing.

Photo 13.1 Vehicle Radio Mount
Vehicles will need modifications and adjustments to handle poor or non-existent roads such as storing tyres on roof-racks, and having extra spares and tyres specific to the environment. Here, a HF radio antenna was mounted to the bumper but soon broke, so that a special additional mount had to be added.

Trip planning

Most NGOs manage vehicle using two means: the trip request form and the movement control board.

Trip request form

Some NGOs find it useful in planning to have a trip request for trips over certain limits. Examples include trips outside the immediate area, trips longer than three hours or overnight trips. Figure 13.1 shows one example, but each NGO will need to develop its own policy based on the context in which they operate.

Movement control board

A movement control board is a simple means of tracking the location and use of vehicles. If available, a large whiteboard works, best but plastic and chalkboards work too. There are at least two ways to design a board. The first method (Table 13.1) provides immediate accountability where drivers must 'sign-out' before departure.

The second (Table 13.2) method allows for better planning.

NGO XYZ

Requestor's Name: _____

Dates of Travel: From _____ to _____

Location: _____

Specific Vehicle Requests: _____

Additional Requests for Logistics: _____

Supervisor's Approval: _____ Logistics Approval: _____

Figure 13.1 Trip request form

Table 13.1 Movement control – 1

Vehicle	Destination and purpose	Driver	Time out	Estimated time of return
Jeep 001	Camp 1/Programme	Kanut	8:45	14:00
Pick-Up 002	Market/Procurement	Willy	9:20	13:30
Jeep 003	Garage	Benoit	8:15	17:00

Table 13.2 Movement control – 2

Vehicle	Time allocation	Comment
Jeep 001	[Camp 1/Programme————————] [UN————]	
Benoit	8 9 10 11 12 13 14 15 16 17 18	
Pick-up 002	[Market/Procurement————-] [Coord Meet]	
Willy	8 9 10 11 12 13 14 15 16 17 18	
Jeep 003		Garage all day for maintenance
Kanut	8 9 10 11 12 13 14 15 16 17 18	

Basic maintenance

Many vehicle problems can be prevented through maintenance. In emergencies, vehicles will need servicing frequently. Emergencies seem to happen most often in areas with the worst roads on the planet. Here are some recommended average service intervals for various conditions.

- **Decent conditions** Service vehicle every 4,000 km; surfaced main and good secondary roads where speeds average 70–80 km/h and good-quality oil and fuels are available.
- **Bad conditions** Service vehicle every 2,500 km; poor roads and tracks, mud, dust, deep water and ruts, with average speeds of less than 50 km/h and medium-quality oils and fuel.
- **Rough conditions** Service vehicle every 1,500 km; rough tracks and terrain, thick mud, dust, deep water and ruts, where average speeds are very slow and oil and fuels are of poor quality.

Because of the complexity of most off-road vehicles, servicing should be carried out by professionals in suitably equipped workshops. Professional mechanics should provide regular services, as described above, at 3,000 km (or 2,000 miles) intervals.

Determining a garage or maintenance shop's capacity

In remote areas, or when a fleet's large size justifies it, an NGO may need to operate its own workshop. In many areas, however, particularly in capital cities and larger towns, a commercial garage may be available and will obviate the need to have a workshop. To decide if a garage or maintenance shop is worth establishing a relationship with, consider the shop's technical capacity, equipment and costs. Probably the most important indicator of capacity, the quality of work, can be difficult to determine. Apart from direct experience, the best way to find out about the quality of work is to seek references from other customers and NGOs.

Table 13.3 provides a maintenance checklist for those NGOs that have their own workshops.

Table 13.3 Vehicle maintenance checklist

Daily	✓	Weekly/Monthly	✓
Fuel level		Fuel filter	
Water level		Oil filter	
Oil quantity and colour		Wiper fluid	
Clean		Tyre air pressure	
Brakes		Engine mounts	
Battery connections		Grease points	
Tyre pressure and damage		Fan and alternator belts	
Vehicle documents		Transmission oil	
Radio check		Brake oil	
Lights: head, rear, hazard, turning and interior		While engine is warm, check fuel system hoses, leaks and other potential problems	
Water and first-aid kit		In gas engine, check spark plugs	
Tool kit		Horn	
Tow and jumper cables		Air filter	
Spare tyres and jack		Battery-acid level	
Snow chains or other items specific to location or travel route			

Note: Routine check-ups based on mileage should be carried out by a qualified mechanic.

Fuel use

There are two main types of fuel: gasoline and diesel. Petrol (gasoline) is common throughout the world for use in automobiles. Diesel is more common for off-road vehicles and trucks and has a variety of advantages over petrol. Diesel is less volatile than gasoline and does not evaporate very quickly, which makes it safer to transport and handle. In some countries, diesel fuel is given a priority over gasoline during shortages, because of its commercial and military importance. Diesel and gasoline engines also function differently. In a diesel motor, fuel is ignited by high-compression heat, instead of by a spark plug, which drives the pistons. An injector pump, which sprays diesel fuel in the right form, also does away with the carburettor.

Diesel fuel also tends to be more economical, although the vehicles that use it tend to be large and demand, especially when air-conditioners are on, considerable amounts of fuel. To determine the fuel requirements for a particular vehicle, it is possible to use this approach.

$$\frac{\text{Litres} \times 60 \text{ minutes (generator) or } 100 \text{ km (vehicles)}}{\text{Cost per litre}}$$

Maintaining the accountability of fuel

Good accountability in fuel procurement is important. NGOs typically use one or more out of three different means of handling and storing fuel: 55-gallon drums, fuel tanks of various sizes and prepaid vouchers or coupons issued through filling stations. The advantages and disadvantages of each method are summarized in Table 13.4.

The main means of maintaining the accountability of drivers and vehicles is through vehicle logbooks (see Table 13.5). These can also be checked against the movement control board as well as eye-witness recollection of passengers and others.

Table 13.4 Fuel accountability

	Drums	Tanks	Vouchers/Coupons
Advantages	Easy transport and storage	Put large amount of fuel in control of organization	Limited access
	Good for small programmes and remote locations	Usually filled by tanker truck which is administratively easy	Less administrative burden
			Station fuel is usually of a good quality
			Good for large programmes
		Decent for medium-sized and large programmes	
Disadvantages	Easily stolen	Can be stolen if not properly secured	Vehicles must be close to established fuelling station
	Contamination of fuel is easier	Requires area in compound to accommodate tank	Arrangements must be formally made
	Small quantities in each drum means that many drums needed	Requires extra safety precautions	Fuel available only during working hours of station
		Needs good record-keeping	Vouchers or coupons can be stolen or traded

Table 13.5 Vehicle log

Date	Destination	Beginning, km	Ending, km	Total km	Driver's name	Fuel in
3/8	Office to warehouse	8.560	8.569	9	Carlos	
3/8	Warehouse to clinic	8.569	8.581	12	Carlos	20 litres
		8.581				

Driving safely

Only drivers with the training and confidence should drive, since NGO vehicles are often exposed to very bad roads. As a general daily precaution, the advice above (about trip planning, vehicle inspections and fleet management) should be adopted as SOPs. Following these instructions, drivers should be competent to safely negotiate a number of different conditions and scenarios described below.

Driving techniques for poor and dangerous conditions

Large or deep obstacles Trenches, large rocks and deep potholes can damage the underside of vehicles and traction can be lost if wheels lift off the ground. To prevent this, the driver should approach obstacles at an angle and enter or cross over the obstacle one wheel at a time in a low gear.

Fords and water crossings Different vehicle makes and models have different abilities to cross water. Before approaching water, check the manufacturer's advice. The electronics and air intake are vulnerable, but most off-road vehicles can handle water as deep as 50 cm without special precautions. If it is a known ford, make sure the water level is low enough for the vehicle to cross and approach the standard route. If the creek or stream is unknown, it will be necessary to scout the water's depth. If the water is judged to be shallow enough, drive slowly and at a consistent speed. If the water is deep but must be crossed, and if tracked vehicles are available, it may be possible to turn off the motor while being towed across.

Snow, sand or mud The best tactic is to avoid the softest stretches by scouting before entering unknown patches. A low gear, using constant, well-controlled momentum should be maintained without spinning the tyre or stopping. If there is no other route, or the vehicle becomes stuck, slightly deflate the tyres to provide better traction. Moving the front wheel from side to side may also give further traction. If the road has deep muddy ruts, once entered the tyres will follow these channels and the vehicle should simply maintain constant speed until out of the ruts. Snow and mud conditions can change over the course of a day, so careful planning is essential.

Climbing an incline Select a low gear, but if it is too low the motor will not have enough power. Try to approach the hill straight on so that the weight is evenly distributed on all wheels. If the climb starts to fail, apply the brakes and put the vehicle in reverse while carefully backing down for a second, or try another route.

Driving in insecure environments

Driving is made even more hazardous for NGOs by the threat of violence. Road travel is the time of greatest vulnerability for relief workers. Careful planning, good driving practices and avoiding dangerous situations are essential in insecure environments. The following suggestions are SOPs for many NGOs.

Pre-trip actions

- Confirm that HQ knows or has approved of the trip, routing, estimated time of departure (ETD) and estimated time of arrival (ETA).
- Lock all doors.
- Fill out logbook unless there is an immediate problem of any sort.
- Fasten seatbelts before leaving.

If there is a threat of terrorism, a number of additional steps should be undertaken. Unless parked inside a secure compound, vehicles should not be left unattended at any time. A driver should guard the vehicle. To do so, the driver or guard must be outside but within 5 m of the vehicle, with a clear view of the entire vehicle. Some drivers may have a tendency to take guarding their vehicle lightly, so they need training and reminders of the importance of this responsibility. If, for some reason, the vehicle has been left unattended, the following checks should be performed.

- On approaching the vehicle, look for suspicious people or activities in the area.
- Walk around the entire vehicle looking for signs of tampering or anything unusual.
- Check to make sure the bonnet (hood) is in a locked position.
- Look around each wheel to see if there are any unusual objects.
- Check underneath the vehicle to see if there are any obstructions or objects.
- Visually inspect the exhaust pipe to make sure it is clear.
- Look inside the windows of the vehicle to make sure there is nothing new or out of place.
- Only once satisfied, enter the vehicle.

Driving

- Ensure drivers are familiar with SOPs and have received training. Many drivers feel empowered to drive recklessly in NGO vehicles. Strict rules should prohibit this behaviour, and sanctions including termination may need to be applied to repeat offenders.

Table 13.6 Accident avoidance

Flat tyre at speed	Traffic suddenly stops	Pedestrian or animal jumps in front of vehicle	Vehicle encounters water	Negotiating an ice patch
Hold steering wheel tightly; vehicle will lean on flat tyre	Depending on the speed and amount of room, first try to brake heavily (for anti-lock brakes) or pump the brake pedal in older vehicles	Try everything to safely avoid collision.	If there is flooding, try avoiding water altogether and if the vehicle stalls, exit to the roof and hope for rescue.	Ease off the accelerator without applying the brakes
Ease off the accelerator and slowly apply the brakes	If a collision is still likely, try steer the vehicle into a clear path (either side of the obstacle/ other vehicles) and then apply brakes	In some countries, mob justice dictates severe revenge for such accidents. Be aware of such customs. If crowds threaten physical violence, decide if it is necessary to get away from the scene, but always immediately report the accident	If in the water already and looks shallow enough to cross, use first gear while revving the engine	Maintain a straight course until the vehicle crosses the ice
Once the vehicle slows, drive off the road to avoid traffic		In some countries, local drivers purposely hit wild animals for their meat and/or pelts. NGOs should have policies that prevent such action	If the vehicle plunges into deep water, after impact try to roll down the windows and exit on to the surface. Water pressure will make it impossible to open the doors until it is equal inside and out.	

- Windows should not be rolled down more than 5 cm, so as to prevent objects (e.g. hands, sticks or grenades) from entering. When driving through crowds, windows should be completely closed.
- Passengers should be instructed (and empowered) to tell drivers to slow down or speed up as needed.
- Always leave an 'out'. When coming to a stop, leave about one vehicle length of space to facilitating pulling out or turning round if the vehicle immediately to the front happens to stall or not move.
- If resources allow it, two vehicles should be used in convoy when heading to remote or insecure areas. The chance of two vehicles breaking down or being involved in the same accident is very low and it allows one to return to safety.
- In rough and remote areas, two spare tyres should be provided for each vehicle.
- Before coming to the destination, slow down and scan the entire area for suspicious people or activities.
- Although frequently used by other types of organizations, NGOs rarely use ballistic protection on vehicles. Cost is strictly prohibitive and it goes against the acceptance strategy of security used by many NGOs (see Chapter 18).
- Park in well-known areas and with the vehicle's front facing out. This facilitates leaving without backing up, which can be dangerous and delay departure if there is an emergency.

Checkpoints

- Drive slowly and according to posted speed limits.
- Do not make sudden movements.
- Follow the police's or soldier's hand signals and verbal instructions.
- Do not take photographs.
- The driver and passengers should keep their hands visible.
- Be polite but show resolve.
- After passing through, drive through at a normal speed and do not look back.
- If the checkpoint is suspected of being unauthorized, prepare to follow the above actions and also be prepared to treat it as a roadblock.

Roadblocks

- If there are large crowds, depending on the SOP decided for that area, either find an alternative route or return to the NGO office.
- If driving through crossfire or a road barricade, maintain an even but fast speed.
- If there is a life-threatening situation and there are no other options, hit objects squarely and, if unavoidable, strike other vehicles in the rear where there is less weight in the vehicle.

Convoys

Convoys are a procession of three or more vehicles and are used for the simple fact that there is safety in numbers. Convoys have two main applications: moving supplies or large numbers of people and evacuations. Convoys may increase security by sheer numbers, but they may also present a bigger target.

Convoys should be planned carefully because of the number of variables and people involved. A convoy leader, who has good leadership qualities and communication skills, should be elected or appointed. The convoy leader or deputy should be able to speak the same language as the drivers. As much information about different routes, such as road conditions, the level of security including the presence of checkpoints and landmines, travel times and distances, should be collected before hand. Weather reports should also be monitored before departure and during the trip.

The convoy leader should hold a pre-departure meeting with the driver of each vehicle to discuss departure time, the route and any alternatives, speed limits and distance between vehicles, planned stops and rally points, communications and what to do in case of an accident or unexpected problems such as a roadblock, landmines or gunfire. The order of movement should also be discussed, as shown in Figure 13.2.

As with many tasks, there is no exact right order or method: what works is what is best. The convoy leader may elect to be in the middle, which makes managing and communicating with other vehicles easier. In difficult areas, or for short periods, they may decide to be in front. Cargo (large trucks) and passengers (buses), usually the slower vehicles, should travel towards the front to help set the pace. In most cases, medical aid and mechanics should be towards the rear or in the trail vehicle so that accidents can be driven to instead of having to backtrack. Ideally, every vehicle will have more than one means of communication (a primary and a back-up system such as VHF and HF). If there are few radios, at a minimum the lead and trail vehicle should be in contact.

Should expatriate staff be allowed to drive?

All staff may feel a strong urge to drive an organizational vehicle, but expatriates are more often accustomed to having a vehicle in their home country and may feel that driving is a right. The more expatriate staff there is, the more there will be a need for a clearly communicated and enforceable policy. There are three options.

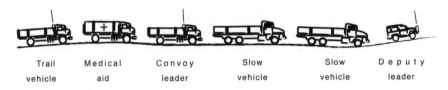

| Trail | Medical | Convoy | Slow | Slow | Deputy |
| vehicle | aid | leader | vehicle | vehicle | leader |

Figure 13.2 Convoy

- **No** General prohibition is equitable and easy to enforce (especially if the expatriates are present for short periods), but it can be inflexible, contribute to cabin fever and create the need for an extra night driver or drivers to match expatriates' schedules. If insecurity is high, this is the preferred option.
- **Restricted to certain staff** This policy allows a few approved expatriates to drive, passing the same test local staff drivers must pass. Usually, those with experience driving in similar conditions and when their position requires it, such as logistics, may drive. This gives some flexibility, but under controlled parameters. Many NGOs adopt this policy as a middle-of-the-road approach.
- **Yes** This option gives the most flexibility but gives the least amount of control, as well as increasing the chance of accidents dramatically. Even in this case, in emergency settings it is best if work-related trips outside or between towns is done by a full-time driver.

Other modes of transport

Aircraft

Here are some points to consider when working with aircraft (see also Chapter 12).

Helicopters Because of their flexibility, helicopters are frequently used in emergency operations. Every word and action of crew members should be followed when near them. In addition:

- If a helicopter is going to land near a camp or other temporary settlement, try to make sure that its flight path and its rotor wash will not significantly affect those on the ground (e.g. damaging tents and other temporary structures).
- People often come to watch aircraft. Help keep others, including animals and children, off the landing zone. According to WFP (2002), a 50-m zone round the landing zone is usually sufficient.
- Passengers and/or loaders should wait immediately off the landing zone in an upwind direction, with their backs to the aircraft until it has landed. Always approach a helicopter from the front. The first person should make eye contact directly with the pilots and/or the loadmaster and wait for their signal to come forward.
- Most helicopter rotors spin at safe height to walk under, but they can move especially it is windy. If the ground is sloping, crouch and try to approach from the downward side.

Air drops On rare occasions, air drops can help to reach remote locations, but they are used as a means of last resort. According to WFP (2002), an air drop reception committee should make arrangements, as follows.

- Local authorities should be contacted for selection and timing of air drops.
- Drop zones should be oriented with the prevailing wind and free of houses, trees and people.

- Although the bigger the better, drop zones should be 600–1,000 m in length and 80–200 m wide.
- As with helicopters, people will almost certainly come to watch, so guards are need to keep the drop zone clear of people and animals. The same guards can be used once the drop is complete to help collect and distribute the supplies.
- Panel markers can be used to indicate the middle of the drop zone and smoke or an improvised windsock (a brightly coloured streamer mounted high on a pole) can help the pilots identify the wind direction.
- Positive communication should be made with the aircraft and dropping should be done only when conditions are safe.

Boats

Boats are a viable source of transport in many parts of the world. From canoes to cargo ships, boats are important for transporting large stocks of commodities and supplies, as well as passengers. Many emergencies happen in coastal areas where the primary means of transport, or only means of access, is by water. NGOs use different type of boats to operate mobile health clinics, distribute commodities and carry out other activities. Although some emergencies happen in landlocked countries, boats may still be encountered, such as ferries and other boats on lakes and at river crossings.

Water rescue systems are universally poor or non-existent in developing countries. There is a considerable difference between rivers and lakes and the sea, although many of the same basic principles can be applied to both. If boats are to be used in emergency programmes, consider the following:

- **Ensure basic survival items are present** At a minimum, there should be personal flotation devices (Pads or life preservers, life jackets) for every passenger. These should be in good condition (compressed kapok, torn fasteners and worn-out nylon are not good signs) and readily accessible in case of problems. On any vessel over 10 m/40 ft, there should also be a lifeboat capable of handling all the passengers. There should also be a functioning marine or ship-to-shore radio on board.
- **Try to determine if the captain and crew are sufficiently skilled** If the boat is large, and making a livelihood is possible, the captain and crew are likely to be properly trained and have years of experience on smaller vessels. On small vessels, however, the captain may be new and have no training. Self-confidence should be evident in the captain and crew's behaviour. They should also be familiar with the boat and water from previous experience.
- **Carry out a seaworthiness inspection** Large boats or ships are likely to be seaworthy in all but exceptional sea conditions. But small boats may be more problematic. For instance, loose hull planking or evidence of leaks is not a good indicator. If the waterline, which indicates the level in which the boat is designed to float, is deeply submerged or if the

water's surface is close to the gunwale (the boat's topside) the vessel is overloaded. Many boats have capsized or sunk when an attempt has been made to carry too many goods and passengers.

- **Have an escape plan** If there are serious concerns, remain close to flotation devices and lifeboats, run through scenarios about what to do in case of sinking, and consider raising your concerns with the captain. If there are really serious problems, abort the trip or do not start it in the first place.

Motorcycles

There are several good reasons to use motorcycles in emergency programmes. First is their low cost: motorcycles can cost a tenth of a good four-wheel vehicle. They are also cheaper to maintain and require less fuel. Second, motorcycles give considerable flexibility and have the ability to go where some four-wheel vehicles cannot. Finally, there is no need for drivers, who consist of yet another expense. The disadvantage of motorcycles is that, of course, they have almost no load-carrying capacity, are more dangerous than four wheel vehicles and the strain on drivers, especially in inclement weather, can be considerable.

Training and tested will be needed for all staff given the responsibility to drive a motorcycle. Licensing should be looked into officially and insurance should cover each motorcycle. A strict policy should be put in place regarding the wearing of helmets and giving lifts to passengers (two helmets should be procured for each motorcycle). Most NGOs buy motorcycles that are no more than 100 cc or 125 cc because they are easier to handle. One way to reduce accidents is to restrict driving to rural areas only, outside cities where the risk of being struck by other vehicles is high.

CHAPTER 14

Communicating using radios and satellites

The difficulty of running emergency programmes can be lessened with good communications. Communication is important because it provides for coordination, information sharing including security, and social reasons. The purpose of this chapter is to provide an understanding to both radios and satellite equipment for both users and managers setting up different systems. This chapter covers the following topics:

- Radio basics
- Radio equipment and uses
- Setting up a communications system
- Organizing a radio room
- Radio procedures
- How to use radios
- Training
- Satellite communications

Despite the wide availability of telephones, radios and other specialized communications equipment will be critical tools for the foreseeable future (Wood, 1996). Like military systems, NGO communications need to be adaptable, transportable, rugged and dependable.

Although telecommunications is a complex discipline in its own right, it is often said that radio communication is as much art as science. There are many variables that can frustrate the uninitiated user, so all NGO staff working in the field need some basic familiarity. Simply, knowing how radios work and how to de-bug some of their problems can go a long way.

The growing availability of inexpensive satellite communications equipment makes it a viable option for even poorly funded NGOs. This equipment has the benefit of general ease of use and the ability to work nearly anywhere in the world. Their applicability to field conditions is discussed on pp. 281–5.

Radio basics

All radios function essentially in the same way. One user (the sender) initiates a transmission sending a signal to another user (the receiver). The signal sent travels through the atmosphere in a discrete segment of the electromagnetic spectrum used by all interactive electronic devices, from radios and mobile telephones, to satellite equipment, remote controls and televisions. Most radios used by NGOs use one of two parts of this spectrum, high-frequency (HF) and very high frequency (VHF) (discussed on pp. 270–2), and three means to broadcast a signal:

1. **Direct line of sight (simplex)** As the name implies, this means that radios directly 'see' each other.
2. **Ground waves** these signals follow along the ground and over objects.
3. **Sky waves** Long-distance communication is made possible by refraction, where a radio signal bounces off of part of the atmosphere known as the ionosphere), allowing for very long distances beyond the horizon. The ionosphere consists of layers of ionized gases that lie 40–500 km above the Earth. This refraction makes it possible for HF communications to cover large distances, as shown in Figure 14.1.

Obviously, radios link together to form a net of users. There are two main types of frequencies typically used by NGOs in the field:

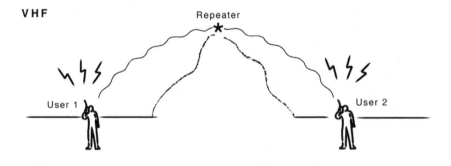

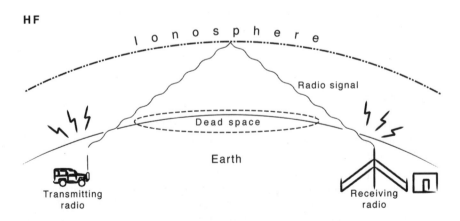

Figure 14.1 HF and VHF radio propagation

High frequency (HF)

HF radios are capable of transmitting signals over long distances of up to 1,000 km (600 miles). HF radios use the section of the electromagnetic spectrum that lies at 3–30 megahertz (MHz), which corresponds to individual wavelengths of 10–100 m. They transmit through three means: ground waves, direct line of sight and sky waves. Generally, with HF radios, the higher the sun and/or the greater the distance, the higher the frequency. Mobile radios are effective over long ranges but generally not as long as base radios.

Some HF radios (e.g. those made by Codan) being used by many NGOs have a feature (Selective Call or SelCall) that allows one radio to directly call another radio by entering a 4-digit number, much like a telephone. If the call is successful, a beeping sound will reply and a person on the other end should respond upon hearing it (if it is not successful, there will be no sound). The Selcall numbers should be available just adjacent to every NGO's radio. Some HF radios can also be linked to a regular landline or satellite phone as well as transmit data (see also pp. 281–5 on satellites). See Table 14.1 for details.

Table 14.1 HF radios

Advantages	Disadvantages
Short to extremely long range communication possible without relay station	Requires registration and frequency licensing in most countries
Less affected by topographical variation than other radio bands	Full-time radio operator often needed for adequate message handling
Messages to multiple destinations can be sent simultaneously	Training of staff needed in order to take full advantage of network
Monitoring simple to perform	Voice messages easily monitored or intercepted by third parties
Well adapted for vehicle use	Networks can be saturated with users, both official and unofficial, if not controlled
Comparatively cheap purchase cost and no directly incurred running costs	May interfere with other electronic equipment if not installed correctly
Easy to network by having multiple stations share frequency	Transmission strength varies at various times of the day due to solar activity
Relatively easy to diversify functions of network (Sitor, Fax, GPS tracking, Voice)	
Requires limited maintenance	
Possible to integrate with other networks	
Selective calling function proves link established	

Source: Lowe (n.d.).

Very high frequency (VHF)

VHF radios are used for communications between short distances. VHF radios come in three varieties: handsets, static base-stations and vehicle-mounted mobile sets. Approximate ranges for these radios depend on terrain and battery output:
- Handset to handset, about 5 km
- Vehicle to vehicle, about 20 km
- Vehicle to base-station, about 30 km
- Base to base – up to approximately 50 km

Frequencies are programmed through a computer and may transmit through either direct line of sight (simplex) or through a repeater device (known as duplex). VHF radios can be affected by terrain and obstacles (such as buildings). Therefore, a VHF radio's performance can be improved by moving to higher ground or the top of a building. A repeater, shown in Figure 14.1, greatly increases the range of VHF radios.

If using a channel on duplex, the user may hear a short beeping sound after each outgoing transmission and there will be a short delay. For this reason, when speaking, the user should delay speaking for roughly one second for the receiver to hear the full transmission. See Table 14.2 for details of VHF radios.

Radio equipment and uses

The industry standards for emergency programmes are Motorola VHF radios and Codan HF radios. Both radios are designed to be rugged and come with many easy-to-use features, both qualities ideal for use in emergency situations. However, they require technical knowledge to set up, especially the newer versions. Many of the gimmicky features rarely get used. Obviously, this book

Table 14.2 VHF radios

Advantages	Disadvantages
Commonly utilized by NGOs and UN	Handheld units frequently lost or stolen
User-friendly; easy to learn to use, limited margin for human error	Limited battery life
Highly portable	Dependent on topography of given area
Well-positioned repeaters can give extended coverage in programme area	Channels easily jammed by third parties
Handheld and mobile units are fairly inexpensive	Inappropriately placed repeaters greatly limit utility of network
24-hour contact with users, provided user is monitoring	VHF scanners are readily available, allowing third parties to monitor all traffic
Casing is usually strongly built; able to withstand rigorous stresses (such as being dropped)	

Source: Lowe (n.d.).

does not endorse either of these companies, and there are several other good radio equipment manufactures, including Icom and Yeasu for VHF and Barret, Icom and Yaeasu for HF.

Frequencies and callsigns

Selecting effective frequencies can be fairly complex and is often best done with technical advice. For VHF radios, NGOs often use established frequencies or are assigned, if there is one, by a functioning government ministry. There are three main ways to determine HF frequencies: by computer, by hand or experimentation. Normally, a specialist needs to determine frequencies and NGOs usually join networks with other organizations.

Because of regulatory red tape and scarce resources, NGOs often need to share radio frequencies. This is especially true of duplex frequencies which cost $2,000 or more for a single-channel repeater antenna. Sharing repeaters is generally easy, when one NGO takes the lead and invites others to share. In cases where an NGO becomes a so-called implementing partner of the UN, it may be able to use frequencies established by their communications teams. The UN has a regional system for assigning callsigns. Examples from West Africa are provided in Table 14.3.

In this example, the director of IOM-Liberia based in the capital Monrovia can be identified by LMM1, while the transport manager for a particular NGO based in the town of Harper would have the callsign LHY7. (See Table 14.5 for the phonetic alphabet.) In larger operations, a second phonetic letter (or 'digit') may be added (between the 3rd and 4th) for NGOs.

To identify specific staff members, a fifth digit can be added, especially with VHF radios that are normally assigned on an individual basis. Following the UN's system, departments are identified as follows: 1 management, 2 administration/finance, 3 logistics, 4 programme, 5 security, 6 NGO-specific, 7 transport, 8 technical support, and 9 visitors. In this way, a deputy director might be identified as 1.1, an assistant logistician as 3.1 and successive programme staff as 4.1, 4.2, 4.3 and so on.

It is important to familiarize all staff with radio callsigns and telephone numbers. Small laminated cards, usually about the size of a credit or identification card, can be made and distributed to each staff member with the explicit instruction that they should carry it at all times. Copies of the cards should be forwarded to selected personnel at HQ as well.

Table 14.3 Callsigns

1st digit Country	2nd digit Location/Town	3rd digit Agency	4th digit Department
Alpha – Ghana	Hotel – Harper	Charlie – UNICEF	1 Management
Golf – Guinea	Kilo – Kakata	Mike – IOM	4 Programme
Lima – Liberia	Mike – Monrovia	Yankee – XYZ NGO	7 Transport

Power supplies

There are several sources of power for radios, which normally have to be combined to maintain a functional communication system:

- **Electrical mains** This is considered to be interruptible because a failure in the supply system will stop base radios from operating. A 110- or 220-volt (depending on the location) alternating current (AC) mains will be supplied by the local electricity authority. In an emergency situation (and in many developing countries), the luxury of constant electrical power is rare.
- **Generators** Also interruptible because generators cannot be run indefinitely and there are frequent failures (e.g. fuel runs out or the generator breaks). For further information, see Chapter 6.
- **Batteries** Considered to be uninterruptible because they normally serve as a back-up when mains and generators fail. The standard connection for a HF radio is a 12-volt car-type direct current (DC) battery. This requires a charger using mains or generator power until those fail, leaving the battery unavailable to provide power. Depending on their size and usage, VHF batteries can last 6–12 hours and thus need daily charging. Most VHF batteries are made from nickel metal so should not be topped up. In other words, they should only be charged when fully used and then they should receive a full charge, although only this can prove problematic with unreliable generators.
- **Solar panels** Although initially an expensive option, solar panels are available for HF radios and may prove a viable option in certain environments.

Setting up a communications system

Determining communications needs

There are several questions worth considering in deciding what radios to procure and use.

- **What already exists?** Is there a simple need of adding more radios or is there a need for more human communication (i.e. between staff members)? Will the radios have the right capacity and frequency range, so that they are compatible with other organizations in the area?
- **How many redundant (back-up) systems are needed?** For example, what happens when the telephone system fails? If handsets or other radio equipment are confiscated, are there other means of communication?
- **What are the regulations?** What laws or government regulations are there concerning each radio? How are the laws in the country where the radios were procured different from where they will be used? How may this affect transport and import? Try to find out all the regulations and legal requirements before procuring communications equipment.

There may also be additional rules for transporting equipment into and around certain countries. In some emergencies, there is no governmental authority. However, preparations should be made for when the relevant ministry does resume authority. Be prepared to pay back fees or at least negotiate a way out of them by banding with other NGOs.

- **What technical support and maintenance might be needed?** Is a technician or specialist needed to set up and maintain the equipment? Is there a reliable supplier available who can fix broken units? Or what is the plan for when this happens?
- **What additional equipment is needed?** What extra equipment or additional accessories are needed for power supplies (e.g. 12-volt battery, charger or cables from generator) or setting up an antenna (e.g. rope for stabilizing the mast)? What about a logbook and training materials?
- **Can resources be shared with others?** For example, can a larger or more established organization (e.g. another NGO, ICRC or UN) help in programming frequencies or erecting antennas? Is it possible to join an existing network?
- **What budget is needed?** Usually, this is the most important question, but as communications are critical, an NGO should set aside private operational funds for it (i.e. ideally, not dependent on the award of grant funds).
- **Who should order the radios and how should it be done?** In other words, who is responsible for procuring communications equipment? If HQ were to order the radios, are they competent enough to request the correct voltage, model and all the accessories?
- **What training is needed?** See below, pp. 280–1.

Antennas

Generally speaking, antennas come in several types: whip, standard for mobile units; horizontal, bi-directional for fixed units; inverted 'V', omni-directional for fixed units.

There are various questions to consider when selecting an antenna.

- Is the antenna selected or supplied technically the proper antenna for the job? If unsure, has a technician been contacted?
- Is there enough physical space for the antenna? Will the antenna extend on to an adjacent property and, if so, has permission been obtained to do this?
- Where and how can the antenna be grounded?
- What kinds of extras need to be carried out, such as trimming branches or cement-mixing for holding the mast? What needs to be procured to do this?

There are several different options for erecting an antenna.

1. **Do-it-yourself** This a fair option for those who are technically minded and have the time to devote to doing hands-on work. This is of course the most cost-efficient.

2. **Employ a knowledgeable local person** After years of the presence of humanitarian organizations, competent persons who can be directly hired to carry out such tasks can be found in the capital cities of some developing countries. Prices will depend on local rates (e.g. in Liberia in 2004 it cost about US $150) and will probably have to be heavily negotiated. In some cases, if the person is looking for work, this can be used to screen potential staff radio operators.

3. **Hire a radio technician** Some countries will have professional suppliers and others who are fully technically competent. They will likely cost slightly more than the option above, but will have a greater likelihood of being technically assured.

4. **Contract a company** As this tends to be expensive and may involve paying the cost of a consultant, it is generally an option more suited to the use of satellite equipment.

If a decision is made to follow any one of the first three options, the following guidelines will help in supervision. Depending on the type of antenna, several steps are involved.

- Radio types and models differ; therefore follow all written instructions provided by the manufacturer.
- Ensure that there is clear ground (around 20 m) in front of the antenna, in the direction the power is to be transmitted.
- If masts (poles) must be installed, make sure there is enough space to emplace guidelines. If there is a building with several floors, make sure there is enough space between other buildings and try not to suspend the antenna above a zinc/tin roof.
- If there are other organizations using HF radio in the immediate area, interference may result if the antennas are installed to close and/or the frequency is similar. If this situation cannot be avoided, do not place the antenna in parallel with others.
- If the office is located in a house with only one floor, check the possibility of using an existing structure (such as a tree or pole) for suspending or supporting the antenna.

Organizing a radio room

A radio room helps facilitate communications and organizing one is rather simple for an NGO to do. Important points to consider include the following.

- The main determining factor in where to locate a radio room is where an antenna and power supply is best located.
- The room should be located in a cool and dry place. The room should be well ventilated to keep the radio transceiver cool and dry. In tropical

areas, for example, rain can be blown through windows. Direct sunlight should not fall directly on the equipment.

- The room must be secure. Extra security measures (e.g. stronger door locks and iron bars on windows) may be needed. There should be no need to move communication equipment in and out of a secure room.
- To keep other office rooms free of radio noise the room should be located separately in a quiet place.
- Antenna coaxial cables should not be tight but rather hung loosely. Excess cable can be tucked away outside the building or underneath the radio table. For cables coming through outside windows, a slack curve should be left so that rainwater does not drip along the cable into the radio room.
- The table on which the components rest should be large enough to have adequate writing space for filling out the radio log and other items.
- Resource materials, such as operator's reference sheets, maps, call sign and frequency lists and a copy of the phonetic alphabet should be either covered in plastic and taped to the radio table itself or hung directly in front of the radio for easy reference.

For obvious reasons, a radio log should be maintained next to each base radio. A simple log is shown in Table 14.4.

Note that in some cases, such as large radio networks, a full recording in the log of all sent and received transmissions is carried out. Depending on the country, it also may be a legal consideration for maintaining a radio operating licence. However, in many cases where NGOs operate in emergency situations, there is simply not the time or necessity to carry out such record-keeping, so a simple action-oriented recording is needed, as in Table 14.4. Logs may be impractical in mobile set-ups; therefore a special decision will have to be made if one is required.

Radio procedures

International SOPs for radios are established to aid in the clarity, uniformity and brevity of radio transmissions. For this reason, radio procedures help not only communication within an organization, but also between them. The phonetic alphabet is a good place to start learning procedures, as shown in Table 14.5.

Table 14.4 Radio log

Date/Time	From/To	Operator	Message
10 Oct 11:15	MC 67 / MC 72	Therese	Medical team arrived safely at sub-office Bravo
10 Oct 10:05	MC 67 / MC 75	Therese	Successful radio check

Table 14.5 The phonetic alphabet

Alpha	November
Bravo	Oscar
Charlie	Papa
Delta	Quebec
Echo	Romeo
Foxtrot	Sierra
Golf	Tango
Hotel	Uniform
India	Victor
Juliet	Whiskey
Kilo	X-ray
Lima	Yankee
Mike	Zulu

Basic rules, some of which are listed below, are essential and must be routinely revisited to ensure compliance.

Dos

- Follow all safety precautions.
- Use standard communication procedures.
- If using a VHF, pre-position yourself to ensure the best line of sight possible (usually on top of hill or building).
- Use established callsigns and code words.
- Ensure there is enough battery power on handheld radios, especially before being away from a power source (such as during a trip).
- Be aware that others use the same radio frequencies.
- Plan what will be said and be as brief and specific as possible.

Don'ts

- Don't disclose sensitive information (such as ethnic details during a conflict or personal details of GBV victims).
- Don't use people's proper names (use callsigns or position titles instead).
- Don't mention specific locations.
- Don't discuss money (such as amounts or transfers).
- Don't transmit over other people's transmissions; wait until they have finished.
- Don't transmit while people are near an HF or satellite antenna (it is potentially dangerous).
- Don't shout, it only distorts the transmission.
- Don't hold the 'press to talk' (PTT) button for longer than 20 seconds.

Standard phrases ('pro-words')

Procedural words or pro-words – predetermined shortcut phrases – help facilitate communications, keeping transmissions clear and brief. Basic examples are shown in Table 14.6.

Code words, in contrast to pro-words, are used to conceal meaning and should be used sparingly by NGOs. Elaborate code systems are laborious to use and generally unnecessary for running emergency programmes. If genuine security issues need to be communicated, there are several options. The easiest method is to use a means that is difficult to eavesdrop (e.g. satellite telephones). For day-to-day communications, word substitution (e.g. 'vitamins' for cash or types of weather for types of violence) and deliberate vagueness (e.g. calling a staff member 'the package') are often used. Another option occasionally used is for two persons to communicate using their native language, which may be obscure in the area (e.g. Gaelic in Central Africa or Serbo-Croat in Asia).

Table 14.6 Standard communication phrases

Pro-word	Meaning
'...this is...'	Use this pro-word when hailing a receiver in the order of 'you *this is* me'. Established callsigns are to be used with this pro-word (e.g. 'CP 72 *this is* CP 71')
Affirmative	Yes or Correct
Break	Use this pro-word to break up a long transmission (radio signals can be distorted during long transmissions, therefore the PTT button should not be held for longer than 20 seconds at a time). This can also be used to interrupt someone else's transmission by saying 'Break, break, break'
Confirm	Did you receive well my last transmission?
Copy	I understood
I spell	I will spell a word using the phonetic alphabet
Negative	No or Incorrect
Out	Used to end a final transmission in which no reply is expected
Over	Used to end each transmission in which a reply is expected
Prepare to copy	Get pen and paper ready before I say important information, I will expect to wait a moment while you do this
Say again	Please repeat your last transmission, I did not understand
Silence	Used when the radio frequency needs to be clear of all traffic. Use 'Silence lifted' to inform others that regular radio use has returned
Standby	Wait for a minute or less
Wait out	Wait for up to 10 minutes
Wilco	I understand and will comply

How to use radios

The procedures below are meant as an *aide-mémoire* for VHF and HF radios most typically used by NGOs running emergency programmes. Radio technology continues to evolve, so always check manufacturers' instructions before using any radio.

Making a call

1. Pick up the handset and listen 5–10 seconds for any other people using the net.
2. If no other person is using the net, attempt to hail the other user, using SOPs (as learned in the procedures above and the practical exercise below).
3. After depressing the PTT for approximately 1 second, begin by stating the user's callsign, then 'this is' and then the callsign, ending the transmission by saying 'Over'.
4. If the user being called does not respond after 5–7 seconds, attempt to call them again.
5. After three failed attempts, end the transmission by saying 'Out'. Wait 5–10 minutes before attempting to call the other user again.

Answering a call

1. If a call (another user) is coming in, respond as soon as possible.
2. If a reply transmission cannot be made within 5–7 seconds, wait for a second call before responding.

Training

Perhaps because so many people are accustomed to easy communications through standard telephone lines, many novices are intimidated by the new words, strange buttons and/or difficulties in transmitting voice messages. For this reason, basic radio training is vital. A minimum standard should be that all staff know the basic functions of each communication device, so that in an emergency they can confidently send and receive messages. Radio operators and those staff members with routine communications responsibilities should receive extended training, as discussed here.

Training staff on the use of radios is most often done as part of security training but ideally, because of its importance, it should not be watered down to

---

Box 14.1 Radio safety

When transmitting, antennas emit dangerously powerful electrical waves. Before pressing the power button or keying the mike of HF and satellite sets, ensure that people -- especially children – are at least several metres away.

a simple overview. Without hands-on practical exercises, few people are able to adequately use equipment that may be entirely new to them. Depending on the number of people, training can usually be accomplished in about an hour, or about 20–30 minutes for individual instruction. A basic overview will cover all the information included in this chapter. Table 14.7 is a checklist for managers.

Even if there is not time to give a full training to every staff member on how to operate the radio as outlined here, every NGO staff member should know how to make emergency calls. Just like the movies, it is done by saying 'Mayday' or 'Pan' three times and giving whatever relevant details.

Satellite communications

Satellite communications technology is rapidly evolving. For the user, there are few downsides: there is increasing range, ease of use and reliability, while at the same time the costs and size of the equipment are decreasing. Here satellites will be discussed in general, describing several current systems and how to select equipment.

Communications satellites circle the earth in two types of orbit. Some satellites orbit relatively close to the earth at 700–800 km above the Earth's surface. These satellites use the earth's gravitational pull to propel them round the planet. GPS and Iridium use groups of such satellites to provide constant signals and transfer signals between satellites as they pass over the horizon. Geosynchronous orbits, on the other hand, are 35,790 km away from the planet's surface. This allows the satellite to rotate at the same speed as the earth turns and maintain a fixed position. These satellites cover specific geographic regions such as East Africa, the Middle East and Central/South Asia. Most communication satellites are geosynchronous and typically offer a higher connectivity rate.

Table 14.7 Training checklist: 10 things every staff member should know

✓	✓
Knows uses of different components such as antenna, button functions, batteries	Shows ability to use callsigns and pro-words
Understands when different radios and telephones should be used, including their ranges	Performs Selcall and other special functions on the radio in use
Can turn equipment on and off and use different buttons on each radio	Can carry out simple trouble-shooting
Knows the uses of different frequencies and how to select them	Knows location and/or carries callsign/frequency information as needed
Demonstrates ability to recite phonetic alphabet	Knows how to properly maintain and charge batteries of handsets

Communication satellites have gone through a number of generations and will so for the foreseeable future. Early commercial satellites were launched and governed by the International Maritime Satellite Organization (INMARSAT) to provide services for ships and other commercial users. More recently, the number of systems available has proliferated.

As with radio communications, there is no standard satellite system used by NGOs and so procuring the right system is the first issue. Before procuring any equipment, first research new options, which will change frequently (at least every few years). Web-searches help, but professional advice is a good idea. Edward and Michael Bizub (pers.comm.) suggest that the NGO's requirements should be familiar, and there are other considerations, as detailed in Table 14.8.

Once some of these basic questions have been clarified, it will possible to narrow down specific systems that are available off-the-shelf. These will change over time, but eight are provided in Table 14.9.

Because satellite communication equipment operates in a broadly similar way to standard mobile telephones, staff require little training. Still, several points are worth considering when first setting up and using satellite communications.

- Show (that is, train) staff so that they can make calls if necessary. All staff should know how to take care of the equipment.
- Establish a call logbook and ensure that staff record all calls made. It is not uncommon for very expensive bills to be accumulated on personal calls, causing administrative problems later on. Because staff welfare is important, a clear policy should be established about telephone use.
- Make sure code numbers (e.g. PIN and PUK) are written down and available to those who need them.
- Programme important numbers into the telephone's memory to help make calls.
- Directional antennas emit powerful electrical signals that can be dangerous to people. While the terminal is transmitting, make sure that people to do not wander in front of the signal.

Internet connections

During the initial phases of an emergency, before equipment is available, NGO staff may have to rely on local internet providers (cafés) and other organizations such as the Humanitarian Information Centre (HIC). If prepared beforehand, this can avoided by using one of the systems described above and combining standard software packages. In practice, problems tend to occur with the software interface, which can sometimes be sorted out from a remote location.

To save costs on systems that charge by the minute, users work offline and then send and receive messages using a programme like AOL or Outlook Express. A further way to save costs is to use software that bundles and compresses messages. Figure 14.2 shows how such a system works using a laptop computer, a portable satellite phone and the internet.

Table 14.8 Satellite communications considerations

Voice: Do you plan to make voice calls?	
Is voice capability included?	While most terminals handle voice calls, not all do. Some are Voice over Internet Protocol (VoIP) capable, but this may raise costs
What type of phone device is needed?	Fixed terminals, which have an antenna that often looks similar to a laptop computer, tend to be more reliable but must be in one place and take longer to set up than mobile units which can be used while moving
Data: Do you need access to e-mail or internet?	
Is data capability included in the unit?	While all terminals have some data capability some require purchasing an extra kit
What data rate is needed?	Measured in kilobytes per second, the data rates range from 2.4 kbps to 144 kbps. For simple sending and receiving e-mails, a lower data rate is needed than for web surfing. Different services provide different costs
What service type is needed?	Both dial-up and always online (broadband) connections are available and depend on users' need
Through what interface(s) does the satellite terminal connect?	A number of connection options are available (e.g. USB, ISDN, Ethernet and Bluetooth) but confirmation is needed that existing computers will connect to satellite terminals and if any adapters or hubs are needed
Location: Where will you take your satellite terminal?	
What coverage area do you need?	Satellites cover different areas of the world but it is best to check future plans as these areas expand. Also, consider power arrangements
What size and weight is best?	Some terminals are only slightly larger than a mobile cellphone while others are larger than a laptop computer. Generally, the heavier the equipment is, the greater its durability
Cost: What is your budget?	
What is the cost of the equipment?	Costs depend on supplier, terminal type and accessories, ranging from several hundred to several thousand US dollars
What are the airtime charges?	Cost vary and may increase with additional fees. Make sure staff are aware and that all calls are logged

Table 14.9 Satellite communications

	Globalstar	Thuraya	Iridium	INMARSAT Mini-M	INMARSAT M4	Thuraya DSL	R-BGAN	BGAN
Voice								
Included?	Yes	Yes	Yes	Yes	Yes	If VoIP added	If VoIP added	*
Phone type	Handheld	Handheld	Handheld	Table-top	Table-top	Table-top	Table-top	Table-top
Data								
Included?	Optional	Optional	Optional	Yes	Yes	Yes	Yes	Yes
Max data rate	9.5 kbps	9.5 kbps	10 kbps	2.4 kbps	64 kbps	144 kbps	144 kbps	492 kbps *
Service type	Dial-up	Dial-up	Dial-up	Dial-up	Dial-up	Always online	Always online	
Interface(s)	Data kit required	Data kit required	Data kit required	RS-232	ISDN, RS-232, USB*	Ethernet	USB, Ethernet, Bluetooth	Both*
Location								
Coverage area	Regional	Regional	Global	Global ex. polar regions	Global ex. polar regions	Regional	Regional	Global ex Pacific Rim
Cost								
Equipment	US$500–1,000	US$500–1,000	Around US$1,500	Around US$2,800	Around US$9,000	Around US$2,500	Under US$1,000	US$1,000–4,000
Airtime charge	Per minute	Per minute	Per minute	Per minute	Per minute	Per megabyte or fixed charge/month	Per megabyte	Per minute or megabyte

Source: Edward and Michael Bizub (www.bizubcomm.com).
Note: INMARSAT will be discontinuing R-BGAN service at end 2008.

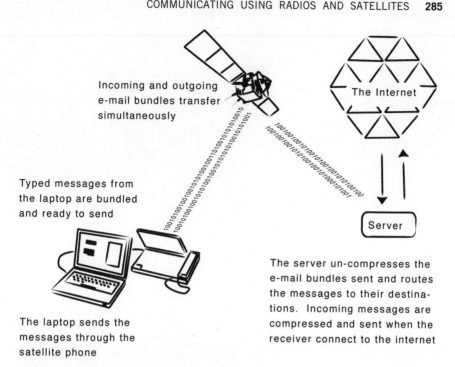

Figure 14.2 Satellite and internet interface
Source: Adopted from www.maflink.org

Such a portable system requires four commonly available items: a Pentium class PC computer with Windows operating system; POP3 e-mail client (e.g. Eudora, Outlook Express, Pegasus); mini-m satellite phone (e.g. NEC, Nera, Thrane & Thrane) with a data cable; and a power source to charge batteries.

Systems like this can provide a reliable e-mail service anywhere an emergency occurs. They also provide a mobile service until higher capacity and more elaborate systems can be established that provide high-speed internet services.

CHAPTER 15
Working with local partners and contractors

The purpose of this chapter is to provide a basis for identifying, assessing and working with other organizations for partnerships and for sub-contracting purposes. This chapter discusses working with local NGOs and assessing their capacity, followed by a brief look at commercial sub-contractors:
- Identifying partners
- Assessing an organization's capacity
- Sub-contractors and the bidding process

With the proliferation of NGOs around the world, international NGOs (INGOs) (or Northern NGOs) have taken on a larger role of working through and with other organizations. These local partners may be from a range of actors and stakeholders such as local government authorities, community groups, parents, professional associations (such as teachers or health workers), but may also be LNGOs (Southern NGOs), CBOs or commercial contractors.

Although there are different types of partnerships (see pp. 287–8), the role of an INGO when working with local partners is most constructive as an enabler and supporter. The partnership forms an inter-organizational relationship beyond basic coordination: not just funds are exchanged but a true partnership is developed with the ultimate aim of achieving objectives that might not have been possible working alone.

Identifying partners

The first consideration in identifying partners is to determine what kind of partner is best suited for the goal, objectives and activities the emergency calls for. Fowler (1997) and Penrose (2000) identify different types of partnership that might be established between an NGO and a local partner:

Ally Organizations agree to cooperate on a mutually agreed agenda often for a set period of time. In a sense, this is a more elaborate form of coordination.

Full partner This type is characterized by full mutual support in all aspects of work. The partnership is holistic and comprehensive, that is, the decision-making authority, both formal and informal, is shared between the organizations. The INGO and the NGO each have decision-making power, or at least substantial influence, over each other's policies and practices at both the organizational and programme level.

Funder or (sub-)contractor In this type of partnership, the emphasis is on financial transactions and so the relationship is narrow and focused. It is usually based on contractual agreements which specify a set period of time. An INGO pays an independent NGO to provide a well-defined package of services under conditions largely established by the INGO.

Institutional supporter This partnership takes the programme support partnership to the next level by supporting the entire organization.

Programme supporter With a particular area of work as its focus, this type of partnership can be characterized by different types of support, including technical advice, networking and funds. Typically the partnership may help either organization achieve its goals by using the comparative advantages of each. The INGO and NGO share decision-making power over planning and implementation by the NGO, with funding and technical support from the INGO.

Spin-off or franchise A formally independent NGO functions as a field office of an INGO, which undertakes most, if not all, of its direction and functioning. A dependent franchise or INGO field office is expected over time to become organizationally and financially independent of the INGO.

Once the reason for and type of partner are decided, the search for potential partners, in the literal sense, is common practice in emergencies. Practical ways to identify partners include:

- Asking other NGOs, donors and local government
- Coordination meetings
- Visibility signs
- Internet or consortia directories
- Assessment information

When in initial contact with partners, it is important to match values, goals and objectives. The type of organization will determine the exact factors to look for. Regardless of the type of organization, the set of questions in Table 15.1 can help determine if partnership might be worthwhile.

Before looking at specific ways to assess the capacity of an organizational partner, it is worth considering how to build and maintain a relationship once the decision has been made. For both organizations, it is important to maintain a professional relationship from the start, as follows.

- Be clear about expectations; put minutes of meetings and especially agreements in writing.
- Be flexible and expect changes.
- Allowing for extra time for tasks like reporting.
- Plan for capacity building.
- Understand that there may be different priorities and ways of looking at things.

Fowler (1997: 110) offers a number of tips for organizations working in partnerships, outlined in Table 15.2.

Table 15.1 Partner considerations

Key considerations	Questions
Goals	Does the organization have compatible goals? As an organization, does it have a demonstrated commitment to basic humanitarian principles?
Approach and Methodology	What approaches and methods does the organization use? Are they appropriate to the situation? If the situation changes, will they be flexible enough to adapt their approach?
Resources	What kind and amount of resources does the organization have? For example, does it currently have enough administrative, logistical and managerial resources to implement new projects? Does it have staff with the right expertise already or would it have to hire new staff to take on additional activities?
History	What projects has the organization successfully completed in the past? Has it worked in the same area or in the same sector before? Does it have references from donors or beneficiary groups? Is it possible to independently verify one or more of its completed projects? Are those completed projects to an appropriate standard?
Funding	Does the organization have other funding to support itself? Can it handle and account for its funding? Is it able to provide budgets and report on accounting?
Communication ability	As an organization, does it have the capacity to interact effectively with your organization? Do staff have appropriate language skills? Does the staff have the capacity to produce timely and professional reports to an acceptable standard? Does the organization have communication infrastructure (e.g. radios or e-mail) appropriate for the area and project?
Absorptive capacity	Will partnering the organization complement its activities or stretch its ability to function? Is the organization in a position to grow? What can be done to contribute to its capacity to help achieve their goals?

Assessing an organization's capacity

Assessing an organization's capacity is an essential step, not just when working with partners but also when carrying out change and organizational development. This section looks at different tools and a process for carrying out participatory assessments. For this reason, the tools described here also apply to Chapter 16.

Table 15.2 Differences between NGOs

Southern NGO	Northern NGO
Be sure of yourself, who you are and what you stand for	Hardest challenges will arise during the move to measures of joint performance
Be credible by being competent – show results	Exercise trust within performance agreements
Have information at your fingertips	Move to partner-based, impact-oriented financing
Be transparent in your internal and external dealings; don't hide failure when it occurs	Share aspects of governance which affect both parties
Demonstrate that you are learning from what you are doing, then challenge donors to show the same	Seek partner's agreement with messages and position adopted on its behalf
Open up decision-making processes to partner's scrutiny	

Note that Fowler is writing about development contexts. Also, Fowler uses the terms 'Southern' for an LNGO and 'Northern' for an INGO. As this might not necessarily be the case in emergencies, the more specific terms 'local' and 'international' are used here.

There are many tools available for assessing organizational capacity, typically using a number of approaches. Some organizations have developed assessments that take months long to complete, but small NGOs and CBOs may be able to carry out a short assessment that will prove of some use, and is certainly better than nothing at all.

The best one will meet the desired results with the constraints present. Carrying out an organizational assessment can be done as an internal self-assessment, with outside support, or it can be carried out by an external organization. There are a number of different tools to help in this process. Some are basic health checks such as the ones provided as managers' tools found in Chapters 3, 9 and 11.

Assessments that focus on organizational capacity often start with a workshop in which the goals, parameters and expectations of the activity are explained. Different activities are undertaken to get participants to reflect and to generate discussions that will contribute to positive change. Here, three basic tools are presented:

Questionnaires

Questionnaires are often used to measure perceptions within an organization and are useful for discovering opinions that others may be typically reluctant to share. Questionnaires are best supported by semi-structured interviews to help triangulate information and expand in areas that may have been highlighted or come to light in the questionnaires. In an attempt to objectify staff opinions, a numeric scale is used; usually 1 to 5 (from lowest to highest). The questionnaire itself can be completed individually or as part of a workshop. An example is provided in Table 15.3 which deals with strategic planning.

The results of the questionnaires need to be analysed and triangulated with other tools.

Force-field analysis

Force-field analysis looks at constraining and supporting factors in an organization's work. The exercise requires flipchart paper and markers and can take 30–60 minutes, depending on the group's size and the amount of discussion. Depending on the group's size, either in plenary or in small groups, the task is to discuss and decide on supporting factors (placed beneath the force field, represented by the horizontal line) that hold up an organization's efforts, as well as those factors (placed on top or pushing down the force field)that hold back, weaken or are simply lacking. The result may look something like the example shown in Figure 15.1.

Table 15.3 Capacity questionnaire

	Strongly disagree	Disagree	Neutral	Agree	Strongly agree
1. We have sufficient skills in strategic planning	1	2	3	4	5
2. When we plan, it involves as many stakeholders as possible	1	2	3	4	5
3. We plan in a top-down fashion	1	2	3	4	5
4. I know what is written in my office's strategic plan	1	2	3	4	5
5. Other members of the staff are adequately familiar with the strategic plan	1	2	3	4	5
6. Adjustments to plans are made when necessary	1	2	3	4	5
7. I make a valuable contribution towards the accomplishment of stated aims and objectives	1	2	3	4	5
8. Our office has enough time to plan	1	2	3	4	5
9. Contingencies, such as staff and structural changes, and emergencies, are adequately taken into account	1	2	3	4	5
10. Project managers are able to set targets and meet them	1	2	3	4	5

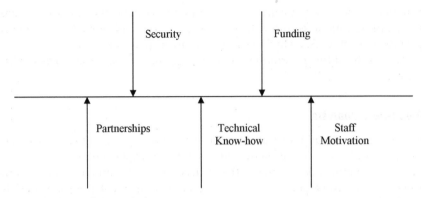

Figure 15.1 Force-field analysis

Strengths, weaknesses, opportunities and threats/constraints (SWOT/C) analysis

SWOT (or SWOC) analysis creates an overall picture of an organization at a given point in time. As such, it can be effective in plotting a path forward for basic improvement. There are different ways to carry out a SWOT analysis, but it usually works best when small groups work out either a single assigned box or all four categories which are then presented in plenary group for discussion. The exercise requires flipchart paper and markers and can take up to an hour depending on the group size and level of discussion in Table 15.4.

Table 15.4 SWOT analysis

Internal	Strengths	Weaknesses
	Available resources	Lack of resources (e.g. financial or human)
	Skills you have and which are necessary to achieve your objectives	Lack of skills
	Capabilities	Lack of capabilities
	Other advantages, e.g. in comparison with other organizations	Disadvantages, for example, in comparison with others
		Lack of organizational infrastructure
External	Opportunities	Threats/Constraints
	Chances you may have due to policy change of government, funders and other stakeholders	Obstacles
	Trends	Increased competition from other organizations
	Events such as workshops where you can explain your programmes and projects	Continued over-spending / under-funding
		Insecurity or reoccurrence of natural disaster

Source: NGO manager (2004).

Sub-contractors and the bidding process

Broadly, NGOs are faced with three modes of implementation. The most appropriate mode of implementation will change with the circumstances of the NGO and the context, as outlined in Table 15.5.

Sub-contracting is a common practice for NGOs, especially for construction and rehabilitation projects. During the post-conflict stages of an emergency, the need for contracting services is likely to be high. Contractors represent a particular type of partner for NGOs. They are most often used for construction projects, but especially in post-emergency settings this can represent a significant series of challenges. It might be appropriate for NGOs working with contractors

Table 15.5 Sub-contracting

Mode of implementation	Pro	Con
Direct: NGO is solely responsible	Use if NGO has capacity especially in technical expertise and manpower	Needs resources in addition to funds
	Control needed and project easy to monitor	Limits community input and ownership
	May be faster as there are few or no other parties to deal with	May increase security risk for staff
Community: Community is mainly responsible	Use if high degree of ownership and participation, especially if design and planning are sought	Projects usually need to be low-tech and uncomplicated
	Good for sustainability as skills are locally available for repair and upkeep	Usually time-consuming
	In-kind labour and material keep costs low	May require technical input if unplanned problems occur
	Good when combined with direct implementation above	
Contractor: Commercial contractor is mainly responsible	Use contractors when technical capacity is limited, such as when the project is one-off	Usually less community input than if directly implemented
	Less of a demand on NGO's resources so good for large sets of projects	NGO must have ability to monitor work's quality and technical and contractual control aspects
	Local experience and contact usually expedite implementation	Sub-contractors will try to maximize profits, so agreements must be ironclad

to call these commercial contracting firms sub-contractors, but they are not really sub-contractors because NGOs almost always work from grants (not contracts associated with profit). For this reason, the contracting process is one which sees the non-profit and commercial sectors overlap.

Step 1 Pre-qualification

Pre-qualification can be either informal or formal. In an informal pre-qualification, NGO staff will look into different contractors' capacity, take recommendations from other organizations and draw up a list of different firms they feel might best qualify for the types of projects they will implement. When time is short, informal pre-qualification may be the only realistic approach, especially when there may be only one or two contractors working in an area. However, the downside is that an informal approach is less transparent, generally less technically robust and may be done just to save time.

Formal pre-qualification involves having interested firms competing for contracts express their interest in writing. A form can be created that asks for evidence of:
- General details about the firm
- Details of past projects
- Accounting statements, including assets and liabilities
- Management's and staff's qualifications and status (full-time or contractors)
- Equipment, plant and vehicle availability
- Available capacity to undertake the work
- References

Step 2 Determining contracting details

In the initial preparation of a proposal, details of the project will likely be part of an initial grant agreement, whether the donor is external or internal funds are used. The contracting requirements can be determined from survey information, including:

Initial survey This element involves simply finding out the location and basic details of the potential project. Coordination, especially to ensure that no other plans or organizations are operative, is crucial at this stage.

Detailed survey Measurements and drawings, bills of quantity (BOQs), work plans, specifications, structural designs, formulation of estimates and existing contracts.

Unlike commercial firms, because emergency project support is humanitarian, specific conditions may be placed on a contractor during the work, depending on the situation. Typical examples include:
- Quality and safety assurances
- Specifics about where supplies can be procured and what can be done with supplies and equipment once the work is finished

- Impartiality in terms of ethnic and gender equity and respect for age
- Good labour relations, in particular fairness in hiring and wages (e.g. prohibition on cartels, wage kickbacks and internal or external commissions)
- Insurance: normally, the contractor is responsible for onsite injury or death of workers, as well loss or damage of supplies, equipment or the work itself and public liabilities. Note that securing credible insurance may be difficult and a plan should be developed in case contractors default and action is taken against the NGO.
- Performance bonds, bid bonds or advance payment bonds may be standard parts of the contract. If no viable banking system exists, contractors may provide a land title or similar collateral as security.

From survey information, a tender can be prepared as described in the next step.

Step 3 Issuing a tender

To promote transparency and help record-keeping, a request for tender (proposals or applications) should be done in writing. A letter or advertisement should be issued containing details of the NGO, and details of the project, as well as when, where and how the tender should be submitted. Normally, the tender should be submitted in a sealed envelope. To circumvent questions from the subcontractors, the letter should also mention when the winner of the tender will be contacted, or there may be a validity period for the tender. The tender should state that the NGO will not reimburse funds for the tender's preparation, is not liable to accept the lowest (or any) price and may annul the tender at any time without explanation.

The BOQ, an example of which is shown in Figure 15.2, is a cost estimation of a construction project that provides material and other (e.g. labour and transport) costs.

The example in Figure 15.2 is abbreviated, and several questions may arise when scrutinizing BOQs. Normally, the BOQ should refer to the detailed written specification of qualities (e.g. type and grading). It is essential to be familiar with the planned project, but the unit costs can be confirmed by logisticians (or procurement staff), as these may vary considerably in each country and over time. Quantities can be checked by someone with technical knowledge and samples, or the contact details of the suppliers can be requested as part of the quality control input. In this example, support costs lack detail and, while they may be reasonable, additional information might be requested to justify the costs. In some areas, labour is open to corruption (e.g. phoney worker lists) and exploitation, so it is important to monitor this as the project progresses. To help reduce cost inflation and shortcuts, commercial companies are also entitled to a profit line-item.

Figure 15.2 Bill of quantity

Item Description	Specification	Quantity	Unit Cost	Total: Local Currency	Total: US Dollars
Part I: Materials and Supplies					
Wooden Beam	5 m	29	80,000	2,320,000	83
Wooden Beam	3 m	60	65,000	3,900,000	139
Wooden Planks	2.5 x 2 m	40	90,000	3,600,000	129
Straw	Uniform qual.	200	10,000	2,000,000	71
Brick	Mud	400	35,000	14,000,000	500
Brick	Fired/cooked	600	55,000	33,000,000	1,179
Stone	Mixed/Lime (kg)	200	20,000	4,000,000	143
Glass	3 mm	48	250,000	12,000,000	429
Wood for Window Frames	Hardwood	1	180,000	18,000,000	6
Glue, Carpentry	Carpentry-grade	5	35,000	175,000	6
Nails	Various sizes	10	75,000	750,000	27
Plywood	3 x 6.2 m	37	175,000	6,475,000	231
Door Locks	Heavy-duty	12	225,000	2,700,000	96
Window Handles	Heavy-duty	24	200,000	4,800,000	171
Hinges	7.6 cm	96	35,000	3,360,000	120
Cement	Portland	25	175,000	4,375,000	156
Sand	Fine	10	50,000	500,000	18
Paint, oil	White	25	100,000	2,500,000	89
Paint, powdered	Blue	50	75,000	3,750,000	134
Paint, plastic	White	20	125,000	2,500,000	89
Paint Mix	White	5	11,000	55,000	2
Iron sheets	2.3 x 4.5 m	17	185,000	3,145,000	112
Patch for Holes in Iron Sheets		1	200,000	200,000	7
Well Deepening		1	8,500,000	8,500,000	304
Pump, water	Afridev	1	10,000,000	10,000,000	357
Sub-Total: Materials				144,285,000	4,599
Part II: Support Costs					
Technical Input/Monitoring					200
Signs (site billboards)					50
Transportation (Truck rental and vehicle operating costs)					1,480
Program Support Costs					500
Sub-Total (Support Costs)					2,230

Item Description	Specification	Quantity	Unit Cost	Total: Local Currency	Total: US Dollars
Part III: Labor Costs (2 Months)					
Skilled Labor (8 man-hours/day)		5	500,000	110,000,000	3,929
Unskilled Labor (8 man-hours/day)		15	300,000	198,000,000	7,071
Sub-Total: Labor				308,000,000	11,000
Totals				**452,285,000**	**17,829**

Step 4 *Assessing applications and awarding the tender*

A standard procedure for many organizations is to collect all the closed bids and, to help with accountability, open them at the same time with a senior manager and a member of the accounting staff present. The project manager should refer back to the pre-qualification to see which organizations are qualified and how their tender measures up. Once a decision has been made on the winner of the tender, the project manager should notify the representative of the sub-contractor. If this is done verbally, a letter should follow so that there is a clear document trail.

A contract should detail the exact expectations of both the NGO and the contractor, including the following.

- Conditions of the contract (length, language and relevant legal system) and the conditions under which the contract will be administered
- Specifics of the work (drawings, BOQs and master plans)
- Work schedule and timeline (usually best produced by the contractor with approval by the NGO)
- Labour specifications
- Penalty for delayed or poor-quality work (local laws should be checked)
- Schedule of payments
- Means for making changes to the contract

Contract details may vary depending on local conditions, translations and the local culture of written documents), the capacity of contractors and the capacity of the NGO to enforce the terms. Contracts should always be fair and equitable. The commercial risks should be recognized and shared equitably under the contract, according to local laws and good practice.

Step 5 *Monitoring work until its completion*

Routine monitoring should occur both at schedule times, to confirm work progress, and as random spot checks to discover inconsistencies and at crucial operations. If changes to the work are needed outside what has been agreed in the original work, a written amendment (called a variation to contract or variation order) should be required. This should have been outlined in the original contract.

Once the contracting firm has met agreed deadlines and feels the work is completed, it should request a review of the work. A joint inspection should be carried out by the contractor's management and qualified NGO staff. If no major faults are found, there will be invariably minor corrections (e.g. doors that do not close properly) that will need fixing before the work can be considered fully completed.

The final handover of the social service infrastructure should be done with representatives of the NGO, local authorities (i.e. community leaders and facility officials) and the contractor all present. During the final handover, another inspection should be carried out so that the work meets the compliance of the local authorities. A certificate of completion should be signed by all three parties, if the work meets their satisfaction, or with a list attached if minor repairs are still needed, with a required completion date.

At completion, unless otherwise agreed upon, the community or government should normally be responsible for the work. The certificate of completion normally stipulates some sort of warranty for the quality of work, but does not extend full liability or damage resulting from wear and tear. Some organizations stipulate in their contracts that the last payment to the contractor is kept back for a period after the completion of all work, in case unsolved problems continue.

CHAPTER 16
Building internal capacity

Capacity building is the process of improvement and change. The purpose of this chapter is to provide an overview of capacity building and improving performance at different levels. It also discusses the concrete skills needed to carry out effective training. The main topics are:
• Capacity building
• Facilitating training
• Giving presentations
• Ice-breakers, energizers and team-builders
• Organizational development

During acute emergencies, when the attention must be focused on programme activities, capacity building will not be possible. However, it should not be ignored during pre- and post-emergency phases. Disregarding its importance will deny staff new skills and professional development opportunities and lessen the chance for the organization to improve. For this reason, successful NGOs plan and make resources available for capacity building.

Using different tools and approaches, capacity building can focus on individuals or on an organization as a whole. Although there is no widely accepted definition, at the individual level capacity building consists of the adoption of new skills, knowledge and behaviour. It can occur in a variety of ways, but the most common way is through informal and formal training. At the organizational level, capacity building is a process that improves efficacy and contributes to sustainability. Different interventions contribute to the process of organizational development, such as strengthening systems and structures to better support the NGO's values and goals. While relief workers often say that they are working themselves out of their jobs, it is important that this approach is incorporated into every project.

Capacity building

Capacity is the ability or potential ability to affect a situation or complete an objective. This ability can be measured by elements such as access and resources, including financial, human, information and material. Capacity building is the process of improvement and increasing capacity. At the field level, capacity building usually focuses on the staff generally or on individuals.

While by no means universal, one of the constraints relief workers often face in the field is a lack of capacity among staff and partners. If the capacity of a staff member is surpassed through too great a workload or too much responsibility (i.e. more than they can handle through unwarranted promotion or change in a work situation), that person will be overwhelmed and will fail to meet expectations. When this occurs, the staff member, the organization and its programmes, and ultimately the beneficiaries, may be adversely affected. Capacity building measures can help staff mitigate these problems and reach their potential.

The typical notion of capacity building may be of a staff member attending an externally-run course, but building the capacity of individual staff can happen in a variety of ways. Some of the issues relating to capacity building and possible remedies are outlined in Table 16.1.

Capacity building is also discussed in Chapter 8 as it is an important element of HRM. Here the focus will be on training and how this can be carried out within an organization using the capacity of existing staff. Organizational development will be briefly discussed on pp. 310–14.

Facilitating training

Training is probably the most common component of capacity building. It should start with an assessment of needs in the organization. This may be done by considering the following.

- **Prioritize** By judging the urgency of training, time can be made. Too often, the emergency is used as an excuse to postpone training. Time must

Table 16.1 Organizational challenges and remedies

	Issue/Example	Possible capacity-building measure
Performance-related	Low output	Counselling
	Failure to meet expectations	Coaching
	Repeated mistakes and/or accidents	Training
	Degradation of skills not used, leading to poor output	Increased access to information
Change	New position (promotion)	Coaching
	New procedures	On-the-job training
	New technology or equipment	Training for new technology or equipment
		Networking
Organizational difficulty	Failure to follow policies and procedures	Review of policies and procedures
Internal conflict	Examination of roles and responsibilities	
	Absenteeism	Staff retreat
	Poor communication	Implementation of capacity-building plan

be made available unless there is truly an urgent programmatic or other need.

- **Determine the specific needs of the participant/s** Training needs most often arise when there is a gap between expectations and abilities. The aim is to determine the staff's knowledge, attitudes and skills, in order to determine how training can improve or influence them. Review job descriptions and, if possible, observe staff work and survey them to find out their perceived needs. Ask staff or beneficiaries (if the training is being done as part of a specific project) what training they received before. Better yet, have them fill out a questionnaire during planning to determine their aptitude and level of knowledge. In some cases, people see training as an excuse to get out of regular duties, as a chance to travel or collect fees like per diems, so the training needs to be as specific as possible.
- **Subject matter** Managers devising training programmes should consider the sequence and usefulness of training. For example, it does not make sense to train on complicated software when participants lack basic computer skills. Because of the large variety of subjects in which to train, Werner and Bower (1982) classify different topics according to importance, following this sequence: 'must know, good to know, nice to know'.
- **Budget** With limited budgets, there will be fewer options available. Although budgets will also put parameters on the duration, location and type of supplies that may be available at the training, this does not mean that training cannot be carried out.

Some staff will be self-motivated and others will need to be coached along. If the staff are self-motivated, they may seek time to train or resources to learn themselves. This can be facilitated by setting time aside for staff to finish early for the day once or twice a week (or allow them to come to work on weekends). Resources, such as computer software or texts that are not locally available, can also be provided. For staff who are not motivated, or if a task is especially boring, it may be helpful to include training or other professional development as part of their evaluation, as discussed in Chapter 8.

More formal training, such as when training activities are the objectives of a programme, should be subjected to more precise budgeting, organization, assessment and planning. Each aspect of the training should undergo evaluation to help modify future training. Too often, pre- and post-testing of the participants are skipped over and it is impossible to measure the training's impact.

Training adults is a challenge. They come with their own experiences and expectations, so reaching understanding on the training needs and methods before training starts is important. Adults' expectations can be met by communicating training goals, deciding mutual expectations, and if the training is participatory, make it engaging and informal. A good approach for training adults is summed up in the Chinese proverb: 'I hear, I forget; I see, I remember; I do, I know.' To accomplish this in training, many avenues should be stimulated in different ways, engaging the eyes, the ears and physical movement.

Three types of training are discussed according to stages of formality. Regardless of the training type, the more participatory a training session is, the more effective it will be.

Coaching

Coaching involves a mentoring approach, where staff members are helped through problems, with the coach serving as a guide and a resource for unanswered questions. Coaching works especially well for the acquisition of skills but is also good for learning and finding out how to carry out complex tasks. An effective coach does not just train, but also inspires and gets people to do their best. In this way, coaching goes hand-in-hand with leading.

On-the-job training

On-the-job (OJT) training involves primarily learning by doing. It is probably best suited for concrete skills which are not highly intricate or require a great deal of background knowledge. Although OJT can follow a formal outline, most often it is achieved informally. Walmsley (2005) sets out seven practical steps:
1.   Set training objective
2.   Describe task
3.   Demonstrate
4.   Let them practise
5.   Answer questions
6.   Reassure
7.   Evaluate

Formal training

Formal training, where groups of people are instructed, is normally carried out in small groups to optimize learning, which is facilitated by one or more training facilitators and presenters. Considerations include the following.

Venue

The venue must support the training. Personal space, lighting, temperature and noise are just some of the issues that should be looked into. Although in many situations the training space and the availability of seating will determine the seating style, seating should suit the type of training being undertaken. Sitting in a circle, for example, is less formal and encourages participation, but is not possible for large groups. Sitting in small groups helps facilitate group work because conversation is easier, but the downside is that some may not be able to see visual aids.

Training schedule

A training schedule is important and it will also act as an agenda for participants and presenters. Most often, training schedules will need to be revised during the training period. Each participant should be provided with their own copy and a master copy should be kept at the training venue. It is important to remember that people's attention typically is highest in the morning and late afternoon, but declines in the early afternoon (after lunch). Good training schedules take this into account and timetable different types of learning at these times.

Methods

A number of formal training methods exist. NGOs often use a 'Training of trainers' methodology (TOT). This allows a few skilled trainers to train selected participants who then train a larger number of people. If available, computer-based training and outsourcing of trainers work well for training in specific skills.

The body of the training should follow a logical progression, but should include varied exercises. In most training situations, learners will have a limited willingness or, in some cases, capacity to listen to lectures, therefore they should be kept to a minimum. Case studies are useful, but the Socratic method, where questions and answers are posed to reach common understanding, is a good way to tailor training to specific contexts. Written exercises and tests may have some application, but these are usually to be used sparingly.

Nearly all training subjects can be delivered in a participatory way. What is limited will be the trainers' creativity. Examples include group or syndicate exercises, including small-group discussions, games, role-plays and presentations involving visual-aids (e.g. maps, pictures or dioramas). This method lets people move around, think in their own terms, share ideas and be creative.

When giving feedback, start with something positive and avoid negative comments which can have a harmful consequence that lasts beyond the training session. Pick key themes and ask questions for clarity. Describe how performance might have been stronger, not just better or other judgemental words.

Presentations

Presentations are made not only in training but also in an organization generally to impart and share information. It is included here because of its importance for carrying out effective training. Presenting is a skill that can be easily learned. Whatever the subject, effective presentations follow a similar structure: the introduction, the delivery or body of the presentation and the conclusion which summarizes. Given the skills and the right amount of preparation, even weak public speakers can give effective presentations. Here, introductions and delivery are briefly discussed.

Introductions

- **Welcome** Ideas for ice-breakers to help start a training session are provided on pp. 305–10.
- **Clarify training objectives** This may be established beforehand or, if time allows, worked out by the participants incorporating their own personal expectations.
- **Go over the training schedule including breaks** This is best done with some sort of visual support such as a flipchart or handout.
- **Establish ground rules for expected behaviour** Practical ground rules include statements about the use of the telephone or radios and what to do when there are questions. Sometimes it is helpful to discuss group values, such as respect for other opinions and participation. If the group is new to training, more time may be needed for this subject.

Delivery

- Practice and preparation are the two main keys to a successful presentation. Have notes ready, know the materials and test the equipment beforehand.
- First impressions are critical. As the subject matter expert, the trainer must display confidence.
- An old saying for presenters is: 'Tell them what you're going to tell them, tell them and then tell them what you told them.'
- When talking, try the 'lighthouse' technique of scanning the audience slowly from side to side. Use appropriate body language and project a loud enough voice.
- If, as a presenter, you are thrown by a difficult question or otherwise get stuck, the best thing is to take it in your stride and maintain a look of confidence. Give yourself time to think. Say, for example, 'That's a good question,' and pose the question to the group (although this tactic cannot be used too often), because the mind can think many times faster than it can form words. Use the question to reinforce the main points covered in the training.
- Instruction through translators can be problematic. Translators extend (often double) the time needed to convey information and are difficult to follow for long periods. If there is no other option but to use translators, consider having a native speaker facilitate the introduction and other aspects of the training that do not require specialist knowledge. Then, work with the translator to go over the material before the training and to clear up new vocabulary.
- Facilitate discussion by asking questions and waiting for responses.

Audiovisual equipment and materials

As mentioned earlier, people learn best when they are stimulated in different ways. In training situations, there are a number of means to share information, depending on the amount of time, the resources and the technology available. A summary of standard materials are provided in Table 16.2.

One golden rule is that if it is difficult for the presenter to see or understand, it will be impossible for the participants, especially those further away from the screen or object. Regardless of the type of audiovisual method used, there is a number of ways to make presentations more effective in their visual presentation. These include the ABC of audiovisual aids (Townsend, 1996):

Attractive

- Number sheets to help keep them organized
- Use bullet points
- Use at least two dark colours on bright backgrounds

Big and bold

- Use thick letters or large fonts
- The visual aid should be legible from the back of the training space

Capital keywords

- Do not use whole sentences

Table 16.3 provides a checklist of preparation, delivery and content, and appearance of a successful presentation.

Ice-breakers, energizers and team-builders

The purpose of these activities is to get participants (staff) to get to know each other better and in different ways which will ultimately improve communication and group dynamics. There is virtually no end to the number and type of ice-breakers, energizers and team-builders out there. The main limitation is the trainer's creativity. With a little preparation and imagination, the momentum of a training session can be started and maintained using the activities suggested here. It is important that the activities are enjoyable on some level and appropriate for the group or geographic location (e.g. some cultures enjoy singing, role-playing and social mixing more than others). For the sake of brevity, activities are categorized into three different types and are outlined below.

Ice-breakers

These activities are used to introduce people and as a way to quickly get to know each other. Typically, one ice-breaker activity is used at the start of a training session. Depending on the group's size, plan about 30 minutes for the entire activity, including explanation, questions and plenary presentations.

1. **Basic interview** Ask each participant to approach someone not known to him or her well or at all and interview him or her, finding

Table 16.2 Audiovisual materials

Material	Pro	Con	Comment
Handout	Participants 'own' the copies	Requires good preparation	Some trainers prefer to give handouts at the start of training, while others prefer to do so at the end. It may also depend on the subject matter
	Participants can refer to information as they need	May cause distractions during distribution	
	Participants can take notes directly on the handout	Participants may focus on handout instead of presentation	
Flipchart/ Poster	Can be used anywhere	Can be awkward to change or move between sheets	As much as possible, prepare flipcharts in advance. Use dark colours. Mark key sheets to locate later on or post each sheet on a wall for reference. If training is going to be carried out many times, considering using cloth sheets instead of paper
	Easy to use	Time-consuming to write and necessitates turning back on group/ students	
	Flexible	Not useful in large groups	
	Excellent for leading discussion and recording contributions		
Video/ Cassette	Good for introducing new topics	Requires a screen (or clean flat wall) and electrical power	Preview material to make sure it fits well and supports training objectives. Introduce material before playing. Set up the equipment well in advance. Have backup if equipment or electricity fails
	Adds variety and enter-tainment to training	Can be expensive	
	Good for provoking follow-up discussion	Prone to be overused	

Overhead projector (OHP)	Relatively easy to use	Requires a screen (or clean flat wall) and electrical power	Preparation is key. Set up the OHP well in advance. Number sheets and put them in order before the session. Have back-up if the OHP bulb or electricity fails. Turn off when changing sheets
	Flexible and allows layering	Requires good presentation	
	Decent for sharing complex information, including photographs		
	Trainer can face participants		
Slide/ Computer projector	Excellent for showing photographs, even in large groups	Not always interactive	Make sure it is set up and working well in advance. The user needs to be competent before starting. Computer presentations, in particular, should be well organized.
	Computers can incorporate infor-mation and images in a professional looking way	Can be distracting	
		Requires projector, screen (or clean flat wall) and electrical power	
Computer-based/ online materials	Good for sharing skills and complex information	Needs extensive set-up	This assumes computer literacy and that there is access to the right hard and software.

Source: Adapted from Townsend (1996).

out their name, home town, nickname and favourite food (or any similar set of questions appropriate to the location). In plenary, each participant introduces their new 'friend' to the rest of the group.

2. **Three truths and a lie** If the participants already know each other, this activity helps them to get to know each other a bit better. In pairs, participants find out four interesting details about each other. In plenary, the pairs present themselves and the group tries to guess which 'fact' is not true. A variation of this activity that works well in large groups has

Table 16.3 Presentation checklist

Preparation ✓	Delivery/Content ✓	Appearance ✓
Identification of training needs	Participants welcomed and attention gained	Professional dress (clothing)
Agenda and materials of preparation	Adherence to cultural norms	Positive body language and voice meet participants' expectations
Venue selection	Presentation flows logically	Visual aids easily understood
Participants notified	Goals and content explained	Visual aids fit with and re-inforce material presented
Venue preparation (seating arrangements)	Relevant and clear examples used	Visual aids can be seen by every participant
Handouts and other materials ready in advance	Approach chosen (e.g. lecture, parti-cipatory and small-group work) appro-priate to topic and participants	Visual aids ready when needed and easily manipulated by trainer
Audiovisual equipment set up and tested before presentation	Opportunities provided for questions and clarification	Time allotted for back and forth if translators used
Practice session carried out if needed	Sufficient time allotted for breaks, ice-breakers, energizers and team-building activities as appropriate	
List of participants available	Strong conclusion summarizing main points covered	

participants write four interesting details about themselves on a sheet of paper which they attach to their chests and, while they mingle, the people they meet try to guess which one of the 'facts' is not true.

3.   **Deserted island** Form participants into small groups and explain that they have been marooned on a remote deserted island. They have five items (or six or seven depending on time) as a group, not individually, which they have brought with them. The group has to discuss which items make up the list, and should explain in plenary why they selected the items they did.

Energizers

These activities are used to maintain a group's energy levels during long training periods. They are designed to get people out of their chairs (or off the floor) and be active. Energizers can typically take 5–10 minutes each to complete.

1.   **Singing** Anything that gets the participants up, clapping and moving around can be a good energizer. In many countries, participants will have traditional or popular songs which may serve the purpose.

2.   **Line-up** Ask participants to form a line in alphabetical order according to their first name. If the group consists of more than 15 participants, and space is an issue, form two or more groups. The first group to get into order wins. Continue by asking the group to get in line according to different categories, such as age, distance travelled to training or workshop, height or years of experience. A more challenging variation of this energizer is to not allow participants to communicate verbally while they get in order.

3.   **'I have never...'** Have the group form a circle with enough chairs for everyone except one person who stands in the centre. The person in the centre says, 'I have never...', inserting an experience or activity they have not done before (e.g. been abroad, been married or seen snow). Anyone who has also not experienced or done this activity must get up and find an empty seat. The last person standing is now in the centre and begins a new round.

Team-builders

These activities are helpful when the participants need to create or improve their interactions or teamwork. They generally are fairly involved and take about 15–20 minutes to complete.

1.   **Confidence walk** Beforehand, obtain enough blindfolds for half the group. Divide the participants into pairs with the task of having one lead the other blindfolded person around the building or immediate area. After five minutes or so, the pair switches the blindfold (roles) for the second round.

2.   **Square the rope** This team-builder needs blindfolds and a length of rope with the ends tied to form a single loop. From the group, select five or six participants who put on the blindfolds. Give the blindfolded participants the rope with the task of creating a square shape with the rope. Participants can talk and use whatever strategy they can until the have completed the task.

Organizational development

Like capacity building, there is no universally accepted definition of organizational development. According to the NGO support organization, Intrac, organizational development is a:

> Planned, systematic and participatory process that aims to facilitate understanding and change in an organization. Organizational development aims to strengthen the alignment between the organization's internal systems and structures, its relationships with stakeholders and its operational activities. Through organizational development, the organization aims to increase its effectiveness and build a reservoir of capacity on which the organization can draw when facing new challenges and changes. (pers. comm., 2005)

The benefits of organizational development are that it:
• Helps improve systems and processes, making work easier
• Prevents crisis and provides stability
• Increases participation, involvement and transparency
• Improves efficiency, lessens bureaucracy and helps to achieve objectives

Ultimately, organizational development is about change. It is easier to change procedures, systems and structures than to change attitudes and culture. Understanding organizations is an important first step in helping them to develop. Three conceptual models are presented here.

Organizational life cycle

During each phase of the life cycle, an organization will go through transition and change. This concept is helpful for staff to understand that every organization undergoes growing pains. Even well-established organizations will experience various phases of growth as new programmes open and close through the course of an emergency. Understanding where an organization is in its life cycle is also useful for deciding if organizational development activities are appropriate. An NGO undergoing change or crisis, low funding or high staff turnover, for example, will likely find such interventions counterproductive.

At the birth stage, funding may be low, the mission unclear and the NGO's founder(s) may hold back the organization by not allowing for growth. The remedies for these problems may include clarifying priorities, including focusing on funding and sharing responsibilities. At the youth stage, when there may be doubts about the way the organization is developing, successful NGOs stress learning and open communication. In adulthood, an NGO may experience internal conflict and commitment may be reduced, with an inward focus developing. At this stage, decentralization may help, as will welcoming new staff as they arrive and fostering further learning.

When mature, an organization's vision may slacken, stagnation may set in and red tape may grow. At this stage, a shake-up may be needed and outside assistance may help. Once decline sets in, major steps, including new and young staff, may be needed to prevent the organization from folding. In many cases, organizations go through cycles of decline and rebirth in what is known as the sigmoid curve. The basic life cycle is shown in Figure 16.1, with each vertical line representing a major change or crisis in the organization.

Conceptually, another way to think of this concept of an organization's life model is through the life of a plant or tree. This metaphor visualizes a tree which grows with the seasons, provides seeds and fruit for other organizations; its wood provides fuel for cooking; and it occasionally sheds leaves (i.e. loses strength). A larger tree has larger roots and provides shelter (shade) for others. In this way, organizations can be seen to follow a similar model.

Three-circles model

This model is a conceptual framework for understanding organizations involving three overlapping circles in the wider or external context. The *Programme – 'To do'* circle represents what an NGO does and its ability to achieve its goals. *External relations – 'To relate'* represents the organization's external linkages with other actors such as government, other NGOs, donors and the commercial

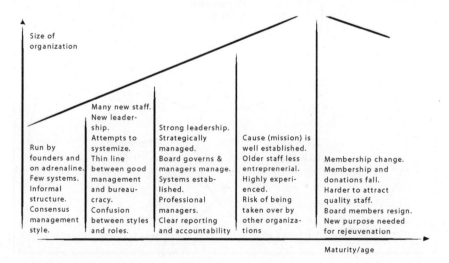

Figure 16.1 Organizational life cycle
Source: Hudson (2002: 365).

sector (e.g. local markets and suppliers). The *Internal organization – 'To be'* circle represents the organization's internal functioning, including its vision, mission or purpose, strategies, structure, systems and resources. Most organizational development activities centre on the, 'To be' internal workings of an organization. This model can be represented, as shown in Figure 16.2.

In this model, the circles are shown overlapping to emphasize the interaction between the three areas of organizational capacity. In other words, limited capacity in one circle will likely have an impact on the other circles, which might have unintended and negative consequences. If an organization places little emphasis on its external relationships, for example, it may have trouble raising funds to support its programme. Similarly, an improvement in staff learning may lead to better programmes and then lead to increased confidence from its donors.

The onion skin model

The 'To be' circle described above can be further thought of using this model. The most visible layers of an organization are its resources, represented on the

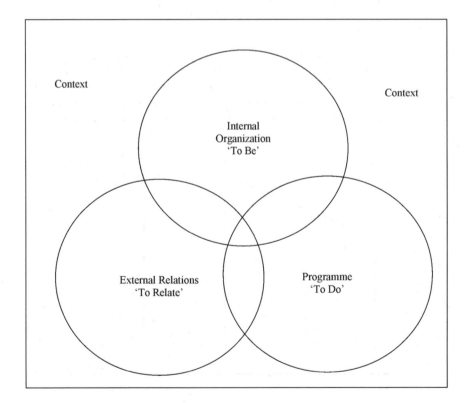

Figure 16.2 Three-circles model
Source: Intrac (2005) (pers. comm.).

outside of the onion, while moving towards the centre are more critical elements, including vision, values and identity, found in the heart. Unless these elements – the onion's layers shown in Figure 16.3 – that make up an organization are appropriately developed and unless the heart is healthy, organizational development activities will not have a lasting impact. Thought of this way, unless the vision, values, identity, mission and strategy of the NGO are well established and clearly understood by all staff, it will matter little how good the structures, systems and staff are and how many resources are available.

How to accomplish organizational development at the field level

The first step is assessing organizational capacity and strengths (see Chapter 15). Once information is collected and analysed, weaknesses or areas for improvement may be revealed. Management or – if more participatory

Figure 16.3 Onion-skin model
Source: Intrac (2005) (pers. comm.).

approaches are used – staff as well may decide to concentrate on one or more areas of improvement and dedicate resources. Usually an action plan needs to be drawn up and commitment from all stakeholders is necessary. Examples of common organizational development needs and possible solutions are provided below:

Strengthen communications Poor communications are often not, as it may appear, due to a lack of equipment (i.e. radios and telephones) but are more commonly the result of a lack of procedures, poor teamwork and bad personal relationships. Following an assessment to identify the real causes of poor communication, an NGO may create an action plan with three main components: first, developing reporting procedures and in so doing establishing a new, more streamlined reporting format; second, holding team-building exercises every month, as conditions allow, to provide face-to-face time between staff who work in different locations so that issues can be ironed out more or less as they arise; and third, in the next new project, making an effort to include more radio equipment and more funds for telephones.

Improve administration and management systems As mentioned above, organizations in their birth phase typically have few systems and those in decline can find it hard to rejuvenate the systems they have. While systems are often equated with hierarchy, a lack of systems or excessive red tape can frustrate efforts in an emergency. To address this issue, an NGO may decide on three steps. The first step is to formalize procedures or review existing ones. To make this effective, managers must agree on the need and the way to do so. They then must enforce the new or revamped procedures in word, in writing and in practice. Without this combination of approaches, the effort will fail. The second step is to bolster the new procedures;, several new forms and tracking systems will be needed. Every attempt must be made to make sure these are efficient and not introducing a level of bureaucracy that makes activities and operations unworkable. The third step, which also supports the first one, is to carry out formal or informal training for all staff.

Enhance monitoring and evaluation (M&E) As it is related to programming, M&E is a critical step in project cycle management. An NGO may find that its M&E systems are weak or non-existent. To address this issue, two steps can be taken. First, if the NGO does not have the resources to hire an external consultant, the programme manager researches M&E systems that might work in their situation, involving internet searches and asking other NGOs for assistance. This results in, among other things, a budget realignment to carry out a formal evaluation for a project during its final month. Second, a greater amount of time is allocated to simple monitoring, involving creating a checklist that any senior manager can use to perform spot checks when in the field. To help accomplish this, managers make specific time for monitoring at least once every two weeks at the project site.

CHAPTER 17
Dealing with the media

Emergencies often draw a lot of media attention and NGO managers need to be able to effectively interact with the media because it is such a powerful tool. This chapter covers not just how to interact with journalists, but also how to go about advocacy efforts and partnership with mass media to help achieve programme objectives. Specifically, this chapter discusses:

- The media and emergency programmes
- Advocacy at the field level
- Giving interviews

Journalists and war correspondents have long been companions of relief workers in the field. This symbiotic relationship brings, for the journalist, leads and stories, access to remote areas and, at times, logistical support. For the relief worker, publicity, visibility and spotlight on their area of concern, and, primarily, increased fundraising for their NGO are in store. The limelight has made people and organizations famous: Florence Nightingale, the Red Cross, Mother Teresa and Médecins Sans Frontières. However, media interest in emergencies ebbs and flows. For every big emergency, there are at least several forgotten ones.

Although recent news coverage of international events has refocused on a few areas, such as the Middle East, and declined in general, mass media remains a powerful means for drawing attention and mobilizing the resources necessary to address the consequences of emergencies.

The media and emergency programmes

Global publicity for emergency programmes may have reached its peak in the mid-1980s when pop stars campaigned with the songs 'Do they know it's Christmas', 'We are the World' and 'Live Aid'. A pattern was created where the media frenzy was intense but the outcome on the ground was negligible and forgotten about shortly thereafter by the public in the developed world.

Since the end of the cold war, media attention has tracked the plague of civil wars, outflows of refugees and massive international responses. In fact, media coverage precipitated many emergencies by bringing international attention to what have often been considered to be remote concerns and distant conflicts. The resulting coverage has brought donors' attention and an influx of those attempting to intervene.

Mass media differs in terms of what it might seek at the field level. Television journalists need accompanying video footage and radio journalists need clear-sounding interviews. Print journalists may be able to go into greater depth but may be more influenced by the slant or bias inherent to their particular daily, journal or magazine. News wire' (e.g. Reuters) are especially important as they are relied on throughout the world to relay the most recent news. There are other types of mass media as well which may be more prone to portray the programme in a positive light: newsletters, fliers, cable television spots, promotional videos, conference displays and various web-based outlets. But at the fundamental level, media must satisfy these basic requirements:

1. **Real news** Humanitarian emergencies, for better or for worse, are often news. It is the human drama of an emergency that makes it news, so simply being present or establishing a programme in itself is almost never newsworthy, although if the NGO is the only one operating in an area or particular sector, and there is nothing more urgent, journalists may take interest in doing a human-interest story. Timeliness also plays a large role in this: journalists avoid yesterday like the plague.

2. **A new twist or angle** There is an old saying that a dog biting a man is not news while a man biting a dog is. A journalist will not cover all points about a programme, but will ask him/herself, 'What's unique about this?' Unless it really catches the eye, they will not spend more than a moment's thought on it.

3. **Something that their readers can relate to** Often it is best to pair an expatriate with a local staff member to provide a more complete picture. The expatriate can help liaise or provide a face for audiences back home, while the local staff member can give a local perspective. He or she may be referred to simply as a relief worker or the programme may be portrayed in simple terms, but this is so that everyone can understand it.

A good story educates and informs people; it can also help to change policy and incite people to help causes. Although certain organizations may find this difficult, the media can also ask hard questions about relief efforts and put an emphasis on local capacity, thereby sidelining international efforts.

On the negative side, the media can be seen as part of a system that generates a certain bias. By their nature, different types of media have different tolerances for understanding depth and nuance. In the past, this has led to a failure to examine root causes of emergencies and the spreading of images that have been labelled disaster pornography. At the field level, NGO staff should be aware of how beneficiaries may be portrayed and should attempt to reveal an honest image of people stricken by disaster. Principle 10 of the Code of Conduct states that ICRC and NGOs agree that: 'In our information, publicity and advertising activities, we shall recognize disaster victims as dignified humans, not hopeless objects' (see also pp. 381–3).

Responsibility for public relations, of which interacting with the media is part, is usually at the HQ level. Individual NGOs may have clearly spelled out policies regarding interaction with the media. Typically, a director or senior manager will be responsible for media relations at the field level unless there is a specialist who has this delegated responsibility. It is best to have the staff member who is most prepared and best suited to handle interviews and who will be helped greatly by knowing the programme inside and out and being able to grasp what simple but profound message should be communicated. This issue is further discussed below.

Advocacy at the field level

Advocacy is the use of a message to encourage backing for particular issue or policy (Wallack et al., 1999). This typically does not rely heavily on the use of mass media as it targets key decision-makers and others in positions of power, with the goal of effecting change in policy, resulting in better treatment for vulnerable people (e.g. refugees, certain women, children and the elderly).

Awareness raising or sensitization, in contrast, is the spreading of information about an issue or problem in the hope that the people (the target group or audience) will be more alert to its dangers or consequences. Examples in an emergency context include hygiene promotion (e.g. maintaining cleaning habits for people who have experienced a disaster) and various protection-related areas, such as children's rights.

Although some NGOs focus exclusively on advocacy and are effective in this role, it is up to individual organizations to decide how much they will advocate for issues in keeping with their overall goals. A significant portion of the NGO sector, usually different organizations from those involved in emergency programmes, play an important role in lobbying for better policies, especially for those who are marginalized or the victims of various types of violence. But a number of programmes carried out during emergencies, especially health-related ones, have components that involve social marketing and public information campaigns.

In some countries and contexts, where it may be seen as political, advocacy can be dangerous and may result in threats to staff or expulsion of the NGO from the country. An organization may be faced with the decision between helping those in need while remaining silent or speaking out about problems and facing the potential consequences. An NGO's presence might go some way towards shedding light on particular issues, but care should be taken to prevent manipulation (or worse) of the NGO's resources, staff or beneficiaries. These are strategic decisions without a clearcut answer, which each organization typically answers for itself.

If policy change is the goal, considerations in carrying out an advocacy campaign using the media include the following.

- Deciding on the objectives and what policy change is likely to have an impact. A plan will be needed deploying similar approaches to those used in project management. However, be realistic about these objectives and remember that smaller organizations have less access and influence.
- Determining which level and who to approach in the campaign. Legislative or governmental policy may be different at different levels (i.e. national, regional, district or community). Organizational policy may be regulatory or procedural, carried out in guidelines or practice.

- Once the level of advocacy has been determined, it will be possible to identify a target audience of people who can change the policy. Examples include leaders and decision-makers and those who can influence these people or groups like community groups and distinguished persons.
- Developing possible messages or sets of themes. Messages are usually framed to get attention. A problem should be identified (the policy, not individuals) that can be addressed or solved through a change in policy. While the message might contain information or references to individuals or events, it should communicate issues and themes in an easily accessible and intelligible way.
- Identifying the most appropriate media outlets. Each type of media has its own advantages and disadvantages and is usually tailored to the local context. You can identify the most effect type or types of media through looking at objectives and the audience.
- If the target is national-level government health policy, then a persuasive report disseminated among decision-makers at an event might be effective. If the target audience includes community members, then simplified messages might work. In some contexts, where literacy may be low, radio may be effective. T-shirts, leaflets and posters all may be relevant over time.
- To ensure effectiveness, messages should pre-tested by selecting a sample of the target audience to try the message on. This process will help to clarify the message or set of themes that will influence the policy. Be sure the problems and the possible solution are clearly communicated.
- Some NGOs find it helpful to develop contact databases based on their relationships with the media. Broadcasters, editors, journalists and others working in the media rely on external sources of information such as NGOs. Media training for staff may be helpful.
- Being prepared to respond to events (i.e. news) as they happen in reference to the policy changes.

Where the objective is to influence public behaviour, not policy, a similar path may be followed when carrying out public service announcements (PSAs). In an emergency context, this may include a range of messages on topics such as family tracing and water use. Regardless of the specific content, each message must be developed by local staff and be pre-tested on potential audience members. The downside of PSAs is their uncertain effectiveness and their expense. Production of a PSA will likely involve editing and production costs such as camera crews, translation and travel expenses.

Writing editorials and press releases

The purposes of these two types of writing are rather different. Editorials take a particular position or argument to influence opinion or action about an issue, while press releases present facts about a programme with the aim of spreading awareness or sharing information. When writing them consider the following points.

Opinions-editorials (op-eds)

- Use persuasive language and convincing arguments shaped to particular audiences.
- Use words like 'urge', 'support' and 'encourage'.
- Emotion should be used rationally to avoid putting off fence-sitters. Rely heavily on facts, and ground the facts in real examples.
- Be prepared to back up every word and fact.
- Always follow a standard style for grammar, punctuation and word usage.

Press releases

- Have a good title or snappy headline.
- Put basic information in the first paragraph or two and explain these facts as the writing goes on. Press releases are typically no more than a page or two.
- Include the date and time. Press releases are usually time-bound on specific events. Therefore they should be used strategically to highlight the start of a new project or a bleak event during an emergency. Do not start with past events. If, for whatever reason, the information contained in a press release should not be out before a particular date or time, write 'embargoed until' with the specific date and time that it should be made public.
- Editorials are for opinions or comments; avoid them in press releases.
- Use a journalistic, active language style with concise and informative sentences.
- Try to be as specific as possible by incorporating concrete facts (e.g. numbers of victims or beneficiaries, location names, or exact amounts of distributions). Comparisons that readers will understand can be especially useful.
- Relevant quotes are helpful and give feeling to the piece.
- Include contact information and a few sentences that describe the NGO at the end of the press release, to allow the readers to follow up if they want additional information.

Taking photographs

Capturing good photographs of activities is more difficult than it might seem. Looking at brochures or posters from organizations with strong media components, such as the UN, may be helpful. It is usually not enough to give a camera to staff and instruct them to take good pictures; the results will likely be an unsatisfactory waste of time. So the following tips should be considered.

- Ensure staff are familiar with how to operate the camera. Digital cameras have largely replaced film-based cameras.
- A digital camera's capacity (usually measured in mega-pixels) should be high-enough resolution to facilitate editing. However, this might need to be balanced with the capacity of the telecommunications to send the photos via the internet.
- Photos should be as action-oriented as possible.
- Close-ups are good for emotional appeal. These should consist of no more than a couple of people; group photos have little external value for an organization.
- The presence of a logo or other clearly identified landmarks is usually important.
- Discuss basic picture composition with staff by showing them photos comparing and compare usable ones with those that are not.
- Above all, ensure that the dignity and, if necessary, the confidentiality of beneficiaries are respected.

Producing audiovisual material

Making audiovisual material, which is most easily done with a standard video camera, is relatively straightforward provided adequate preparations are made. Press releases called video news releases (VNRs) can be done in video form which news agencies can then edit and use for broadcast.

First, determine the exact audience. If the material is not just for news release, is it useful for presentation at a public or internal meeting, professional seminar or training? Second, consider the material's distribution to television news channels. An 'A-roll' VNR is pre-packaged narrative material (or 'talking-heads'), while a 'B-roll' is made up of miscellaneous original footage with no narration. Of course, none of these options is mutually exclusive.

Third, consider different distribution options:

- At a press conference, consider handing out cassettes and have a staff member ready to be interviewed.
- Via satellite, expensive if special agreement with an operator (e.g. the European Broadcast Union) is arranged.
- Cassette shipment.
- Internet (web) cast.

In most cases, VHS quality material is good enough. Standard TV systems are BETACAM SP Pal or NTSC (US and Latin American standard).

Finally, determine the content. Any audiovisual product can be multi-purposed for presentations, news and web distribution, but the more objectives and audiences targeted with one audiovisual production project the better pre-production work needs to be.

- Establish the story line.
- Provide baseline information about the programme, such as when it was established and what objectives it has achieved.

- Demonstrate in what way this video will be different from previous efforts from other organizations.
- Develop a few shooting ideas.
- Include context material, such as a B-roll of the location, economic activity, daily life (past and present, footage of walls with signs of the past war and other shots of brand new building).
- Inject the human dimension by selecting a character to follow and showing the impact of the project on his or her life.
- If possible, include a comment from an NGO senior representative about the initiative and its readiness to be rolled out in other countries or one from a practitioner who lived the project.
- Include a comment from a neutral observer about the importance of the programme.

Giving interviews

If the NGO has specific guidelines, they will need to be followed. All the same, consider the following points:
- Always be professional. Being antagonistic with a journalist (for example, who may show little concern for local people or who parachutes in with little understanding of the situation) will not be likely to help in any way. There may be a dividend later on if you provide them with assistance, information or a greater appreciation of the context.
- If possible, try to cultivate a friendly and ongoing professional relationship with a journalist who shows interest in the organization's work. If a media person works for the NGO, they will develop lists of the media present around the emergency and they will try to interact with them on a social level. They will also keep them abreast of plans and preparations as well as ongoing activities.
- Think of personal stories and anecdotes to share with reporters. One-word answers and basic facts are not enough. They will most probably want to know about direct experiences and details about the beneficiaries. Site visits and personal interactions with beneficiaries are important for this reason.
- Realize that the journalist's story may already be written. In other words, a journalist carries out interviews to get supporting sound bites or quotes. If the subject is sensitive, weigh carefully what you will say in order to minimize the chances of being misquoted or to prevent the journalist from misconstruing what is said or shown.

Before the interview

- If possible, prepare a press pack containing basic information about the NGO and facts about the programme (see Box 17.1). Often a one-page fact

---

Box 17.1 Press pack content list

- Cover letter with contact details
- Annual report
- Organizational brochure(s)
- Programme photos including dates, location names and descriptive captions
- News stories and published articles
- One-page detail about programme
- List of needs and future plans
- Purpose-written letters from staff to give personal side of story

---

sheet with the details of the programme and a paragraph about the NGO will suffice.

- Consider your organization's activities and plans in order to prepare to respond to questions. Try to confirm details about the emergency and beneficiaries beforehand. If the journalist will receive a tour of a project site, for example, will the interview be before, during or afterwards? Ask what questions will be asked.
- If there need to be ground rules, establish them beforehand and stick to them professionally. If they are not provided, try to anticipate questions that might be asked and avoid situations which may dehumanize or misrepresent the beneficiaries' situation.
- Remember that they are after a story, so try to share one with them. Tell them about the challenges as well as the successes the programme has undergone. The interviewer will most likely already have the big-picture facts and figures and is seeking an interesting story or anecdote.

During the interview

- There is little need to be nervous – you are the subject-matter expert. Try to relax and explain the situation in everyday terms.
- Remember the KISS principle (i.e. keep it simple, silly). Explain the situation in simple, everyday language. Try to avoid jargon (e.g. wat/san) and acronyms (e.g. NGO, PHC). Always explain terms that may not be familiar.

Box 17.2 Points to remember for an interview

Be available.
Be friendly.
Be accurate.
Be concise.
Be descriptive and personal.
Repeat your message simply and more than once.
Be sure to get their contact details in case you need to follow-up.

- Retention is achieved through repetition. Say the message clearly, as the public will remember what they see, hear, and read repeatedly in the media.
- Speak clearly and loudly enough to be heard. When speaking into microphones, talk close but a little off-centre to avoid distortions. When interviewed for television, think about appearances and look at the interviewer, not the camera. On camera, try to remain still and try to keep your hands out of the camera shot as much as possible.
- Journalists spend their lives uncovering information so it is not worth saying that everything is going well or covering up bad situations. Try to put the situation in context. It is best to assume what is said and done will appear in print or on the air. There is no such thing as off the record.
- Consider what is meant by emergency, and only use words like 'disaster' and 'catastrophe' if they really apply to (at least a part of) the population. In the last 15 years, every war and genocide-related adjective has been overused. If it is a genuine emergency, try comparing it with other well-known disasters.
- If the journalist is using a confrontational style, ask for clarification to questions.
- While it is often helpful to be critical, be careful about openly disparaging other organizations. If another organization could do more about a particular issue, say it diplomatically and back it up with publicly available facts.

After the interview

- Inform others so that copies can be retrieved for later public relations use.
- Try to follow up the interview with additional facts or information. If one of your facts or answers was uncertain, get back to the journalist as soon as possible.
- If something has been misquoted, it is important to contact both the journalist and others inside your NGO so that corrections can be made. Once a story is public, however, it is essentially too late, although some form of correction should be made.

CHAPTER 18
Managing security

Working for an NGO can be dangerous, especially in areas of ongoing conflict. The purpose of this chapter is to provide an overview supported by practical information. The chapter covers:

- NGO security fundamentals
- Security phases
- Security planning cycle
- Security management
- Developing an effective security plan
- Security audit: a manager's tool

During a field assignment, staff may be exposed to hostile checkpoints, landmines, violent crime and even activities of open war such as snipers and shelling. Security cuts through all aspects of an NGO's work. Poor security can hamstring activities, threaten staff and beneficiaries, and have a significant or even catastrophic impact on an organization. For these reasons, good security management is a key part of good programme management.

Part of the reason more aid workers are at risk is simply because there are more NGOs, and therefore more staff, working in more conflict zones, and greater numbers are prepared to do so. Since the late 1980s, NGOs have grown exponentially in number and are now a constant and significant player in humanitarian emergencies. This has increased the amount of people, many of who are new to the field, operating in more parts of the developing world.

Another reason for the increased risk is that the nature of conflict itself has changed. Since the end of the cold war, a succession of wars spread in different regions of the world, including the Balkans and parts of Africa. Wars are no longer solely the business of states: national, religious and other groups pose a significant threat to civilians. These wars are characterized by an absence of order, disrespect for rules that had been established historically and the politicization of humanitarian aid itself. For NGOs, the disrespect of the positions and symbols of neutrality are an increased threat to those implementing humanitarian relief.

NGO security fundamentals

What is meant by NGO security?

NGO security is complicated because of the difficult environments in which NGOs operate. Research indicates that although accidental death may be underreported, most aid worker deaths occur as a result of violence. This violence is often the result of war, and it is important to remember that no two conflicts are the same. NGOs have operated in active war zones in some areas where the level of violence is lower, while also being evacuated from other areas because of specifically targeted threats. In Bosnia and Afghanistan, for example, some NGOs carried out programmes very close to the front lines, while in Iraq and Chechnya NGOs withdrew after kidnappings and other terrorism. What mattered in these cases was the directness of the threat faced and how the NGOs carried out their mandates.

Security can be defined as an act (or acts) or potential threats of manmade violence. For the purposes of NGO management, security can be contrasted with safety, which covers accidents and diseases. Obviously, the concepts of safety and security are intimately related in at least two ways. One reason is that NGOs have moral and legal obligations to protect their staff from both insecurity and unsafe conditions. Another reason is that good accident prevention and safety measures are often similar or identical to sound security practices. For example, ensuring that vehicles are correctly maintained has both safety and security ramifications. Still, accident prevention is a normal part of everyone's daily life, whereas security (at least at the level NGOs face) is not. Therefore, security deserves particular attention as well as special ways of thinking about the dangers faced.

Because of their mandate and the way they operate to fulfil this mandate, NGOs view security differently from business and governments. One starting point from which to think about security is to break it down into three component parts: threat (the potential violent act); vulnerability (to the potential threat); and risk (the impact the threat will have). Together, they can be thought of as shown in Table 18.1.

Table 18.1 Threat, vulnerability and risk

Threat	Vulnerability	Risk
Abduction/kidnapping	Affiliations (e.g. UN, EU, US)	Damage to reputation
Arson	Community relations	Inefficient operations
Battle/shelling	Cultural sensitivity	Loss of donor support
Bombing/Terrorism	Location	Lost/damaged property
Burglary/Robbery	Mandate/Mission	Programme closure
Carjacking	Profile/Visibility	Staff casualties
Death threats	Quality of information and coordination coordination	
Disgruntled staff	Staff background	
Illegal checkpoints	Staff experience/training	
Landmines	Staff stress/attitude	
Mobs/riots	Time	
Sexual assault	Transport capacity	
Sniper/random gunfire		

Source: Adapted from Van Brabant (2000).

In practice, certain threats may present themselves more regularly. The vulnerability to the threat is increased or decreased depending on staff behaviour and actions, or other elements. If carjacking is a probable threat, driving an expensive, well-equipped and thus desirable off-road vehicle (as opposed to an inexpensive automobile) at night increases the threat. The likely risk will be loss of the asset and possible physical harm to staff.

Security phases

A simple tool that helps some organizations with their security management practice is a phase system for determining the level of a violent environment. General indicators determine at which level a particular geographic finds itself. This may or may not match what NGOs typically might do in a given situation. These are summarized in Table 18.2.

In Table 18.2, differences between the 'UN label' and 'typical NGO actions' are very evident. This is because most relief-oriented NGOs typically do not follow the UN security phases. One reason is that, in many instances, the security phases remain in place long after the situation has improved. They are also dependent on key events such as the arrival of peacekeeping forces. In such cases, NGOs often continue with activities while civilian UN staff stay out of the field.

Another reason is that the linear nature of the phase system is difficult, if not impossible, to accurately reflect reality. In practice, the security phase tool is an ideal example and each conflict will present different challenges. In many countries in conflict, it is normal to have areas or regions at a 'higher' phase than others. This inconsistency can make the creation and enforcement of policies difficult. It can also affect programming in which developmental relief (discussed in Chapter 1) is carried out.

Following UN security guidance can pose difficulties for NGOs for other reasons. In some cases, the UN Security Coordinator may ask NGOs to sign a formal MOU which obliges implementing partners (i.e. NGOs working under contract to the UN) to follow their guidance and share in some costs, while the risk and liability remains with the NGO. Although the UN has devoted some attention to how it might promote closer cooperation with NGOs, it seems best if NGOs proceed cautiously with both agreement and action connected with the UN. Based on UN models, Interaction, the American NGO umbrella organization, has attempted to raise the standards of their members' security through a document called the Minimum Operating Security Standards (MOSS). Like Sphere Standards, the MOSS offer guidance for NGOs with providing better policy and practice related to security. The MOSS covers five areas: organizational security policy and plans, resources to address security, personnel management, accountability and sense of community.

Table 18.2 Security phases

Level/UN Label	Indicative conditions	Typical NGO actions
0 Normal	Normal living conditions. Active police and emergency services. Little threat of violence. Typical non-emergency, developmental situation	Expatriate staff register with their respective embassy. Staff follow commonsense regarding safety and security. Strong community relations established by NGO
I Precautionary	No outward signs of insecurity but perhaps a history of violence or growing political tension that could lead to greater insecurity.	Security managers monitor situation for deterioration. Staff receive specific security briefings. ID badges carried at all times. Security files are developed and maintained
II Restricted movement	High amounts of crime, ineffective police, some political unrest including demonstrations, poor economic conditions, local towards international hostility (including NGO) presence	Contact is maintained with security personnel from a number of organizations. Ensure basic security measures are in place including guards. Reconsider organizational visibility. Emplace effective and redundant communication system. Evacuation plan put in place. Heighten staff awareness and precautions during movement. Vehicle security practices used (e.g. varying routes used, never leaving unattended, always parking with front facing out)
III Relocation	General lawlessness, weak government structures, rioting, possible terrorism, markets routinely closed or disrupted, fighting in proximity of staff or programme	Regular staff briefings. Continuation of life-saving programmes only. Possible use of two-vehicle minimum when travelling. Possible curfew and other travel restrictions (such as the buddy system). Restrictions on visitors from outside programme area. Mandatory radio checks. Stocks for hibernation prepared

IV
Programme suspension | Widespread looting or rioting, absence of public services, fighting in close proximity of staff or programme | Staff maintain continuous contact with head of office or security officer. Essential travel only. Curfew and other restrictions possibly introduced. Possible evacuation of non-essential staff and prevention of new staff arriving. Consider putting all programmes on hold. Preparations for evacuation made

V
Evacuation | Clear and imminent threats posed by civil unrest or fighting in the immediate vicinity of staff housing or offices | Regular communication maintained with external security personnel. All programme activities closed. Consider advantages and disadvantages of hibernation and evacuation. All staff are prepared for immediate evacuation

Note: Levels information adapted from the UN Department of Safety and Security (UNDSS).

Security planning cycle

With so much to consider, especially when working in an unfamiliar place and perhaps with a new environment or organization, it helps to use a framework for organizing security management. Figure 18.1 presents critical elements of security management.

Step 1 Assessment

Who are we?

Knowing who you are and who you represent is a fundamental question. It is the starting point not just for security but also for programme management. There is a number of questions worth considering, such as: What is our mission? What is our mandate? How do our activities represent our NGO? How do we perceive ourselves as a group and how might our actions affect that perception? A further critical question is to carefully consider and ask HQ how risk-averse is the organization. This will help determine when to consider when to withdraw from dangerous areas.

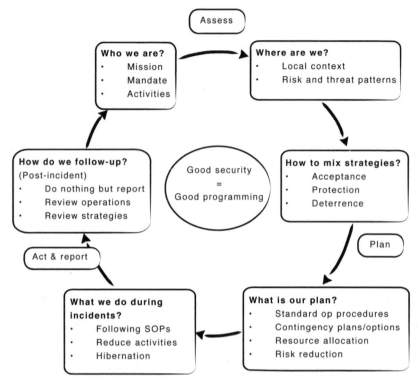

Figure 18.1 Security management cycle
Source: Adapted from materials produced by Van Brabant (2000).

Where are we?

In thinking about security, the context is critical. How do you gather information? Of course, the situation in conflict areas constantly changes. An effective assessment includes not just threats but also vulnerabilities, the exposure to the threat, as well as the risk or impact of the threat.

Although specialists should carry out an initial security assessment, it may fall to the manager to consider the security risks. This list should then be followed.

1. **Plan** who will be responsible for the assessment among the staff and how they will go about it.
2. **Collect** information. Use as many sources as possible and consider carefully the reliability of each source. From a larger perspective, the easiest sources are to ask local staff, other NGOs, the UN, read local news papers. The internet is usually helpful.
3. **Analyse** historical, geographic, political, socio-economic and current development contexts.
4. **Present** in writing for analysis and use by others. Some narrative is good, but the key is to put forward the information in a digestible form. A summary format is shown in Table 18.3.

Table 18.3 Threat analysis

Threat	Vulnerability	Location	Comment
Kidnapping	High visibility	Capital: very high	Recommend establishing routine radio checks before and during travel at well-known waypoints
	Lack of variation during travel	Countryside: low	Reduce movements during spates of kidnappings
	Presence in low-traffic urban areas		
Landmines	Frequent travel to unfamiliar areas (during programme assessments)	Capital: nil	Need to coordinate with both local and international officials to identify specific suspected landmine areas
	Untrained staff	Countryside: very high	Landmine awareness training needed for all staff and should be included in induction from this point forward
Riots	Slow information sharing with other organizations	Capital: high	Greater coordination, even if arranged informally, with UN (UNDSS) and other INGOs needed
	Unspecific incident procedures	Countryside: low	New version of security plan required with specific procedures, including rally points, for violent demonstrations

Step 2 Planning

How will we mix strategies?

In the following discussion, three security strategies (i.e. acceptance, protection and deterrence) are outlined, followed by specific examples. An effective security approach brings elements of each strategy together. Some NGOs fall into the trap of relying on a single strategy, which might leave the organization vulnerable. For example, reliance on acceptance by itself, without adequate protection and deterrence measures, will likely expose the NGO open to many kinds of threat. Similarly, some may advocate an overreliance on protection measures, but this may give the impression that the organization is a high-value target. For this reason, security strategies are presented in a balanced triangle in Figure 18.2.

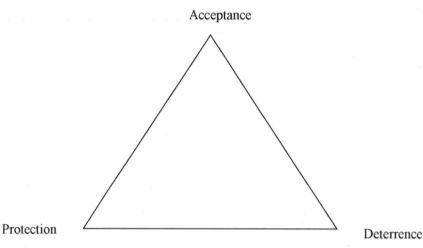

Figure 18.2 Security triangle
Source: Adapted from Van Brabant (2000: 57).

Acceptance takes advantage of relationships with external actors to help ensure the security of an NGO. In this strategy, security is based on an NGO's acceptance in a community, so measures typically work best in rural areas where relations are more easily established than in urban areas. For an NGO, this is probably the most natural strategy and it is the most cost-effective. Steps may include seeking out the approval of locals, especially key individuals, such as authorities like village elders or a similar group. Fostering acceptance can be as simple as earning the respect of common people through project results, giving appropriate respect in accord to local custom or paying attention to special groups like the elderly and children.

Image is especially crucial in gaining acceptance. A number of factors can influence image, including staff's behaviour and appearance. In some cultures, for example, male-female interactions and use of alcohol are viewed very negatively. NGOs that disrespect (or even generate a perception of disrespect of) local customs can face an increased level of threat. Even simpler issues, like the way staff dress, can influence image and should be carefully considered.

Protection uses equipment and devices to harden a target. Protection strategy consists of a litany of objects that may be needed in an insecure environment, from bars on windows to radios to flak jackets. Often, it is employed in incremental steps, for example:

1. No fence, no guards, no floodlights, doors left open at night
2. Fence, no guards, floodlights left on at night, doors locked
3. Fence with barbed wire, guards at night, floodlights left on at night, doors locked
4. Fence with barbed wire, guards on duty 24 hours, floodlights left on at night, doors locked and reinforced

Obviously there will be more severe steps that can be taken. NGO managers should carefully consider the image this might portray in relation to the security cycle.

Deterrence involves presenting a counter-threat. In rare cases, deterrence may include the use of armed guards, while more typically the threat of withdrawing a programme or contacting relevant and more powerful authorities (e.g. peacekeeping forces) is used. For obvious reasons, this is often a difficult and problematic strategy for NGOs to follow.

To help illustrate how mixing strategies might work in practice, three specific threats and possible measures for different strategies are outlined in Table 18.4.

Standard Operating Procedures (SOPs)

SOPs create a regular system for carrying out specified tasks. In security, this can create an understanding of a range of different expected or required actions. If,

Table 18.4 Security strategies

Carjacking

Acceptance	Protection	Deterrence
Strong community acceptance will likely decrease threat as community members may identify likely perpetrators and help recover stolen vehicle	Staff should know avoidance and evasion measures, such as locking doors, parking with front facing out, restrictions on routes and travel times. Special anti-theft devices may be installed	If a large enough problem, NGOs may declare certain areas off limits until situation improves. Working with government or other groups (e.g. UN) may also help mitigate this threat

Burglary/Robbery

Acceptance	Protection	Deterrence
Good community relations can reduce threat by having observant neighbours notify authorities before incidents	Staff training, curfews, travel restrictions, appropriate office and residence physical security (e.g. adequate guard coverage, perimeter fences/walls, floodlights	An able guard force is imperative in many areas. Closeness to international military/policy may also help

Open conflict

Acceptance	Protection	Deterrence
Local community members may alert NGO to possible threats and provide safe passage or housing if needed	Robust protection measures needed, including reliable and redundant communications, clear and well-thought-out SOPs and protective equipment (e.g. flak vests, helmets, sandbags, bomb shelters	Generally, activities should not be carried out outside the coordination of a larger international presence (e.g. the UN)

for example, all staff members understand that they are expected to congregate in a particular area during an emergency, this will help managers account for staff and proceed with further action.

SOPs may or may not be put in writing. Some procedures, such as where keys are maintained or how radio checks are done, need not necessarily be on paper, but generally procedures are more easily enforced and transferred to new staff when in writing. A large part of a SOP may consist of a written security plan, which is further discussed below.

Contingency planning

No one can know for sure what may happen in any environment and this is especially true in an insecure place. Still, speculation about potential security incidents can help when the time comes to react to them. There are models for considering potential incidents, but the most unencumbered means is simply developing different scenarios. Suppose, for example, an NGO is carrying out programmes in a refugee camp along a frontier. If fighting crosses the border encircling the camp, is there more than one route in case of evacuation? Or suppose there is high criminality in the neighbourhood around the office. If the office were robbed, is there a way to call for help (and ideally more than one)? The key is proactive thinking to help prevent or avoid incidents.

Resource allocation

In planning, there is a critical need to allocate funds for information collection, equipment and training from the start. Often, the largest amount of funds goes to communications equipment, but these funds may also be spent on training and specific protection measures such as stronger locks or floodlights. These resources should be made available regardless of the availability of donor funds. Those in the field may need to persuade HQ to use the organization's own money.

Step 3 Act and report

What we do during incidents

While there are useful guidelines for surviving dangerous situations, such as those listed in Box 18.1, nothing can replace good judgement and commonsense. But running emergency programmes is not easy. What might sound like practical advice in reality may prove impossible. Before 11 September 2001, the best security advice said that hostages should follow whatever instructions terrorist hostages might deliver (this recommendation, of course, proved fatal on that day). Advice such as avoiding walking may be inappropriate in emergency situations if walking to a programme area is necessary. Or, if the advice is to travel with others, it may be unclear what do you do if there is only one representative or staff member of the NGO present.

How will we follow up?

Not every incident deserves the same response. Follow-up can be either individual or organizational.

Individual level Managers must be proactive in doing what is best for their staff. In mild cases, this may involve giving time off to staff or advising them to take an early break (holiday or R&R) from the field. In more serious incidents, this should involve providing the opportunity for professional counselling and/or mandatory departure from the field (see Chapter 10). The difficulty for managers is to determine what should be optional and what should be obligatory. In either case, in put from HQ may be helpful and necessary.

Organizational level At the field level, there are at least three options, including:

1. **Do nothing, but report** In minor incidents, sometimes there is nothing to do but report to others what is happening. Still, sharing information at all levels, regardless of how seemingly unimportant, is critical for those who are responsible for security: it helps to form a bigger picture. On more than one occasion, relief workers have been aware of things, but did not report information that later made a difference in a larger and more significant violent incident.

2. **Review operations** There may be certain times of day or geographic locations that can be avoided to prevent further incidents. Perhaps a certain group perceives the NGO as favouring another side and a slight change in programming may prevent violence in the future. Policies and procedures should be reviewed in light of newly perceived threats.

3. **Review strategies** At times, especially following a significant incident, a more thorough examination of the NGO's strategies is needed. Perhaps there has been an overreliance on acceptance as a strategy, so more protection measures (e.g. vehicle convoys or more guards) are needed. Maybe the hope was that violence could be avoided through protection, but after analysing the incident reveals that greater acceptance by the community would have prevented

---

Box 18.1 10 recommendations for surviving incidents

1. Learn as much as possible about your surroundings.
2. Stay alert.
3. Be a team player and share information.
4. Keep a low profile by trying to blend in.
5. In times of high threat, avoid crowded areas.
6. Drive safely and wear seatbelts.
7. Always lock doors (i.e. car doors and bedroom doors).
8. Alert others of your whereabouts.
9. Know when and how to call for help.
10. Remain cautious.

violence. The key is to be open to review and flexible to meet changing situations.

Security management

Throughout this chapter, an effort has been made to show that good security is linked to good management and hence good programming. While there are a number of complex issues to consider, three key challenges face managers when implementing security policies and procedures.

Key challenge no. 1: authority In emergencies, managers have an explicit responsibility to look after their staff while staff have an implicit responsibility not just to follow directives but also to share information and be a constructive team player. As suggested in Chapter 3, NGOs often adopt flat organizational structures and make decisions through consensus. But emergency situations require decisive leadership. Building legitimacy and organizational clarity are important. For this reason, and although it has its own pitfalls, an NGO may adapt its structure during insecure situations to establish a stronger (i.e. top-down) authority. Ways to create a conducive environment are discussed below (pp. 337–9).

Key challenge no. 2: enforcement Since staff members want both to live a normal life and carry out the programme's activities regardless of the danger, enforcement of security policies and measures is often difficult. In many ways, the extreme ends of the security spectrum (i.e. phases 1 and 5) are the easiest to manage. In other words, in the grey area in between where the situation is ambiguous or changing, staff may expect certain freedoms, which will make enforcement of policy difficult. As a situation worsens, staff members may have to suffer a curfew, for example, and may find it difficult to live with other restrictions imposed on them. As situations apparently improve, it may also be difficult to get staff to remain security-conscious. In such instances, the best measures to follow are usually found in good management practices: keep people informed, be consistent and set a personal example.

Key challenge no. 3: equity Balancing different interests is always a challenge. From a security perspective, there are often additional challenges. Should national staff be treated differently and, if so, how? In certain countries gender lines are very clearly defined; how might this influence security practices? If an evacuation of non-essential staff is made, who should be determined non-essential? These are challenging questions without easy solutions. At the least, they should be addressed in a proactive way at a senior level in each NGO. Like security strategies, the keys to the good security management of staff include:

- **Information and awareness** Good communication and multiple flows of information make the difference.
- **Behaviour** Create an atmosphere in which people know how to modify, adapt and react to dangerous situations.
- **Teamwork** There is safety in numbers.

Security staff

Safety and security are the responsibilities of senior management. Having the senior representative (or CD) responsible for day-to-day security management has the advantage that the person in this position normally attends many meetings and has access to sources of information. He or she also has the explicit authority to enforce whatever course of action is decided. The disadvantage is that this person is simply too busy to gather, analyse and disseminate security information.

Some NGOs opt to have their senior representative manage security; others pass the function of day-to-day security management to a logistician (or similar), or employ a full-time security officer. In this case, there are several considerations.

Logistician (or similar position) Many NGO senior managers delegate security responsibilities to a logistician or administrator. In some cases, it makes sense in that it frees up the CD's time and the logistician or administrator is responsible for resources. The disadvantage is that such a person typically does not have direct access to information nor the authority of a country director. In addition, a logistician might also feel pressure to place more emphasis on logistical duties, at the expense of security.

Full-time security officer or consultant To focus scarce resources on programmes, many NGOs opt for a short-term consultant to evaluate the security situation, train staff, write security plans and develop policies. This is can be a very pragmatic approach if a full-time security officer based in the field is not necessary. As with all consultants, it is important that they have clear and realistic TOR or scope of work that outlines exactly what is expected of them. Additionally, a security consultant's background should be checked, because the security needs of NGOs differ significantly from other organizations in conflict zones.

Former police and military personnel may possess many skills that are useful in the environments in which NGOs work, but their specific background should be carefully considered. What is important is the exact experience they had while in uniform. The most successful applicants usually have experiences working directly with civilian populations in places with poor resources.

Security awareness training

If a qualified instructor is available to carry out security training, it is good idea to do so in all but the most acute emergencies where there is not enough time. There are many ways to carry out security awareness training at the field level. As with any training, there are several elements to consider:

- **Who should attend** Ideally, security training should be attended by all staff, but this may not be realistic for logistical (e.g. staff are in different locations or work different shifts) or other pragmatic reasons (e.g. language or position). However, training should always be organized in groups. At the least, staff should receive versions of the same training which has been modified for the best fit possible. In certain cases, specific training, such as for drivers and guards, may be needed, while in other cases simple awareness raising is called for. An assumption, however, should not be made that certain staff (e.g. office accountants compared with doctors on mobile medical teams) do not need training (such as landmine awareness), because all staff may encounter threats at one time or another. Training needs assessment is discussed further in Chapter 16.

- **Place and length** Like other training, a suitable training location will be free of distractions, have good lighting and ventilation, and have toilet and refreshment facilities. The length of the training should be flexible, depending on time constraints and the time needed to impart the skills and information. One option is to set aside up to a full single day, work permitting, or splitting up the training over the course of several days or weeks to allow for reflection and investigation of options or other information.

- **Suggested topics** The list of topics to be covered should be tailored to the intended audience. Staff members who are new to field conditions will need more basic instructions, while experienced staff and those from the area (i.e. national staff) will benefit from learning about how the NGO might react to particular incidents. If there is any action planning associated with the training, be sure to follow through and keep the expectations for the time needed to implement new policies and procedures realistic.

Training should be hands-on and participatory. Discussions are preferred to lectures. Exercises that generate the exchange of ideas and awareness raising are best. One such exercise is analysing what level of risk is considered acceptable to the NGO (see Chapter 5).

When people lack situational awareness, they are more likely to be caught off-guard and have a slower reaction to threats. All NGO staff should be able to be clearly aware of immediate threats they might face. The following tool (known as Cooper's colour code) can help maintain individual situational awareness in insecure environments. It can be introduced during initial induction or formal training:

Level Green The staff member is essentially unaware of the security situation as he or she may be in their home country. In emergency settings, no one should be at this level.

Level Yellow The staff member actively assesses potential threats. This should be the basic standard in emergencies. For example, if their vehicle approaches the office gate, he or she makes a mental note of unknown persons standing nearby.

Level Red The staff member deals with the threats identified in Level Yellow. If in the vehicle again with potentially threatening individuals standing outside, he or she sound the horn to draw attention, drive forward or drive in reverse depending on what is the best option.

Level Black The staff member carries out the action decided on while in Level Red. Continuing the example, the staff member sounds the horn to draw the attention of the guards and the suspicious-looking persons. Moving from Level Yellow to Level Black, in this example, would only last a few seconds. Depending on the situation, the staff would also be wise to report the incident.

Developing an effective security plan

Written security plans are a problem for many NGOs. On the one hand, plans tend not to be useful. A review of various NGO security guidelines shows that too many of them are either too vague, with gems of advice like 'Don't take risks', or are too specific, suggesting unfeasible physical security improvements to residences. On the other hand, plans can turn into thick manuals people do not read and so they spend time in a drawer or on a shelf collecting dust.

For a plan to be effective it must be kept up-to-date and provide the precise information needed. This is not always easy to do and having a lengthy security plan may substitute for continued awareness and alertness of staff. Where and when possible, it is usually best produced with information generated by several sources, including local staff members and external people (e.g. UN or military). To do this, information must be up-to-date, based on the best information available and drawn from different sources.

Some NGOs find it effective to write plans in a participatory way, like holding a workshop or forming a working group composed of selected members of staff (e.g. management, programme and programme support). This method may not be feasible during the initial draft when getting something on paper is the priority. In such cases, it is important this draft be reviewed by others.

Many NGOs have global security manuals produced by HQ, which tend to be lengthy and nearly impossible to quickly adapt for local conditions. Because people find long documents less useful, plans are more likely to be used if they are no more than 10–15 pages in total length. Most NGOs feel it is better for sub-offices to have a separate plan that is an extension of the main security plan. Box 18.4 presents a basic security plan for a refugee situation.

Box 18.2 Radios and security

Many people, it seems, equate radios with security. Radios by themselves are not security devices. If someone mugs you on the street, there will be little more you can do but throw the radio at them. Still, radio can fill an important role in providing timely information which can make the difference between life and death. Every staff member should be fully trained in their use even if they do not normally carry one. See Chapter 14 for further discussion of radio communications.

Box 18.3 Security plan

I Background and location context

History, recent events and current developments should be discussed with an eye to the threats faced. Questions that should be answered are: How has conflict affected the area? Who was involved and how? What specific areas witnessed fighting or unrest? What are potential flash points? Analysis of different stakeholders and their relationships may be included in this section.

II Threat analysis

This should be specific to the local context. Points to consider include: What specific threats are faced? What is the level and pattern of crime? Have other NGOs been targeted in the past? If so, how? The threats faced should be reviewed, using trusted local contacts and staff, other NGOs and other organizations such as the UN. Past patterns should be noted in the light of current and possible future developments.

Specific indicators may help determine what measures to take and if security phases should change. These can then be linked to what to do before, during and after an incident. A simple action plan can be put in place such as this one for a refugee camp.

1. **Pattern/Indicator**
    - Negative rumours spread by the disempowered
    - Disenchantment among the local populace over the disparities in aid provided
    - Violence in one camp spreading to others by refugees modelling behaviour
2. **Preventative measures**
    - Raise the NGO's profile in the camp.
    - Make refugees and locals aware of the NGO's mission and objectives.
    - Collaborate closely with camp management structure.
3. **Incident action**
    - Monitor VHF Channel 2.
    - On instruction, staff will rally at main gate or, if not possible, proceed to the camp manager's tent.
    - If the situation worsens, leave the camp with all staff members.
4. **Post-incident follow-up**
    - Increase availability of VHF radios among staff.
    - Strengthen reporting and information sharing.
    - Consider deterrent measures.

III Specific policies

Based on the threat analysis, rules and other details including contingency plans should be outlined. Specifics are needed, since some staff may push the limits of commonsense unless limits are set. Examples include: office closing procedures, curfews, no-go areas and travel regulations, reporting procedures, how to handle cash and 'what to do when' scenarios. In certain areas, additional information may be needed for evacuation, landmines or other topics.

IV Maps

At least one map should be included in the plan, which shows the evacuation routes. Maps should be of a scale that can be used to navigate and pinpoint the major and easily recognizable features. Hand-drawn maps can be used until detailed professional maps are available. The maps used in the plan may be versions of maps used to brief staff on high- and low-risk areas found in the emergency.

V List of important contacts/phone numbers

The list should contain all standard emergency numbers (e.g. fire and police) where available, relevant security forces and emergency HQ numbers, since staff may not have already have these important numbers. In some plans this information is on the first page, but in others it is at the end, so that the page can be easily detached.

Note that care should be taken that the document does not contain any sensitive information. Sections I and II should merely provide information for the uninitiated (e.g. new expatriate staff), and should be in language that does not offend any present or future authorities. Also, if it is not spelled out somewhere else, it will also be important to clearly define security responsibilities, including who will act as the security focal point.

Security audit: a manager's tool

An audit can help those concerned with security to examine different vulnerabilities and examine preventative measures. There are literally thousands of pertinent questions to consider, so only a sample of 110 (deliberately leading) questions are presented in Table 18.5.

Table 18.5 Security audit

Category	Points of inquiry
General	What is your NGO's policy towards security (i.e. is it committed and aware)? What mix of security strategies does your NGO typically follow? What is its stance towards neutrality and impartiality?
	Does your NGO have a policy for the use of armed guards? Is there a realistic plan for dealing with hostage situations?
	Is there a satisfactory way of handling the death of a staff member?
	Does your NGO have the resources to address the security threat posed where you are currently operating and can more equipment be procured if needed?
Assessments and plans	Does your NGO have a standard format or list of questions for security assessments? Is it comprehensive enough? Is the assessment well-rounded, including threats, vulnerabilities and risks? Are the sources used realistic and reliable?
	What is done with the assessment once it is finalized? Is there a clear action plan and is someone responsible for taking the process forward?
	Is an adequate security plan in place? How many people and how many sources of information were used in completing it? Is the written plan a living document, i.e. is there a way to ensure staff are familiar with its contents, and when was it last revised?
Site security (resident, office or project site)	Is property adequately protected against the current and potential threats faced?

cont.

cont.

Category	Points of inquiry
	Are there any areas (e.g. windows, doors roofs) that can be strengthened for greater protection? Specifically, are doors and locks of a high enough standard? Are fences/walls high enough and equipped with enough concertina/barbed wire to thwart criminals and others? If there are bars on windows, are they all secure and thick enough? Is there sufficient lighting? Is there a peephole or other safe means of viewing the outside of each door or gate?
	Are poles, tree limbs or other objects that may aid intruders to enter the property sufficiently secured or trimmed to prevent their use?
	Is there adequate means of escape, such as a ladder large enough to reach over concertina-topped walls? Is there a secure room staff can flee to in the event of invasion? If there is a bomb shelter or similar protective measures, and will it actually protect against the threat faced (i.e. was expert/ technical advice used in its emplacement)?
	Is there an opening and closing procedure? Is it followed by staff? Are residence doors locked whenever staff are not present and during the night? How are visitors handled: are identifications checked, is there a badge system, is there a sign-in book?
	If guards are employed, are they vetted and trained? Do they have a clear idea of what is expected of them? Do they have a means of communication and appropriate equipment (e.g. working flashlights, club or other defensive weapon)? Does someone routinely check to make sure they do not sleep (unless that is the local norm) in the middle of their shift?
Vehicles	Are vehicles adequately maintained (i.e. is there a regular maintenance schedule and are the mechanics reliable)? Are vehicles robust enough to handle evacuation by road? Do they have tools, tyre jack, extra fuel and other items appropriate for the area (such as a second spare tyre, snow-chains and axes for cutting felled trees)?
	Are drivers skilled enough to drive off-road? What are drivers instructed to do in different security incidents, such as being caught in crossfire or entering a suspected landmine area? What will a driver do if he causes an accident or hits a pedestrian?
Travel	Are staff instructed on what precautions they should follow when travelling? Are they obliged to communicate their whereabouts? Do they understand when and by what means? Is there a heightened state of insecurity at the international level that makes travel outside your area more dangerous?

Category	Points of inquiry
	Do staff have enough preparation and the right equipment (e.g. radios and water) for their trip? Are maps good enough to navigate with?
	Do staff know what to do at checkpoints, how to behave around military personnel and in other sensitive areas? If landmines are present, are staff prepared to safely handle them by negotiating a direction away from the danger? Are there restricted or off-limit/no-go areas and are these known?
Money	Are adequate controls in place to prevent theft (e.g. strong safes and back-up records)? How often is the money counted and recorded?
	What is the procedure for banking? If banks are not functioning, how are funds moved (i.e. transferring cash by hand and using an informal cash transfer system), and is it as safe as possible? Are the limits set for petty cash low enough so that a large amount cannot be lost, but is enough to meet operational needs?
	If a safe is being used, is it strong enough? Is it mounted correctly? Are keys and combination sufficiently protected? If the money is simply hidden, is this sufficient to deter theft?
Communications	Are the types of communications equipment of the appropriate standard? Are there enough radios for your staff to communicate in an emergency?
	Is it (technically) possible to communicate with other organizations when needed? Has some prearranged contact been formed with relevant organizations in the event of a security incident?
	Are staff adequately trained? Do they know standard radio protocols and do they properly use the radio? Do they know how to use satellite telephones?
	Do all staff members possess all pertinent callsigns, Sel-call and telephone numbers? Are these posted in accessible locations, such as bulletin boards, radio rooms and vehicles?
Evacuation	Is there a clear, sufficiently detailed and realistic plan? Are alternatives to this plan likewise thought out and workable? Are staff mentally and physically prepared if it should come to evacuation? Is there a checklist or similar available?
	If there is an unplanned evacuation (e.g. caused by a credible death threat), do staff have a clear idea of where to go (e.g. local police, embassy or international military presence) and what actions to take?
	Are there enough stocks of food, water and other supplies to last through a period of hibernation and evacuation?

Category	Points of inquiry
	What national staff will be informed? Is there an arrangement for nationals either to evacuate with expatriates or continue activities while at the same time being compensated?
	Are steps in place to effect the evacuation? To what level are HQ and other organizations involved?
Human resources	Have staff been screened and vetted? Do records exist for their references and up-to-date contact information, which includes information such as their next-of-kin? Are you aware of your staff's abilities (e.g. prior security training or first-aid skills) and limitations (e.g. phobias and illnesses)?
	Do all staff members have access to the security plan and other security-related information? How is this information shared with them? Are they clear what their responsibilities are in the event of an emergency?
	How is security included in staff recruitment, orientation and while on the job? How are briefings and training conducted? How can the security competence of staff be raised? Is there information that allows every staff member's family to be contacted in the event of an emergency? Are staff adequately covered by insurance?
	How are national and expatriate staff treated differently in terms of security? What information is withheld and why? Can certain local staff members be relied on to share information or play an active role in security-related matters? Conversely, are there local staff members who may be a liability because of their backgrounds or affiliations?
	Do all staff members receive the same briefing and training? How much of a facto is experience in transferring skills and knowledge to staff members (i.e. is it assumed that staff with a lot of experience automatically know the ropes)?
	Are staff present in the field for long periods monitored for burnout, complacency and/or stress? How does your NGO approach staff stress? Is there a way to handle cases of post-traumatic stress?
Reporting	How are incidents reported in the field and to HQ? Who does the reporting and when? Is there a specific mode or format?
	How is coordination handled with other NGOs and organizations like the UN? Does an embassy or the UN have a warden system? If a warden, are the role and expectations clear?
	Do all staff know who to report incidents to and how? Is there a standard format or does one need to be created?
	Are the lessons learned from incidents fed back into the organization so that improvements can be made? How often are reviews of security policy done? Is it a top-down, externally driven (e.g. by a consultant) or participatory process?

CHAPTER 19
Monitoring and evaluating a project

Monitoring and evaluation (M&E) are two important management tasks. Monitoring is an ongoing process of review and appraisal. Evaluation is a planned appraisal of a project or programme. The purpose of this chapter is to focus on the monitoring and evaluation of project activities. It covers:
- M&E basics
- Monitoring
- Evaluation

M&E might cover any aspect of an NGO's activities, including, for example, financial resources, administrative procedures and strategic directions. The success or failure of a project or programme will ultimately be determined by whether or not it has, or will have, achieved its objectives. Paired together, at least in an informal setting, monitoring occurs frequently, while evaluations are done periodically. In emergencies, too often, M&E is done as a half-hearted afterthought of project cycle management. Both should be considered an integral part of managing projects and part of a process of improvement (SCF, 2001).

M&E basics

M&E in emergencies has several distinctive differences from M&E in development practice. These differences include: rapid change in situations and thus information, instability and security, missing information including baseline data and pressures on staff such as lack of time and turnover. Despite these challenges, however, M&E is a critical element in the project cycle management process.

There are two primary reasons for carrying out M&E: first, for accountability. NGOs are responsible to project beneficiaries and to their donors. M&E information can help maintain these relationships and provide proof where there is no clear bottom line. The second reason is in order to improve performance. When done properly, monitoring can involve an exchange where lessons learned are elements incorporated into future activities. In this way, M&E can contribute to learning and form the basis of lessons for the existing project and the ones that follow.

According to Bakewell (2003), each M&E system should incorporate the following basic principles:
- Participation
- Cost-effectiveness
- Consistent, good-quality information
- Gender awareness

- Capacity building
- Emphasis on analysis and decision making
- Awareness of unintended consequences
- Openness to other sources of information

As explained by Twigg (2004), M&E systems should be planned carefully, as each project is unique. Although generalities apply, a shelter project, for example, will be different in Central Asia from Central Africa. When designing a system, some considerations include:

- Providing a clear method and focus to the M&E activities
- Using existing indicators
- Unit of assessment: M&E can take place at individual, household, group, community or institutional levels
- Sampling size and methods
- Geographical coverage, including hazards and risks and the number and types of vulnerable people assisted
- Existing information sources, such as past surveys
- Who should be involved in collecting, providing and discussing evidence
- Scheduling – M&E takes time
- Tools and methods to be used, such as those outlined in Chapter 4
- Matching inputs and outputs
- Reporting back to all the stakeholders concerned in a way that they can understand how findings will be acted upon
- Clear TOR which reflect the main decisions

According to Save the Children (SCF) (1995), there are a number of key questions to consider before carrying out M&E:

1. **Purpose** Why is the evaluation necessary? What is its aim?
2. **Results** Who is the evaluation for? How will the results be used?
3. **Objectives and key questions** What are the objectives and what specific questions should it address?
4. **Information collection and analysis** What information is needed to answer these questions? Where will the information come from? What indicators can be used to measure the impact and the progress of the work? How should information be collected, analysed and presented?
5. **Presenting the results** What are the conclusions and recommendations? How will the findings be recorded and presented to different users? What feedback will there be about the findings and about the process to the people involved in the work?
6. **Organization** How will it be directed and managed? Who should be involved? What are their tasks and responsibilities? What is the timescale? What resources will be needed?

Many of the approaches and tools discussed in Chapter 4 can be applied to M&E. FGDs, ranking and mapping, for example, can be used at different times during the project cycle. In this way, participation is initiated and managers get a clear picture of the status of a project.

Monitoring

Monitoring is the continuous process of reviewing the progress of a work towards planned objectives. At a basic level, it is simply checking to make sure that project activities are on track. To be truly effective, monitoring should look at programme support elements, as well as specific programmes. Effective monitoring is normally also participatory, both in its methods and by involving stakeholders as well as directly involved staff.

Monitoring plan

The purpose of the monitoring plan is to set expectations and track achievements, improve performance through problem identification and programme improvement and examine costs against outputs and outcomes. Monitoring information can come from a variety of sources and should be measured against stated indicators. It is important to focus on the quality and quantity of project inputs and outputs and how they lead towards the achievement of objectives. Table 19.1 shows an example based on a typical PHC project.

Some NGOs develop a means to carry out the monitoring. A check, such as that shown in Box 19.1, helps facilitate a uniform and objective means for monitoring.

Table 19.1 Monitoring plan

Programme component	Indicators	Data source	Frequency	Staff responsible
Reducing morbidity and mortality among community members	Percentage of total population to have access to quality PHC by the end of the project	Evaluation data	End of project	CD and project manager
Strengthening the capacity of community structures to deliver PHC	Number of community health workers proficient in new skills	Records, interviews, staff reviews	Monthly	Project manager
Training health workers and skills upgrades	Improved understanding of PHC among community health workers	Training records and observation	End of training	Project manager and trainer

Box 19.1 Food distribution monitoring checklist
1. **The organization of the distribution area**
   - Are people waiting in an orderly manner in line?
   - Is the food being handled properly? Are bags open or is food spilled on the ground?
   - Is the distribution area properly sheltered?
   - Is the distribution area kept clean?
   - Is there enough security provided to ensure an orderly distribution?
   - Are there enough crowd-controllers present?
   - Is the area clearly defined by rope or plastic?
2. **Distribution process and name verification**
   - Is the ration card verified to check the holder's identity and to check whether the holder is on the beneficiary list?
   - Is the ration card punched or otherwise marked upon entry into the distribution site/upon receiving food?
   - Does the agency use a computerized beneficiary list?
   - Do all food distribution staff wear gloves (and are they observing additional hygienic rules)?
   - Do all beneficiaries sign on having received their ration?
   - Have family sizes increased during food distribution?
   - Are loudspeakers used to call out the names of the beneficiaries?
3. **Distribution equity and vulnerable beneficiaries**
   - Is there a separate line for easy access for the more vulnerable persons?
   - Are staff involved to assist the more vulnerable persons in receiving their ration?
   - Are staff monitoring the line for the more vulnerable persons?
   - Are persons who are not on the list given food? Is any action undertaken to sort out why they are not on the list?
   - Does everybody receive the same agreed food ration?
4. **If scoops are being used:**
   - Are standard scoops used?
   - Are all scoops precise and marked (to show the exact quantity)?
   - Are the same scoops used for different food items?
   - If scoops change in between distributions while food ration remains the same, is this clearly explained to the beneficiaries
5. **Information sharing on the distribution**
   - Have all beneficiaries been informed about the distribution day, the food items and their quality?
   - Are all beneficiaries well informed on the quantity of food contained per scoop?
   - Are beneficiaries properly informed on changes in food rations?
   - How and when is this information disseminated?
   - Are there different approaches used to inform the most vulnerable people (including minors, deaf persons, elderly persons)?
   - Are the standards of accountability displayed by the implementing partner?
6. **Timeliness of distribution**
   - Did the distribution start on time?
   - Did the implementing partner arrive on time?
   - Was food offloaded and handled in a proper and safe way?
   - Was a WFP, UNHCR or implementing partner on the ground throughout the distribution process

Source: NRC (2004: 192).

Once the monitoring has been carried out and analysed by management, it is important to also consider how findings will be shared. This sharing should be clear, concise and easy to relate to the main aims of the project.

Evaluation

An evaluation is an appraisal of a project's progress at a single point in time. The purpose of evaluation is to confirm that the objective has been achieved and to provide evidence for accountability. Evaluations are considered more involved than monitoring reviews, which are a quick check of the status or health of a project.

Evaluations can happen at different times during a project: during it, usually in the middle, at the end as a final evaluation, or afterwards as 'ex post'. Evaluations can also take place before a project, sometimes called ex ante evaluations, feasibility studies or appraisals, which are the same as the assessments described earlier in this book.

Photo 19.1 Monitoring Construction
Where there is no engineer: Only an appropriately qualified and experienced engineer can properly oversee a construction or rehabilitation project, but it does not take an engineer to tell that these well rings are of poor quality. Staffs with various backgrounds will likely visit project sites during the course of their duties and their visits, if properly prepared, can help monitor progress.

The most effective evaluations focus on the beneficiaries' perceptions regarding the outputs and outcomes they receive over the process of outputs delivered. It is important to make it clear that problems and mistakes will treated as opportunities for learning, not as a reason for punishment. When done effectively, evaluations help to improve future projects and help staff learn. An evaluation should not be perceived as an inspection, which may be perceived as threatening and lead to staff covering up information. Thus the concepts discussed in Chapter 4 under participatory methods may be of particular use in gaining insight into these perceptions. They can be adapted to the evaluation of a project.

CHAPTER 20
Coordinating with other organizations

Coordination is a process of sharing information, reaching common understanding and, in many cases, reaching common positions. The purpose of this chapter is to outline what is commonly understood by coordination and how NGOs can best interact with other organizations often present in emergencies. Specifically, this chapter discusses:
- Understanding coordination
- Coordination between NGOs
- Coordination between NGOs and the UN
- Coordination between NGOs and the military
- Coordination between NGOs and host governments

Coordination should be a two-way street based on respect and trust; it is a process but not an end in itself. A quick view of humanitarian coordination generally reveals two schools of thought. The first group emphasizes strong coordination and sees a lack of coordination as wasteful. This group places a priority on coordination through a centralized approach dominated by influential organizations and agencies.

The second group emphasizes a loose decentralized approach and is more common among those who work for NGOs. This second group tends to see centralized coordination efforts as a means of control and is not ready or willing to devote the time to it. There is insufficient evidence that centrally coordinated relief efforts are more effective. In fact, a diversity of efforts and approaches helps to ensure success: if one fails, all do not fail. Those following this school feel that NGOs may have to protect themselves, to preserve their humanitarian principles, by making sure they are being coordinated with, rather than being coordinated by or for.

Regardless of view, NGOs that are not clear about their own goals and values and lack good systems of accountability are more likely to be manipulated by other organizations. Unless all stakeholders understand the role of coordination, optimal programming is usually not achieved, because of the potential for overlap, wasted effort and probable gap areas being unaddressed. Part of figuring this out is to reach agreement on whether coordination is a luxury add-on or an important element of running emergency programmes.

Understanding coordination

The term 'coordination' can be defined in different ways: in this context it involves people or organizations working together towards a common objective and is roughly synonymous with being in synchronization. It involves filling gaps and preventing the overlap of activities. But maybe an exact definition is not necessary. In an emergency, it is obvious when coordination is lacking or dysfunctional. For this reason, it is easier to focus on why coordination is important, and the answers are that it:

- Facilitates information sharing
- Serves to fill gaps and prevent or eliminate overlap
- Creates uniformity: for example in salaries, sitting fees for training and programme standards

This chapter takes a fairly wide view of coordination as defined by collaboration, cooperating and working with. An NGO's two most important partners, beneficiaries and donors, as well as formal partnerships (Chapter 15) are fully discussed in other parts of this book. For other organizations (i.e. other NGOs, the UN, the military and host governments), issues of power, control and sovereignty may be equally or more prominent, but each manifest themselves in different ways.

When coordination is absent or somehow inadequate, competition, waste and inefficiency usually result. Coordination is rarely easy but it remains an important management task. Although some feel coordination takes time away from real work, it also takes deliberate effort.

One of the main challenges of coordination at the field level is that there are many actors in emergencies, but for the right or the wrong reasons, they mostly have different aims. Some have financial, political or military aims with humanitarianism, as a distant secondary concern. According to Bennett (1997), when coordination problems arise between NGOs, there are several ways to troubleshoot. These include:

Key challenge no. 1: poor attendance at meetings People typically skip meetings when they do not believe that what will be covered is important to them. The first thing to confirm with meeting participants is if they feel the agenda meets their needs. A survey can be carried out to find out why organizations are not attending, based on different reasons, such as meeting content or focus, frequency and location. If the meeting is held by a formal coordination body, a temporary measure in such cases can be to lower the quorum. Finally, the most active participants, or the executive of the coordination body, can visit individuals who should normally attend to appeal for their participation.

Key challenge no. 2: unrealistic expectations Early coordination efforts, such as over customs duties or programme standards, may create high expectations that are unmet over time. Organizations should be familiar with the purpose and role of formal coordination efforts. If necessary, different organizations can offer resources to address the problem.

Key challenge no. 3: renegade organizations In formal coordination bodies, where participation is voluntary, it can be a challenge to reach consensus and follow through on difficult issues. If renegade organizations do not belong to the body, they should be encouraged to join if only as an observer.

Key challenge no. 4: local or international NGOs Inherent differences may make having a coordination meetings or bodies that include both local and international NGOs difficult. Different perspectives, cost and language may be just some of the things that force local NGOs to shy away from joining their international counterparts. A survey of NGOs' needs, different types of membership and partner bodies are some of the options available.

Key challenge no. 5: lack of funds to support coordination Most donors understand the need for funding coordination, but it is still important to stress the importance of funding the activities necessary to achieve coordination. Within an NGO as well, the field may need to appeal to HQ to make funds available. There are also non-financial ways to support coordination as well, such as providing office space or equipment and technical advice.

When coordinating between organizations, another challenge is working within (or around) different organizational levels. NGO managers, and CDs in particular, perhaps more than any other organizational managers have to coordinate and interact simultaneously at different levels. Although there are many ways that organizations interact with each other, one way to put order into the chaos is to think of the different levels that often, but not always, correspond to geographic locations, as shown in Table 20.1.

Coordination in practice

Although formal meetings represent a common type of coordination, in practice coordination can take place informally and at almost any location. Examples include programme staff sharing information with local government authorities and beneficiaries or logisticians sharing the use of expensive resources.

Formal coordination usually falls to managers with the responsibility for external representation. Holding meetings in general is also discussed on pp. 195–7. If you are tasked with chairing a coordination meeting, you need to think about the following things you need to do:

- Prepare an agenda on paper beforehand (see Box 20.1). The objective(s) of the meeting should be clear.
- If possible, try to circulate the agenda several days beforehand.

Table 20.1 Levels of coordination

NGOs	UN	Military	Government
HQ/International office	HQ (e.g. New York or Geneva)	Strategic	National capital
Regional or national office	Region	Operational	District, county, province
Sub-office or programme site	Country office and field office	Tactical	City, town, village community

- Although adequate space is usually limited during emergencies, try to provide a seat for everyone. As much as possible, try to make sure the space is free of outside noise and is the right temperature.
- During the meeting, follow the agenda as closely as possible. If a major decision or work is needed on a particular item, suggest a separate meeting afterwards to work out the details.
- Have another person keep notes or minutes of the meeting. Allow time for understanding and translation.
- Encourage participation. Ask participants if they agree or have suggestions.
- Give everyone with something to say a chance to speak, but keep the discussion focused.
- Try to summarize for everyone key points and, if necessary, ask participants for clarification.
- If necessary, ensure there is time to follow up.

One useful tool to synchronize the activities of different organizations in an emergency is a matrix that confirms ongoing activities or those that are starting shortly. An example of managing camps, where gaps are identified by blank space, is presented in Table 20.2.

During the initial stages of an emergency, identifying gaps using this tool can be done at meetings or at a focal point such as a humanitarian operation or information centre, or through an NGO coordinating body, if it has the capacity. During secondary phases, a system detailing who does what, where is often set up by one of the UN organizations to help identify gaps and prevent overlap.

Box 20.1 Suggestions for a coordination meeting agenda

1. **Introductions** In an emergency there is high turnover at meetings and, unless it is an exceptionally large one for sharing information, each meeting should begin with all present introducing themselves and their organization.
2. **Present the agenda** Review the objectives of the meeting and outline what points will be covered. Reach consensus on the agenda and ask if there are any suggestions for additions to the agenda.
3. **Follow-up from previous meeting** If this is a routine meeting, allow people to raise any issues from the previous meeting that may not be addressed in the following points of discussion.
4. **Points of discussion** As the main body of the meeting this may be divided up into different sections. For information meetings, a common way is to first discuss geographic and then sectoral points. For decision making or consultative meetings, it is common to follow action points in the agenda. Try not to cram too much into the meeting and arrange the points in a logical order. Some prefer to discuss difficult points last, while others prefer to work on these first and then move to easier points. Consider the participants and plan accordingly.
5. **Any other business (AOB)** This is a chance for participants to make announcements or raise issues for the next meeting. The time and place for the next meeting should be the last point discussed.

Table 20.2 Coordination matrix

Sector	Camp 'A'	Camp 'B'	Camp 'C'
Camp management	BINGO	BINGO	BINGO
Registration	Local gov't	Local gov't	Local gov't
Water and sanitation	Wat/San NGO	Wat/San NGO	
Shelter			Local supply NGO
Food distribution	Food NGO	Food NGO	Food NGO
Non-Food Items (NFIs)		Local supply NGO	
Health	Health NGO	Health NGO	Health NGO
Protection		UNHCR	UNHCR
Psychosocial	Children's NGO		Children's NGO

Source: Modified from UNHCR (2000: 65).
Note: Other sectors might include camp infrastructure (e.g. construction, water systems, shelter/tents and latrine construction), information, community services, income generation, supplementary and therapeutic feeding, food basket monitoring, health promotion, referral hospitals, the environment and animal breeding.

Using geographic information systems (GIS), detailed maps can be generated and this is often a task taken up by NGO coordinating bodies or the UN Office for the Coordination of Humanitarian Affairs (UNOCHA), Humanitarian Information Centre (HIC); it is available through the internet and has detailed information for affected countries.

Coordination between NGOs

How an NGO coordination body is organized and run

Based on the idea that the sum can be greater than its parts, NGO interaction helps to improve the efficiency and effectiveness of programmes. Although some may feel that coordination between NGOs is a bit like herding cats, depending on the situation and the generally accepted goals of coordination, NGO coordination can occur in a variety of ways and levels. Like other organizations, coordination between NGOs may happen formally or informally and at international levels or through personal contacts. Fowler (1997) identifies three levels of collaboration:

1. **Networks** In emergencies, where organizations might be very different but share similar interests, NGOs may form loose collaborations such as information sharing meetings or informal exchanges.
2. **Alliances** Where there is a need for closer collaboration, alliances can provide a more formalized mechanism for coordination. They usually focus on specific sectors, but may be larger than a single emergency programme.

3. **Coalitions and consortia** The highest level of collaboration involves increased resources, but heightens an NGO's profile and leverage. Coalitions offer the organization increased profile and leverage while consortia typically offer increased access to resources.

In emergencies, there are likely to be many organizations present, such as commercial firms, military units and missionary groups. To help preserve NGO independence, clarity about which organizations are actually NGOs may be needed at the start of coordination meetings and other fora. At the international level, there are some NGO consortia of relief and development NGOs. In Geneva, the ICVA was founded in 1962 and has over 70 members. In Brussels, created in 1993, the consortium Voluntary Organizations in Cooperation in Emergencies (VOICE) has about 90 members. In Washington, DC, InterAction was established in 1984 and comprises about 160 member NGOs. In the UK, a group of the most active NGOs involved in relief have formed the Disasters Executive Committee (DEC) to coordinate responses to emergencies, including fundraising and advocacy.

At the national level, most countries have one or more NGO coordinating bodies. The main variable is the level of governmental support or control. There are also good examples of coordination bodies in which there has been a long history of conflict and intervention by NGOs, such as the Consortium of Humanitarian Agencies (CHA) in Sri Lanka. Afghanistan has several NGO coordination organizations including the Agency Coordinating Body for Afghan Relief (ACBAR), which was founded in 1988 and now represents over 90 NGOs in the country. As ACBAR describes it, it fulfils a range of roles:

*   Coordination to avoid duplication of work and to identify gaps to be filled
*   Planning NGO strategy to meet humanitarian aims
*   Collection and dissemination of information relevant to humanitarian assistance and development
*   Facilitation of research through a resource and information centre
*   Advocacy and policy

The rest of this section discusses coordination bodies, which tend to function as coalitions at the country or emergency programme level.

Typical interaction

There are a number of reasons NGOs will want to meet together. InterAction has developed a Field Cooperation Protocol, where NGO members have agreed to reach consensus on a number of issues. In effect, it is a list of reasons why NGOs should coordinate:

*   Establishment of an NGO forum in emergencies for responding organizations to meet, including holding regular meetings and a jointly supported office for coordination
*   Relations with local authorities over such issues as registration and taxation

- Local human resource practices, including pay scales, increasing access for the employment of different groups and capacity building
- Leasing, contracting and procurement practices, such as payment of fees
- Media relations, including criticism of other organizations' efforts
- Security arrangements, such as communication and evacuation planning
- Relations with local NGOs, including training and funding
- Relations with other organizations including the UN and the military
- Project planning and division of labour, adoption of programme approaches and information sharing

Points to consider when interacting with other NGOs

- Try to make meetings inclusive but efficient. Schedule meetings for different purposes, but resist having too many
- Routine formal meetings are helpful in that they bring people together. Meetings provide a mechanism of discussion of not just the formal agenda, but also an opportunity for people to discuss things before and after the principal meeting
- Mix formal and informal. Social gatherings apart from formal meetings foster understanding and the exchange of views
- It is often necessary to have a forum separate from the standard ones that involve the government and/or the UN
- International organizations (IOs) typically work in similar ways as NGOs, but may maintain different mandates, such as human rights or migration. The best visible IO is the Red Cross movement which is represented by the ICRC in manmade emergencies and the IFRC in natural disasters

Coordination between NGOs and the UN

How the UN is organized and run

As a consensus-driven organization, the UN is made up of member states (currently 192), who belong to the General Assembly. For humanitarian emergencies, the IASC, chaired by the Emergency Relief Coordinator, determines policy direction and response. At the country level, the UN manages its emergency response in one of two ways. In sudden-onset emergencies, the country representative (or resident coordinator) of UNDP typically is responsible for overseeing the UN's response. All UN agencies present in a particular country will follow the UNDP Representative's lead.

In larger and long-term emergencies, the UN's Secretary-General is usually represented by an appointed Special Representative. Reporting to the Special Representative is a Humanitarian Coordinator who is responsible for several lead agencies that look after specific programme sectoral issues. These agencies are found under the UN General Assembly, which has a number of programmes and funds that address specific social concerns ranging from women's development to the environment. In emergencies, NGOs typically interact with several specialized UN agencies.

- **OCHA** (Office for the Coordination of Humanitarian Affairs) Originally created as the Department of Humanitarian Affairs in 1991 to address the urgent need for coordination within the UN in humanitarian operations. In 1998, it was reorganized to become an office-sized agency with three main functions in the field: coordination of humanitarian activities, policy development and advocacy. With HQ in New York and Geneva, OCHA maintains about 450 staff in various offices around the world. From an NGO perspective, OCHA can provide an on-the-ground coordination function and information through its HIC) set up during or soon after emergencies.

- **UNHCR** (UN High Commissioner for Refugees) In emergencies, UNHCR's aim is to provide protection to persons of concern to UNHCR and to provide timely assistance. Although the origin of the High Commissioner for refugees dates to the 1920s, under the auspices of the League of Nations, UNHCR was not formally organized until 1950. UNHCR has over 6,000 staff in about 115 countries, with its HQ in Geneva. UNHCR has had varied periods of growth and contraction, although their budget through most of the 1990s was US$1 billion per year, with both success and failure. UNHCR often takes a lead role in key sectors and is a frequent sub-contractor of NGOs in all sectors relating to refugees.

- **UNICEF** (UN International Children's Emergency Fund) UNICEF was founded in 1946 to respond to the postwar needs of children in Europe and China. Since 1950, its mandate has gradually expanded to include sectors and countries where children need assistance. With its HQ in New York, UNICEF employs over 7,000 people in nearly 160 countries. Unlike other components of the UN, which rely on the contributions of member states, UNICEF is authorized to carry out private fundraising through sales of gift cards and through national committees. In 2001, nearly 40 per cent of UNICEF's funds were from these private sources. Like UNHCR, NGOs are often the sub-contractors in implementing UNICEF projects.

- **WFP** (World Food Programme) Established in 1963 as a temporary programme, but has remained a continual necessity since then. With its HQ in Rome, WFP has nearly 9,000 staff overseeing its programmes in more than 80 countries. Over 90 per cent of food and funds donated to WFP goes toward emergency relief aid. NGOs often sub-contract with WFP to distribute food and related items as well as carry out projects such as school feeding and FFW.

In conflicts that experience significant international intervention, there may be a UN-led peace operation, which reports to the UN Department for Peacekeeping Operations (UNDPKO) in New York. Member states contribute funds and military contingents to the UN Secretariat, to which UNDPKO reports. In addition to traditional peacekeeping, UNDPKO may support a number of different types of missions. such as observers, interim administration, interim and stabilization forces, truce supervision and peace enforcement. NGOs may coordinate activities and share information with UNDPKO, but likely have little other contact.

There are a number of other agencies that may be present during an emergency or may (re)establish themselves during a post-emergency situation. These include many of the specialized agencies such as, among others, the World Health Organization (WHO), the Food and Agriculture Organization (FAO) and the UN Family Planning Organization (UNFPA). Although some UN agencies maintain their own air transport services, the UN Humanitarian Air Service (UNHAS) is typically responsible for flights in many emergencies, and these are often available to NGO staff members.

In 2005, the UN established the cluster approach in an attempt to improve the predictability, timeliness and effectiveness of its relief efforts. According to the UN, the approach, working through IASC Cluster Working Groups, tries to enhance partnerships and complementarity among the UN, the Red Cross movement and NGOs at both the global and field levels. The cluster approach consists of three elements covering service provision, relief and assistance; a number of cross-cutting issues; and nine specific areas described by the IASC, as follows:

1. **Logistics** chaired by WFP
2. **Emergency telecommunications** chaired by OCHA as process owner, with UNICEF as the common data communications service provider and WFP as the common security telecommunications service provider
3. **Emergency shelter** chaired by UNHCR for conflict-generated IDPs
4. **Health** chaired by WHO
5. **Nutrition** chaired by UNICEF
6. **Water, sanitation and hygiene** chaired by UNICEF
7. **Early recovery** chaired by UNDP
8. **Camp coordination and camp management** chaired by UNHCR (for conflict-generated IDPs) and by the International Organization for Migration (IOM) (for natural disasters)
9. **Protection** chaired by UNHCR for conflict-generated IDPs

In the cluster approach, NGOs are seen as the implementers following UN direction. For this reason, and because (as mentioned earlier) centrally organized efforts have not been proved to be the most effective, some NGOs have voiced concern about this approach. Yet the cluster approach looks as if it will be an instrumental coordination mechanism for some time to come.

Points to consider when interacting with the UN

- UN agencies normally need written agreements, in the form of international and regional instruments, as well as MOUs at the local level, in order to have formal coordination between organizations.

- As a donor, the UN often practises cheque-book coordination. In such cases, NGOs should adopt a strong but flexible position.
- Ask for decisions in writing. UN staff notoriously shy away from this, but one tactic is to write a letter (or e-mail if available) outlining the conclusions of meetings or discussions and request an acknowledgement.
- When working on an agreement, it is a good idea to insist on having the UN agency's proposal and reporting guidelines and budget formats. Ask if there are established rates, or what is provided to other implementing partners, for standard items like vehicles, fuel, office rent and staff salaries.
- Beware of agreements or MOUs where all the responsibility rests with the NGO. If the UN insists on calling it a partnership, then insist on some measure of equity.
- Beware of promises of in-kind supplies and assistance. Ask if the promised supplies are already in a local warehouse or are in the supply pipeline, and so could take months or longer to arrive. If they promise training, try to establish a specific start date during negotiations and ask for an agenda beforehand.
- Unless their offer of in-kind supplies fits with the needs of the beneficiaries and programme, firmly but politely decline it. Consider citing technical concerns. Some commodities, such as food, are dumped by donors on the UN, and they may be detrimental to the local economy.
- Be sure to know the UN requirements for visibility. UN staff members have been known to put signs on projects (especially before an official visit or in front of the media) for which they have no responsibility.
- Pay attention to personnel movements and changes. Negotiations are between organizations and not between individuals, but often new staff try to undo prior commitments that are not in writing. Also, in emergencies, UN staff are typically entitled to a week's holiday for every six weeks worked. This leaves significant periods when decision-makers are out of the area, or are preparing to leave, or adjusting to coming back. Local staff are rarely empowered to carry on in their absence.

Coordination between NGOs and the military

How militaries are organized and run

Because there is sometimes a fine line between different types of military, it is important to understand military organizations that may be present during an emergency. (See pp. 363–64 for interaction with peacekeeping forces.)

Western militaries, especially those of the NATO countries, have well developed and organized units that interact with civilians, called Civil Affairs or, following the NATO acronym, CIMIC. Most, if not all, militaries of developing countries model their organization and methods on Western militaries, although they do not have the same amount of resources. The primary military mission of

Table 20.3 Types of military organization

Military organizations	Characteristics	Historical examples from emergencies
Peacekeeping forces	Legitimacy conferred by the UN under specific resolutions as supported by Chapter 6 of the UN Charter. The military force keeps the peace but has limited power to deal with issues that arise. Made up of either troops contributed to the UN or under the leadership of a specific power (e.g. the US or the African Union)	NATO military contingents in the former Yugoslavia and Afghanistan; UN peacekeeping forces in many other countries
Peace enforcement forces	Legitimacy conferred by the UN under specific resolutions as supported by Chapter 7 of the UN Charter. Military units formed to enforce a particular agreement and able to use force to do it. Made up of either troops contributed to the UN or under the leadership of a specific power (e.g. the US)	Korea 1952, Kuwait–Iraq 1991
International forces and coalitions	Legitimacy nominally or not at all bestowed through the UN or regional body. Almost always highly organized, trained and well equipped (especially in relation to the opposing forces they face)	US-led coalitions in Iraq and Afghanistan; Russian forces in the former Soviet republics
National governments	Legitimacy earned from the people governed, on historic rights or by force of arms. Generally well organized but with varying levels of training and equipment	Armed forces of any country party to a conflict
Local militias	Legitimacy extended from national government. Act in support of governments, national groups or local people. Usually lightly armed and may be supported by the govern-ment. Like national government forces, they may maintain bases, checkpoints and other types of presence in the field	Nationally aligned paramilitary forces (e.g. Serbian forces in Bosnia, various factions in Afghanistan, Janjaweed in the Sudan)

cont.

cont.

Military organizations	Characteristics	Historical examples from emergencies
Rebels and guerrilla insurgents	Legitimacy typically only found among local populace in certain geographic regions. Usually nationalist-based, anti-government forces which have varying degrees of organization. Motivated by national, anti-government or religious causes, basing their legitimacy on perceived rights and/or beliefs. While there are many variables, these groups may become legitimate rulers based on political and military outcomes. Groups involved in terrorism (actions directed at civilians designed to cause fear) may behave operationally and claim legitimacy under this type of organization, but rarely hold the same legitimacy and their contact with NGOs is certainly limited to attacks on civilians	The KLA in Kosovo, post-Saddam Iraqi insurgents, RPF in Rwanda, SPLA in Sudan, LURD and MODEL in Liberia, RUF in Sierra Leone, FARC in Colombia
Criminal groups	Legitimacy, if it exists, rarely extends beyond its immediate geographic base. These groups may be either full-time and well-organized or part-time and ad hoc. They can also be off-duty individuals from one of the categories above or on-duty members undertaking fund- and profile-raising activities	Organized criminal gangs including narco-traffickers and warlords in several countries

these forces in wartime is to minimize collateral damage and keep civilians clear of military operations, including main supply routes (MSRs), which typically are the only usable roads found in some countries.

In peacetime, their mission focuses on activities that support the re-establishment of effective civil control as well as winning the hearts and minds of local populations, to reduce tension and the likelihood that forces will come under threat. To accomplish this mission, Civil Affairs units may include soldiers with a number of practical skills, including engineering, health, transport and public administration, including legal issues.

Typical interaction

Interacting with the military is a controversial issue among NGOs. Though some relief workers have little problem with it, some feel very strongly opposed to coordination with the military. Some feel strongly that NGOs cannot maintain their impartiality and independence if they coordinate with the military and do not want their actions to confer any humanitarian legitimacy onto the military which it does not deserve. One way to think about this relationship is a spectrum, where NGOs hold different views in which they tolerate interacting with the military, as shown in Figure 20.1.

Western militaries have sought to address the need for coordination through the establishment of centres during emergencies. These centres may have different labels, such as Civil Military Operation Centre (CMOC), Civil Military Coordination Centre (CMCC) or Civil Military Information Centre (CIMIC), but they have similar roles of providing a means for civilian interaction, sharing information and coordination with civilian organizations, including NGOs.

Points to consider when interacting with the military

In the past, a number of problems have been identified in connection with interaction between the military and NGOs. These include roles and missions that are at odds, perceived encroachment on NGO independence, poor coordination and a different mandate or way of operating that causes tension. The following points address these issues:

- Understand the NGO's position regarding the military. If necessary, draw up a draft policy and share it with HQ.
- Appreciate the context and players in the situation. Some UN peacekeeping operations are now integrated, combining civilian and military structures.
- Acknowledge and be understanding of the policies of other organizations. If an NGO tends to be closed to cooperation, understand that other NGOs may try to achieve their objectives by using the best means possible. If the NGO tends toward openness, realize that closely interacting with the military, may, among other things, blur the distinction between combatants and civilians; and that other NGOs may have genuine concerns about this.

'Close' collaboration whenever called for. This NGO would consider accepting assistance and even funds from the 'right' military. This type of NGO probably does not have any specific policy for interacting with the military

Neutrality is important to this type of NGO but they may weigh the benefits and context of their interaction with the military. They may consider accepting limited assistance from the 'right' military. This type of NGO may or may not have a policy for interacting with the military

Little or 'zero' interaction allowed. This type of NGO may consider even limited interaction with the military as a threat to its neutrality. This type of NGO probably has a very specific policy for interacting with the military and may train staff to be outspoken against interaction with the military.

◄- ►

Figure 20.1 Spectrum of cooperation between NGOs and the military

- If the NGO is willing to interact with the military, consider designating specific staff members, perhaps those with prior military experience, with interacting with the military.
- If the military is involved in humanitarian projects, it is best suited to provide logistics, some types of medical support (military medicine is designed to care for soldiers not refugees) and limited reconstruction activities. They may also obtain basic assessment information. But the military does not have skills or resources for projects much beyond this, and they are unfamiliar with community-driven approaches. The appropriateness of military supplies and services also needs to be examined carefully.
- While it may be a secondary goal of the military, those units that are tasked with interacting with civilians are likely to be highly dedicated and at least somewhat knowledgeable, and will work hard to provide what assistance they can. Many militaries have shown a readiness to change and adapt procedures to better fit humanitarian efforts.
- Members of the military need help to understand the emergency situation from a humanitarian perspective. NGOs whose policies permit it should share information to ensure that the military's humanitarian efforts are in line as much as possible with the work of others and are in the best interests of the beneficiaries. This can be done formally and informally, but understand that the sharing of information may not be completely equitable.
- If the military breaches any laws, rules or codes of behaviour, be sure to obtain all factual details before raising the issue. Because militaries are organized on a clearly defined chain of command, commanders should be approached first, but they will not be able to act without as many details as possible.

Coordination with host governments

Host governments are simply the national government in whose country an emergency occurs. They are in effect host to the mob of NGOs and others that often show up during and after an emergency.

How some governments are organized and run

The breadth of different types of governments is too large a subject, so only a brief overview is provided here. At the national level, the ministry responsible for the particular sector often provides accreditation for NGOs, overseeing or approving of projects to ensure they are part of overall strategies. These line-ministries usually cover the range of social services, such as health, education, water resources, and urban and rural development. Traditionally, vulnerable groups (e.g. women, children and the elderly) may have sections within some line-ministries devoted to them or, in some cases, may have whole ministries looking after their concerns (e.g. ministries of youth or women's affairs).

At the sub-national level, there are districts and towns, or their equivalents. Regardless of their label or how land is divided, NGOs usually have to seek officials at this level. The officials at this level are responsible for how policies are implemented and thus need a close coordination with NGOs. In most cases, these officials will be local residents, having been raised in the area, and having a keen interest in seeing the area improve. There will also be representatives from line-ministries working in designated areas like schools and health clinics.

Typical interaction

NGOs' views on relations with government occupy a range similar to that of relations with military forces. This is in part based on NGOs' view of the government's legitimacy, human rights record and the degree of cooperation. In some countries, coordination with the host government is a requirement. NGOs must typically coordinate at all three levels, and this can be a burden for managers who are involved in all aspects of running an emergency programme. Senior managers normally delegate coordination at the local level.

Interaction between NGOs and the host government may take the form of technical input, either from the government or from the NGOs. The host government may take an observer role or become more directly involved as a controller, depending on its approach. In some cases, different types of partnership may be formed between NGOs and a host government.

Points to consider when interacting with host governments

- Understand that the host government is stretched, by the nature of an emergency, beyond its normal capacity. In the developing world, the normal capacity of the government is often weak to begin with, especially in the social sector.
- Be patient and respectful – it is their country after all. However, depending on the NGO's policies, be forthright about rights and in your concern for the beneficiaries.
- In some conflict-affected countries, when the top politicians and leadership often change, most government staff remain the same. Civil servants may continue to hold posts, and show up to work a few hours a day, based on their dedication and in the hope of a return to normality. In these cases, the civil servants may hold other jobs as their primary livelihood.
- If appropriate, support capacity building for line-ministries. NGOs cannot replace the government but more objectives can be met by working together with the government.

CHAPTER 21
Closing an emergency programme

By design, all emergency programmes come to an end. Closing an emergency programme is a process that requires planning and strategy. The purpose of this chapter is to present three types of closing: handovers that foresee activities sustained beyond the involvement of a particular organization and phase-out, where no other activities will continue. To help relief workers close an emergency programme, the chapter covers:
- Handover strategies
- Phase-out strategies

There are different reasons for closing a programme, depending on the situations of the emergency. The reasons include such factors as beneficiaries no longer needing assistance to changing situations, like security and the withdrawal of funds. Projects that comprise a programme normally have different end dates and should be linked to other developmental efforts.

In ideal situations, programmes can be handed over in a phased approach, as appropriate to the context. But because emergencies are rarely if ever ideal, there may be situations that require an exit that has not been planned. Hasty and unplanned closure results in poor accountability, the loss of lessons learned and a potential break in the sustainability of the programme activities.

Regardless of the reason, closing a programme should be anticipated and planned. Unfortunately, many emergencies are the result of insecurity and funding does not always correspond with need. While a security incident or funding shortfall may require a hasty departure, this should be anticipated and many of the steps are the same as with a planned handover or closure.

Handover strategies

A handover strategy is a means for either continuing activities beyond the departure of staff or, depending on the sustainability of the activities, continuing the impact of an activity after a project ends, either through another organization or with the beneficiaries themselves. Effective handovers are seamless transitions where responsibility is shifted from one organization (or individual) to another. This involves one of two types of handover: that of programme and that of staff:

Programme handover

Programmes are handed over when the activities are going to continue either with local partners or by with beneficiaries themselves (e.g. through a municipality or CBO). For this reason, selection of a good local partner is essential.

The local partner's capacity, resources, experience and potential need to be carefully weighed to determine their likelihood of successfully continuing the project's activities. Ideally, an action plan will need to be developed covering a period of a minimum of 3–6 months, comprising an evaluation of lessons learned, training and supervision, during a gradual withdrawal and handover.

Programme concerns should be second only to security. Special attention is needed for certain types of programmes whose basis goes beyond the life of the project. Activities that are especially dependent on external input (e.g. food or cooking/heating fuel) or technical advice or supervision (e.g. AIDS or TB health programming) will need longer and more extensive capacity building, transition period, and supervision and monitoring.

Specific plans will need to be made as early as possible and will differ from one emergency to another. Generally, there are six important considerations in a programme handover:

1. **Planning**
   - Who? (Beneficiaries, staff and partners)
   - What? (Goals, objectives and activities)
   - Why? (Reasons and timing)
   - When? (Timeline)
   - How? (Expectations)
2. **Resources**
   - Funding
   - Staff
   - Asset transfers
3. **Partner(s)**
   Clarity of roles, responsibilities and expectations:
   - UN
   - LNGOs
   - CBOs
   - Local government
4. **Capacity building**
   - Training
   - Material and staff needs
   - Systems and procedures
5. **Transition**
   - Formal agreement
   - Staff handovers
6. **Supervision and monitoring**
   - Follow-up
   - Post-handover assistance (if needed)

During a programme handover, many aspects covered in other parts of this book may be important. A local partner (Chapter 15), for instance, may need assistance building their capacity (Chapter 16) and obtaining funds (Chapter 7); and a period of monitoring might be called for (Chapter 19). Ultimately, a significant element of handover from one person to another will be necessary, as discussed in the next section.

Staff handover

A staff handover is when a staff member departs and is replaced by a new staff member either new externally or promoted internally. Handover from one staff member to another is far more common, especially because of the high turnover of NGOs involved in emergencies. To successfully carry out the handover, consider the following steps.

Step 1 Preparation

Preparation for a handover should be approached in the same way as any other task, by developing a timeframe and an action plan. This plan should cover a period of months or weeks, not days. Considerations include:

- Review the proposal and existing tools (e.g. a logframe) to see if these are applicable to the handover. The aim should be to have a seamless transition that contributes to sustainability. Changes can be made gradually by the new staff.
- Review the job description and update it to reflect accurately what is done on a daily, weekly and monthly basis.
- Prepare the work space, files and other work-related items so that they are ready to be turned over to the replacement.
- Try to find out about the replacement staff before their arrival, so as to adjust the handover to their background and experience. Allow time for gaining familiarity and training (if needed).
- Make a handover schedule and take into account the needs of external stakeholders, by making appointments if needed and allowing travel time to project areas as appropriate.
- As part of the induction (see Chapter 8), prepare a complete briefing for the replacement.

Step 2 Lessons learned

Take time to reflect on what has been learned during the contract term. This may be informal and consist of working notes and observations, so that others may absorb what has been learned. In some instances, a more formal appraisal will be called for which includes the review of original programme proposals and other documents and meeting beneficiaries and staff. An action plan will be needed to benefit from analysing the lessons learned. Some questions to consider are:

- What went well and why?
- What might have been better handled and why?

- How well were objectives met?
- How closely do the organization's vision, values and identity match the objectives and activities carried out?
- Were the right strategies followed? What might have been done differently?
- How well were systems and structures to the tasks required?
- Did staff have the right skills and competencies? What capacity building is needed?
- Was there the right amount of financial and physical resources available; if not, why not?
- Can any of the lessons be applied to other emergency programmes?

Step 3 Handover

Welcome the replacement and, before starting the briefing, make sure that any immediate needs (e.g. lost luggage, contacting home and refreshment) are met, so that the person can give their full attention. Many organizations have outlines for such handovers, which include:

- **Context** What are the unique characteristics of the emergency and area? Why was the project or programme started? What strategy is used? What are the goals? If these goals have changed, how and why? When will the project objectives be achieved? What are the activities? What problems have been experienced, how were they overcome and what obstacles remain? What are future plans and anticipated issues?
- **Relationships** Who are the main partners, including donors? What is the history of these partnerships, including problems and successes? What are the relationships with other stakeholders and major players in the area, such as beneficiaries, government authorities, the UN, commercial entities and military forces? Which of these are beneficial and which ones are detrimental? What are the contact details for different partners, including donors and other NGOs?
- **Skills** Are there any skills that the replacement does not have or is not especially strong in? Can those skills be learned during the handover period or do other arrangements need to be made so that the person can carry out their responsibilities?
- **Administration/Logistics** What administrative and logistical arrangements need to be made during the handover? Does the replacement have all the tools and other materials (e.g. computers/passwords, keys, ID cards and documents) to carry out his or her responsibilities?

The briefing should include a discussion and introduction to supervisory and subordinate staff, policies and procedures, where to find assistance and the upcoming handover schedule. It is usually best to allow the more time for the briefing to discuss the history of the organization and details about the project, and provide detailed written handover notes. Following the introduction and briefing, a handover period should be set up for the time available. In some cases, a brief introduction and description of these relationships will suffice during the handover, as the new person will likely want to get to know each staff member in his or her own time.

One effective way of organizing the handover is to set a pre-departure date halfway through the remaining time. Before this halfway point, the replacement follows or shadows and after this, the departing staff member provides advice as the replacement takes on full responsibility. This schedule follows a 'listen, watch, do' approach, like in on-the-job training.

While emergencies usually allow far less time, two weeks is a good amount of time for a proper handover. Any longer and the departing staff member will have little to do or retain responsibilities for too long. In some cases, HQ staff will want assurances that problems will not surface after departure and may want feedback on the replacement's performance.

A final part of the handover should be to provide handover notes, business cards and contact information, passwords, keys, ICT equipment and any other organizational property for the replacement.

Step 4 Departure

Everyone handles departure differently. One of the main issues is to maintain safety and security precautions to the end. In many situations, it is also important to maintain professionalism until the end, since it is possible to build up a good work record and then have it largely erased by trailing off at the end. In some cases, celebration(s) or a party may be called for, and on behalf of those staying behind this should not be dismissed or overlooked. Consensus should be reached in this case. According to Scheyvens and Storey (2003: 202), there are number of factors influencing leaving:

- Nature of emergency
- NGO organizational culture
- Length of time spent in one place
- Nature of relationships formed
- Degree of culture and local immersion in the field
- Degree of similarity or difference between staff members and beneficiaries
- Commitments and obligations to fellow staff and beneficiaries
- Success or otherwise of programme
- Expectations and feelings of family members and friends
- Cultural norms and expectations associated with leaving
- Time available for the leaving process

Returning home can be more of a challenge than leaving in the first place. Most staff simply re-adapt but others face challenges. Life back home may need to be re-started by finding follow-on work, dealing with relocation and other adjustments. Traditionally, NGOs have done little to help returning staff. This may be changing to some degree in relation to health and mental wellbeing.

Strong emotions may also surface with leaving, including reluctance or resistance, disappointment, sadness or loss, guilt, anxiety, relief or the satisfaction of accomplishment. People may appear to have changed, or more commonly, they may have seemed to stay the same. However, relief workers have changed as a result of their experience. Away from the emergency, there may seem to be less camaraderie, a slower pace of life and less excitement. If escape from one's family or other problems was the original reason for working as a relief worker, the problems will be waiting for them on their return.

Phase-out strategies

Programme phase-out, when a programme is closed with no further activities, should be planned carefully. The achievement of goals and objectives, based on measurable indicators, signals the need to close activities. In some cases, NGOs will develop new programmes to meet developmental (i.e. non-emergency) needs. It is important that this is envisioned and planned from the start. For this reason, good programme design will help. As the programme goes through its cycle, M&E is needed. When programmes do not close, a number of adverse consequences may result, such as unnecessary costs, directionless staff and, most worryingly, undermining or degrading local coping strategies.

In some cases, the programme's objectives may be reached before it was originally intended. Examples include evidence of reduction in malnutrition, eliminating the need for feeding activities, changes in a government's provision of social services such as health clinics and the initiation of a peace plan and repatriation. Such changes are generally positive and NGOs should remain flexible and ready to support such processes. Insecurity may also lead to closing a programme. While this may not be expected, following good security management, it can be anticipated and planned for (see also Chapters 1 and 18).

When closing an office there are many things to think about. Table 21.1 provides a checklist.

Table 21.1 Checklist for closing an office

Planning	✓

Informed decision-making determined that closing was necessary

Plan developed taking balancing staff and programmatic needs

Timeframe/schedule developed listing activities, closing day and final working day of staff

Notice provided to relevant stakeholders

Human resource management

Determine last payments and severance if necessary

Ensure accounting staff have enough money to pay all outstanding salary payments

Meet staff to inform them of the closing, address concerns and discuss related issues

Provide assistance to staff in finding new work, reference letters and CV updating

Following standard end of contract procedures (see Chapter 15) collect keys, ITC equipment, ID cards and other NGO property

Finance/Accounting

Ensure financial needs are adequately covered during through the closing period

Arrange for final payments and ensure (ideally, in writing) that no outstanding balances remain

If needed, create system of payments if support will continue through a handover

Arrange closing of all bank accounts and provide HQ address for remaining follow-on correspondence, such as the final statement

If post-closure accounting is needed, make appropriate arrangements (e.g. agreement with local accounting firm)

Determine what to do with remaining records (most NGOs will have a procedure for this)

Legal considerations

Ensure all legal agreements are available, up-to-date, copies available and back-up copies filed in secure, separate location

Consult attorney about registration, contracts in progress and tax. Determine if their services will be needed after departure and make appropriate arrangements (e.g. available documentation and payment)

Contact government offices about closing to complete any required paperwork

Determine if there is a need to maintain the NGO's registration in the country and make necessary steps to accomplish the process

Logistical property/Assets

If not already up-to-date, review and update inventory list

cont.

cont.

Planning	✓

As applicable, check with donor and governmental regulations about retention or disposal of assets

Group assets into three categories such as high-value assets, low-value items and disposal items, with the aim of having no excess or leftover items

Turn over high-value items such as vehicles, radios and computers to partners, or return them to donor organizations or transfer to other programmes/countries of the NGO

Sell locally or pass on to partners low-value items such as office furniture

Sell locally, pass on to partners, or otherwise dispose of disposable items such as office supplies

Files and records

Decide final disposition – storage, transport or disposal – of files and records of each department and location

If local storage is used, make arrangements following a realistic timeline

According to organizational requirements, prepare report of final records

Office and residence

Using inventories and original agreements/leases, determine what property (if any) should remain

Notify landlord of departure and make arrangements for return of property and deposits (if any)

Secure evidence of final agreement with property landlord to ensure that there are no outstanding disputes or payments

External relations

Notify and meet beneficiaries to inform about and discuss organization's departure. Special care will be needed for any uncompleted activities and certain types of programming (e.g. especially health)

Inform partners, government, donors and other stakeholders of the organization's departure

Prepare and distribute document containing lessons learned for relevant and interested stakeholders

Leave follow-up contact information at relevant places (e.g. HIC or office door/gate)

Source: Modified from EngenderHealth (2005).

Appendix

The Humanitarian Charter of the Sphere Project

We reaffirm our belief in the humanitarian imperative and its primacy. By this we mean the belief that all possible steps should be taken to prevent or alleviate human suffering arising out of conflict or calamity, and that civilians so affected have a right to protection and assistance. It is on the basis of this belief, reflected in international humanitarian law and based on the principle of humanity, that we offer our services as humanitarian agencies. We will act in accordance with the principles of humanity and impartiality, and with the other principles set out in Humanitarian agencies committed to this Charter and to the Minimum Standards will aim to achieve defined levels of service for people affected by calamity or armed conflict, and to promote the observance of fundamental humanitarian principles.

1 Charter

The Humanitarian Charter affirms the fundamental importance of the following principles.

1.1 The right to life with dignity

This right is reflected in the legal measures concerning the right to life, to an adequate standard of living and to freedom from cruel, inhuman or degrading treatment or punishment. We understand an individual's right to life to entail the right to have steps taken to preserve life where it is threatened, and a corresponding duty on others to take such steps. Implicit in this is the duty not to withhold or frustrate the provision of life-saving assistance. In addition, international humanitarian law makes specific provision for assistance to civilian populations during conflict, obliging states and other parties to agree to the provision of humanitarian and impartial assistance when the civilian population lacks essential supplies.

1.2 The distinction between combatants and non-combatants

This is the distinction which underpins the 1949 Geneva Conventions and their Additional Protocols of 1977. This fundamental principle has been increasingly eroded, as reflected in the enormously increased proportion of civilian casualties during the second half of the twentieth century. That internal conflict is often referred to as 'civil war' must not blind us to the need to distinguish between those actively engaged in hostilities, and civilians and others (including the sick, wounded and prisoners) who play no direct part. Non-combatants are protected under international humanitarian law and are entitled to immunity from attack.

1.3 The principle of non-refoulement

This is the principle that no refugee shall be sent (back) to a country in which his or her life or freedom would be threatened on account of race, religion, nationality, membership of a particular social group or political opinion; or where there are substantial grounds for believing that s/he would be in danger of being subjected to torture.

2 Roles and responsibilities

2.1 We recognize that it is firstly through their own efforts that the basic needs of people affected by calamity or armed conflict are met, and we acknowledge the primary role and responsibility of the state to provide assistance when people's capacity to cope has been exceeded.

2.2 International law recognizes that those affected are entitled to protection and assistance. It defines legal obligations on states or warring parties to provide such assistance or to allow it to be provided, as well as to prevent and refrain from behaviour that violates fundamental human rights. These rights and obligations are contained in the body of international human rights law, international humanitarian law and refugee law (see sources listed below).

2.3 As humanitarian agencies, we define our role in relation to these primary roles and responsibilities. Our role in providing humanitarian assistance reflects the reality that those with primary responsibility are not always able or willing to perform this role themselves. This is sometimes a matter of capacity. Sometimes it constitutes a wilful disregard of fundamental legal and ethical obligations, the result of which is much avoidable human suffering.

2.4 The frequent failure of warring parties to respect the humanitarian purpose of interventions has shown that the attempt to provide assistance in situations of conflict may potentially render civilians more vulnerable to attack, or may on occasion bring unintended advantage to one or more of the warring parties. We are committed to minimizing any such adverse effects of our interventions in so far as this is consistent with the obligations outlined above. It is the obligation of warring parties to respect the humanitarian nature of such interventions.

2.5 In relation to the principles set out above and more generally, we recognize and support the protection and assistance mandates of the International Committee of the Red Cross and of the United Nations High Commissioner for Refugees under international law.

3 Minimum standards

The Minimum Standards which follow are based on agencies' experience of providing humanitarian assistance. Though the achievement of the standards depends on a range of factors, many of which may be beyond our control, we commit ourselves to attempt consistently to achieve them and we expect to be held to account accordingly. We invite other humanitarian actors, including states themselves, to adopt these standards as accepted norms. By adhering to the standards set out in Chapters 1–5 we commit ourselves to make every effort to ensure that people affected by disasters have access to at least the minimum requirements (water, sanitation, food, nutrition, shelter and health care) to satisfy their basic right to life with dignity. To this end we will continue to advocate that governments and other parties meet their obligations under international human rights law, international humanitarian law and refugee law. We expect to be held accountable to this commitment and undertake to develop systems for accountability within our respective agencies, consortia and federations. We acknowledge that our fundamental accountability must be to those we seek to assist.

(See www.sphereproject.org/dmdocuments/handbook/hdbkpdf/hdbk_hc.pdf)

Comparison chart of Sphere Standards and UNHCR Emergency Handbook

Topic/Area/Issue	Sphere Project	UNHCR Emergency Handbook
Water		
Quantity	7.5–15 litres per person per day (l/p/d) collected. Survival need 2.5–3 litre/person/day; basic hygiene 2–6 l/p/d; cooking 3–6 l/p/d	15 litres per person per day, absolute minimum for short term survival is 7 l/p/d
System/Delivery	Taps provide flow rate of at least 0.125 l per second	At least one water point per 250 people, 'at least one tap per 80–100 refugees and no more than 200 refugees per hand-pump or per well with one rope and bucket'
Quality	No more than 10 faecal coliforms per 100 ml at point of delivery	1–10 faecal coliforms per 100 ml is 'reasonable quality'
	For piped systems residual free chlorine at tap is 0.2–0.5 mg/l and turbidity is less than 5 NTU (nephelometric turbidity units)	Residual free chlorine at tap is 0.2–0.5 mg/l at distribution point
	Dissolved solids no more than 1,000 mg/l	

Topic/Area/Issue	Sphere Project	UNHCR Emergency Handbook
Hygiene – sanitation		
Soap	250 g soap per person per month	
	200 g of laundry soap per person per month	
Laundry	1 washing basin per 100 people	
Toilets/latrines	Maximum 20 people per toilet. Arranged by household and/or gender	1 latrine per family or as second option, 1 per 20 persons, or third option 1 per 100 persons or defecation field
Refuse bins	I container per 10 families	I container per 10 families or 50 persons
Refuse pits	No shelter further than 15 m from container or 100 m from communal refuse pit	1 pit 2 m × 5 m × 2 m deep per 500 persons
Camp site planning		
Gross area	45 m² per person (inclusive of all uses except agriculture or garden)	30 m2 per person (inclusive of all uses except agriculture or garden space)
Dimensions/Distances	Maximum distance between shelter and toilets 50 m	Maximum distance between shelter and toilets 50 m
Firebreaks	2 m between shelters, 6 m between clusters of shelters, 15 m between blocks and clusters .	30 m per every 300 m of built-up area
Distance between wells/springs and latrines	Latrines farther than 30 m from groundwater sources and 1.5 m above water table	Latrines further than 30 m from groundwater sources and 1.5 m above water table
	Maximum distance from any shelter to water point 500 m: 'No dwelling should be further than 100 m or a few minutes' walk from distribution points'	
Elevation/Drainage	3 m above high water table. 2–4% gradient (ideal) and not more than 7% without extensive site engineering	
Shelter		
Shelter area	3.5–4.5 m² covered area per person	3.5 m² covered area per person in tropical climates
		4.5–5.5 m² covered area per person in cold or urban situations
Plastic sheeting for temporary shelter	4 m × 6 m sheet per household of 5 people (UNHCR material specifications)	4 m × 5 m reinforced plastic tarpaulins in sheets with aluminium eyelets all four sides

Topic/Area/Issue	Sphere Project	UNHCR Emergency Handbook
Food/Nutrition		
Calories	2,100 kcals/d (initial planning figure to be modified based on thorough demographic analysis of population	2.100 kcals/d (initial planning figure)
Make-up	10–12% total energy from protein	10–12% total energy from protein
	17% total energy from fat	17% total energy from fat
Health		
Excess mortality/ Crude Mortality Rate (CMR)	1/10,000 CMR	Normal rate among settled population 0.3–0.5/10,000/ deaths (d)
Under 5 yrs mortality rate	2/10,000/d under 5 CMR	Emergency programme under control <1/10,000/d
		Emergency programme in serious trouble >1/10,000/d
		Emergency: out of control >2/10,000/d
		Major catastrophe >5/10,000/d
		Normal rate among settled population 1.0/10,000/d
		Emergency programme under control <2.0/10,000/d
		Emergency programme in serious trouble >2.0/10,000/d
		Emergency: out of control
Measles vaccination coverage	95% of all children 6 months–12 years	
	Measles vaccine needs 140% of target group (15%waste, 25% stockpile)	UNHCR advocates immunization of children from 6 months to 12 or even 15 years (rather than the more usual 5 years) because of increased risk from living conditions in refugee emergencies. As an emergency indicator, 'Any reported cases, 10% or more unimmunized in age group 6 months to 5 years'
Medical staff	1 home visitor for each 500–1,000 population	Approximate staffing levels for refugee health and sanitation services for population of 10,000–20,000

cont.

cont.

Topic/Area/Issue	Sphere Project	UNHCR Emergency Handbook
	1 TBA for each 2,000	Community health worker: 10–20
	1 supervisor for each 10 home visitors	Traditional birth attendant: 6–10
	1 senior supervisor	Public health nurse: 1
	1 peripheral health facility per 10,000 population	Clinic nurses, midwives: 3–4
	1 central health facility for each 10,000 population	Doctors/Medical assistants: 1–3
		Pharmacy attendant: 1
		Laboratory technician: 1
		Dressers/Assistants: 10
		Sanitarians: 2–4
		Sanitation assistants: 20
Non-food items (domestic needs)		
Water containers	2 vessels of 10–20 l each for collecting plus 1 20-l vessel for water storage (i.e. 4 l per person depending on availability of supplies), should have narrow necks and covers	Ability to transport 10 l, and ability to store 20 l per 5-person household
Eating utensils	• 1 cooking pot with lid • 1 basin • 1 kitchen knife • 2 wooden spoons • 1 plate per person • 1 spoon per person • 1 mug per person	
Protection and security		
Location	50 km from threat	'a reasonable distance'
Staff competency		
Staff	Qualifications	
Attitude		
Experience		
Management	All staff receive proper supervision and support including sound HRM practices such as capacity building and security training	

Source: Originally compiled by Interworks, February 2001
(www.interworksmadison.com/index.htm)

Code of Conduct: Principles of Conduct for the International Red Cross and Red Crescent movement and NGOs in disaster response programmes

1 The humanitarian imperative comes first

The right to receive humanitarian assistance, and to offer it, is a fundamental humanitarian principle which should be enjoyed by all citizens of all countries. As members of the international community, we recognize our obligation to provide humanitarian assistance wherever it is needed. Hence the need for unimpeded access to affected populations is of fundamental importance in exercising that responsibility. The prime motivation of our response to disaster is to alleviate human suffering amongst those least able to withstand the stress caused by disaster. When we give humanitarian aid it is not a partisan or political act and should not be viewed as such.

2 Aid is given regardless of the race, creed or nationality of the recipients and without adverse distinction of any kind.

Aid priorities are calculated on the basis of need alone. Wherever possible, we will base the provision of relief aid upon a thorough assessment of the needs of the disaster victims and the local capacities already in place to meet those needs. Within the entirety of our programmes, we will reflect considerations of proportionality. Human suffering must be alleviated whenever it is found; life is as precious in one part of a country as another. Thus, our provision of aid will reflect the degree of suffering it seeks to alleviate. In implementing this approach, we recognize the crucial role played by women in disaster-prone communities and will ensure that this role is supported, not diminished, by our aid programmes. The implementation of such a universal, impartial and independent policy, can only be effective if we and our partners have access to the necessary resources to provide for such equitable relief, and have equal access to all disaster victims.

3 Aid will not be used to further a particular political or religious standpoint

Humanitarian aid will be given according to the need of individuals, families and communities. Notwithstanding the right of non-governmental humanitarian agencies (NGHAs) to espouse particular political or religious opinions, we affirm that assistance will not be dependent on the adherence of the recipients to those opinions. We will not tie the promise, delivery or distribution of assistance to the embracing or acceptance of a particular political or religious creed.

4 We shall endeavour not to act as instruments of government foreign policy

NGHAs are agencies which act independently from governments. We therefore formulate our own policies and implementation strategies and do not seek to implement the policy of any government, except in so far as it coincides with our own independent policy. We will never knowingly – or through negligence – allow ourselves, or our employees, to be used to gather information of a political, military or economically sensitive nature for governments or other bodies that may serve purposes other than those which are strictly humanitarian, nor will we act as instruments of foreign policy of donor governments. We will use the assistance we receive to respond to needs and this assistance should not be driven by the need to dispose of donor commodity surpluses, nor by the political interest of any particular donor. We value and promote the voluntary giving of labour and finances by concerned individuals to support our work and recognize the independence of action promoted by such voluntary motivation. In order to protect our independence we will seek to avoid dependence upon a single funding source.

5 We shall respect culture and custom

We will endeavour to respect the culture, structures and customs of the communities and countries we are working in.

6 We shall attempt to build disaster response on local capacities

All people and communities – even in disaster – possess capacities as well as vulnerabilities. Where possible, we will strengthen these capacities by employing local staff, purchasing local materials and trading with local companies. Where possible, we will work through local NGHAs as partners in planning and implementation, and cooperate with local government structures where appropriate. We will place a high priority on the proper coordination of our emergency responses. This is best done within the countries concerned by those most directly involved in the relief operations, and should include representatives of the relevant UN bodies.

7 Ways shall be found to involve programme beneficiaries in the management of relief aid

Disaster response assistance should never be imposed upon the beneficiaries. Effective relief and lasting rehabilitation can best be achieved where the intended beneficiaries are involved in the design, management and implementation of the assistance programme. We will strive to achieve full community participation in our relief and rehabilitation programmes.

8 Relief aid must strive to reduce future vulnerabilities to disaster as well as meeting basic needs

All relief actions affect the prospects for long-term development, either in a positive or a negative fashion. Recognizing this, we will strive to implement relief programmes which actively reduce the beneficiaries' vulnerability to future disasters and help create sustainable lifestyles. We will pay particular attention to environmental concerns in the design and management of relief programmes. We will also endeavour to minimize the negative impact of humanitarian assistance, seeking to avoid long-term beneficiary dependence upon external aid.

9 We hold ourselves accountable to both those we seek to assist and those from whom we accept resources

We often act as an institutional link in the partnership between those who wish to assist and those who need assistance during disasters. We therefore hold ourselves accountable to both constituencies. All our dealings with donors and beneficiaries shall reflect an attitude of openness and transparency. We recognize the need to report on our activities, both from a financial perspective and the perspective of effectiveness. We recognize the obligation to ensure appropriate monitoring of aid distributions and to carry out regular assessments of the impact of disaster assistance. We will also seek to report, in an open fashion, upon the impact of our work, and the factors limiting or enhancing that impact. Our programmes will be based upon high standards of professionalism and expertise in order to minimize the wasting of valuable resources.

10 In our information, publicity and advertising activities, we shall recognize disaster victims as dignified humans, not hopeless objects

Respect for the disaster victim as an equal partner in action should never be lost. In our public information we shall portray an objective image of the disaster situation where the capacities and aspirations of disaster victims are highlighted, and not just their vulnerabilities and fears. While we will cooperate with the media in order to enhance public response, we will not allow external or internal demands for publicity to take precedence over the principle of maximizing overall relief assistance. We will avoid competing with other disaster response agencies for media coverage in situations where such coverage may be to the detriment of the service provided to the beneficiaries or to the security of our staff or the beneficiaries.

(See http://www.ifrc.org/PUBLICAT/conduct/code.asp)

Summary of international humanitarian law, human rights law and refugee law

Treaty/Document	Relevant provisions
Geneva Convention 1864	Provides protection to wounded soldiers and those in non-combatant roles (e.g. chaplains and civilians serving with militaries) as well as medical personnel, facilities and equipment (symbolized by a red cross, a protected emblem from 1977). Sets out the idea that militaries do not have unlimited means of waging war which are first spelled out in the Hague Conventions of 1899 and 1907
Geneva Conventions (I–IV) 1949	(I) Strengthens the provisions of the first Geneva convention for the 'amelioration of the condition of the wounded and sick in armed forces in the field'. (II) Extends provisions of the First Geneva Convention to the sea and naval forces. (III) Sets out protection for prisoners of war including their right to health care, contact with families and freedom from torture, experimentation and public display. (IV) Protects civilians in areas occupied by military forces. Civilians are entitled to live under 'normal' conditions including right to health care, food and work. Civilians can only be detained or deported for security reasons and are not to carry out military-related labour
1977 Protocols	Further protects civilians from indiscriminate attacks on certain structures (e.g. cultural or religious locations, dams, crops and long-term damage to the environment). Outlaws recruitment of children under 15 years of age for military purposes. Permits impartial relief organizations to carry out humanitarian activities. 'Common Article 3' extends these protocols to non-international conflict
Universal Declaration of Human Rights 1948	Non-binding treaty adopted by UN General Assembly followed by a number of legally binding international treaties including the Convention on the Elimination of All Forms of Racial Discrimination (1965), the International Covenant on Civil and Political Rights (1966), the International Covenant on Economic, Social and Cultural Rights (1966), the Convention on the Elimination of All Forms of Discrimination against Women (1979), the Convention against Torture and Other Cruel, Inhuman or Degrading Treatment or Punishment (1984) and the Convention on the Rights of the Child (1989)
Convention relating to the Status of Refugees 1951	Refugees are entitled to full human rights and states are not permitted to expel or return refugees if it will threaten their life or freedom (principle of non-refoulement). Refugee protection does not extend to persons who have committed a non-political crime. States are also obliged to cooperate with UNHCR. Later bolstered by the Protocol relating to the Status of Refugees (1967), OAU Convention Governing the Specific Aspects of Refugee Problems in Africa (1969), and the Cartagena Declaration (1984) and San Jose Declaration (1994) for Latin America

Treaty/Document	Relevant provisions
Guiding Principles on Internal Displacement 1998	As a supplement to IHL, UN Secretary General statement designed to extend refugee-type protection to IDPs. Government authorities and international actors are to prevent arbitrary displacement and provide protection to those who have been displaced.
Rome Statute 1998	Establishes the permanent International Criminal Court to reside over grave breaches of IHL. War crimes include murder, mutilation, cruel treatment and torture, hostage taking, denial of fair trail, intentionally attacking civilians, pillaging, rape and other acts of sexual violence and, in absence of military necessity, ordering displacement of civilian populations. Crimes against humanity include murder, extermination, enslavement, deportation, torture and enforced disappearances

Sources: IASC(2004); Bouchet-Saumier (2001).

The Humanitarian Accountability Project Principles of Accountability

1. Commitment to humanitarian standards and rights

Members state their commitment to respect and foster humanitarian standards and the rights of beneficiaries.

2. Setting standards and building capacity

Members set a framework of accountability to their stakeholders.

Members set and periodically review their standards and performance indicators, and revise them if necessary.

Members provide appropriate training in the use and implementation of standards.

3. Communication

Members inform, and consult with, stakeholders, particularly beneficiaries and staff, about the standards adopted, programmes to be undertaken and mechanisms available for addressing concerns.

4. Participation in programmes

Members involve beneficiaries in the planning, implementation, monitoring and evaluation of programmes and report to them on progress, subject only to serious operational constraints.

5. Monitoring and reporting on compliance

Members involve beneficiaries and staff when they monitor and revise standards.

Members regularly monitor and evaluate compliance with standards, using robust processes.

Members report at least annually to stakeholders, including beneficiaries, on compliance with standards. Reporting may take a variety of forms.

6. Addressing complaints

Members enable beneficiaries and staff to report complaints and seek redress safely.

7. Implementing partners

Members are committed to the implementation of these principles if and when working through implementation partners.

Note: The framework of accountability includes standards, quality standards, principles, policies, guidelines, training and other capacity-building work, etc. The framework must include measurable performance indicators. Standards may be internal to the organisation or they may be collective, e.g. Sphere or People in Aid.
(See http://www.hapinternational.org/en/page.php?IDpage=3&IDcat=10)

People in Aid Code

Principle 1 Human resources strategy

Human resources are an integral part of our strategic and operational plans.

Indicators

1 Our organizational strategy or business plan explicitly values staff for their contribution to organizational and operational objectives.
2 The organizational strategy allocates sufficient human and financial resources to achieve the objectives of the human resources strategy.
3 Operational plans and budgets aim to reflect fully our responsibilities for staff management, support, development and wellbeing. The monitoring of these plans and budgets feeds into any necessary improvements.
4 Our human resources strategy reflects our commitment to promote inclusiveness and diversity.

Principle 2 Staff policies and practices

Our human resources policies aim to be effective, fair and transparent.

Indicators

1   Policies and practices that relate to staff employment are set out in writing and are monitored and reviewed, particularly when significant changes in the legal or working environment take place.
2   The policies and practices we implement are consistent in their application to all staff except while taking into account relevant legal provisions and cultural norms.
3   Staff are familiarized with policies and practices that affect them.
4   Appropriate guidance is provided to managers so that they are equipped to implement policies effectively.
5   The rewards and benefits for each role are clearly identified and applied in a fair and consistent manner.
6   Policies and practices are monitored according to how well they meet:
    • organizational and programme aims
    • reasonable considerations of effectiveness, fairness and transparency.

Principle 3 Managing people

Good support, management and leadership of our staff is key to our effectiveness.

Indicators

1   Relevant training, support and resources are provided to managers to fulfil their responsibilities. Leadership is a part of this training.
2   Staff have clear work objectives and performance standards, know whom they report to and what management support they will receive. A mechanism for reviewing staff performance exists and is clearly understood by all staff.
3   In assessing performance, managers will adhere to the organization's procedures and values.
4   All staff are aware of grievance and disciplinary procedures.

Principle 4 Consultation and communication

Dialogue with staff on matters likely to affect their employment enhances the quality and effectiveness of our policies and practices.

Indicators

1   Staff are informed and adequately consulted when we develop or review human resources policies or practices that affect them.
2   Managers and staff understand the scope of consultation and how to participate, individually or collectively.

Principle 5 Recruitment and selection

Our policies and practices aim to attract and select a diverse workforce with the skills and capabilities to fulfil our requirements.

Indicators

1   Written policies and procedures outline how staff are recruited and selected to positions in our organization.
2   Recruitment methods aim to attract the widest pool of suitably qualified candidates.
3   Our selection process is fair, transparent and consistent to ensure the most appropriate person is appointed.
4   Appropriate documentation is maintained and responses are given to candidates regarding their selection/non-selection to posts. We will provide feedback if necessary.
5   The effectiveness and fairness of our recruitment and selection procedures are monitored.

Principle 6 Learning, training and development

Learning, training and staff development are promoted throughout the organization.

Indicators

1   Adequate induction, and briefing specific to each role, is given to all staff.
2   Written policies outline the training, development and learning opportunities staff can expect from the organization.
3   Plans and budgets are explicit about training provision. Relevant training is provided to all staff.
4   Managers know how to assess the learning needs of staff so they can facilitate individual development. Where appropriate training and development will be linked to external qualifications.
5   The methods we have in place to monitor learning and training ensure that the organization also learns. They also monitor the effectiveness of learning and training in meeting organizational and programme aims as well as staff expectations of fairness and transparency.

Principle 7 Health, safety and security

The security, good health and safety of our staff are a prime responsibility of our organization.

Indicators

1   Written policies are available to staff on security, individual health, care and support, health and safety.
2   Programme plans include written assessment of security, travel and health risks specific to the country or region, reviewed at appropriate intervals.
3   Before an international assignment all staff receive health clearance. In addition they and accompanying dependants receive verbal and written briefing on all risks relevant to the role to be undertaken, and the measures in place to mitigate those risks, including insurance. Agency obligations and individual responsibilities in relation to possible risks are clearly communicated. Briefings are updated when new equipment, procedures or risks are identified.
4   Security plans, with evacuation procedures, are reviewed regularly.
5   Records are maintained of work-related injuries, sickness, accidents and fatalities, and are monitored to help assess and reduce future risk to staff.
6   Work plans do not require more hours' work than are set out in individual contracts. Time off and leave periods, based on written policies, are mandatory.
7   All staff have a debriefing or exit interview at the end of any contract or assignment. Health checks, personal counselling and careers advice are available. Managers are trained to ensure these services are provided.
8   In the case of staff on emergency rosters, managers should ensure that health clearance, immunizations and procedures for obtaining the correct prophylaxes and other essential supplies are arranged well in advance.

(Abridged from: http://www.peopleinaid.org/pool/files/code/code-en.pdf)

Content of UN standard kits

Complete details about the kits listed below, as well as other relief items, can be found on UNICEF's Supply Website (http://www.supply.unicef.dk/catalogue/). Located in Copenhagen, Denmark, there are about 17,000 items available through UNICEF's supply warehouse. Once registered, NGOs are supposed to be eligible to place orders. Prices include freight, although the cost and shipping time may be disadvantageous for NGOs in most emergency programmes.

1 Emergency health kits

The kit, often available from WHO or UNICEF but developed by a team of agencies for emergency situations where there are no working medical facilities, are designed to meet the primary health needs of 10,000 persons for 3 months or 30,000 persons for 1 month. A basic manual (treatment guidelines) comes with each kit intended for training purposes.

The Basic Unit consists of 10 identical boxes, each weighing 41 kg, and costs approximately US$2,194. The Basic Unit is intended for primary health care workers and contains basic supplies, including 12 non-injectable drugs.

The Supplementary Unit contains 14 boxes (3 boxes of drugs, 5 boxes of infusions, 3 boxes of renewable supplies and 3 boxes of equipment). It weighs 420 kg and costs approximately US$2,752. The Supplementary Unit contains drugs and medical supplies and is to be used only by professional health workers or physicians. The Supplementary Unit does not contain any drugs and supplies from the basic units and can therefore only be used when these are available as well. Supplementary Kit no. 1a contains drugs that may need import authorizations (psychotropic + narcotic) and/or drugs that need to be stored at specific temperatures (cold chain) and antimalarial drugs. Supplementary Kit no. 3 contains renewable health supplies.

2 Children's recreational kits

Programming focused on children is an integral part of emergency programmes. UNICEF's recreation kit comes with 21 separate parts: 13 teachers' items and 8 students' items packed in a metal box weighing 28kg. The Recreational Kit is designed to serve up to 90 children playing simultaneously.

3 Basic family water kit

As a means to help collect and distribute water during an emergency, UNICEF's basic family water kit is designed to be sufficient for 10 families. The kit weighs 21 kg and contains collapsible water containers, buckets, soap and water purification tablets.

4 School-in-a-box

Restocking and reopening schools is a critical emergency and post-conflict task. UNICEF's School-in-a-box kit for 80 students has 37 components: 26 teachers' items and 11 students' items. It weighs 52 kg. School-in-a-box comes in a steel metal lockable box. There is also a 'school-in-a-carton' that has the same contents but comes in a cardboard box instead.

5 UNFPA Reproductive health kits

These sets of kits help implement the MISP in emergencies. They are designed to be distributed to health facilities at different levels (Block 1 for PHC posts/ 10,000 persons, Block 2 for health clinics/30,000 persons and Block 3 for referral hospitals/150,000 persons) and last for a period of three months. The kits are designed to help implement reproductive health activities, including sexual health, post-rape management and medical supplies for safe deliveries of babies.

References

Armstrong, M. (2004) *How To Be an Even Better Manager*, 6th edn, Kogan, London.

Ashmore, J. (2004) *Tents: A Guide to the Use and Logistics of Family in Humanitarian Relief* (Reference Number: OCHA/ESB/2004/19), OCHA, Geneva.

Bakewell, O. (2003) *Sharpening the Development Process: A Practical Guide to Monitoring and Evaluation*, Intrac, Oxford.

Bennett, J. (1997) *NGO Coordination at the Field Level*, Intrac, Oxford.

Blake, R., and Mouton, J., (1968) *Corporate Excellence Through GRID Organization Development*, Gulf, Houston, TX.

Bouchet-Saumier, F. (2001) *The Practical Guide to Humanitarian Law*, Rowman and Little, Lanham, MD.

Bounds, G. and Woods, J. (1998) *Supervision*, South-Western College Publishing, Cincinnati. OH.

Bryson, J. and Hansch, S. (1993) *Food/Cash for Work Interventions in Famine Mitigation*, Famine Mitigation Strategy Paper, Office of US Foreign Disaster Assistance, Washington, DC.

Cahill, K. (ed.) (2003) *Basics of International Humanitarian Missions*, Fordham University Press, New York.

Cammack, J. (1999) *Financial Management for Development*, Intrac, Oxford.

Chambers, R. (1992) 'Rural appraisal: rapid, relaxed, and participatory', Discussion Paper 311, Institute of Development Studies, Sussex.

Chin, J. (ed.) (2000) *Control of Communicable Diseases Manual*, APHA, Washington, DC.

Cook, C. (2005) *Just Enough Project Management*, McGraw Hill, New York.

Corbett, J. (1997) 'Where there is no telephone'. Available online at: www.reliefweb.int/library/wtint/toc.html

Corsellis, T. and Vitale, A. (2004) *Transitional Shelter: Displaced Persons*, Shelter Project/Cambridge University Press, Cambridge.

Cross, T. (2001) 'Comfortable with chaos: working with UNHCR and the NGOs: reflections from the 1999 Kosovo refugee crisis. New issues in refugee research', Working Paper No. 42, UNHCR, Geneva. Available online at: http://www.jha.ac/articles/u042.htm#_edn25

Cuny, F. (1999) *Famine, Conflict and Response*, Kumarian Press, Bloomfield, CT.

Davies, A. (1997) *Managing for a Change*, IT Publishers, London.

Davis, J. and Lambert, R., (2002) *Engineering in Emergencies: A practical guide for relief workers*, ITDG Publishing and RedR-Engineers for Disaster Relief, London.

de Beer, A. and Rossouw, D. (eds.), (2005) *Focus On Operational Management*, JUTA and Co. Publisher, Cape Town.

de Bono, E. (2000) *Six Thinking Hats*, 2nd edn, London, Penguin.

de Waal, A. (1998) *Famine Crimes*, Indiana University Press, Bloomington, IN.

Department for International Development, UK (DFID) (1999) Sustainable Livelihood Guidance Sheets, DFID, London. Available online at: http://www.livelihoods.org/info/info_guidancesheets.html#5

DFID (2000) *Working with the Media in Conflicts and Other Emergencies*, DFID, London.

Drucker, P. (1967) *The Effective Executive*, Heinemann, London.

EngenderHealth (2005) *Field Office Closing Procedures Manual*, Engenderhealth, New York.

Fisher, R. and Ury, W. (1991) *Getting to Yes*, Penguin, London.

Fowler, A. (1997). *Striking a Balance*, Earthscan, London.

Gabarro, J. and Kotter, J. (1979) 'Managing your boss', *Harvard Business Review*, 85(7/8): 30–9 (updated 2005).

Handy, C. (1985) *Understanding Organizations*, London, Penguin.

Heller, R. (1998) *Essential Managers: Managing Teams*, DK Publishers, London.

Henderson, N. (2007) *Resiliency in Action: Practical Ideas for Overcoming Risks and Building Strengths in Youth, Families, and Communities*, Resiliency In Action, Ojai, CA.

Hudson, M. (2002) *Managing Without Profit*, Directory of Social Change, London.

Inter-Agency Standing Committee (IASC) (1994) 'Working paper on the definition of complex emergency' (December), IASC, Geneva.

Inter-Agency Standing Committee Task Force on Humanitarian Action and Human Rights (2004) *FAQ on International Humanitarian, Human Rights and Refugee Law in the Context of Armed Conflict*, IASC, Geneva.

IASC (2005) *Guidelines for GBV Interventions in Humanitarian Emergencies: Focusing on Prevention and Response to Sexual Violence*, ISAC, Geneva.

Interagency Working-Group (2004) 'Refugee Repatriation Process', unpublished working paper, Monrovia, Liberia.

International Federation of the Red Cross (IFRC) (1996) *World Disasters Report 1996*, Oxford University Press/IFRC, Oxford.

IFRC (2001) 'Coping with stress', IFRC, Geneva. Available online at: www.ifrc.org/cgi/pdf_pubs.pl?health/stress.pdf

Johnson, D. (1998) *Distributing Seeds and Tools in Emergencies*, Oxfam, Oxford.

Lindenberg, M. (1999) 'Complex Emergencies and NGOs: CARE', in J. Leaning (ed.), *Humanitarian Crisis*, Harvard University Press, Cambridge, MA.

Lowe, R. (n.d.) *Telecommunications Training Module*, RedR, Bristol.

McCurley, S. (1993) 'Alternatives to termination', *Grapevine* (Jan/Feb). Available online at: www.casanet.org/programme-management/personnel/sins.htm

McGregor, D. (1960) *Human Side of Enterprise,* McGraw Hill, New York.

Mango (2003) 'Financial management health check: how healthy is the financial management of your NGO?' (June).

Maren, M. (2002) *Road to Hell*, Free Press, New York.

Maslow, A. (1987) *Motivation and Personality*, 3rd edn, Harper and Row, New York.

MSF (1997) *Refugee Health*, MacMillan, London.

MSF (1998) *Logistic Catalogue*, MSF, Paris.

NGO Manager (2004) 'Organizational assessment tool (OAT)'. Available online at: www.ngomanager.org/tools/OAT_July_2004.pdf

Nicolai, S. (2003) *Education in Emergencies: A Toolkit for Starting and Managing Education in Emergencies*, Save the Children, London.

Norwegian Refugee Council (NRC) (2004) *Camp Management Toolkit*, NRC, Oslo.

Oxfam (n.d.) *Guidelines for Public Health Promotion*, Oxfam, Oxford. Available online at: www.oxfam.org.uk/what_we_do/emergencies/how_we_work/downloads/public_health.pdf

Pan-American Health Organization (PAHO) (2001) *Humanitarian and Supply Management and Logistics*, PAHO, Washington, DC.

PAHO/WHO (2004) *Management of Dead Bodies in Disaster Situations*, PAHO, Washington, DC.

Penrose, A. (2000) 'Partnership', in R. Dorcas, T. Hewitt and J. Harriss (eds) (2000) *Managing Development: Understanding Inter-Organizational Relationships*, Open University Press and Sage Publications, Milton Keynes.

Peppiatt, D., Mitchell, J. and Holzmann, P. (2001) *Cash Transfers in Emergencies: Evaluating Benefits and Assessing Risks*, Humanitarian Practice Network Papers No. 35, Overseas Development Institute, London.

Prendergast, J. (1996) *Frontline Diplomacy: Humanitarian Aid and Conflict in Africa*, Lynne Rienner, Boulder, CO.

Saade, A. and Burnham, G. (eds) (2000) *Public Health Guide for Emergencies*, Johns Hopkins Press and IFRC, Baltimore, MD. Available online at: www.ifrc.org/what/health/relief/guide.asp

Save the Children (SCF) (1995) *Development Manual 5: A Practical Guide to Assessment, Monitoring, Review and Evaluation*, SCF, London.

SCF (2001) *Toolkits: A Practical Guide to Assessments, Monitoring, Review and Evaluation*, Development Manual 5. Save the Children, London.

Scheyvens, R. and Storey, D. (eds) (2003) *Development Fieldwork: A Practical Guide*, Sage, London.

Sphere Project (2004) *Sphere Handbook*, revised edn, Sphere Project, Geneva.

Telford, J. (1997) *Counting and Identification of Beneficiary Population: Registration and its Alternatives*, Good Practice Review No. 5, Overseas Development Institute (ODI), London.

Terry, F. (2002) *Condemned to Repeat? The Paradox of Humanitarian Action*, Cornell University Press, Ithaca, NY.

Thomas, K. (1976) *Conflict and Conflict Management* McGraw-Hill, New York.

Townsend, J. (1996) *The Trainer's Pocketbook*, Management Pocket Book Series, Alresford Press, Alresford.

Twigg, J. (2004) *Disaster Risk Reduction: Mitigation and Preparedness in Development and Emergency Programming*, Humanitarian Practice Network, Good Practice Review No. 9, ODI, London.

UN Food and Agriculture Organization (FAO) (1998) *Emergency Activities: Technical Handbook Series*, FAO, Rome.

United Nations Childrens Fund (UNICEF) (2005) *Emergency Field Handbook*, UNICEF, New York. Available online at: http://www.unicef.org/publications/ files/UNICEF_EFH_2005.pdf

United Nations High Commissioner for Refugees (UNHCR) (1994) *Refugee Children: Guidelines on Protection and Care*, UNHCR, Geneva.

UNHCR (1999) *Protecting Refugees: A Field Guide for NGOs*, UNHCR, Geneva.

UNHCR (2000) *Handbook for Emergencies*, 3rd edn, UNHCR, Geneva.

UNHCR (2003) *Sexual and Gender-Based Violence against Refugees, Returnees and Internally Displaced Persons: Guidelines for Prevention and Response*, UNHCR, Geneva.

USAID/OFDA (2005) *Field Operations Guide*, USAID, Washington, DC.

Van Brabant, K. (2000) *Operational Security Management in Violent Environments*, Humanitarian Practice Network Papers No. 8, Overseas Development Institute, London.

Wallack, L., Woodruff, K., Dorfman, L. and Diaz, I. (1999) *News for a Change: An Advocate's Guide to Working with the Media*. Sage, Thousand Oaks, CA.

Walmsley, B. (2005) *Teach Yourself Training*, Teach Yourself, Chicago, IL, and London.

Wells, J. (2005) *Protecting and assisting older people in emergencies*, HPN Paper 53, Overseas Development Institute, London.

Werner, D., and Bower, B., (1982), *Helping Health Workers Learn: A Book of Methods, Aids and Ideas for Instructors at the Village Level*, Hesperian Foundation, Berkeley, CA.

Wisner, B., Blaikie, P., Cannon, T. and Davis, I. (2005) *At Risk: Natural Hazards, People's Vulnerability and Disaster*, 2nd edn, Routledge, London.

Wood, M. (1996) 'Disaster Communications'. Available online at: www.reliefweb.int/library/dc1/dcc1.html

World Food Programme (WFP) (2002) *Emergency Field Operations Pocketbook*, WFP, Rome.

WFP (2002) *Guidelines for Selective Feeding Programmes in Emergencies*. WFP, Rome.

World Health Organization (WHO) (1999) *Guidelines for Safe Disposal of Unwanted Pharmaceuticals in and after Emergencies*, WHO, Geneva.

WHO (2005) *Communicable Diseases Control In Emergencies – A Field Manual*, WHO, Geneva.

Useful websites

Action Without Borders: www.psychosocial.org

Agency Coordinating Body for Afghan Relief (ACBAR): www.acbar.org

Aid Data: www.oecd.org/statsportal

Aid Workers Network: http://aidworkers.net

Alertnet: www.alertnet.org

Antares Foundation (stress management): www.antaresfoundation.org

Bioforce: www.bioforce.asso.fr

Center for Disease Control (US): www.cdc.gov

Centre for Humanitarian Psychology: www.humanitarian-psy.org

CHA: www.humanitarian-srilanka.org

Collaborative for Development Action (Do No Harm): www.cdainc.com

Communications information: www.maflink.org

Compas Qualité: www.compasqualite.org

Development Executive Group: www.developmentex.com

Devnet Jobs: www.devnetjobs.org

Disaster information: www.gdacs.org

Discussion-Oriented Organizational Self-Assessment (DOSA): www.edc.org/
    GLG/CapDev/dosapage

ECHO: http://europa.eu.int/comm/echo/index_en.htm

Emergency Nutrition Network: www.ennonline.net

European Foundation Centre: www.efc.be

Famine Early Warning System: www.usaid.gov/fews

Fanta Project (Nutrition): www.fantaproject.org

Foodaid: www.foodaid.org

Forced Migration Online: www.forcedmigration.org

Forced Migration Review: www.fmreview.org

Foundation Center: www.fdncenter.org

Fritz Institute (Logistics): www.fritzinstitute.org

Global Action Network: www.globalactionnetwork.org

Good Humanitarian Donorship project: www.goodhumanitariandonorship.org

Global Humanitarian Platform: www.globalhumanitarianplatform.org

Group URD: www.urd.org

Headington Institute (stress management): www.headington-institute.org

Health Workers Without Borders: www.mhwwb.org

HIC: www.humanitarianinfo.org

HIV/AIDS (UN): www.unaids.org

Humanitarian Accountability Project: www.hapgeneva.org

Humanitarian Communications: www.humaninet.org

Humanitarian information: www.humanitarianinfo.org/iasc

Humanitarian Practice Network: www.odi.org.uk

Indicators: www.smartindicators.org

InterAction: www.interaction.org

Interagency Network for Education in Emergencies: www.ineesite.org

International Committee of the Red Cross: www.icrc.org

International Council of Voluntary Agencies (ICVA): www.icva.ch

International Crisis Group: www.crisisgroup.org

International Federation of the Red Cross: www.ifrc.org

International Water and Sanitation Centre: www.irc.nl

InterWorks: www.interworksmadison.com

Intrac: www.intrac.org/pages/praxis

Journal of Humanitarian Assistance: www.jha.ac

Livelihoods: www.livelihoods.org

Livestock Emergency Guidelines and Standards (LEGS): www.livestock-emergency.net

Mango (Finance): www.mango.org.uk

Microfinance Gateway: www.microfinancegateway.org

Mindtools: www.mindtools.com

MISP: www.unfpa.org/emergencies/manual/2.htm

Networklearning: www.networklearning.org

New Partnerships Partnering (measuring capacity): www.usaid.gov/pubs/npi/index

NGO Café: www.gdrc.org/ngo/ncafe-ks.html

NGO Manager: www.ngomanager.org

Nutrition Net: www.nutritionnet.net/everyone

Nutrition Survey: www.nutrisurvey.de

OCHA: www.ochaonline.un.org

OFDA: www.usaid.gov/our_work/humanitarian_assistance

One World: www.oneworld.net

Overseas Development Institute: www.odi.org.uk

PACT: www.pactworld.org

Participatory Organizational Evaluation Tool (POET): www.undp.org/csopp/
poet

People in Aid: www.peopleinaid.org

Reality of Aid Project: www.realityofaid.org

RedR: www.redr.org

Relief Web (UN): www.reliefweb.int

Reproductive health www.rhrc.org

Self-Reflection Project (OSR): www.reflect-learn.org/EN/tools/comparar

Shelter Project: www.shelterproject.org

Sidran Institute: www.sidran.org/trauma

Sphere Project: www.sphereproject.org

Trauma Resource Institute: www.traumaresourceinstitute.com

Tsunami Evaluation Coalition (TEC): www.tsunami-evaluation.org

UN International Strategy for Disaster Reduction (ISDR): www.unisdr.org

UNDPKO: www.un.org/depts/dpko

UNFPA: www.unfpa.org/emergencies

UNHCR: www.unhcr.ch

UNICEF: www.unicef.org

Vehicle information: http://home.planet.nl/~serem000/mech.html

VOICE: www.ngovoice.org

Waterlines: www.itdgpublishing.org.uk/waterlines.htm

WFP: www.wfp.org

WHO: www.who.int

World Bank Assessment Information: www.worldbank.org/wbi/sourcebook/
sba1.htm.

World Hunger: http://www.worldhunger.org/articles/global/armedconflict/
anderson.htm

WWF (organizational development information): www.wwfknowledge.org

Glossary of common terms

This glossary provides working definitions of key terms used in this book. Some of the terms and concepts used here are complex and can be defined in different ways. An attempt has been made to use generally accepted terms used in the field.

Acceptance: Security strategy that improves security through relationships with external actors such as neighbours and beneficiaries.

Accountability: The ability to justify actions and report on the use of resources and the progress of results.

Activity: Any action or work done to achieve an objective. A process of transforming inputs into outputs and outcomes.

Advocacy: Actions taken, usually through the use of a specific message, to encourage backing for a particular issue or policy.

Anthropometric measurement: Measurement of the body, often using scales or tape measures, to identify changes that reflect health and nutritional status.

Aquifer: Ground layer or material that contains water and may be accessed through wells or through springs.

Asset: (1) Items or other resources possessed by or available to beneficiaries. (2) Items owned by an organization. In some cases, assets are divided between capital assets of more than a particular monetary amount (e.g. US$5,000) and non-capital assets and disposable assets less than amount.

Assumptions: The potential of external factors (i.e. risks or constraints that an NGO has no direct control over) that may influence the progress towards stated objectives.

Asylum: Shelter, protection or a place of safety for refugees.

Audit: Independent assessment of an organization's finances by an independent person, an auditor, or organization such as an accounting firm.

Base-station/radio: The stationary (as opposed to mobile) radio, often manned by a radio operator, which serves to control or monitor a radio communications net.

Baseline survey/assessment/data: Information or analysis of a situation prior to a project or programme that can be used for comparisons or to measure progress towards objectives.

Benchmark: An indicator, metric or standard used to measure progress or achievements of a project.

Beneficiaries: People who are the intended recipients of the output and outcome of activities. Often further delineated as direct and indirect or between primary, secondary and tertiary beneficiaries.

Bias: Predisposition or partiality that causes error while collecting or interpreting data.

Bill of quantity (BOQ): Document that contains the cost-estimation of a construction project.

Budget: Document detailing a spending plan for a given period of time, project or activity.

Callsign: Name for an individual (usually based on their position) used to keep communications brief.

Capacity: Ability or potential ability to affect a situation or complete an objective which can be measured by elements such as access and resources, including financial, human, information and material.

Capacity building: Process of improvement and change usually focused on the staff or individual level.

Cashbook: Record or ledger of money coming in and out of an organization; kept in chronological order.

Catchment area: The physical area where beneficiaries are present.

Child: A person up to the age of 18 years (UN definition).

Cluster sampling: Sampling method that is comprised of groups (e.g. households or communities) rather than individuals. A common cluster is made up of 30 samples.

Cold-chain: System for maintaining vaccines in a usable (cold) condition, using refrigerators and other equipment, from the point of manufacture to the beneficiary.

Community mobilization: Activities intended to raise the awareness of beneficiaries around particular issues at the grassroots level or in conjunction with a project involving significant community buy-in, such as microfinance or child protection.

Complex emergency: An emergency caused by more than one event or condition, leading to the breakdown of authority and social support systems, requiring an external response. Also called complex humanitarian emergency, complex political emergency and situation of chronic political instability. (See also Emergency below.)

Concept paper: Concise document which sets out the basic idea behind a planned project or programme.

Conflict resolution: Activities that help reduce tension and put an end to discord; seen as a step beyond settlement.

Coordination: People or organizations working together towards a common objective, preventing overlap of activities.

Cost-share: Contributions to a grant-funded project from more than one donor. Also called 'matching funds'.

Country Director (CD): Although separate organizations may attach specific roles to such titles, in this book, Country Director is a catch-all title for the top staff member in a particular country and is thus synonymous with head of mission, head of delegation, chief of party, representative and national director.

Country office: The head office of an NGO in a country where programming is carried out. Sometimes called a national office or emergency programme office.

Culture: The norms, traditions and ways of doing things within a group of people.

Deterrence: Security strategy that improves security by presenting a counter-threat.

Development: Generally, the alleviation of poverty and need through improvements in various freedoms such as economic opportunity and political liberty.

Direct beneficiaries: The people who are the primary recipients or intended clients of a project or programme. Also called the target population or intended beneficiaries.

Donor: Organization or person providing money to an NGO. In some cases, NGOs can act as donors to other organizations.

Emergency: An exceptional circumstance that causes human suffering and requires assistance beyond what is locally available. May occur suddenly ('rapid onset') or slowly over time ('slow onset') and be caused by political violence or natural hazard. Can be used interchangeably with 'disaster'.

Evaluation: Planned appraisal of a project or programme.

Expatriate staff: Organizational staff whose permanent residence is outside the country where an emergency occurs. Also called international staff.

Food basket: The food consumed by a person, as a ration or dietary regime, that is made up of a healthy mixture of energy, protein, fat and nutrients.

Food security: Access to food needed at any time to achieve an active and healthy life.

Gender: Socially determined attitudes and values stemming from differences in sexual characteristics.

Gender-based violence (GBV): Physical or emotional force (violence) directed at a person because of their gender or sex.

Goal: The overarching purpose or desired impact of a project or programme. Sometimes called aim or overall objective.

GPS: Global Positioning System. This allows someone to determine their (almost) exact location on the planet using a small handheld device. The information is essentially useless unless used in conjunction with the correct type of map.

Handset: Short for radio handset and typically refers to a VHF radio.

Hazard: Threat to people's welfare; either natural (e.g. volcanoes, severe storms and seismic activity) or man-made (e.g. violence and armed conflict).

Headquarters (HQ): For an organization as a whole, the head office and seat of the executive director and support staff of an NGO, which be in either the global North or the global South. At the country level, this usually refers to the head office typically based in the capital city and seat of the Country Director), whose primary purpose is to represent the organization and oversee field offices or sub-offices. Field level refers to the next lowest level or area where programming is carried out.

Human resources management (HRM): Broad concept that includes the administration and supervision of staff from recruitment through to their departure from an organization.

Implementation: The process of carrying out a project.

Implementing partner: Label used by some donors to indicate their relationship with an NGO, in which there is a contractual agreement to carry out a project.

Incidence: Number of health cases (morbidity) during a defined time period, usually expressed divided by a total given population. Often expressed as a rate (e.g. X cases per 1,000 people).

Indicator: Expressed in a quantifiable statement, a standard or reference point in which progress towards an objective can be measured. Very similar to a benchmark, which may be an interim indicator.

Indirect beneficiaries: The people who are the secondary recipients of a project or programme. For example, if particular teachers are the direct beneficiaries, students are often considered indirect beneficiaries.

Input: The resources (e.g. financial, human, information and material) that are attributed to a project or programme to achieve desired outputs/outcomes for beneficiaries.

Internally displaced person (IDP): Person who flees their residence, without crossing an international frontier, to escape danger or persecution.

International humanitarian law (IHL): The set of rules, treaties and customs intended to protect civilians, both beneficiaries and relief workers, in times of armed conflict.

Inventory: A record of assets or amount of stock.

Ionosphere: Part of the atmosphere that reflects HF radio sky waves.

Kwashiorkor: Severe form of malnutrition resulting from inadequate protein intake and/or the stress of infection.

Lead agency: An organization (e.g. an NGO or a UN agency) appointed to coordinate activities in a particular sector. When done properly, this involves leadership and advocacy, not control.

Line-ministry: A government office (ministry) responsible for a particular sector, such as health, education, rural development and women's affairs.

Livelihood: The capacities, resources and activities that generate an income. Examples include any occupation or employment. In emergency contexts, the focus is on durable livelihoods that reduce vulnerability and enable people to withstand shocks.

Logical framework analysis (LFA or logframe): Management tool intended to improve the design and internal logic of projects by analysing the relationship of different elements (i.e. input, activities, objectives and goal).

Logistics: The acquisition, control, handling, transport, storage and removal of goods or supplies.

Mainstreaming: The effort to integrate specific themes and issues (e.g. gender or security) into an organization and its activities as much as possible and thus raise its awareness and importance.

Marasmus: Severe form of acute malnutrition resulting from rapid weight loss or failure to gain weight.

Mass casualty incident (MCI): Event involving injuries and destruction, caused by a large accident or significant violence, that exceeds the capacity of a single organization to respond to.

Microfinance: Sector that focuses on the smallest types of enterprise and encompasses the provision of advice, the establishment of cooperatives (or other community-based financial institution) and micro-enterprise development, as well as the provision of credit in the form of loans.

Monitoring: An ongoing process of review and appraisal.

Morbidity: Incidence or prevalence of illness.

Mortality: Incidence or prevalence of death.

National staff: Organizational staff permanently resident in the host country where an emergency occurs. Also known as local staff.

Non-Refoulement: Concept from international refugee law that prohibits states and governments from returning refugees to situations in which their lives or freedom may be threatened.

Objective: An objectively verifiable statement describing the end sought in a project or programme.

Older person: A person over the age of 60 years (UN definition). Also called the elderly.

Operations: The combination of logistics, procurement, transport, security and other programme support functions within an NGO.

Organizational development: Process of improvement and change usually focused on the organizational or institutional level.

Outcome: The effects of a project or programme, such as improved education.

Output: The tangible results of a project or programme, such as rehabilitated school buildings and supplies delivered.

Participation: Process of involving stakeholders, particularly beneficiaries, in planning, carrying out and evaluating a project or programme.

Partnership: Two or more organizations with similar or compatible aims, working together towards common objectives and goals, usually focused on specific issues or programmes.

Petty cash: Money held by a staff member for small expenses that is not part of the main accounting system or cashbook.

Phonetic alphabet: Terms assigned for each letter of the alphabet to ease communication transmissions.

Plenary: All attendants or participants present at a meeting or workshop. This full group may be divided into small groups for exercises or to work on specific issues.

Prevalence: Number of health cases (morbidity) at a given point in time.

Primary health care (PHC): The most basic type of health care which people need; most often focuses on prevention and refers cases to next levels of care, based on a person's condition.

Programme: Set of projects which might combine sectors, for example, health and shelter. Also used as shorthand for an emergency operation in a particular country.

Project: An activity or set of activities carried out to achieve specific objectives using a set of resources (staff and budget) and within a specific timeframe; for example, latrine construction or provision of care for children under 5 years of age.

Proposal document: A document, longer than a concept paper (see p. 400), that describes in detail a proposed project or plan and usually supported by assessment data, implementation plans and detailed budgetary information.

Protection: (1) Activities designed to prevent abuse or deal with its consequences through various types of programming; usually targets vulnerable people such as refugees and children. (2) A security strategy that improves security by relying on physical objects and equipment.

Pro-words: Terms used for brevity and to facilitate radio communications.

Psychosocial: Adjective used to describe a project or activities aimed at improving a person's wellbeing in both a psychological (e.g. thinking and feelings) and a social (e.g. culture, family and friends) sense.

Qualitative data: Information using comparisons, such as camp conditions or characteristics of health practices.

Quantifiable data: Information using numbers, such as caloric intake per day and extent of immunization coverage.

Redundant communications: Having several means to communicate so that, if one system no longer works or is inaccessible, at least one back-up communication device is available.

Refugee: A person who flees a country, crossing an international frontier, to escape danger or persecution.

Relief official: A representative or staff member of a donor organization, government or the UN.

Relief worker: A field-based local or international (paid or volunteer) member of an organization involved in responding to emergencies. Someone who implements or runs programmes.

Repeater: Type of antenna that takes a VHF transmission and repeats it at a greater strength and distance.

Risk: Likelihood in which a hazard will have adverse consequences on a project, programme or organization.

Sector: Programme component. In development and humanitarian programming, examples include nutrition, health, wat/san and shelter.

Shock: Event/s that affect a person's or group's vulnerability and ability to cope with disasters and emergencies.

Soak-away: The area, usually containing rocks and gravel, where excess water from a well head or spigot spreads and is absorbed by the ground.

Social service infrastructure: Structures built and available for public or community use, such as schools, health clinics, public latrines, water wells and roads.

Spring box: Structure constructed to store and dispense water from a spring.

Stakeholder: Any person, group or organization that has an interest in or is affected by an NGO's activities. In this sense, stakeholders are a much larger group than beneficiaries and include staff, commercial entities and government authorities.

Stunting: Shortness indicated by a low height-for-age index.

Supplementary feeding: Nutrition provided in addition to what people can obtain for themselves, with the purpose of preventing malnutrition.

Sustainability: The ability or likelihood of results continuing after the end of a project or programme (i.e. once support is withdrawn and responsibility moves to local capacity). Sustainable development refers to development activities that do not harm the ability of future generations to achieve their own development.

Sustainable livelihood: Means for making a living that can withstand shocks.

Terms of reference (TOR): Job description for a short-term professional position. Often used interchangeably with Scope of Work (SOW).

Therapeutic feeding: Nutrition provided for people, usually children, who have become severely malnourished.

Threat: Potential act that may result in harm or injury to staff or loss or damage to property or programmes.

Tracing: Looking for displaced or missing persons for the purposes of reunification, typically children with parents.

Traffic: Set of radio transmissions or regular chatter.

Transmission: Radio signal or broadcast between a sender and a receiver.

Triangulation: Confirming information using three or more sources of information.

Unaccompanied minor (UAM): Child up to 16 years of age (or older if the child perceives him/herself as vulnerable and in need of support), whose parents or relatives cannot be found (UNHCR definition).

Unexploded ordnance (UXO): An explosive device, such as artillery shells, mortar rounds and bomblets, that has yet to be detonated.

Vulnerability: Likelihood of being affected by a hazard or exposure to threat.

Wasting: Rapid loss of body fat and muscle indicated by a low weight for height or body mass index resulting in thinness and other clinical signs.

Wat/san: Of or relating to the water and sanitation sector.

Well head: The parapet, cover (which typically holds the pump) and apron of a well.

Young person: Any Person whose age is between 10 and 24 years old.

Youth: Any People whose ages are between 15 and 24 years old.

Z-score: Measurement used in nutritional surveillance and assessments to show the standard deviation in weight-for-height (WFH) measurement above or below the median.

Notes on Basic Conversions

Weight	Volume (Liquid)
1 gram (g) = 0.035 ounce	1 litre (l) = 0.26 gallons = 2.11 pints
1 kilogram (kg) = 2.2 pounds (lbs) = 1 litre	1 gallon (US) = 4 quarts = 3.785 litres
1 UK tonne = 2240 lbs	1 gallon (US) = 0.822 gallon (UK)
1 US tonne = 2000 lbs	1 gallon (UK) = 10 pounds = 4.54 litres
Length/Distance/Area	**Temperature:** Celsius (C)/Fahrenheit (F)
1 millimetre (mm) = 0.0394 inch	C to F multiply by 1.8 + 32
1 centimetre (cm) = 0.39 inch	F to C divide by 1.8 − 32
1 metre (m) = 3.28 feet	Freezing = 0°C = 32.3°F
1 kilometre (km) = 0.62 mile	Hot day = 40°C = 104°F
1 hectare = 2.47 acres	Boiling = 100°C = 212°F

Index

The following abbreviations are used in the Index:
f = Figure; *t* = Table